Chicano Renaissance

Chicano Renaissance

CONTEMPORARY CULTURAL TRENDS

edited by

David R. Maciel

Isidro D. Ortiz

María Herrera-Sobek

THE UNIVERSITY OF ARIZONA PRESS   TUCSON

The University of Arizona Press
© 2000 The Arizona Board of Regents
First Printing
All rights reserved

♾ This book is printed on acid-free, archival-quality paper.
Manufactured in the United States of America

05   04   03   02   01   00   6   5   4   3   2   1

Library of Congress Cataloging-in-Publication Data
Chicano renaissance : contemporary cultural trends / edited by David R. Maciel,
Isidro D. Ortiz, and María Herrera-Sobek.
p. cm.
Includes bibliographical references and index.
ISBN 0-8165-2020-8 (acid-free paper) —
ISBN 0-8165-2021-6 (pbk.: acid-free paper)
1. Mexican Americans—Intellectual life—20th century.
2. Mexican Americans—Social life and customs—20th century.
3. Mexican American arts—History—20th century.
I. Maciel, David. II. Ortiz, Isidro D., 1949–   . III. Herrera-Sobek, María.
E184.M5 C453 2000   00-008073

British Library Cataloguing-in-Publication Data
A catalogue record for this book is available from the British Library.

Publication of this book is made possible in part by the proceeds of a permanent
endowment created with the assistance of a Challenge Grant from the National
Endowment for the Humanities, a federal agency.

Dedicated to
Don Luis Leal
and to the memory of
Don Américo Paredes

Pioneer scholars and true
exponents of Chicano culture

Contents

Preface

*F*or the three editors, this book is the culmination of a lengthy professional and personal odyssey. We have all been observers and active participants of the historical period that this book covers. The book itself began as an idea in the late 1980s. The project was conceived as a reaction to the lack of scholarly materials available on the current status of the Chicano community. Originally the project was designed to be published in a one-volume work. However, it became apparent that in attempting to address questions of politics, economics, education, Chicana/o studies, women's issues, and culture, a single-volume format was not enough. Therefore, we decided to offer our assessment of the last two decades of the Chicano experience in two volumes.

The initial study *Chicanas/Chicanos at the Crossroads: Social, Economic, and Political Change* was edited by Maciel and Ortiz and published in 1996. Much to our delight, the book has been well received. We began work on the companion volume even before the completion of the first. Because the second volume was going to be devoted to art and culture, we invited one of the foremost cultural studies scholars, Professor María Herrera-Sobek, to serve as coeditor with us.

Together we shared the responsibilities, joys, and concerns of an edited work. It has been a rich and rewarding learning experience to work with such professional and committed scholars. I have learned much from these original and creative collaborations. It is an experience that I will always cherish and remember fondly as one of the highlights of my professional career.

DAVID R. MACIEL

Acknowledgments

*F*or any anthology to succeed, particularly one that includes a multitude of perspectives and themes, the assistance and support of many individuals and institutions are critical. Foremost we are indebted to our contributors. Each delivered highly original, innovative, and comprehensive essays. We learned a great deal from them and profited from their observations and suggestions for the project.

We are grateful to the countless gifted Chicana and Chicano artists and scholars. Their works have inspired us and are the basis for this book. Indeed, their artistry has enhanced and elevated our lives and our community. At times creating under adverse conditions, Chicana/o artists nevertheless have brought forth a cultural flowering that has been acclaimed by U.S. audiences as well as international ones.

Invaluable and indispensable clerical assistance was provided on three campuses. At California State University, Domínguez Hills, Virginia Rodríguez, Alfonso González, and Claudia Rodríguez skillfully, patiently, and with great professionalism converted and formatted diskettes, processed manuscripts, and performed other necessary tasks in the final preparation of the book. At San Diego State University, Janice Miller and Laurel Dyke enthusiastically processed different versions of the text and helped at critical times with computer issues. Fatima Mujcinovic from the University of California at Santa Barbara patiently typed different drafts of the manuscript.

Special resources that made possible the hiring of the necessary staff to aid the editors were made available by the office of the president and vice president of academic affairs at California State University, Domínguez Hills. This assistance was invaluable for the completion of the project. We are also grateful to the Luis Leal Endowed Chair for the funds received.

The editorial staff at the University of Arizona Press has been a model of professionalism and support. From the onset of this project, we have received strong support and necessary guidance whenever necessary. Our previous acquisitions editor, Joanne O'Hare, and our current one, Patti

Hartmann, voiced a deep personal commitment to our project. In a similar vein, Steve Cox, former director of the University of Arizona Press, was an advisor and advocate of this anthology. We also express our gratitude to Nancy Arora for her fine work as our manuscript editor. One would be hard-pressed to find a better press to work with.

Introduction

The late 1960s witnessed the emergence of a social upheaval in the United States known as the Chicano Movement. According to historian Ignacio García, the Chicano Movement became "a full-fledged transformation of the way Mexican Americans thought, played politics, and promoted their culture. Chicanas/os[1] embarked on a struggle to make fundamental changes, because only fundamental changes could make them active participants in their lives."[2] The Movement was guided by a militant political ethos or consciousness, commonly known as Chicanismo. The term "Chicanismo" encompassed both political and cultural constructs related to being both a Chicana/o and a participant of the Mexican American experience.

The Movement, as analyzed by García, had four distinct phases. The first phase was that of critique and revisionism: "Mexican American intellectuals, politicians, students, and others came to believe that the liberal agenda, which had been seen as the solution to the community's problems, was simply morally corrupt and a failure."[3] García further adds that "[h]istory, once used to perpetuate stereotypes and rationalize Mexican American backwardness [by Anglo historians], became a weapon for liberation [by Chicano scholars]. It also allowed for a growth of an academic as well as an organic or homegrown Chicano intellectual elite that sought to give meaning to the Mexican American experience."[4] The first step in this process was a critical examination of existing scholarship and interpretations of the Chicano experience. As a generation of Movimiento students reached graduate and professional status in the late 1960s and early 1970s, it quickly became evident to them that traditional scholarship and perspectives on the Chicana/o community were seriously flawed for the most part. Indeed, traditional scholarship contributed to negative views and assumptions by society with regard to the Mexican-origin population in the United States. Thus, a rigorous in-depth examination of social science and humanities literature focusing on the Chicano experience was undertaken. This initial Movimiento generation of scholars, such as Rodolfo Acuña, Jesús Chavarría, Marta Cotera, Juan Gómez-Quiñones, Margarita Melville, Miguel Montiel, Octavio Romano, Rosaura Sánchez, Nick Vaca, and others, harshly critiqued the state and nature of the extant scholarship available on Chicanos. These scholars suggested much-needed revisions and alternative models of analysis.[5]

Early Chicano scholars were well aware that mainstream journals and academic presses were indifferent or even downright hostile toward Chicano scholarly contributions. Chicanas/os had no choice but to found their own publishing outlets. Thus, in 1967 Octavio Romano and others founded *El Grito: A Journal of Contemporary Mexican American Thought,* a pioneer journal devoted exclusively to publishing creative and academic writings of the Movimiento generation. In 1970, a second and equally important journal, *Aztlán: Chicano Journal of the Social Sciences and the Arts,* began publication at the Chicano Studies Research Center of the University of California, Los Angeles. In contrast to *El Grito,* which stressed the humanities and education, *Aztlán* focused on history and the social sciences. Both became instrumental in the evolution and dissemination of Chicano scholarly and creative production. The articles and other literary writings published by both journals clearly reflected a new scholarship that addressed critical issues and offered revisionist perspectives on the Chicana/o experience.[6] The creative works that appeared in the new Chicano journals also initiated a new literary canon that challenged the traditional Eurocentric vision prevalent in American colleges and universities.

Soon thereafter, other specialized journals and periodicals were founded. They disseminated Chicana/o cultural productions throughout the Southwest and the Midwest, and for the first time, writings on the Chicana/o experience began to be widely read and discussed. Thus, from the very onset of the Chicano Movement, a heightened awareness of the importance of culture and the desire for alternative artistic manifestations that reflected and extolled the creativity and richness of the Chicana/o experience was paramount. It was in such a climate that an artistic and cultural renaissance began to flourish. A revolutionary fervor in the arts ensued and is one of the greatest and most lasting contributions of the Chicano civil rights struggle.

The second phase of the Chicano Movement focused on the development of theoretical models that would aid us in the hermeneutics of the Chicano experience. The most often employed and popular theoretical model used to explain the oppression of Chicanos in the United States was the "internal colonial model." This framework offered a critical and useful analytical tool for the study of the dynamics of oppression of the Chicana/o community. Besides the internal colonial model, Chicana/o scholars incorporated other conceptual and methodological constructs such as Marxism.[7] They explored related disciplines and perspectives that were useful in the definition of the Chicano experience. Particularly significant areas of research were gender studies, cultural studies, and comparative ethnic studies.

History as a discipline became an area of study where the internal colonial model was initially applied. The critical perspectives that emerged in the Movimiento and post-Movimiento years clearly revealed that Chicanas and Chicanos had been badly misrepresented or ignored by existing historical narratives. Their contributions and struggles in the United States were nowhere to be found in the writings or teachings of American history. Realizing that a people without a historical memory would be subordinated to ideas generated by the dominant order, nascent Chicana/o academics turned their skills toward recovering their historical legacy and exciting past. From the 1970s on, an impressive amount of scholarly articles were produced and published in Chicano and mainstream journals with a historical focus. Doctoral dissertations increasingly were turned into impressive monographs that began to place the Chicana/o community within the structure of national historical narratives. A multitude of areas related to Chicana/o history began to be developed. These included labor, urban studies, women's history, social and cultural histories, the family, and biographical studies, to name a few.[8]

Ignacio García perceived the third phase of the Chicano Movimiento as characterized by a sense of affirmation. Chicano activists, intellectuals, and artists declared "a rediscovered pride in their racial and class status and in their sense of peoplehood." According to García:

> This affirmation of race and class brought about a sense of solidarity with Third World movements for liberation and united Chicanos with a worldwide revolution against oppression. It also spurred a renaissance of Chicano literature, theater, and art. Artists and writers now took the barrio as the setting for their work, and the working people or their indigenous ancestors as their protagonists. The attempt by earlier artists to integrate their works into the mainstream ceased among many of the new and some of the old artists of the barrio. The search began for a "uniquely Chicano" literature, theater, and art.[9]

The remarkable Chicano cultural flowering encompassed the arts, so-cial sciences, and literary production. Chicano cultural workers appropri-ated in their discursive strategies both established and popular culture motifs and manifestations, including such indigenous cultural icons as Quetzalcoatl and Coatlicue as well as historical figures from the Mexican Revolution (1910–17) such as Francisco Villa and Emiliano Zapata. Novels, poetry, short stories, ballads, and so forth emerged as a direct result of the energy released by Chicana/o artists and writers as they became involved in the various phases of the civil rights movement. Such political activities as the drive by César Chávez and Dolores Huerta to unionize the farm workers; the land struggle of Reies López-Tijerina; the formation of the La Raza Unida party; the Crusade for Justice; the sit-ins, love-ins, and marches against the Viet-nam War; the feminist movement; and the gay and lesbian liberation move-ment all contributed in no small part to inspire Chicana/o artists.

Nowhere was the flowering more evident than in the production of theatrical plays. In California, the Teatro Campesino emerged on the scene specifically to help the farmworkers organize themselves and form a labor union through which they could obtain humane working conditions. Luis Valdez, as well as both male and female actors, produced plays targeting agribusiness and its exploitative treatment of farmworkers. Other theater groups came into being in the early years of the Movement. The Teatro de la Esperanza in Santa Barbara, California, under the direction of Jorge Huerta, is one example.[10]

Literary works in other genres quickly began to surface as well: the poetry of Alurista, the novels of Tomás Rivera and Rolando Hinojosa, and the short stories of Estela Portillo Trambley contributed to a cultural revolu-tion propelled by the Chicano Movement. With the explosion of literary works, Chicana/o literary criticism appeared on the scene and began a vigorous analysis of the works published. Rejecting the old Eurocentric literary canon, Chicanas/os proposed a new, more inclusive canon in tune with the social and cultural context of the Chicano population. This new discourse embraced the works of ethnic writers, who insisted that they be included in the halls of academia.[11]

Filmmaking also emerged as a critical and innovative cultural expres-sion. Chicana/o film students wrote, directed, and produced an impres-sive number of powerful, well-crafted documentaries that brought the Chi-cana/o experience to the screen. Chicanas were particularly influential in documentary filmmaking. In the last three decades Chicano narrative films have made their mark on the silver screen.[12]

Chicano Studies departments and programs also began to surface in many universities and colleges as Chicanas/os breached the ramparts of academia. Departments were challenged for their exclusionary practices, and they gradually began to open their doors (although some hesitantly and others unwillingly) to Chicano and Chicana course material. Across the Southwest, the walls built a century and a half ago (after the U.S.–Mexican War of 1848) to keep the Mexican American population in a marginalized state began to crack, and in these small but significant cracks, the creative works of Chicanas/os took root and flourished.[13]

While literary scholars engaged in these academic battles, Chicano and Chicana painters waged artistic war with their murals. Chicana/o history was inscribed onto walls, storefronts, and buildings. Public spaces were appropriated to boldly proclaim the history and grievances of the Mexican American people, who had been silenced for more than a century. Judith Baca, Manuel Hernández, Carmen Lomas-Garza, José Montoya, Santa Barraza, Salvador "Queso" Torres, the Royal Chicano Air Force, and many others took up the paintbrush and in bold strokes outlined the history, the myths, the oppression, and the heroes and heroines of the Chicano people.[14]

Although the Chicano Movement was never homogeneous, certain themes predominated in early Chicano cultural productions. This was to be expected, because the artistic movements were a direct result of political initiatives. Lack of educational opportunities, police brutality, economic and social oppression, racial and class discrimination, immigrant rights, and discrimination in the workplace were some of the issues expounded in literary and artistic cultural productions.

The Chicano Movement was never univocal but rather was characterized by multiple perspectives yearning and struggling to be recognized in the evolving cultural spaces. Even the term that Chicanas/os used to refer to themselves became a bone of contention. Some groups preferred "Hispanic," others used "Mexican American," still others opted for "Chicano," and more recently the term "Latino" has become acceptable. Residents of Mexican descent in New Mexico and Colorado often described themselves as having a "Spanish American" heritage, whereas Texans preferred to describe themselves as "Hispanic" or "Mexican American." The heterogeneity of naming, and thus of political and philosophical trends, manifested itself in the diverse naming of research centers. At the University of Texas, Austin, the research center was named the Mexican American Studies Research Center. In New Mexico, the major center at the University of New Mexico was named the Southwest Hispanic Research Institute. In contrast, by 1979, universities in California, such as Stanford and the University of California campuses at Los Angeles, Santa Barbara, Berkeley, and Davis had opted for "Chicano" research centers. At each campus, Chicanas/os grappled with what name to use, with the final name serving as a reflection of the philosophy of each group's founders. The political and philosophical roots and purposes of the various academic units, nevertheless, had much in common.

From the very onset of the Chicana/o cultural renaissance, artists and scholars viewed their contributions as an essential part of the Movimiento. They defined themselves as cultural workers who contributed their scholarship and motifs to the goals of providing ethnic pride, raising a critical awareness of the Chicano experience vis-à-vis the dominant society, and offering rich and vibrant cultural works. The role and position of social critics and analysts became paramount in Movimiento and post-Movimiento writings and artistic manifestations. Chicana/o intellectuals denied that their work was produced as "art for art's sake." Rather, they viewed their effort as a committed political endeavor with a clear ideological premise: to create a cultural production that is sensitive to and representative of its community and that is an essential element in the community's quest for social justice and artistic acclaim.[15] This defined role of Chicana/o artists, scholars, and writers has remained unchanged.

In the fourth phase of the Chicano Movement, activists engaged in oppositional politics, "the politics of Aztlán." The political ideas supporting this strategy "were developed within a new framework that saw Mexican Americans as a historically and culturally rich community seeking to liberate itself from Anglo-American racism."[16] Chicana/o activists' goals were those of self-determination and cultural solidarity. As members of a community that was outside the American mainstream, they promoted cultural nationalism as part of an anticolonial struggle. The Movimiento rocked the political and cultural landscape of the Southwest. During the late seventies, however, it experienced a significant decline in intensity, cohesion, and scope.

The Chicano Movement left a significant cultural legacy, although it did not accomplish all of its major goals. In fact, while the activist phase and confrontational nature of the Movimiento declined or moved in a different direction, the cultural renaissance never wavered, its momentum and creative force continued and even gained a new generation of artists in the decades that followed. The Movement "institutionalized a political counterculture that define[d] itself through its ethnicity and historical experience."[17] One of the most visible signs of this institutionalization has been the establishment of the Chicano community's cultural centers throughout the nation. The Guadalupe Cultural Center in San Antonio, Texas, and the Centro Cultural de la Raza in San Diego, California, are outstanding examples of such institutions. These and other similar centers were most responsible for the promotion and appreciation of Chicana/o culture at the grassroots level; they were instrumental in the representation and diffusion of Chicana/o culture; and they made artistic works accessible to community audiences. Their valuable efforts have continued through the decades of the 1980s and 1990s.

Another significant example of the continuing influence of the Chicano Movement is the sprouting and flowering of a distinctive Chicana literature. Chicana writers, many of them former Movement activists, have become a powerful force in Chicano literary circles. Through their creative writings, Chicanas have manifested a specific (but not exclusive) concern for issues of identity, gender, and social justice. Most Chicana writers have evinced a feminist position, and thus many of their protagonists are preadolescent girls, young women, and older women struggling against a patriarchal order. Ana Castillo, Denise Chávez, Sandra Cisneros, Demetria Martínez, Helena María Viramontes, and others have filtered their fictional universes through the lens of a feminist optic.[18] Their literary works are currently at the forefront of Chicano letters.

Another salient issue of paramount importance to Chicana writers is their concern for the rights of lesbian Chicanas and gay Chicanos. Chicana writers continue to battle against what they perceive to be a homophobic and antilesbian society; it is particularly painful for Chicana/o homosexuals to experience sexism and sexual oppression from Chicano society itself. Writers such as Gloria Anzaldúa, Alicia Gaspar de Alba, and Cherríe Moraga have eloquently inscribed within their literary discourse a critique of oppressive policies and actions on the part of both the hegemonic culture and Chicano society. Through their critiques, they extend and reflect the adversarial position against oppression that was and remains an integral component of the Chicano counterculture.

In the literary realm, another concrete example of the influence of the

Chicano Movement is the existence of Chicano-oriented publishers. Two prime examples are Arte Público Press at the University of Houston and the Bilingual Review Press at Arizona State University. Both presses have sought out, published, and distributed numerous monographs and individual literary works by Chicana/o writers. Their efforts encouraged a steady production of Chicana/o literature. The two presses published emerging writers as well as more established ones. Through excellent publicity, and on the strength of the works themselves, these presses quickly became important vehicles for placing Chicana/o writings on the national scene. In the wake of the success and popularity of Chicano presses, established university presses also began publishing Chicana/o authors. Commercial presses have also followed suit. As a consequence, more and more Chicana/o scholars and writers are being published nationally by mainstream presses.

Since the 1970s, Chicano cultural production has not only been influential and significant in American society but has also transcended borders. Currently, Chicano culture has generated a great deal of interest and fascination in Latin America and Europe.[19] Even Mexico began to take a more positive attitude toward her U.S. descendants. In the past, Mexico had ignored or, worse yet, had stereotyped Chicanos as *pochos.* The pejorative term "pocho" indicated Americanized people of Mexican origin, who consciously turned their back on Mexico or even denied their Mexican roots. However, the advent and development of the Chicano Movement reversed this process. Because the Movimiento stressed its Mexican roots and cultural legacy, Mexican society began to rediscover *el México de afuera* (the other Mexico) and to re-evaluate the Chicana/o community and its cultural expressions. Chicano writers and scholars have since become increasingly known and read in Mexico.

Prominent Chicana/o authors who are particularly recognized in Mexico are Sandra Cisneros, Miguel Méndez, and Alejandro Morales. Méndez and Morales, in particular, first published their initial novels in Mexico. Subsequently, select Mexican mainstream presses such as Fondo de Cultura Económica, Siglo XXI, and era have translated and published various Chicana/o monographs and anthologies. Further, editorial projects by the Secretaría de Educación, the Universidad Nacional Autónoma de México, and other Mexican state university presses have sought out and published original studies on Chicana/o themes. Although the great majority of scholarship and artistic works on Chicanas/os have been authored by Chicanas/os themselves, a small number of Mexican scholars and artists have begun to examine, write, and creatively represent the Chicano experience. A Chicano influence has permeated Mexican contemporary art. The art movement known as the "Nuevomexicanistas" has acknowledged that one of its principal influences has been Chicano culture and art as well as the Chicano civil rights struggle. Their artistic works include diverse Chicano themes and icons such as *pachucos* (zoot suiters) and representations of Mexican American women.

During the 1980s, Chicana/o literary and cultural production made an impact on European scholarship. Germany was one of the first European countries to focus on and explore the intricacies of Chicana/o creative writings. Wolfgang Binder, a professor at a major university in Germany, began interviewing Chicana/o scholars and analyzing their works in the 1970s. In the following decades, conferences on Chicana/o topics were held in France, Germany, Holland, and Spain. In the nineties, Spain led the way and sponsored several conferences. European countries have shown a great interest in Chicana/o political issues and literary and artistic expressions. They view Chicana/o cultural production not only as interesting in terms of its artistic merit but also as a model for understanding ethnic groups within their own countries. Such interest reflects the international appeal of Chicana/o contemporary art and culture.

Chicano Counterculture

In the post-Movimiento decades—the 1980s and 1990s—Chicana/o cultural and artistic trends became more complex; they matured and reflected various tendencies and perspectives. In addition, a new generation of artists, filmmakers, writers, and scholars emerged and made their presence known. This most recent Chicana/o generation encompassed its own unique characteristics. Like the Movimiento's artistic generation, which developed concurrently with and was influenced by the civil rights movement, the post-Movimiento generation sought to address their artistic and cultural concerns by reflecting the political and ideological climate of the 1980s and 1990s. Chicana/o artists and writers have been structuring their cultural works through a discursive framework that appeals to a wider audience. Thus, political and nationalistic themes in art and culture are linked with issues of gender, alternative lifestyles, sexuality, and the challenges of the new millennium.

The Chicana/o counterculture was one of several counterculture movements (along with the feminist movement, the gay and lesbian liberation movement, and so forth) that surfaced in the United States in the late sixties and has continued up to the present. Such counterculture movements have attracted scholarly attention. In particular, the youth counterculture has received considerable notice because of a preoccupation with the so-called "culture wars." An assessment of the future fate of the counterculture movement is not encouraging to activists of the 1960s. According to Thomas Frank, this counterculture has experienced co-optation by the culture industry (for example, movie producers, television networks, radio stations, publishing houses). He argues that dissent has been "commodified": the rebellious youth counterculture has become today's "hip commercial culture."[20]

An important question to be asked is whether the Chicano counterculture and its cultural production has suffered the same fate as the youth counterculture. In other words, has the Chicano counterculture been assimilated into the mainstream and become institutionalized? Has it been subjected to co-optation and commodification, key processes of cultural imperialism? An examination of selected areas of Chicano cultural production, in particular Chicano theater and art, offers conflicting answers vis-à-vis possible co-optation. For example, one analysis of the trajectory of Latino art suggests that commodification emerged at the beginning of the 1980s when mainstream institutions began to recognize Latino arts and artists.[21] Yolanda Broyles-González, in her seminal study of the Teatro Campesino, offers a perspective that includes the cultural imperialism thesis.[22] Tomás Ybarra-Frausto, on the other hand, asserts that:

> They [Chicano artists] change not because a museum starts buying their work, but because they're onto another phase of their *inquietud* and their expression, and as long as they do that, I don't think there's any possibility of containment. Containment only happens when you stop creating and keep producing. I think most of our artists are still creating rather than just producing. Their work is not commodified, they still have too many stories to tell.[23]

Although the fate of the Chicano counterculture is an important issue, it is one of many issues that need to be examined in depth. Clarification of these and related issues is an important goal of Chicano Studies research centers and Chicana/o intellectuals as well as other scholars interested in the development and evolution of Mexican American cultural production and cultural thought.

Overview of Chapters

The nine scholarly articles included in this anthology address various artistic fields of contemporary Chicano culture. They offer the reader a discussion and analysis of the major issues and directions of contemporary Chicana/o culture and artistic production.

In his article "All Over the Map: *La Onda Tejana* and the Making of Selena," Roberto R. Calderón discusses how, throughout most of the twentieth century, the Mexican Texas–based music known as *Tejano* has enjoyed great popularity. Until recently, this particular genre of music tended to appeal regionally, mainly among Texans of Mexican heritage and among the Mexican American community along the Southwest border. The Chicano historian documents that during the 1990s, however, the music began to transcend geographical and social boundaries, experiencing an unprecedented rise in reach and popularity among audiences across the United States, Mexico, and Latin America. Calderón points out as evidence an increase in Tejano record sales worldwide, and the meteoric rise of the young late Tejano recording artist, Selena Quintanilla-Pérez. In short, Tejano music has become a transnational phenomenon appealing to audiences "all over the map."

Calderón traces the rise of Tejano music to social and economic developments within and outside the Chicana/o population. These developments included the rapid growth of the Latino population in the United States, extensive Mexican immigration during the 1980s and 1990s, and increased purchasing power among Chicanas/os and other Latinos. Other factors contributing to the success of Tejano music were the entrance of multinational recording companies into the Tejano music market and their cultivation of the careers and music of Tejano artists. Of added importance was the distribution of this musical genre through major retail chains, and the growth of Spanish-language radio and television stations. After examining these developments and their specific contributions to Tejano music, Calderón focuses on the phenomenal rise of the young recording artist Selena. During the 1990s, Selena became known as the "queen of Tejano music." According to Calderón, her success aided in the breaking down of gender barriers within the Tejano music industry and marked the beginnings of a more gender-integrated industry. Calderón's article provides an excellent analysis of the Tejano music industry, Selena's rise to fame and fortune, and her positive impact on the Tejano music industry. Of additional interest is his analysis of Selena's significance as a cultural icon.

Historian Juan Gómez-Quiñones's study "Outside Inside—The Immigrant Workers: Creating Popular Myths, Cultural Expressions, and Personal Politics in Borderlands Southern California" offers incisive insights regarding the cultural production of Mexican immigrant communities along the border and, in particular, in southern California. His analysis focuses on the 1986–96 period and examines various genres of Mexican immigrant popular culture. With respect to music, for example, he chronicles and examines songs ranging from Chicano punk bands such as Los Illegals to such groups as Banda Machos. These performers have given a voice to immigrants, underscored the trials and tribulations of the immigrant journey and experience, and revealed the texture of immigrant society and life. Gómez-Quiñones provides an illuminating discussion of the nature and significance of the borderlands' cultural expressions in terms of identity, myth construction, and social change.

According to Gómez-Quiñones, the cultural practices of the borderlanders challenge the stereotype of immigrant nonagency found in scholarly and journalistic discussions. The Chicano historian underlines how these cultural practices constitute "modes through which the political and the personal are expressed and [through which] simultaneously cultural ideals and practices themselves are changed and redefined" across national boundaries. In the face of efforts to "annihilate" them culturally, socially, and politically, these borderlanders, Gómez-Quiñones argues, have challenged and affirmed themselves and their "surrounding order." In the process they have created views of themselves at significant odds with the pejorative images evoked by popular and scholarly discussions. Mexican immigrants, through their expressive cultural traditions, document an evolving consciousness as they affirm themselves and their culture. Their creations have been frequently infused with insurgent tendencies, which have manifested themselves in humor, poetry, literature, theater, graphic and mural arts, and music. In short, they have created and sustained a dynamic culture.

David R. Maciel and Susan Racho, in their contribution " 'Yo soy chicano': The Turbulent and Heroic Life of Chicanas/os in Cinema and Television," focus on the significance of two broad areas related to the mass media—cinema and television—and how these two media have affected the Chicana/o experience. The authors initiate their discussion by underscoring the detrimental effects that the mass media has had on Chicanas/os. According to Maciel and Racho, the media have promoted institutionalized racism toward this ethnic group. In particular, institutionalized racism has occurred in the form of stereotyping, appropriation of Chicano culture, negative portrayals of Chicanas/os, exclusion of Chicanas/os with respect to employment, and the lack of opportunity for the development of their artistic projects. Among the consequences of these practices have been the legitimization of discrimination against Chicanas/os and the near invisibility of Chicanas/os on screen and behind cameras. Yet Maciel and Racho point out how Chicanas/os have not been passive victims of these practices. Chicanas/os repeatedly have fought for access to film schools and television stations and for other types of resources needed. They have also explored alternative ways to achieve their goals, such as undertaking independent film productions and seeking coproductions with their Mexican counterparts.

Chicanas/os have also fought for the right to be represented in television and film scripts. Oftentimes this has been achieved only when Mexican Americans became filmmakers themselves. Initially, attention was focused on the production of film documentaries. By the 1990s, Chicanas/os had been involved in more than 100 documentaries covering a diverse array of subjects, including such noted ones as the history of the Chicano Movement: *Chicano: History of the Mexican American Civil Rights Movement.* Today, the documentary remains the dominant cinematic genre for Chicana/o filmmakers. A recent development, however, has been in narrative cinema. Maciel and Racho point out how this genre has developed despite serious obstacles placed before it.

After critically reviewing some of the major Chicano narrative films, Maciel and Racho examine the role of Chicanas/os in narrative television. In this arena, Chicana/o participation at all levels is even lower than in film. The only area where progress in commercial television has occurred is in local and national television news programs. A serious consequence of such neglect is a lack of reporting on Chicano issues.

Although Spanish-language television has grown substantially since the late eighties and is a potential source of news/entertainment and employment opportunities for Chicanas/os, the networks have been largely indifferent to producing Chicano works. On the positive side, Spanish-language television networks have devoted greater attention to issues of concern to Chicanas/os and other Spanish-language audiences such as California's recent anti-immigration legislation (Proposition 187) and "English Only" drives.

Maciel and Racho propose a series of changes that must be implemented if the status of Chicanas/os in cinema and television is to improve.

In the absence of such changes, the future of Chicanas/os in the industry will continue to be bleak and the vibrancy and complexity of the Mexican-origin population in the United States will continue to be ignored. This is unfortunate, because Chicanas/os and other Latinos will become the nation's largest minority in the twenty-first century.

Communications scholar Virginia Escalante, in her contribution "The Politics of Chicano Representation in the Media," critically examines the emergence of "Hispanic" or "Latino" media and the significance of this development. Escalante posits that in order for the "Latino" or "Hispanic" media phenomenon to be understood, it must be placed in the contexts of the struggle over cultural representation, the political economy, the racialized social structure of the United States, and the role of the dominant media among Chicanas/os.

Escalante argues that the dominant media historically have bolstered, legitimated, and reproduced the social hierarchy in which Chicanas/os occupy a subordinate position and are largely subjected to an invisible state or negative representation. Chicanas/os, however, have not been passive victims in the process. Capitalizing on the changing demographics, Chicanas/os have created community-based communications vehicles. In particular, they have published newspapers with at least alternative, if not oppositional possibilities, as typified by *El Sol de San Diego*. Confronted by competing cultural products and an expanding market, and driven by market and profit incentives, the dominant media have begun to reach out and incorporate community-based media. One major negative consequence of this was the imposition of an increasingly commercialized culture that eclipsed alternative or oppositional cultural forms. As a result, the production of popular culture has been inhibited and the emphasis on consumerism has discouraged dissent. In addition, there has been a demise of alternative forms of communication necessary for the achievement of an equitable redistribution of information resources and a more democratic media system.

Although the 1980s were heavily promoted as an era when Chicanas/os were supposed to achieve visibility and recognition at the national level, they did not witness substantial advancement in media representation or employment. Furthermore, Chicanas/os have remained marginal in communication studies departments at colleges and universities throughout the United States. Theories that can serve to explain the nature of the relationship between Chicanas/os and the media have not been developed, although the absence of such theoretical work has dire consequences.

Diana I. Ríos, in her article "Chicana/o and Latina/o Gazing: Audiences of the Mass Media," takes as her point of departure the current state of theoretical underdevelopment and argues for serious work to be undertaken in this area. Ríos posits that the construction of explanatory models is needed in three vital areas of communication studies research: Chicano audience exposure (to determine how much time individuals spend with different forms of media), functional media use and gratification (to determine what rewards viewers obtain from media exposure), and feminist popular culture theory on spectators, fans, and readers of film and/or print media (to determine the effects of media on female audiences).

Ríos asserts that a careful examination of the contributions and limitations of the above areas are vital to the understanding of the nature of the Chicano gaze. ("Gaze" is defined as the manner in which one perceives reality by looking at the world and the way it is represented.) She offers theoretical models for the extant gaps in communication studies and Chicano audiences. Her analysis reveals a complex portrait of the links between communication studies and Chicana/o audiences and their importance in theoretical and instrumental applications. In Ríos's view, the development of theoretical models for understanding the media vis-à-vis Chicana/o audiences is important. However, in the current political and social climate, studies of this sort are unlikely to occur. Thus, the guarded qualities of the Chicano gaze will become even more accentuated as the result of unresponsive media.

In his article "A Historical Overview/Update on the State of Chicano Art," art historian George Vargas offers an in-depth study of the evolution of Chicana/o art. His analysis focuses on the art produced during the late sixties and early seventies. Vargas points out that Chicana/o art is a socially sensitive phenomenon that serves the Chicana/o population as well as the larger community. He underscores its origins in the social and political conditions extant in Chicano communities. Even though it is often perceived as monolithic protest art, Chicano art is characterized by diversity in techniques, media, and content. Vargas points out how various art forms are used to validate Mexican American identity.

Vargas's analysis seeks to stimulate dialogue and offer analytical models vis-à-vis the development of Chicana/o art. His careful examination of the evolution of Chicana/o art reveals continuity in the experiences of these artists. Among these experiences is the sense of continued marginalization. Nevertheless, since the late sixties and early seventies, the world of Chicana/o art has witnessed change. During the 1980s, the features of this ethnic art changed as the socioeconomic standing of the population underwent a transformation. Moreover, Mexican American artists journeyed into new territories, exploring other artistic theories and media; they organized groups to explore and study Chicana/o participation in a global society, and they embraced new forms of artistic expressions. They recognized the importance of our postmodern society. Some even began crossing over into new commercial art markets.

The 1990s have seen a shift in the Chicana/o artists' intended audience. In the 1960s and early seventies, Chicana/o artists appealed primarily to Mexican American audiences. In the present decade, Chicana/o artists have crossed over to larger mainstream audiences. Indeed, some artists have joined the mainstream graphic arts/advertising industry. As a result of these changes, Vargas argues, "the new Chicano art" is more fluid, organic, multifaceted, and multicultural, expressing/communicating a worldview of unlimited possibilities and diminished nationalism. Vargas concludes his essay by offering an optimistic prognosis for the future of Chicana/o art. He foresees this art as achieving greater prominence in the future and believes it will continue to have the potential to unify Chicanas/os. It will also continue to provide them with insights into their consciousness.

The emergence of Chicano theater in the late 1960s was one of the most exciting developments associated with the rise of the Chicano Movement. The theater produced within the Chicano community survived the demise of social protest, which the initial theatrical productions vividly and dramatically articulated in the barrios, on college campuses, and in agricultural fields. Literary critic Arturo Ramírez, in his work "Contemporary Chicano Theater," examines the evolution of Chicano theater from its formative years, during which the *actos* format was developed by Luis Valdez and El Teatro Campesino presented its Chicano-specific content, characters, and themes, to its current multidimensional character.

Ramírez discusses the history of Chicano theater, which he views as being characterized by both continuity and change during the past three decades. Luis Valdez, whose works initially defined "Chicano teatro," provides a sense of continuity throughout the changes seen in the institutionalization, professionalization, commercialization, and diversification of Chicano theater. Gains and losses have accompanied these developments. For example, commercialization has softened the more strident social protest nature of Chicano theater; institutionalization, however, has meant movement away from the barrios. Such developments, nevertheless, have brought benefits. Diversification, for example, has allowed Chicana feminist playwrights and productions to flourish. Their presence has brought a new level of sophistication and a new range of experiences, insights, and perspectives to Chicano theater. As the twenty-first century begins, Chicana/o theater remains distinct and diverse, but it is no longer unconnected to the rest of the theater world; rather, it is a part of the whole. Furthermore, its vibrancy and vitality remain connected to the community, to social activism, and to the struggle for social change.

The emergence of Chicana voices in the Chicana/o political, economic, social, and cultural life has been one of the most exciting developments in the last decades of the twentieth century. Political scientist Edwina Barvosa-Carter, in her essay "Breaking the Silence: Developments in the Publication and Politics of Chicana Creative Writing, 1973–1998," offers insights into the rise of a Chicana literary voice. According to Barvosa-Carter, Chicana writers experienced obstacles in the publication and dissemination of their literary works. Nevertheless, they have refused to remain silent, tenaciously struggling to continue their work. Accordingly, the years since the 1970s have witnessed an increase in the number and in the dissemination of their publications. This has brought previously marginalized voices to the general public's attention. Indeed, Barvosa-Carter asserts that in the late 1990s literature by Chicanas "stands closer than ever before to taking a central place in the literary landscape."

The story of Chicanas breaking the silence, Barvosa-Carter argues, has not been fully told. In her essay, she traces the publication history of Chicana writers, focusing in particular on the publication of poetry, prose fiction, and drama during 1973–98. Barvosa-Carter examines the social and historical context in which contemporary Chicana writing arose, underscoring the changing opportunities and trends as well as highlighting the social and political significance of the themes encompassed in the writings. It is clear that Chicana writers have not only shattered the literary silence but have also offered critical, exploratory, and dissenting voices. The process of claiming a voice constitutes an act of courage because it defies existing forms of marginalization based on gender, sexuality, physical ability, class, ethnicity, and race. Chicana writers are powerful actors in the process of social and political transformation.

In our closing article, "Trends and Themes in Chicana/o Writings in Postmodern Times," Francisco A. Lomelí, Teresa Márquez, and María Herrera-Sobek explore the trends in Chicana/o literary production in the 1980s and 1990s. The contemporary postmodern age has seen an unprecedented number of Chicana literary voices emerge and offer original and distinctive perspectives and insights. In addition, two new trends have appeared: the rise of the Chicana/o detective novel and a resurgence of Mexican immigrant themes.

According to Lomelí, Márquez, and Herrera-Sobek, the socioeconomic and political conditions of the early eighties were unfavorable for the Mexican-origin population in the United States, despite the media hype surrounding the so-called "Decade of the Hispanic." Nevertheless, this state of affairs did not daunt the creative spirit of Chicana/o writers. A new poetics emerged, rooted in a Chicana desire to experiment with forms and in a deep concern for gender egalitarianism. Mexican American women authors also capitalized on the opportunity afforded by a new-found interest in ethnic writers on the part of commercial publishing companies. As the postmodern rubric of diversity gained ground, Chicana/o authors began to capture international attention. Spearheaded by writers such as Helena María Viramontes and Sandra Cisneros, Chicana writers transformed the decade of the 1980s into the literary "Decade of the Chicana" through a prolific outpouring of creative works, thus becoming one of the most important postmodern trendsetters and innovators in Chicano literature. Their contributions included laying the foundation for the creation of a body of literary writings by Latinos of diverse national origins, resulting in a second "Latino literary boom."

The 1990s witnessed the emergence of a new wave of Latino writers as Chicana/o literature matured. Chicana/o writers increasingly produced texts that defied easy classification, as authors blended form and subject in unprecedented ways. Writers prominent in the era of postmodernity included Luis Rodríguez, Ana Castillo, Denise Chávez, and others. These writers, like their predecessors before them, eschewed exclusive subscription to a specific literary agenda or trend. In their writings they created images of Chicanas/os as complex beings. Some of the writers, such as Manuel Ramos, established the Raza/Aztlán detective/mystery novel as a new literary model, using the genre as a vehicle for commentary on issues of class, race, gender, and sexual orientation or preference. Rapidly increasing in quantity, these works exhibited distinguishing attributes, such as a difference in worldview, and promise to become forceful agents for social and political change.

Chicano Renaissance: A Dialogue with the Future

Since the advent of cultural studies in the late seventies, Chicana/o culture has increasingly attracted the attention of scholars. Although Chicana/o culture has evoked extensive commentary and scholarship, existing studies have tended to focus on a particular cultural manifestation. Seldom does one find in contemporary scholarship a comprehensive examination of Chicano culture. A second limitation of published scholarly studies has been the time frame of the material covered. The great majority of scholarly works do not encompass the 1990s. Thus, to meet and partially address this scholarly neglect, we offer our collection of scholarly essays entitled *Chicano Renaissance: Contemporary Cultural Trends.*

Rarely does a single scholarly work offer definitive answers about questions as diverse and complex as those associated with the nature of contemporary Chicano culture. This anthology is not an exception. Instead, it is offered in the spirit of providing timely, useful, and instructive insights and thought-provoking discussions. Our collection of essays seeks to engage in a scholarly dialogue that will aid in the clarification of the many issues associated with the continuing vitality of Chicano culture. Our goals are to frame tentative answers, advance understanding, and contribute to the body of knowledge emerging with regard to critical issues in contemporary Chicano culture.

In these essays the various contributors reveal that, contrary to the popular notion that Chicanas/os have succumbed to a victim mentality, Chicanas/os actively struggle to shape the conditions of their lives and the direction of American society through their artistic projects. It is their labors that enable Chicana/o cultural production to continue to remain influential. Moreover, contrary to the idea that the eighties and nineties have been decades of self-interested individualism and narcissism, a humanitarianism and a commitment to collective community improvement continue to infuse Chicano cultural production and expression. One area where these themes persist is the depiction of the Mexican immigrant experience. Mexican immigration to the United States, a process with human dimensions of tremendous depth and complexity, has been a central concern of Chicana/o cultural workers. The experience of Mexican immigrants has been made more difficult by the rise of nativism and immigrant bashing encountered in the United States over the last twenty-five to thirty years.

However, resistance, struggle, defiance, autonomous cultural production, and change have not been the only currents the scholars highlight. Other trends are also at work within the Chicana/o cultural arena. Evidence of accommodation can be found in the production of Chicana/o work by non-Chicana/o sponsors and other organizations. In short, the essays included in this anthology reveal that dynamism, diversity, and complexity characterize Chicana/o contemporary expressions.

Notes

1. Historically, the entire Mexican-origin community was recognized by the term "Chicano." In this book, "Chicanas/os" and "Chicanos" are used interchangeably to refer to Mexican Americans and reflect current trends in scholarship that acknowledge the contributions of women. This usage is consistent with the name changes of academic departments and of the most important professional academic organization in the field, the National Association of Chicana and Chicano Studies. Also, the terms "Latinos" and "Latinas" are used here instead of the terms "Hispanic" and "Hispanics," unless otherwise noted. The criticisms are discussed in Diana Griego Erwin, "No Need to Collar the Dog," *The Sacramento Bee*, 16 July 1998, 1-1.

2. See Ignacio García, *Chicanismo: The Forging of a Militant Ethos* (Tucson: University of Arizona Press, 1997).

3. Ibid., 9.

4. Ibid., 12.

5. See Carlos Muñoz, Jr., *Youth Identity, Power: The Chicano Movement* (London: Verso, 1989).

6. Ibid., 143–45.

7. Ibid., 146–49.

8. The major studies in the areas of history and other disciplines are examined by various scholars in *Chicanos and the Social Sciences: A Decade of Research and Development (1970–1980)*, ed. Isidro D. Ortiz (Santa Barbara: Center for Chicano Studies, University of California, Santa Barbara, 1983).

9. García, *Chicanismo*, 12.

10. See Yolanda Broyles-González, *El Teatro Campesino: Theater in the Chicano Movement* (Austin: University of Texas Press, 1994).

11. An excellent overview of these developments is provided in *Handbook of Hispanic Cultures in the United States,* ed. Francisco Lomelí (Houston: Arte Público Press, 1993).

12. These developments are critically examined in Rosa Linda Fregoso, *The Bronze Screen: Chicana and Chicano Film Culture* (Minneapolis: University of Minnesota Press, 1994).

13. Carl Muñoz, Jr., "The Development of Chicano Studies," in *Chicano Studies: A Multidisciplinary Approach,* eds. Eugene E. García, Francisco Lomelí, and Isidro D. Ortiz (New York: Teachers College Press, 1984).

14. Eva Sperling Cockroft, "From Barrio to Mainstream: The Panorama of Latino Art" in *Handbook of Hispanic Cultures in the United States,* ed. Francisco Lomelí (Houston: Arte Público Press, 1993), 192–217.

15. The clearest expression of this position is found in Juan Gómez-Quiñones, "On Culture," *Revista Chicano–Riqueña* 5, no. 2 (1977): 29–47.

16. García, *Chicanismo,* 13.

17. Ibid., 145.

18. For a survey of range and value of the contributions of Chicana writers prior to the nineties, see Cordelia Chávez Candelaria, "Latina Women Writers: Chicana, Cuban American and Puerto Rican Voices," in *Handbook of Hispanic Cultures in the United States,* ed. Francisco Lomelí (Houston: Arte Público Press, 1993); María Herrera-Sobek and Helena María Viramontes, *Chicana Creativity and Criticism: New Frontiers in American Literature* (Albuquerque: University of New Mexico Press, 1996); Herrera-Sobek and Viramontes, *Chicana (W)rites: On Word and Film* (Berkeley: Third Woman Press, 1995); Alma M. García, *Chicana Feminist Thought: The Basic Historical Writings* (New York: Routledge, 1970); and Carla Trujillo, ed., *Living Chicana Theory* (Berkeley: Third Woman Press, 1998).

19. The roots of interest in Europe, in particular Spain, are discussed by Nicolás Kanellos and Claudio Esteva-Fabregat in the introduction to Lomelí, ed., *Handbook of Hispanic Cultures in the United States,* 11–12.

20. Thomas Frank, *The Conquest of Cool: Business Culture, Countercultures, and the Rise of Hip Consumerism* (Chicago: University of Chicago Press, 1998).

21. Eva Sperling Cockroft, "From Barrio to Mainstream: The Panorama of Latino Art" in Lomelí, ed., *Handbook of Hispanic Cultures in the United States,* 208.

22. Broyles-González, *El Teatro Campesino,* 214–15.

23. Quoted in Alicia Gaspar de Alba, *Chicano Art: Inside and Outside the Master's House* (Austin: University of Texas Press, 1998), 218.

Chicano Renaissance

All Over the Map: La Onda Tejana and the Making of Selena

ROBERTO R. CALDERÓN

El corazón no se hace viejo, es el cuero el que se arruga.
Leonardo "Flaco" Jiménez

*T*he 1990s proved to be a defining decade for "La Onda Tejana," variously known as "La Onda Chicana" in the 1960s and 1970s and as "Tex-Mex" in other circles. By the early 1980s the regional Mexican Texas–based music, which was meant to be danced to, came to be identified as "Tejano" music.[1] This music was supported by the growing Mexican and Latino population in the United States, and during the 1990s, the combined *conjunto,* polka, *cumbia,* country, pop, and rock sounds underlying the style eclipsed previous modes. It also established itself as a new sound among music audiences everywhere.

The rise of Tejano music was paralleled by a related trend within the Spanish-speaking music industry in the United States and Latin America. This trend, which had emerged over the course of the previous ten to fifteen years, reduced the musical presence of acts from Spain by the late 1980s.[2] It climaxed in 1989, when Spanish acts ceased to rule *Billboard's* U.S. Latin music charts.[3] In Mexico, Jesús López, vice president of Latin North America at BMG International, noted how the musical sounds produced in countries such as Mexico and Argentina were getting closer and closer to Spain's. He added, "Now there are fewer artists [from Spain] because Mexico has its own artists who can compete."[4] Further, the retail value of the Latin American music market during the early to mid-1990s experienced continued growth at the expense of some European countries; by 1994 the market was worth $2 billion, or 5.6 percent of the world's total sales.[5]

The major recording companies with interests in worldwide music markets began cultivating the careers and music of regional and national artists, especially in the United States and selected Latin American countries. Changing tastes in popular music among Latino audiences paralleled corporate record industry commitments, which reflected the trend. José Behar, president of EMI Latin and a leading player in signing Tejano artists to major labels, observed that "[t]he signing of Gloria Estefan in the U.S. opened a lot of people's eyes to the possibilities of local talent. So the market gradually changed and evolved as we gained confidence in the potential of local artists."[6] Consequently, recording artists in the Tejano and other Latino music genres became more likely to sign recording packages with the industry's global companies.

Capitalizing on these trends, the major record labels began signing Tejano artists to long-term and multiple-record contracts as quickly as possible.[7] The role of major record labels in the Tejano music industry was accompanied by increased promotion and distribution for the music at most of the mainstream record chains nationwide.[8] But Tejano went even further and entered international Latin American markets, where the music had not found a hold before.[9] This experience was colored by unprecedented music sales worldwide, with sales in Southeast Asia and Latin America driving world sales beyond the $30-billion barrier in 1992 (excluding music video sales).[10] Helping this intensified marketing and promotional environment was the fact that the U.S. music market led the world in sales. Moreover, Mexico, despite huge problems with piracy, emerged among the top ten leading music markets worldwide as well.[11]

La Onda Tejana was poised to take off commercially, sweeping all kinds of new sales records and audiences. The industry became big business, influencing corporate decisions, concert venues, syndication, and corporate sponsorships. It also furthered the careers of established and new performers. Among the most renowned of the new performers was a young Tejana, Selena, who, along with her band, Los Dinos, typified Tejano's new amplified style and success in the music industry. In this chapter I offer a cultural history of La Onda Tejana's increasing popularity and commercialization during the 1990s; I conclude the examination with a discussion of the rise and significance of the Tejana star, Selena, whose untimely death in 1995 evoked immense grief in the Tejano music universe (fig. 1.1).

FIGURE 1.1 One month before her death, Selena dominated the Texas music industry, winning six Tejano Music Awards, including Best Female Vocalist and Best Female Entertainer. Selena at the Alamodome in San Antonio, Texas, site of the Fifteenth Annual Tejano Music Awards, February 1995. (Courtesy of the *Eagle Pass Business Journal.*)

La Onda Tejana a Rising Genre

Tejano music's boom during the nineties was an integral part of an explosive cultural phenomenon occurring within Latin music generally. All the Latino musical genres—pop, salsa, regional Mexican, tropical, and jazz—were experiencing significant growth. Moreover, "Latin rap and hip-hop, born in Hispanic neighborhoods of the inner cities, were created by a new generation of artists who, just like those who gave impulse to salsa in the early sixties, learned their music in the streets."[12] Heightened Latino demographic growth accompanied by greater purchasing power, the entrance of the multinational recording companies into the market, distribution through major retail chains, and the cumulative increase of Spanish-language radio and television outlets contributed to the making of this major music and artistic trend. Latino music ceased being a marginal business. By the 1990s the emerging patterns of the 1980s had turned into a full-fledged remaking of the Latino recording industry. Markets that had been confined to regional audiences ten years earlier, during the 1990s "evolved into new artistic expressions."[13] The roots of Tejano's boom as a rising musical genre lie in these developments.

During the early nineties, the album sales of Tejano acts such as La Mafia, Grupo Mazz, La Sombra, and Selena, among others, increased with each release, though the former three (all-male) "established" acts led the way.[14] Industry observers noted the substantive change. Some characterized the period from 1989 to 1991 as years during which the Tejano music industry emerged as "the most active and fastest-expanding genre of all regional forms of Mexican music."[15] Global record companies contracted the top acts for their labels and pursued the "no-names" as well for extra measure lest the competition discover them first. Still, the industry's mood was ebullient but cautious. In question was whether the Tejano market in the United States had yet reached its zenith. The market was hot enough, however, to entice both major and independent (indie) record labels to continue to pursue their share of the market.

The trend by the major recording companies into the Tejano music market began in 1985 when Little Joe y La Familia were signed by José Behar to Discos CBS (now Sony Discos). Behar, who later switched to Capitol/EMI Latin, signed Selena in 1989 to the latter label and learned firsthand about the significant consequences of the acquisition of a major record contract for a Tejano act. Commenting in 1991 on the effect of Little Joe's contract with Discos CBS he stated:

> Six years ago, it was unheard of that a Tex-Mex artist would be signed to a major. But the next thing you know, he was doing TV shows out of Puerto Rico and the next thing the national spotlight was on him. There was a ripple effect as far as image and sales were concerned.
>
> When I signed Little Joe, to sell 25,000 to 30,000 units was considered a major feat. Today when I release [Grupo] Mazz, to go platinum is no longer a huge undertaking.[16]

The promotion of Tejano music by both major and independent record companies paralleled the aggressive marketing of regional Mexican music.[17] Despite the difficulty in establishing accurate figures for the stateside Latino music market, distributors and recording label executives estimated in 1991 that album sales for the U.S. Latino market had climbed to approximately $60 million. Regional Mexican music accounted for approximately 50 percent ($30 million) of the total sales. Within the overall context of this market, by comparison, Tejano's wholesale revenue in 1991 was estimated to be between $3 and $4 million. Record executives' optimistic forecasts that Tejano's growing sales in the previous five years would continue proved to be correct.[18]

Another banner year was reported by industry insiders in 1993. Estimates placed sales of Tejano products stateside at $14 million, an increase over 1992's estimated wholesale volume of $9 million. In Mexico, the wholesale value of Tejano music for 1993 was estimated to have been between $5 and $6 million. EMI/Latin's José Behar was profuse in his optimism as he spoke about the burgeoning market for the Texas-based sound: "I know for a fact that [Tejano artists] are not achieving those sales based on their success in Texas alone. Those artists have crossed over into California, Atlanta, New York, and Florida. [And] Tejano music has hit like an atomic bomb in Mexico. This year [1994], I see the market selling close to $20 million here [stateside]. And in Mexico I see Tejano selling about half that figure."[19]

Behar's Sony Discos counterpart, George Zamora, refusing to disclose specific figures for his label's Tejano acts, admitted that sales in 1993 had improved by as much as 25 percent over the previous year.[20]

Within three short years, revised gross wholesale figures for the U.S. Latino music market pegged its value in 1990 at about $80 million. Within three short years the wholesale figure had nearly doubled to approximately $150 million. Industry observers attributed this increase to improved distribution and increased CD sales. The annual growth rate for the Latino record industry, however, was increasing by 10 percent. While pop artists such as Barrio Boyzz, Gloria Estefan, Jon Secada, and Selena were certainly crossing over into the Anglo market in terms of sales, the greatest overall share in the Latino wholesale music market was coming from artists performing *rancheras,* cumbias, and salsa. As *Billboard* writer John Lannert put it, "Take a look at a typical *Billboard* Latin 50 chart and usually at least 60 percent of the artists making up the chart are ranchero-based *grupos,* Tejano or Tex-Mex artists, and Afro-Caribbean tropical acts."[21]

In the case of Tejano music, industry insiders anticipated continued growth in sales revenue to come partly from the spreading contact of the genre with new audiences previously beyond the reach of the more marginal and traditional independent arrangements that had prevailed in the industry. As sales increased, independent labels became more scarce due in large measure to the general restructuring of the music industry. Vigorous marketing and the infusion of capital by the major labels expanded the genre's performance infrastructure and financial potential.

Tejano artists also became more aware of the appeal of their music beyond the boundaries of Texas, their traditional audience base. For all involved, this appeal translated into greater economic leverage. Before Tejano music's tentative crossover into the English-language markets, the Tejano sound had already crossed over into the Spanish-language markets of the regional Mexican genre both in Mexico and stateside. Through television, the genre also penetrated Latin American markets that had been unfamiliar with the music's contagious rhythms.

Latino Markets and Spanish-Language Radio

As a primary form of mass communication in the nineties, Spanish-language radio exemplified the surge in Latino media markets in the United States. Radio fueled Tejano (and Latino) music's expanding audience base and economic horizons. San Antonio, considered by many to be the heart of the Tejano music industry, made Spanish-language radio history in 1992. Tejano powerhouse radio station KXTN-FM, which changed formats in 1991, became the first primarily Spanish-language (bilingual) music format station to seize the number-one position in the twelve-plus Arbitron ratings. The switch to a 90 percent Tejano format catapulted KXTN, according to program director Rudy Rocha, from "worst to first."[22] In the wake of this unprecedented development, station owners and programmers scrambled to take advantage of the breaking event, which was no fluke.

In Los Angeles, California, "La Equis" (KLAX-FM) replicated KXTN's ratings precedent during the autumn of 1992. Its regional Mexican Spanish-language music (ranchera-*banda*-tropical) format took top honors in the City of Angels' Arbitron ratings, a first in California for Spanish-language radio.[23] Shortly after, another Spanish-language radio station, KGBT in McAllen/Brownsville on the Texas-Mexican border, joined KXTN and KLAX in the ratings sweep. KGBT had long been a ratings contender in a market with an 87-percent Mexican population.

All three stations were located among the top 100 radio markets nationwide.[24] Notably, between 1992 and 1995 KXTN did not relinquish its number-one position in San Antonio's metro radio market.[25] Although Spanish-programming stations generally did not draw the increased advertising revenue to their stations commensurate with top Arbitron ratings, at least some stations in San Antonio reported in 1994 that station revenues increased 35 percent.[26] Though station owners refused to reveal precise figures, industry sources estimated that KXTN was billing advertisers between $5 and $6 million, "an unheard of tally for a Tejano station."[27]

KLAX's market-topping ascent was particularly distinguished as it "became the first, and fastest, Spanish station to top the ratings in a top-20 market." Prior to changing its playlist in August 1992, KLAX had featured a combination of romantic international hits. Between August 1992 and February 1993, having changed to a contemporary presentation and música banda, its Arbitron ratings soared from 2.0 to a "jaw-dropping" 8.4, enabling the station to make Los Angeles radio history. The last station in any single ratings period to score nearly as high had been KPRW-FM, attaining a 7.5 during the autumn of 1987. La Equis's (The X's) historic feat was achieved in a Los Angeles radio market where more than 30 percent of listeners were Latinos, but only six major stations served them. KLAX's achievement, moreover, was distinguished by its ability to attract and retain young listeners, especially Mexican and Latino immigrant youth, who could have tuned in to Top 40 stations.[28]

Although KLAX's historic breakthrough of the overall ratings barrier in the Los Angeles market established the precedent, it subsequently relinquished the top position to the Heftel Broadcasting Company's Spanish-language station, KLVE-FM (Radio Amor), during the ratings period from January to March 1995. KLVE catapulted from a twelfth-place Arbitron rating in the autumn of 1994 to first place during the ratings period from January to March 1995 because of the popularity of its morning program. The program was hosted by Pepe Barreto and emphasized romantic music on its playlist. KLVE's ratings jump pushed KLAX down to eighth place in the same market.

Based on Arbitron ratings, KLVE has since consistently captured the number-one or number-two position. However, KLAX has continued to rank among the top ten most popular stations in Los Angeles. By the 1990s, the new realities for Los Angeles radio were that Mexican and Latino audiences would determine the top positions in the medium and that a new era in mass-media trends had arrived to stay.[29] A rapidly changing radio market perhaps reflected not only a growing Latino population but also a listening audience that paid particularly close attention to Spanish-language radio.

Today the Los Angeles and Orange County metro market is the fastest-growing Spanish-language radio market in the nation. Among the region's eighty-two stations, eighteen are Spanish outlets, including the most recent conversion of English-language station KWNK-AM, in Simi Valley, to a Central American news, music, and sports format. Forty years ago (in 1957), the same Los Angeles metropolitan market featured only one full-time outlet in Spanish, KWKW-AM. By 1987, there were half a dozen, "none of them major players."[30]

In retrospect, the moment had been long in arriving. Spanish-language (Mexican) radio broadcasts in the Los Angeles market date from the late 1920s. The debut of the program *Los Madrugadores* (The Early Risers) at the onset of the Great Depression in 1929 on KMPC "had perhaps the greatest commercial impact."[31] Writing from the pre-KLAX perspective, ethnomusicologist Steven Loza stated that six principal stations served the Los Angeles Spanish-language market. One radio station, KALI, began Spanish broadcasts in 1952 and estimated that at the time 60 percent of Latinos in Los Angeles listened to its programming daily. KALI's rival, KWKW, which began operating in 1942 but switched to Spanish programming in 1962, enjoyed an estimated daily audience of one million listeners in Los Angeles and Orange counties after it switched to all-Spanish broadcasts. KWKW featured Spanish broadcasts of L.A. Dodgers baseball games in its repertoire. More recent competitor stations KLVE and KTNQ claimed a weekly audience of more than a million listeners, before KLAX's zoom to ratings history. KKHJ, meanwhile, was introduced to Angelinos in April 1990. From Mexico City, Radio Express (KXPRES) beamed its powerful signal to the Los Angeles Spanish-language market.[32]

Commenting on KXTN's and KLAX's influential standard-setting performance in heavily Latino U.S. metropolitan radio markets, Casey Monahan, program director at the Texas Music Office, stated in 1993 that "The success of KXTN and KLAX [in] Los Angeles is indicative of Tejano and Latin music's growth in the market. Radio stations respond to ratings, and you can't argue with the success of these two flagship stations."[33] The success of Tejano music in San Antonio and Los Angeles resulted in the conversion to a Tejano music format by more than thirty radio stations in generally smaller markets, including more than a dozen stations in 1992 alone. These new Tejano stations opened from Texas to California, in some cases converting from other forms of Latino music. Even in Guadalajara, Jalisco, radio stations KEKMA-AM and KEKSX-AM began spinning Tejano tunes to their audiences. Meanwhile, in San Antonio one of the first Tejano stations, KEDA-AM, celebrated its twenty-seventh year on the air with a two-day *pachanga* featuring Tejano artists playing the genre's various styles. Television executives and producers capitalized on the industry's popularity, with several producing Tejano music specials for local, national, and international audiences.[34]

Tejano radio used a novel (by existing all-Spanish or all-English format standards) bilingual and bicultural format. Whether commercials, disc jockeys spinning their *rollos,* or the music itself, the bilingual sound of Tejano radio had been a tradition since the fifties for Texas-based AM radio listeners.[35] Only in the nineties did the bilingual tradition hit the FM radio waves through stations such as KXTN and others that followed suit. Johnny Canales, for example, who began his career as an on-air personality in radio, carried the tradition to television in the 1980s.[36] The innovative radio format reflected the bilingual reality of large segments of Mexican and Latino audiences north and south of the U.S.–Mexico border. By 1993 some 350 radio stations in the United States alone were playing Latino music. Among this group were an estimated fifty stations whose programming was all-Tejano and another 100 that reserved some portion of their programming for Tejano music.[37]

Moreover, the number of stations with Tejano music on their playlists kept growing. For example, Dallas acquired its first Tejano station, KICK-FM/AM, in December 1993, while Houston acquired its second FM Tejano station, KXTJ-FM in spring 1993.[38] In addition, another dozen U.S.–Mexico border stations either added Tejano to their programming or converted entirely to the format.[39] As competition stiffened in the Tejano radio market, KXTJ's owners, El Dorado Communications, resorted to buying out the competing FM Tejano station in Houston, KQQK-FM, for a reported $11.5 million.[40]

By 1995, perhaps the most acute competition anywhere within the Tejano radio market occurred in the greater Corpus Christi, Texas, area. Seven FM Tejano stations covered the market, including four in the seaside city: KMIQ, KSAB, KBSO, and KNDA; another three operated in nearby cities: KFLZ in Bishop, KUKA in Alice, and KBIL in Beeville. On the AM dial four stations had a Tejano format: KCCT, KUNO, and KINE in Robstown, and KBIL. The last stood alone in presenting a mixed playlist of Tejano and other genres such as *norteño,* banda, and conjunto.

Four additional FM Tejano stations were heard for the first time in 1995: Colorado's KNKN-FM (Pueblo), New Mexico's KLBO-FM (Albuquerque) and KLMA-FM (Hobbs), and Texas's KQFX-FM (Amarillo).[41] In southern California and other regions of the country, Tejano music programs also appeared on college radio stations during the nineties. Often barely noticed by private-sector competitors, college radio reaches mostly young audiences. These audiences generally tune in to hear a variety of musical genres in highly segmented programming schedules, resulting in the building of a loyal following. One example of Tejano programming by a college radio station is the University of California at Riverside's Radio Aztlán, whose signal reaches a population that is approaching 40 percent Latino in the Inland Empire (Riverside/San Bernardino metropolitan area). Radio Aztlán veteran programmer Alfredo Figueroa launched the one-and-a-half-hour *Tejano Sounds* program in 1995, "because we were playing the music like Little Joe and others, mostly older, brassier sounds, but decided to focus it more. We felt there was a following out there. And it [Tejano music] wasn't being played a lot." Their expectations have since been confirmed. Figueroa discovered that Tejano fans were already organized in southern California and has since built a close relationship with the Tejano Music Club of Southern California, a nonprofit organization dedicated to furthering appreciation of the genre among its members through a newsletter, dances, and *tardeadas.*[42]

Increased access through AM and FM radio expanded marketing directions for Tejano music. One instance of this was the opening in the early nineties of several modern, glitzy nightclubs that were unlike previous smaller, older local dance halls in cities such as Houston and San Antonio.[43] The new nightclubs attracted audiences of all ages, but the emphasis was on drawing younger crowds to appreciate and support the artists. San Antonio's clubs Desperados and T-Town and Houston's ZAZZ led the trend. Artists were in turn paying more attention to the image they portrayed to audiences. Similarly, retail merchandising of artist paraphernalia assumed greater importance and increased accordingly.

Historically, the use of videos to further the careers of Tejano musicians was practically unheard of, and where it did occur, these were low-budget productions generally funded by the artists themselves. But by the early nineties and without any outlet comparable to MTV, which focused on English-language pop and rock music, labels began supporting Tejano artists in the production of music videos to accompany promotion and sales and increase name recognition. La Mafia (and Sony Discos) was a pioneer in the music video arena with their 1991 video of hit songs from their mega-album *Estás Tocando Fuego,* costing an estimated $50,000 to produce. Sony Discos's video of Ram Herrera's hit single "Si mañana nunca llega" (If Tomorrow Never Comes) was another effort that cost $50,000 to produce. More typically, however, even by the early to mid-1990s, music videos for Tejano artists were being produced for $15,000 to $25,000. Some acts continued to shoot their videos in Mexico for costs as low as $5,000, but these tended to be lower-quality productions. Nevertheless, Tejano Music Awards video producer, Jaime Vera, stated in 1993 that "[w]ith few exceptions, videos in Tejano are way behind the times."[44] Vera's assessment aside, the trends were begun toward improved quality in video production, expanded retail merchandising, and increased live performance venues readily available to artists, and further improvements appeared sure to follow.

The Johnny Canales Show

Perhaps the most influential television program to present La Onda Tejana to new and established audiences is the *Johnny Canales Show.* The show was launched locally in Corpus Christi by Juan José "Johnny" Canales in 1980, while he worked with Radio Jalapeño, KCCT-AM. Canales was approached by the Coors beer distributor to conduct a half-hour television program on "border music," scheduled to air on Corpus Christi's NBC affiliate. The venture marked the beginning of Tejano television programming, which was quickly adopted by television station programmers in Laredo, San Antonio, and the Río Grande Valley.[45] So successful was the *Johnny Canales Show* in Texas that in 1988 the SIN television network (now Univisión) contracted to show the program nationwide.[46]

By late 1989, Canales's program was being viewed in the United States, Mexico, and Latin America. SIN's 522 affiliates in the Western Hemisphere provided "a potential viewing audience estimated in the millions."[47] Canales stayed with Univisión for more than six years, but switched over to the competing Telemundo network in 1996. He claimed that his viewers were often confused and upset over Univisión's failure to consistently schedule the *Johnny Canales Show* at a fixed hour.

Telemundo's executives sensed the problem and offered Canales a better deal. They scheduled the program at a fixed time and date. Canales's syndicated show promoted live performances of Tejano, norteño, tropical ballads, and Tejano-country. By the mid-1990s Canales had added banda to his show's repertoire because of the genre's great popularity among regional Mexican music fans who comprised a significant part of his viewing audience in Mexico and the United States. Canales was fortunate to have had the opportunity to introduce such emerging Tejano and regional Mexican greats as Selena, Grupo Mazz, and Bronco, to cite but a few, to national (and international) audiences.[48] These music industry relationships were mutually beneficial.

The Tejano Music Awards

In 1980, another inaugural event, barely noticed except by those most closely tied to the Tejano music circuit, transpired in San Antonio. Enter the Texas Talent Musicians Association (TTMA), a nonprofit organization formed to showcase and recognize Tejano musicians, songwriters, producers, in short, the full spectrum of talent comprising the heart and soul of La Onda. TTMA's executive director from 1980 to 1998 was Rudy R. Treviño. TTMA's foremost innovation and contribution was the creation of the Tejano Music Awards (TMA). The first annual event was held at the Convention Center's North Banquet Hall on March 1, 1981, and drew 1,300 participants.[49]

By 1991, the TMA event was drawing upwards of 13,000 participants, with most of the industry's officials taking part. Furthermore, the event was being held in the Convention Center Arena where delayed television broadcasts were estimated to have reached an additional thirteen million people.[50] The first live broadcast of the TMA occurred in 1993, when it was beamed directly via satellite to thirty-two markets in the Southwest, including California.[51] A year later, the TMA went global when it was broadcast for the first time by the U.S. Armed Forces Radio and Television Network.[52] Notwithstanding the appearance of numerous copycat shows across the country, by 1997 the TMA was considered to be the industry's premiere annual awards event, one sure sign that the TMA was popular and that word about the event had become widespread. More than 40,000 attended the 1997 (seventeenth annual) awards ceremony at the 65,000-seat Alamodome, where TMA events have been held since 1994.[53]

By 1997, moreover, the economic impact of the TMA and associated initiatives had become impressive. One event timed to coincide with the March date of the TMA was the Tejano Music Fanfare at Market Square, which drew an estimated 35,000 persons. In a city where tourism is an important economic enterprise, the TMA and related events contributed an estimated $14.5 million to San Antonio's economy. Further, approximately 250 million people viewed the TMA by satellite and delayed-tape television in the United States and 134 countries, while more than fifteen million other audience members were reached through related radio programs in the United States alone. Similarly, more than seventy-five newspapers, magazines, and other publications with a combined estimated readership of more than ten million covered the latest version of the awards extravaganza.[54] Further, the TMA continued its induction of members into the Tejano Music Hall of Fame,[55] whose purpose, according to Sam Zuñiga, TTMA Hall of Fame archivist, was to honor

> [t]he best of the best. It is our goal to recognize and pay tribute to those musicians, composers, and performers who have contributed significantly to the foundation of the Tejano music industry.
>
> [T]he Tejano Music Hall of Fame was established to preserve the history, culture, and the continued development of Tejano music. The performers and composers we honor have broken barriers and overcome tremendous obstacles in an industry where personal sacrifice and perseverance are the price of success.[56]

Crisis and Resolution: The Boycott

Amid the growing popularity of the TMA, as demonstrated by the increasing thousands of fans who attended the event every year, the awards experienced a major crisis in 1992, when Capitol/EMI Latin artists swept all thirteen categories in two consecutive years (1991–92). Believing they were being excluded, four competing labels, Fonovisa, Freddie Records, Sony Discos, and TH Rodven, announced a boycott of the genre's main event after the 1992 TMA event. At issue was the nomination and selection process. This was expressed in a statement to the TMA by boycott participant Sony Discos: "[I]t is clear there are no procedures in place to protect the integrity of the nominations and awards process."[57]

The TTMA responded promptly, and specific steps to appease the critics were undertaken. In July and August, TTMA executive director, Rudy R.

Treviño, organized several meetings to "redraw the playing field and hope-fully lure back the disgruntled labels," which held firm and avoided direct participation.[58] A fifty-seven–member Tejano Music Awards Committee comprised of industry volunteers was formed and divided into four sub-committees. The individual subcommittees were assigned to establish guide-lines for nominations, vote tabulation, new awards categories, and lifetime achievement awards.[59] The committee's summer work resulted in several immediate changes.[60]

The boycott signaled the TMA's premiere role in the Tejano music indus-try. It was an expression of the extent to which the industry's competing la-bels would go to ensure that they turned an acceptable profit on the millions they had invested on the genre's future, the artists they represented, and the music product they marketed. Record executives knew that recognition at the TMA meant artistic and label success.[61] They were willing to wager that a temporary absence from the gala event would influence its future direction.

The TMA boycott lasted two years, with the labels and their stable of artists returning to the fold in 1995. Though the four labels made peace with the TMA during the fall of 1994 and allowed artists signed to their labels to attend, most did not show up. Among those Tejano acts conspicuous by their absence were at least two veteran Tejano acts, Grammy winner Little Joe y La Familia and La Mafia, Sony's lead Tejano/pop act, who expressed continued displeasure with the TMA.[62] Meanwhile, the awards had become divided into two broad sets of categories—the general (popular) awards and the industry awards—as a result of the 1992–94 boycott and subsequent reforms that were implemented. Winners of the industry awards were deter-mined only by Tejano artists, and in 1994 at the Alamodome "Selena was the only general award honoree to garner an Industry Award, winning best Tejano international artist prize."[63]

The TMA, the staff, and the board of the TTMA acted responsibly and professionally to avert the boycott against its principal program. During the boycott, the television broadcast of the TMA was expanded to include live broadcasts stateside and globally through the Armed Forces Radio and Tele-vision Service Network. The TTMA also expanded the live audience at the event between 1993 and 1994, when it moved the TMA event from the 15,000-seat Convention Center Arena to the Alamodome, with more than four times the seating capacity (attendance rose from 15,000 to 35,000) (fig. 1.2).[64]

In addition, the TTMA continued to innovate ways to support Tejano music. For example, it presented the first Tejano Music and Media Con-

FIGURE 1.2 Emilio Navaira accepts the Male Entertainer of the Year Award at the Fifteenth Annual Tejano Music Awards at the Alamodome, San Antonio, Texas, February 1995. (Courtesy of the *Eagle Pass Business Journal.*)

ference at the Institute of Texan Cultures in San Antonio at the end of 1994.[65] The inaugural conference addressed many topics central to the ongoing and future success of the industry such as radio airplay, royalty payouts, video exposure, and corporate sponsorships. While they were under the most intense scrutiny, the TTMA and the TMA worked impressively to surmount the difficulties, demonstrating ingenuity, tenacity, and creative management of the crisis. Critics aside, the popular support shown by thousands of Mexican Texans—the core consumer group—for the goals and programs developed by the TTMA paved the way out of the boycott. The people's vote inspired confidence and purpose. Even the critics' heavyweight clout was unable to shut down the TTMA's highly popular awards event, and in any case, additional labels wanted to enter the market.

Sin Fronteras: *Tejano Acts in Mexico*

Unprecedented performance, recording, and marketing opportunities for Tejano artists emerged in the 1990s. Many new events and increasing record sales accompanied this period of growth, a reflection of the groundbreaking work done in previous years by countless Tejano performers, promoters, distributors, and audiences. In many ways, the new mix for success in the industry was due to the decisions made by Tejano artists and the success of their careers, the recording labels dependent upon the artists' careers, and the belief that tapping new markets and expanding existing outlets was not only possible but long overdue.

At the 1990 Tejano Music Awards the veteran band from Brownsville, Texas, Grupo Mazz, and rising recording star Emilio Navaira, dominated the show, winning six of the twelve categories. Mazz then signed to EMI Latin and was feted for the sales success (50,000 units) of its latest album, *No te olvidaré* (I Won't Forget You); Mazz's former label, Discos CBS, likewise recognized the band for its previous album, *Straight from the Heart*.[66] Together with a few other seasoned groups such as La Mafia and Roberto Pulido y Los Clásicos, Mazz became among the first Tejano acts to tour in Mexico. During the summer of 1990, Mazz's first EMI Latin album surpassed the 75,000 unit sales; *No te olvidaré* captured the number-one spot on the *Billboard* Top Latin Albums chart.[67] Industry insiders generally understood in 1990 that albums which sold 50,000 units had reached what were previously considered heady limits for the genre, an industry standard that harked back to La Onda Chicana's 1960s and 1970s heyday.

Grupo Mazz was credited within Tejano circles as being a successful innovator who had effectively utilized the synthesizer and assimilated rock-and-roll sounds into what passed for traditional Tejano sounds in the mid-1980s. Yet even this sound was steeped heavily in the norteño, cumbia, polka, and ballad music familiar to fans in northern Mexico. Part of the rationale behind Mazz's first Mexico tour was based on the realization that, in touring the Southwest, the band typically played before audiences that contained large numbers of Mexican immigrants. By extension, if this same audience segment liked the sounds north of the U.S.–Mexico border, then they would likely appreciate them south of it as well.

Increased Mexican immigration to the United States during the 1980s and 1990s provided an economic incentive that could not be ignored by the artists and recording companies. As Mexican immigrants moved back and forth across the border and visited family and friends, they became willing promoters of the music among those *en el otro lado* (on the other side). Insertion of Tejano music into the transnational Mexican immigrant circuit, culturally speaking, translated into an expanded marketing base and sales. This same phenomenon explained the success of Mexican music acts both in Mexican and U.S. Latin markets. The careers of artists such as Los Tigres del Norte (who were based in San Jose, California), Ramón Ayala, Bronco, Los Bukis, and international Latin pop stars such as Luis Miguel, Daniela Romo, José José, Alejandra Guzmán, and many others reflected the success of these combined industry, migration, and marketing trends. Many of these Mexican artists already lived part of each year in U.S. cities such as Los Angeles and elsewhere. Thus, Tejano artists only adopted what was already established practice for Mexican acts from south of the border; the idea was to get the music going in the other direction, too. Significantly, Mazz's tour of northern Mexico distinguished itself from any other tour by a Tejano act because it represented the first such tour coordinated by "Mexican and U.S. record officials from the same multinational label."[68] Such industry support for Tejano music's success in Mexico had been virtually nonexistent prior to the entrance of the major recording companies into the genre.

Other veteran Tejano performers, however, had toured northern Mexico and points farther south before Grupo Mazz did in 1990. These included Roberto Pulido y Los Clásicos and La Mafia. It was La Mafia, however, that, before any other Tejano act began touring in Mexico, made the deepest inroads into the Mexican market directly through their live-on-the-road performances and later through huge sales of their music in Mexico and stateside. Moreover, La Mafia toured Mexico without the label-orchestrated support that had defined the Mazz experience. Doing it the hard way, La Mafia sailed forth on their own and only later connected with a major Mexican promoter who helped them sort out the sometimes impossible paperwork of Mexican customs at the northern border crossings into Mexico. In September 1990, while Mazz was just getting started with live appearances in Mexico (despite being based on the Texas-Mexico border), Oscar Leonard y La Mafia headlined along with Los Tigres del Norte before 30,000 appreciative fans at the *Super Baile* (Super Dance) in Monterrey, Nuevo León. La Mafia's accomplishment was unique because virtually no

other Tejano act had appeared in Mexico, except for occasional performances by some artists in Texas-Mexico border cities. At the Monterrey
event, moreover, Los Tigres del Norte took 50 percent of the entrance fees;
La Mafia earned $15,000 for two one-hour sets performed at one of the four
stages that fans had paid six to eight dollars to enjoy.[69]

During its fall 1990 Mexican tour, La Mafia performed in Sabinas Hidalgo, Matamoros, Monterrey, Guadalajara, San Luis Potosí, and other Mexican cities. In retrospect, it is somewhat incredible to imagine that a music
genre such as Tejano, derived and produced from a Mexican and Spanish-
language tradition, had not yet seen its leading acts successfully tour in
Mexico. But that was largely the case until the early 1990s. Henry González,
La Mafia's manager, reasoned clearly why the timing for touring Mexico was
right: "The immigration from Mexico isn't going to stop anytime soon. We
just wanted to play with the best [groups] of Mexico, to play to the same
audience. In this way, we can build a new audience."[70]

By late 1991, La Mafia was prepared to draw upon their extensive Mex-
ico touring experience and debut what was termed the first Tejano album
ever to be released and promoted simultaneously in both Mexico and the
United States. Two years later, La Mafia scored another first-time Tejano
achievement when its hit single, "Me estoy enamorando" (I Am Falling in
Love), "became the first song by a Tejano act to reign supreme over the Hot
Latin Tracks. The touching ballad logged more weeks, twenty-four, on the
Hot Latin Tracks chart than any other tune."[71] In 1995, La Mafia again made
Tejano chart history when their hit single, "Toma mi amor" (Take My Love),
from their album *Éxitos en vivo* (Live Hits) became the first norteña song to
top at number one on the Hot Latin Tracks.[72]

The band's incredible Mexico/U.S. crossover success was further evident in the more than 900,000 units sold of their hit album, *Estás tocando
fuego* (You're Touching Fire). La Mafia's sales performance got hot after they
signed with Sony Discos in 1991. Their sales jumped from 60,000 to 70,000
units per album prior to 1991, to several hundreds of thousands per album in
subsequent years. In Mexico alone, by 1994 the Tejano group's first two Sony
albums had sold more than 400,000 units each, and La Mafia was actively
courting its newer audiences in Chile, Central America, Colombia, and
Puerto Rico. La Mafia's two strongest markets stateside were in California
and Texas. The original deal with Sony had the long-term goal of enabling
the group to cross over into the English-language market.

Founded in 1980, La Mafia signed their first recording contract with

Cara/cbs in 1981. Based in Houston, the group developed a loyal following in central and east Texas. Their breakthrough came in 1986 with the album *La Mafia 1986*, containing the hit single, "Si tú supieras" (If You Knew), which was popular in both the United States and Mexico. Commercial success afforded them the opportunity to build their own recording studio, Houston Sound Studios, in 1994, at a reported cost of $500,000.[73]

Sony Discos had a large stable of Tejano artists by 1993; the company emphasized "cumbia/grupo grooves that remain so popular in California and Mexico." Marketed north and south of the border, its Tejano acts included Alex Móntez, Anna Román, Bob Gallarza, Grupo Águila, Grupo Zuave, Jay Pérez, Fama, Los Palominos, and Ram Herrera.[74]

By 1991 at least two major record companies, Sony Discos and Capitol/emi Latin, had coordinated resources to promote newly minted Tejano releases simultaneously in Mexico and the United States.[75] Indeed, leading Tejano acts signed to these (and other) labels, such as La Mafia, Grupo Mazz, La Sombra, Selena, and Emilio Navaira to name a few, had broken into mainstream performance venues in both the United States and Mexico by 1992. Stateside, they were drawing record crowds "at Houston's George R. Brown Convention Center (15,000), Houston's Livestock Show and Rodeo (56,000); at New York City's Roseland Ballroom (5,000); and at Fort Bend County's [Texas] County Fairgrounds (32,000). They also reached headliner status in Mexico, the largest Hispanic [Latino] market, with stadium tours that included Mexico's biggest groups, such as Los Bukis, Ana Gabriel, and Los Tigres del Norte."[76] For her part, Shelly Lares's appearances at the El Paso and San Antonio livestock shows in 1993 were "held in 10,000 capacity coliseums."[77] These performances drew the attention of U.S. mainstream promoters such as Houston's Pace Concerts and San Antonio's Glenn Smith Presents. The new business endeavors undertaken by artists and labels sought to tap receptive markets that the Tejano independent labels had failed to pursue with organized, well-funded marketing and promotion campaigns because they lacked the financial resources to engage in such wide-ranging industry ventures.

Other Crossover Trends

By the early nineties, while Tejano acts were beginning to tour Mexico and sales of their music were increasing, other trends manifested themselves with respect to the crossover of Tejano performers into new English- or Spanish-language audiences. One trend was the move by Tejano acts such as the Texas Tornados and Emilio Navaira, among others, to record in English and expand to country Western audiences. Another was the novel surge of foreign English-speaking acts that performed at sold-out major venues in Mexico, especially Mexico City. For example, in late 1992, Elton John's two-day tour stop in Mexico City's Estadio Azteca drew 176,000 avid fans. In response to Tejano music's growing number of tour performances before various Mexican audiences, the multinational record industry actively promoted these trends. At the same time, Tower Records opened its first megastore in Mexico City's trendy Zona Rosa.[78]

Yet another trend in the opposite direction was the growing number and success of Mexican pop and regional acts performing in the United States from California to New York. One example was the first-ever *baile* (dance) held at the Los Angeles Coliseum in October 1993. Headlined by Los Bukis, the multi-act concert drew approximately 25,000 people who paid between $30 and $35 to attend; the gross gate receipts reached $750,000. Based on this initial success, additional bailes were planned for 1994 with acts such as Banda Móvil, Banda Toro, Banda Vallarta Show, Grupo Mojado, Los Rehenes, and Los Tiranos del Norte.[79] And in April 1994, at the Rosemont Convention Center near Chicago, the romantic pop/ballad quintet Los Temerarios headlined a baile that drew 18,000 fans. Accompanying Los Temerarios were regional Mexican groups such as the pop/ballad Grupo Samuray, the cumbia-driven Banda Campeche Show, and the veteran Tejano band, Grupo Mazz.[80] Similarly, on the East Coast, recording artist Ana Gabriel's two-day concert appearance at New York's Radio City Music Hall in February 1995 grossed $525,780 at the box office.[81]

Where Mexican and Latino audiences were concerned, the early 1990s was a period in which the rules and former paradigms within the music industry in the United States and Mexico ceased to apply. The emphasis was on change and innovation, with improved production quality being one of the results. Transnational marketing and promotion structures were rapidly becoming the rule, not the exception. Whether they appreciated music in Spanish, English, or both, audiences from all economic classes readily embraced these new trends. Similarly, English-speaking listeners were gradually accepting crossover Tejano (and Latino) artists, most of whom are bilingual in English and Spanish.

In 1990, the Texas Tornados—Doug Sahm, Freddie Fender, Flaco Jiménez, and Augie Meyers—proved that crossing over into the country market was not only possible but lucrative. Their eponymous Warner/Reprise debut album sold 300,000 units, a feat accomplished without a hit single. The recording industry took note. Released in Spanish, the group's debut cut led to a nomination for best new group in the regional Mexican category at the Lo Nuestro Latin (1990) music awards. In the wake of the group's second release, *Zone of Our Own,* Fender introduced his "greatest hits" solo album, *The Freddie Fender Collection,* a work that featured reworked bilingual songs. Fender described Tejano country as accordion-based "country music in Spanish," and warily observed that it might suffer commercial dilution as Nashville accepted the style.[82]

Still, the uninhibited Texas Tornados recorded a segment on The Nashville Network's music show, *The Texas Connection,* in February 1993 that featured their first *Billboard* Hot Latin Track single, "Tus mentiras" (Your Lies). Tish Hinojosa, with her "Tejano/folk hybrid" style, followed on the show with a taping of her own. The results led to additional tapings of other Tejano artists.[83] Like it or not, Tejano was going Nashville.

As the Texas Tornados were crossing over to country audiences with their "Tejanofied" sound, other Tejano groups such as La Mafia, Grupo Mazz, and La Sombra were selling upwards of 100,000 units with each new release. But the door to Tejano country in the U.S. market promised to open even wider. Sony Discos obtained license from San Antonio–based R.P. Records to issue the album *This Is Tejano Country.* Recorded in English, the album included the work of veteran Tejano performers such as Sunny Ozuna and Jimmy Edward, plus newcomers Richard Castillón and Shelly Lares. Immediately after the album's release, some Texas country stations played cuts from it.[84]

Subsequently, Grammy winner Flaco Jiménez released a mostly English solo album, *Partners,* under contract with Warner/Reprise. Jiménez was accompanied by a stellar lineup of artists known to country and pop audiences, including Holly Dunn, Emmylou Harris, John Hiatt, Linda Ronstadt, Los Lobos, Ry Cooder, Stephen Stills, and Dwight Yoakam. This was Jiménez's first release with a major label, though he had recorded more than sixty albums with independent labels. Within a few months *Partners* succeeded in entering the top ten on *Billboard's* regional Mexican and world music charts.[85] Jiménez commented on what his latest crossover achievement represented personally and for Tejano (or "Tex-Mex" as he called it) music in

general: "My roots I have never forgotten or abandoned. I have been recording for years and years on independent labels, but they didn't have the
money to be able to expose or promote me to the outside world. So I was
pleased to do this with Warner Brothers. I like combining different cultures
in English and Spanish—which we did—because it opens more roads for
Tex-Mex."[86]

Jiménez added that the major difference between conjunto and Tex-
Mex was that the former's twelve-stringed bass guitar *(bajo sexto)* and accordion had been replaced by the latter's synthesizer or electric bass guitar and
saxophone. Nonetheless, he noted, "it's all Tex-Mex." Whether Tejano, particularly its country and pop idioms, had already succeeded in crossing over
to the respective English-speaking audiences by late 1992 was debatable,
according to *Billboard's* Latino music critic John Lannert, who believed that
"Tex-Mex has yet to make its long-awaited crossover to mainstream country
or pop music audiences." Jiménez, on the other hand, felt then that the genre
was beginning to attract a wider following.[87] His solo tours and tours with
his fellow band members contributed to the widening of audiences in Bel-
gium, France, Germany, Japan, Mexico, and Spain.[88]

Leonardo "Flaco" Jiménez was not alone in his assessment. Two years
later, Tejano music critic Ramiro Burr in 1994 waxed enthusiastic about the
multiple crossover successes for Tejano artists. Within the industry, EMI
Latin and Sony Discos executives, José Behar and George Zamora, agreed
with Burr. The moment's exuberance led Burr to write: "Anchored by talented young artists armed with fresh musical perspectives, Tejano has never
enjoyed a stronger potential for crossover prosperity. An essential element of
Tejano's widening popularity is the music's ongoing evolution and absorp-
tion of country, pop, rock, rap, and R&B. The resulting blends have attracted
young audiences who grew up only on synth-powered polkas and romantic
cumbias."[89]

In Burr's opinion, the crossover of Tejano groups into new markets
equaled improved economic success. Behar pinned his assessment on the
bicultural and bilingual mix most Tejano artists brought to their music
and careers; biculturalism was the source for the genre's continued success. Behar believed that Tejano "artists are exposed to what's happening
in the pop world and the Latin world. They pick and choose what they
like, and then they blend it together and re-invent it for the new, young
generation."[90]

George Zamora, for his part, was also bent on crossing over his label's Tejano artists to Mexico's and the non-Latino U.S. markets. According to Zamora, "The artists who have that capability will be worked towards that objective. Basically, what we do is build a base in Texas. When the sales numbers are sufficient, then we talk about bringing them to Sony Mexico. And if they have potential to break into Monterrey [Nuevo León], then we start there and work back into Los Angeles and Chicago."[91]

But the bottom line was always increased record sales. In 1991 Stuart Dill, president of Refugee Management in Nashville, was instrumental in signing Emilio Navaira and Texas Tornados's Flaco Jiménez and Freddie Fender to its agency's roster of country artists. Furthermore, Warner Nashville established its subsidiary Warner Discos specifically for Tejano acts crossing over to a country venue. One year later Arista Nashville created its Austin-based Tex-Mex label, Arista Texas, with similar objectives.[92] Two years later Arista Texas had signed five artists, including Flaco Jiménez, Freddie Fender, Joel Nava, La Diferenzia, and San Antonio newcomer Rick Orozco. Moreover, Emilio Navaira made Tejano music history when he became the first Tex-Mex act "to headline at the San Antonio Livestock Show and Rodeo. He performed two sold-out shows [on] February 13 at the San Antonio Freeman Coliseum."[93] By late 1994, Emilio had signed a concurrent recording deal with Nashville's Liberty Records, one which José Behar insisted the EMI sister label executives fulfill. With Navaira's signing by Liberty Records, four Nashville-based labels now carried Tejano artists. The other three were Arista Nashville, Sony Nashville, and Warner Nashville.[94] In 1994, along with Rick Treviño, Emilio Navaira signed booking deals with William Morris's Nashville office to "maximize the booking potential of Tejano artists," claiming that the agency wanted for crossover Tejano acts what they had accomplished for Latino acts Jon Secada and Gloria Estefan.[95] Subsequently, Emilio Navaira dropped the "Navaira" part of his name and became known simply as "Emilio" (fig. 1.3).[96]

These developments confirmed that Nashville had finally warmed to the idea of marketing Tejano country acts to wider audiences. This possibility had been predicted by Stuart Dill in 1991. He had described the audiences as "Hispanic Americans in tune with country music. They [country labels] need to develop Hispanics who really are country. That's what we've been trying to develop here—artists who are completely legitimate in both art forms. And as major players come in, they will spend more money

FIGURE 1.3 Emilio Navaira and his brother, Raul "Raulito" Navaira, are considered among the best Tejano music entertainers. They are shown here performing a duo at the Tejano Country Island Jam '98, South Padre Island, Texas, April 1998. (Courtesy of the *Eagle Pass Business Journal.*)

on the albums, make the records better, and make the radio formats sound better. It makes more people buy more records."[97]

All Over the Map

If Emilio Navaira, Flaco Jiménez, Freddie Fender, the Texas Tornados, Rick Treviño, Joel Nava, and other young talents were leading the way by crossing over into country, in the pop category it was Selena y Los Dinos who were making waves by the mid-1990s with a unique head-turning crossover Tejano pop act that was distinguished by the band's performance of original material. Exceptional among Tejano's artists, the young but experienced Selena was the sole female performer whose career accomplishments matched and arguably surpassed those of the industry's best male artists.

The 1994 Grammy Awards, according to *Billboard*, were the "grandest Grammy day for the Latino market." At the event Selena scored her first Grammy for best Mexican American album *(Live!)*, joining Gloria Estefan who won her own first award for best tropical Latin album, *Mi tierra* (My Land), and Luis Miguel who won his award for best Latin pop album, *Aries*.[98] Months earlier in November 1993, Selena had signed a worldwide recording deal with SBK Records, sister label to her EMI Latin label. In signing with SBK Selena became the third crossover artist with the label, joining Jon Secada and Barrio Boyzz. Selena's signing was touted as evidence of SBK's continued commercial commitment to a growing bilingual market. Indeed, under EMI Latin's contract, Selena had become in the previous five years a "top-selling artist in the Hispanic market."[99] The SBK deal represented Selena's crossover into the pop English-language market, which made her the first Tejano artist to land a pop music contract.

By late 1993, Selena's four EMI albums had sold nearly one million units in the United States, and she was already hitting the pop charts with her music. Her fifth EMI album, *Amor prohibido* (Forbidden Love), was released in April, a month after her Grammy win.[100] Daniel Glass, president and CEO of EMI Records Group, saw a pop star in the making when he remarked on Selena's SBK contract, "I don't like to compare artists, but Selena is the closest artist I've got to Madonna. She has that same control, and I love artists that know where they want to go and how to get there. She's definitely a pop star. What's more, it's rare to find an artist so self-contained and well-organized. She has been touring for ten years with her own sponsor [Coca Cola], entourage, bus, and eight trucks carrying her sound and light equipment."[101]

José Behar felt he had signed Selena to EMI Latin in 1989 because he believed that she would become an English-language star. He stated, "I never in my wildest dreams thought she would be such a big Latin act. If I had been looking for a Latin act, I don't know if I would have signed Selena."[102]

Selena took her success in stride and spoke of the crossover challenge and her Chicano/Latino fans, "I hope we're able to expand in a different [musical direction]. This market is a whole new ballpark for us. Just because we signed a contract with a worldwide English company that doesn't mean we're going to leave our base. I think a lot of people that have supported us would be very disappointed if we were just to turn our backs and go on to something else."[103]

Selena was riding atop the Latino music world at the time she signed her SBK English-language recording contract (fig. 1.4). *Corpitos* (Corpus Christi) was sure to be proud of its native daughter. Just under a year away from what would be her untimely death, Selena also managed to score a first for Tejano music with her album *Amor prohibido*, becoming the first Tejano

FIGURE 1.4 Accompanied at the podium by her brother A. B. Quintanilla and Los Dinos band member Pete Astudillo (to her left), Selena accepts the Best Female Vocalist of the Year Award at the Tejano Music Awards at the Alamodome, San Antonio, Texas, February 1995. (Courtesy of the *Eagle Pass Business Journal*.)

artist ever to scale the top of the *Billboard* Latin 50 chart. Two of her other albums were also on the chart. Between touring dates she was busy scheduling recording sessions for the first SBK album due out in 1995. With respect to Selena's feverish pace in spring 1994, *Billboard's* John Lannert remarked that "Selena now is the hottest artist in the Latino market."[104] Indeed, in under a year *Amor prohibido* sold 200,000 units, and her eponymous duet with the Barrio Boyzz on their SBK album, *Dondequiera que estés* (Wherever You Are), sold 100,000 units.[105] Selena's third sweep of the number-one spot on the Hot Latin Tracks arrived when her hit single, "Bidi bidi bom bom," reached the top of the chart, making it the second song from the album *Amor prohibido* to capture the honor.[106] Unfortunately, Selena's meteoric rise concluded in tragedy when she was murdered on March 31, 1995, in Corpus Christi, Texas. At her death, many affectionately ascribed the title of "Reina de la Música Tejana" (Queen of Tejano Music) to Selena.[107]

With Selena gone, the Latino community in the United States and Latin America experienced a sense of loss and tragedy. Perhaps this loss was most deeply felt by the Tejano community in Texas, which had embraced and supported the Latina music star's career long before it became fashionable. Selena had the talent and bold creative spirit to expand her circle of appreciative music fans ever more widely. How far Selena might have gone in her artistic career is a question in part answered by the widespread popular response to her death. In the wake of her death, it became clear that she had already crossed over, broken cultural, social, and economic precedents. The response to her death was indicative of the success that would have awaited her, whether she sang in English or Spanish or performed different musical styles. Selena's career promised a plethora of possibilities. In a brief span of time Selena had carried Tejano music to a new level of popularity, opening new opportunities and establishing new expectations for those coming behind her.[108]

To admit that we harbored distant or close support for Selena's career, and all that it offered us either vicariously or directly, the sheer pleasure of seeing her succeed and crossing all kinds of artistic *fronteras,* brought a sense of joy and affirmation. Certainly, Texas Mexicans were right to be proud of her achievements. Many already looked forward to her much-anticipated crossover album in English. Selena recorded four tracks of this English-language album, which was scheduled to be completed by May 1, 1995, and due in the stores by late summer. The tracks had been recorded in Nashville, Los Angeles, and her own Corpus Christi studio, Q Productions.[109] In retrospect we shared her hopes that the album would succeed, as it was predicted to do. With the release of her English-language CD, Selena was expected to break language and cultural barriers in the entertainment industry much like Gloria Estefan, Jon Secada, Julio Iglesias, Los Lobos, Luis Miguel, Linda Ronstadt, and others had done in recent years.[110] But for her tragic death, Selena, "Southern Texas's ambassador to the world," as the *Los Angeles Times* put it, would have been among this select group of accomplished Latina and Latino recording artists.[111] In so many ways Selena was just about to start an entirely new career, and we were all cheering her on.[112]

Summing Up

The Tejano music of the 1990s was born in a norteño Mexican tradition extending back generations to southern Texas and northeastern Mexico. Over time, numerous influences have shaped the various performance styles and musical genres. Many artists have understood and interpreted these influences and charted the direction of change in their lifetimes. In so doing, these artists have left a major imprint upon the collective Tejano music experience. The twentieth century clearly was one in which American musical influences combined with Mexican norteño traditions to produce an evolving bicultural genre, but one that was still distinctively Mexican in its sound, cadences, and language. Tejano music is deeply appreciated by multiple generations, classes, and listening audiences, who concur on at least one point: The music is not meant solely to be listened to, but to be danced to as well. Regardless of change, Tejano music has always represented a ritualized performance between audience and artist. In the nineties, the euphemism for this process became known in the language of the record company executives and performing artists as "developing a base." Indeed, no base, no music.

Beginning in the 1920s and continuing into the 1990s, Tejano music has continuously adapted to technological innovation. If the 1920s was a period in which the music was first recorded and appreciated by radio transmission, then the 1990s brought forth equally heady technological innovations. In each period, moreover, the cultural and social consumption of the music has kept pace qualitatively and quantitatively with the tenor of the opportunities and challenges presented by technology. Then as now, major recording companies representing economic interests based outside the Tejano community, which both generates and provides a market for the music, have played a leading role in cultivating the genre.[113]

Tejano music's much vaunted success in the nineties resulted in the creation of literally dozens of benchmarks. Whether established or not-so-established, Tejano artists will henceforth have to measure their contributions to the industry against these achievements. The decade constitutes one in which the community of Tejano artists, big names and no-names, women and men, succeeded in making the market for their music grow beyond all previous limits and conceptions. With significant numbers of Mexicans immigrating to the United States throughout the late twentieth century, Tejano artists were acquiring a substantial audience outside the Texas-Mexico border region. Artists such as La Mafia, Grupo Mazz, Roberto Pulido y Los Clásicos, and Selena y Los Dinos, among others, ventured farther afield than any of their predecessors had done. These and other Tejano artists also played alongside many of the very best contemporary Mexican artists in Mexico, touring with them and performing at major Mexican venues, as well as at venues in major urban areas in the United States where Tejano music had simply not held sway in the past. From 1985 onward, with the signing of

Little Joe y La Familia by a major recording company and with the far-sighted efforts of recording executives such as José Behar of EMI Latin, a trend was set in motion. The 1990s came to be defined as the decade in which many Tejano artists stepped from recording with independently owned companies to signing with multinational recording labels. Distribution and promotion strategies and supportive budgets contributed greatly to the annual growth in sales of Tejano music throughout the decade.

To their credit, Tejano music fans across the country embraced the changes. They also welcomed the appreciation of their music by newer audiences in Mexico, Puerto Rico, Central America, and countries such as Colombia in South America. Television and radio, despite their own self-interests and limitations, brought the talents of the Tejano recording industry to these newly developing markets. But the artists also actively labored to ensure the success of the process. Tejano artists took their tours to places they had never been; some (for example, veteran artist Flaco Jiménez, solo and with the Texas Tornados) took the music to Europe and the Far East. Moreover, Tejano music witnessed the establishment of its own major awards program, the Tejano Music Awards, and the renaissance of conjunto and the accordion as central to the Tejano music recording industry, a development fueled in part by the founding of the Tejano Conjunto Festival. Both industry events were founded in the early 1980s and have been held continuously since then in San Antonio. Since then, numerous other Tejano music awards shows have been launched elsewhere. However, the tens of thousands of fans who attend the San Antonio events make these events the leaders in their field.

Key developments also occurred when Tejano acts crossed over into English-language markets, particularly the country music market. Moreover, Selena made headway in taking Tejano music into the international pop market, both the Spanish-language market (into which she had already begun to make big inroads) and the English-language one, becoming the first Tejano star to sign an English pop music contract from a major recording label, SBK Records. Selena's huge success also signaled the breaking down of the gender barrier within the Tejano recording industry, which had been dominated by male artists. In the post-Selena era the Tejano music industry has become much more gender-integrated. Tejana music artists have become more acceptable to audiences, especially younger ones.

Highly significant too is the trend toward the establishment of independent recording studios by many of the industry's major artists such as

Little Joe y La Familia, Emilio Navaira, La Mafia, the Quintanilla family (Q Productions), and others. Closely tied to this is the creation by many of these leading industry artists of management agencies for younger Tejano music talent seeking opportunities to develop their own careers. Several of the major recording labels that have entered the Tejano music market have signed promotion and distribution contracts with these new artist-generated talent agencies, thus forging new links between the established artists and the new generation of performers. Collectively, these promising trends raise the hope and expectation that artistic control and maximum profit, as a result of the growth of the industry, may come to rest in the hands of the Tejano artists themselves, not solely as performers, but as producers, promoters, agents, and executives of the developing infrastructure. It may be too soon to tell, but the promise of such possibilities is suggested by these developments.

Like all periods of cultural renaissance, Tejano music's recent nineties renaissance has come full circle. Late in 1995 a down cycle in the market for Tejano music appeared. Buoyed by sales of Tejano music in part generated by the tragedy of Selena's death (particularly sales of Selena's own music), this emerging pattern was not publicly noticed until 1996. By then, major record companies had begun to withdraw their contractual and promotional commitments made during the first half of the decade. Major recording companies retained with their labels only the most commercially viable of the artists in the genre. In this shifting financial environment, even some of the major Tejano artists were released from their recording contracts. Many of the artists who had less commercial success at the retail level were dumped even earlier and have since returned to recording with independent record companies. Fortunately, most of these indies are still owned and operated by Tejano music entrepreneurs. Thus, the independent Tejano recording labels that survived the intensified economic competition of the first half of the nineties decade, and those indies that have appeared because of it, particularly artist-owned labels, will once again assume a leading role in determining the future aesthetic and stylistic directions that the industry will take in the years ahead. Scholars of this music such as Manuel Peña view this new challenge as a positive result for the genre because the music will once again move closer to its base, rooted primarily in Texas. Arguably, the late nineties down cycle in the market for Tejano music has called forth a return to the genre's roots, marked by the renewed predominance of norteño's influence on the music as a whole. Meanwhile, the unprecedented push to the top in the Arbitron ratings among Alamo City radio stations achieved by KXTN-FM during the nineties has dwindled in the latter years of the decade. The Tejano power station assumed instead a more modest though still formidable fifth-place ranking by 1998. The KXTN-FM ratings shift is symbolic of the larger changes occurring throughout the industry.[114]

Another significant change reflecting the ongoing internal restructuring brought about by the Tejano music industry's late nineties down cycle was the split that occurred in the leading Tejano music awards show and organization—the TTMA's Tejano Music Awards. TTMA cofounder Rudy Treviño and the organization's board of directors developed irreconcilable differences regarding which direction the organization should take in fomenting continued and growing financial success for the artists, labels, promoters, songwriters, and others affiliated with Tejano music. Arguing that Tejano music needed new visions, directions, and horizons, Treviño resigned as executive director of TTMA on July 14, 1998, and incorporated a new nonprofit organization called Tejano Entertainers and Music Association (TEMA) on July 16, 1998. TEMA staged its first press conference in San Antonio on July 22, 1998, and on February 28, 1999, held the first TEMA Music Awards program in San Antonio at the Municipal Auditorium. It was attended by approximately 2,000 Tejano artists and fans. For its part, the TTMA held the nineteenth Annual Tejano Music Awards at the Alamodome on March 6, 1999, for the first time without Rudy Treviño acting as executive director of the organization. An estimated 12,000 artists and fans attended this music event, a notably smaller number than had been attending the TMAs in the years previous to the split within the TTMA leadership. TEMA intends to alternate hosting its annual TEMA Music Awards in various Texas cities and will not be keeping the event tied to San Antonio, which the TTMA had always done with its awards show. Such discord among those who would presumably promote the music is a reflection of the challenges faced by industry leaders in capturing and keeping the potential audience's imagination, loyalty, and entertainment dollars. Whatever outcomes result from these particular organizational changes that are occurring, it is to be hoped that the net effect will ultimately benefit and further the interests of the music genre's artists and fans.[115]

Many of the gains made by the recording artists, labels, and promoters, not to mention the sizeable growth in audiences that occurred in the 1990s and the expansion of independent artist-led management agencies, recording studios, and labels, have resulted in a vigorous infrastructure that leaves the industry ahead of where it stood before the late 1980s when the boom in Tejano initially appeared. The future outlook ought to be one of optimism rather than pessimism. Hard times provide an opportunity to critically review where things stand, the better to come out ahead with more fresh, creative, original, and dynamic ideas than before. This view was well captured by longtime Tejano veteran and San Antonio native Flaco Jiménez, who told an interviewer for *La Opinión* in mid-1996 as the down cycle was being acknowledged: *"El corazón no se hace viejo, es el cuero el que se arruga."* (The heart does not age, it is the skin that wrinkles.) Indeed, Tejano music has added a new wrinkle to its history. Yet there are as many old and young hearts—artists—making music in the genre today as there have ever been. While the global recording giants are without any loyalty except to the bottom line, and they have more or less come and gone for now, La Onda Tejana is as vital as it will ever be.

Perhaps the premiere Tejana star of the nineties is the one who is no longer living, Selena. Selena's untimely death hurt many, most acutely her own family, but also the hundreds of thousands who believed in her career, her music, and her authentic Mexican soul, bilingual and bicultural as she was. Her life provides a word of caution to those in the industry who are in the position of making sure that the Tejano music industry survives into the twenty-first century with continued growth and vitality. Selena's talent and ambition knew no bounds, or so it seemed to many who, through her, took pride in who they were and in their communities, whether Tejano, Mexicano, or Latino. Selena was at the cutting edge of a new and emerging Latino identity in the United States. And it was an identity based in a solid norteño Mexican tradition, however infused it might have been with the soul and rhythm of the American pop music of the seventies and eighties. Selena bridged new and old, Mexican and Puerto Rican, Mexican and Salvadoreño, Mexican and Chicano, Mexican and Anglo, Mexican and black, song and dance, languages and cultures, music and life. This was the spirit that moved her. A young artist, businesswoman, designer, and border-crossing architect, Selena broke barriers as if they were made of clay and made it look so easy, so fantastic. She struck a collective chord in the soul of the Mexican, Mexican American, and Latino communities everywhere, at home and abroad. And in death, Selena wrote her own tribute to the possibility for tomorrow when she became the first U.S. Latina to be honored with a feature-length film about her life story. Selena's film is the first. But it will not be the last; that is her legacy. A young Chicana who achieved and established countless unprecedented accomplishments in her chosen field, Selena managed to do it through her music, her family, her fan base, and the infinite ritual performance between audience and artist. From Tejana star to Tejana legend, Selena embodied the best of the change and innovation that the Tejano music industry had to offer during the nineties.

Notes

Author's note: The author would like to acknowledge the following persons: Juan Gómez-Quiñones and David R. Maciel for reading an earlier draft of this essay and urging its completion, María T. Jiménez for commenting on an earlier draft and providing technical assistance, and Ricardo E. Calderón for his support and contribution of several sources. The author would also like to acknowledge receipt of a Dean's Faculty Research Incentive Grant, College of Humanities, Arts and Social Sciences, University of California, Riverside, 1996–97.

Epigraph quote cited in Luis Manuel González, "Hay 'Flaco' Jiménez 'pa' rato'," *La Opinión*, 31 July 1996, 3D. Between 1986 and 1996, Flaco became a three-time Grammy winner, once with the Texas Tornados.

1. Ramiro Burr, "Tejano Takes Off and Labels, Radio, Retail Catch On," *Billboard*, 20 March 1993, 41.

2. John Lannert, "While Their Hold on U.S. and Mexican Markets May Be Loosening, Spanish Acts Break into Chile and Argentina," *Billboard*, 8 July 1995, 46.

3. Ibid. Lannert writes: "Take the U.S. Latin market, for example. In 1989, four of the top five entries listed in *Billboard's* year-end Top Pop Latin Albums chart were recorded by stars from Spain; nine of that year's 40 Top Hot Latin Tracks were from Spanish acts. In 1994, only one Spanish artist—Sony's Julio Iglesias—graced the year-end *Billboard* Latin 50 retail chart."

4. Ibid. The pop/rock music of particular Mexican artists such as Luis Miguel, Maná, Alejandra Guzmán, and Caifanes was also being increasingly heard in Spain. Spanish acts continued to have an audience, but the overall impact was diminished.

5. Jeff Clark-Meads, "IFPI Says Sales in Latin Markets Up 33 Percent: Brazil, Mexico Lead Way; Piracy Casts Shadow," *Billboard*, 19 August 1995, 3.

6. Lannert, "While Their Hold on U.S.," *Billboard*, 46. Behar also cited the high cost of bringing Spanish acts stateside as an impediment to the "accessibility necessary to effectively work the U.S. Latin market."

7. Ibid. Prior to 1990 only one major label was marketing Tejano acts. By early 1993, five of the major record labels had become involved in producing, marketing, and promotion within the Tejano music industry: Capitol/EMI Latin, Fonovisa, TH Rodven, Sony, and WEA Latina.

8. Ibid. Also see Ramiro Burr, "Acculturation in America: Retailers Open Doors to Tejano," *Billboard*, 20 March 1993, 46. Drawn by accelerating record sales, major

music retail chains that began participating in the marketing of Tejano music products in the early 1990s were Sound Warehouse, Hastings, Musicland, Tower Records,
Best Buy, and others. Retail giants such as K-Mart and Wal-Mart also entered the
market and either included or expanded the Tejano music products in their Spanish-
language racks. Mom-and-pop stores and independent distributors, which had been
the principal distributors of the music previously, felt the competition, and in some
cases disappeared altogether from the market. Some independent record retailers
thrived under the increased competitive environment, as they proved capable of
customizing their service whereas major retailers were incapable of doing so. See
Ramiro Burr, "Mainstream Rivals Fail to Faze San Antonio's El Norteño," *Billboard,*
21 August 1993, 47, 51.

9. Accompanying the burgeoning U.S. Latin music market was the increased sale of
pirated Latino music products. The Recording Industry Association of America
(RIAA) reported in mid-1995 that "counterfeit Latin music product makes up 60
percent of RIAA's seizures." Piracy in all other genres was declining. Pirate music
factories were reported to be down everywhere in the United States except the
Southwest. See Bill Holland, "Latin Music Piracy on the Rise in the U.S.: Genre
Makes Up 60 Percent of Pirate-Product Seizures," *Billboard,* 2 September 1995, 111.

10. Dominic Price, "World Music Sales Up 5.9 Percent in '93: Latin America, Southeast Asia Spur Growth," *Billboard,* 14 May 1994, 8, 51. Noting the effects of the North
American Free-Trade Agreement (NAFTA) on the world music market, Price writes:
"In 1994, with the NAFTA treaty in effect, the free-trade block formed between the
U.S., Mexico, and Canada will become the largest single market: If the three nations
had been counted together in 1993, the block would have represented 37.1 percent of
all [worldwide] sales, with $11.3 billion."

11. Ramiro Burr, "Publishers Battle Pirates but Foresee Smoother Sailing Buoyed by
Sync Rights and CD Sales," *Billboard,* 19 September 1992; James G. Fifield, "Mexico
Must Curb Piracy in Order to Grow," *Billboard,* 8 October 1994, 5; Adam White, "IFPI
Targets Mexico in Pirate Talks," *Billboard,* 29 October 1994, 54; Clark-Meads, "IFPI
Says Sales in Latin Markets," *Billboard,* 3. International recording companies were
pressing the Mexican government to enforce copyright laws in the post-NAFTA period, much as Southeast Asian nations such as Singapore, Malaysia, Taiwan, and
Korea had done between 1987 and 1992, when these markets reduced piracy to 15 percent of sales. The industry argued that those who benefited most were the recording
artists and the governments involved, which stood to gain in the taxes collected from
legal sales. Less sanguine but no less powerful a motive behind the industry's efforts
to curb piracy was the generally acknowledged fact that Mexicans have a high per
capita spending on music.

Mexico in 1993 was the world's eighth largest international music market, a figure industry leaders noted would increase to fourth place (and in excess of $2 bil-
lion) were piracy controlled as it had been in the Asian markets. If piracy were

controlled, Mexico's market would rank in value and volume behind only the world's leading markets: the United States, Japan, and Germany. According to Fifield (president of EMI Music): "In 1993, legitimate music sales in Mexico reached 62 million units with a retail value of more than $572 million [dollars]. In that same year, though, 100 million pirated units were sold, representing nearly $1 billion [dollars] in lost revenue, royalties, and taxes. In terms of sheer number of pirated units sold, Mexico's plague of piracy has been exceeded by only one other country, China."

Mexico's world-ranked record industry in the post-NAFTA period invariably faced the discontent of the multinational recording companies, which complained not only about piracy, but also about the problems associated with collecting royalties on their copyrighted products. See John Lannert, "Suit Shows Muddy Mexican Royalties," *Billboard*, 30 September 1995, 1, 109; and Edward P. Murphy, "Mexico's Royalty Issues Depend on NAFTA," *Billboard*, 30 September 1995, 6.

12. "The Latin Market in the 90s," *Billboard*, 26 May 1990 (special insert).

13. Ibid.

14. La Mafia was based in Houston, Texas, Grupo Mazz operated out of the Texas-Mexico border at Brownsville, and La Sombra and Selena y Los Dinos claimed Corpus Christi as their home. See John Lannert, "Top Mexican Acts Follow Population Flow to Penetrate New U.S. Markets," *Billboard*, 21 September 1991.

15. Ramiro Burr, "The Future Looks Bright, but There's Still Plenty of Room for Growth," *Billboard*, 21 September 1991.

16. Quoted in Lannert, "Top Mexican Acts Follow," *Billboard*. Note that platinum status varies by market depending on the overall size of the individual national market. In this instance, platinum entails sales of 100,000 units.

17. Sam Quiñones, "Norteña's Corridos Paint Underbelly of Mexican Life," *Billboard*, 25 February 1995, 1, 48. One of the regional Mexican music's leading genres, *música norteña*, which Quiñones described as "a hybrid, polka rooted genre from the northern Mexico/southern U.S. border, tied inexorably to colorful parables about Mexico's social-political ills, such as drug-related violence, unemployment, and immigration," was subject to intense interest by Mexico-based multinational recording labels in 1994. The labels were actively courting artists to sign. Warner Music Mexico debuted a label, Raza, specifically to sign norteño acts to its roster, and based its promotion director in Monterrey, Nuevo León. EMI Latin Music Mexico, meanwhile, was negotiating to acquire DLV, "home of Los Invasores del Norte, as well as the deep catalog of norteña icon Ramón Ayala, Sr." EMI Mexico's president, Mario Ruiz, believed the market for norteño music was set to expand based on its having "gone over from the lower class to the middle class. It's accepted as original Mexican music."

Sony also maintained an office in Monterrey, and BMG International's vice president of its Latin, North America label, Jesús López, was about to sign two norteño acts and planned to sign another five or six more. Quiñones attributed the growing success of the norteño market to Mexican immigrants who, upon listening to the genre (Los Tigres del Norte, for example) at dances in places such as central California, "provided much of the cross-pollination that took norteña from the California cantinas to Mexican stadiums." The music was now popular in regions from whence the Mexican immigrants originated; Guerrero and Michoacán, states in central Mexico, are two examples.

18. Lannert, "Top Mexican Acts Follow," *Billboard*. Also see John Lannert, "Tejano Gaining Foothold in Country Market: Texas Tornados Blow Open Doors for Other Acts," *Billboard*, 7 December 1991, 35; and Burr, "The Future Looks Bright," *Billboard*. Among the Tejano artists who benefited from these changing industry conditions was none other than Selena. According to José Behar, who became a cheerleader and architect for the crossover careers of Tejano artists signed to his label in this period (including Selena), he believed that:

> [T]he Tejano market has been blown wide open. The fact that the majors have gone in there, has brought a spotlight to that region [when it] was really handled by independents, which unfortunately didn't have the clout that the majors do as far as nationalizing and internationalizing this kind of product.
>
> Selena is probably going to go gold in a few weeks [Behar stated in July 1991]. For somebody who was selling 2,000 units on a little independent [label] to be able to sell 50,000 units is impressive. Now you know, you have a lot of huge pop artists—and my competitors know this—who don't go gold. They have great images, sell out shows everywhere they go, but they can't sell 50,000 units.

19. Ramiro Burr, "Luring Labels, Reawakening Radio and Securing Sponsorships, Tejano Music Is Burning Hot and Spreading Fast," *Billboard*, 23 April 1994, 30, 32, 34.
20. Ibid., 30.
21. John Lannert, "Showcased Artists and Panel Experts Take the Fifth Annual Latin Music Conference into the Genre's Golden Age," *Billboard*, 21 May 1994, LM-4.
22. Burr, "Tejano Takes Off and Labels," *Billboard*, 41; Eric Boehlert, "Contemporary Mix Makes Market-Toppers: Spanish Stations Boost Ratings with Tejano, Banda," *Billboard*, 3 April 1993, 84.
23. Elena de la Cruz, "Triunfo de radio en español despierta espinosas reacciones," *La Opinión*, 11 January 1996, 1D, 3D.
24. Boehlert, "Contemporary Mix Makes Market-Toppers," *Billboard*, 84.
25. Ramiro Burr, "Growth of Labels, Radio and Mass Merchandising Cap a Fifth Year of Phenomenal Growth," *Billboard*, 2 September 1995, 39, 42, 44, 46.
26. For a critical discussion of how corporate and commercial advertisers in the United States have insisted on paying lower prices for advertising their products on Spanish-language radio in contrast to English-language stations, see Boehlert, "Con-

temporary Mix Makes Market-Toppers," *Billboard,* 84; de la Cruz, "Triunfo de radio en español," *La Opinión,* 1D, 3D; and Elena de la Cruz, "La radio hispana ya llegó al año 2000," *La Opinión,* 2 February 1996, 1D, 3D.

27. Burr, "Luring Labels, Reawakening Radio," *Billboard,* 34.

28. Boehlert, "Contemporary Mix Makes Market-Toppers," *Billboard,* 84.

29. See de la Cruz, "Triunfo de radio en español," *La Opinión,* 1D, 3D; de la Cruz, "La radio hispana ya llegó," *La Opinión,* 1D, 3D; "KLVE al tope de las radios," *La Opinión,* 22 April 1995, 3D; and Steve Hochman, "KSCA Fans Fear New Owner Will Touch Dial," *Los Angeles Times,* 21 December 1996, F-1, F-20. In Los Angeles much controversy has been created by competing English-language station owners as the result of their Spanish-language competitors' seemingly unnerving persistency in securing high rankings in the market. English-language station owners have even thrown into question the methodology utilized by Arbitron to measure the market, a point never contested prior to "La Equis's" epic break to the top.

30. Judith Michaelson, "More Radio Stations Say Adios to English," *Los Angeles Times,* 17 March 1997, F-1, F-7.

31. Steven Loza, *Barrio Rhythm: Mexican American Music in Los Angeles* (Urbana: University of Illinois Press, 1993), 21–36. In 1931, Los Madrugadores's early morning program moved "to radio station KELW in Burbank, where it aired daily from 4:00 to 6:00 A.M."

32. Ibid., 53.

33. Burr, "Tejano Takes Off and Labels," *Billboard,* 41–42.

34. Ibid. Among the new radio stations playing Tejano full time or part time by 1993 were (in Texas) KRIO-FM (San Antonio), which made the Alamo City the only city with two FM Tejano stations at that time, KBSO-FM (Corpus Christi), KBMA (Bryan/College Station), KKPS-FM (McAllen), KTNO-AM (Dallas); (in New Mexico) KABQ-AM and KANQ-AM (Albuquerque), KSWV-AM (Santa Fe); (in California) KHDC-FM (Salinas); and (in Arizona) KOHT-FM (Tucson).

35. Joe Nick Patoski, *Selena: Como La Flor* (Boston: Little, Brown and Company, 1996), 16–28, 48. For example, San Antonio radio stations and personalities who began to make their way on the airwaves showcasing *conjunto, trío,* and *orquesta,* as well as rock and roll and rhythm and blues included Henry "Pepsi" Peña, Manuel Dávila, Sr., and Little Junior Jesse on KUKA, and Scratch Phillips on KCOR. Miguel Ríos in Alice played recent releases by Juan Colorado, Tony de la Rosa, and Isidro López on KOPY; in Kingsville, Mike Chávez's bilingual program on KINE featured Top 40 and La Onda Chicana hits. Tejano deejays in Corpus Christi promoting Tex-Mex included Johnny Canales, Freddie Martínez, and Domingo Peña. San Antonio's KEDA-AM changed to a bilingual format to include the sounds of Flaco Jiménez, Little Joe and the Latinaires, and Sunny Ozuna and the Sunliners, which played next to Little Richard and B. B. King. KEDA became known as "Radio Jalapeño."

In 1974, Radio Jalapeño's Dávila family bought radio station KCCT-AM in Corpus Christi and promptly reformatted the station playlist to fit their Onda Chicana format used in San Antonio. KCCT ceased playing Mexican mariachi and international Spanish hits. Rechristened Radio Jalapeño like its sister station, KEDA, KCCT's format was novel for Corpus Christi and immediately seized an audience. As Patoski noted, "Proof was the crowd of 10,000 that flocked to an outdoor concert that KCCT organized at Cole Park."

36. Ibid., 21–22. Actually, during the early 1960s before Canales managed to make it into television, his colleague and contemporary, Corpus Christi Onda Chicana deejay and promoter, Domingo Peña, opened on channel 3 with his *Domingo Peña Show.* Apparently, Peña was the first Tejano on local television, and at the time, his was the only such show in the entire region. Peña favored Tejano acts from Corpus Christi and south Texas, but regional Anglo acts lacking any similar television venues also appeared.

37. Burr, "Tejano Takes Off and Labels," *Billboard,* 41–42.

38. John Lannert, "Top Acts Flock to Winter Festivals," *Billboard,* 11 February 1995, 35. The task of providing programming on a networkwide basis in the Tejano and regional Mexican music genres was undertaken by giant, Las Vegas–based Heftel Broadcast Corporation (HBC), which owned a network of fifty affiliates in 1995. HBC was and continues to be one of the largest international Spanish-language radio broadcast companies. According to Lannert, Heftel had "announced the formation of two Super Station radio networks for Tejano and regional Mexican formats. Heftel's Dallas stations KICK-FM and KMRT-AM will be the broadcast source for all programming for the two networks. Heftel will introduce 'Hot Tejano Hits' and the regional Mexican-rooted 'Exitos Calientes' to an estimated fifty affiliates in the U.S. and Mexico."

39. Burr, "Luring Labels, Reawakening Radio," *Billboard,* 34.

40. Burr, "Growth of Labels, Radio," *Billboard,* 42. For more on Spanish-language radio, particularly in Texas, see Manuel Peña, *The Texas-Mexican Conjunto: A History of a Working-class Music* (Austin: University of Texas Press, 1985), 108, 150–51. Also, for a pre-1980s assessment of Spanish-language radio, see Félix F. Gutiérrez, *Spanish Language Radio in the Southwestern United States* (Austin: University of Texas, Center for Mexican American Studies, 1979).

41. Ibid.

42. Alfredo Figueroa, personal interview, Riverside, California, 9 May 1997. The newsletter of the Tejano Music Club of Southern California provides its members with the dates Tejano artists will be performing in the area and also offers a listing (with dates and hours) of the region's radio stations that offer Tejano music. Club members tend to be active in calling in their requests and even assist in expanding the "Tejano Sounds" library by sending in music not available to the deejays. Older club members tend to request Tejano oldies. Many, but not all, of the club's members

have some sort of connection to Texas, Figueroa asserted. Further, the club has a web site on the Internet. Also, Radio Aztlán acquired its first web site in May 1997: http://www.corona.ca.com.

43. Burr, "Tejano Takes Off and Labels," *Billboard*, 41–42. In San Antonio, prior to this phase of the industry's development the most popular dance halls went by names such as Arturo's (Ballroom), the Blanco Ballroom, or Venturas. These dance halls, moreover, used to promote the artists more infrequently, as they were rented for many other purposes besides Tejano dance concerts.

44. Ibid.; Ramiro Burr, "Fresh Images: New Rules in the Vid Age. Artists Clean Up Their Acts for Maximum Exposure," *Billboard*, 20 March 1993, 42.

45. Ramiro Burr, "Industry Focus: The Key Players," *Billboard*, 21 September 1991; Victoria Infante, "Nueva cadena y nuevo horario, pero sigue el mismo Johnny Canales," *La Opinión*, 10 July 1996, 1D–2D, 6D. Canales was born in General Treviño, Nuevo León, Mexico, of a Tejano father and Mexican mother, although he has resided in Corpus Christi since he was a month old. Canales began his musical career when he was but six years old. His father used to take him to local bars to sing. He later learned to play the accordion and eventually formed his own musical group. Canales stated: "I played during the decade of the seventies, in the Freddie Martínez epoch. I had my own *orquesta de metales:* two trumpets, two saxophones, guitar, bass, contrabass, *tambora*, drums, and organ." See Joseph Treviño, "Johnny Canales y esas músicas hermanas: la tejana y la norteña," *La Opinión*, 8 October 1995, 3D.

Canales was also a pioneer in promoting Tejano music on radio. Tejano acts were largely excluded from south Texas radio stations because Anglo station owners favored programmers and announcers from Mexico, as they supposedly spoke better Spanish than the Tejanos. The selection of music "the mustache guys," as they were called, played included whatever was popular in Mexico. This "Mexico First" policy on south Texas radio first began to break in the late 1950s, and personalities such as Domingo Peña, Freddie Martínez, and Johnny Canales in Corpus Christi, and Manuel Dávila, Jr., in San Antonio were among the first to break through this exclusionary practice that inhibited the development of a regional Tejano sound. The issue was significant because radio was the "most important form of mass communication in Texas Spanish-speaking [Mexican] communities." For a discussion of these points, see Patoski, *Selena*, 3–28.

46. Burr, "Industry Focus," *Billboard*.

47. Ibid.; Infante, "Nueva cadena y nuevo horario," *La Opinión*, 1D–2D, 6D.

48. Ibid. Canales, in conjunction with his wife, Nora Pérez, hosted at the Bronco Bowl in Dallas, Texas, the first "You Got It Awards," whose intent according to Canales was to recognize more than forty groups that had not been recognized before, even though their songs have been popular with the public. The new awards program was also televised on Telemundo's network affiliates.

49. Rudy R. Treviño, "Tejano Music: A Historical Perspective," *Eagle Pass Business Journal* 4 (1997): 7; Ricardo E. Calderón, "Tejano Music Awards Founder: Rudy R. Treviño," *Eagle Pass Business Journal* 4 (1997): 3, 22–23; and "Rudy Treviño and TTMA," *Texas Hispanic* (1997): 33–36. Treviño was born on March 25, 1945, in Eagle Pass, Texas, to Miguel Hernández Treviño (born in Texas) and Minerva Rodríguez de Treviño (born in Coahuila, Mexico). He attended elementary schools in both Eagle Pass and Crystal City before his family moved to San Antonio, where he graduated from Fox Tech High School. In 1967 he graduated from the University of Texas at Austin. An artist and former high school teacher (until 1990), Treviño once published the magazine, *Picante*, where he made many of his initial contacts with Tejano musicians. He and a friend, Gilbert Escobedo, first thought of creating a Tejano music awards event in 1976.

Treviño has claimed to have been responsible for rechristening the genre, which was then popularly known as "La Onda Chicana" or "Tex-Mex," as "Tejano music," by which it has generally come to be known ever since. His reasons for choosing the term "Tejano" are explained in his article cited above. In short, Tejano was a term of "self-designation," he wrote.

50. Burr, "Industry Focus," *Billboard.* In 1990, at its tenth annual edition, more than sixty-two radio and thirty-one television stations in several states covered the TMA through syndication. Sponsoring the awards were Budweiser; Coca-Cola, USA; and the City of San Antonio. See Ramiro Burr, "Grupo Mazz, Navaira Take Top Tejano Music Trophies," *Billboard*, 14 April 1990, 6, 89. The eleventh annual (1991) version of the TMA marked the second consecutive year in which more than 13,000 fans attended. The awards were taped for later broadcast through thirty-three television and sixty-five radio stations. The sole live broadcast was made by San Antonio's official Tejano Music Awards radio stations, KXTN-FM and KZVE-FM. See Ramiro Burr, "Tejano Music Awards Nominations Announced," *Billboard,* 23 February 1991, 67; Ramiro Burr, "Mazz Dazzles Tejano Voters, Taking 6 of 12 Awards," *Billboard*, 23 March 1991, 58.

51. Ramiro Burr, "Capitol/EMI Latin Again Sizzles at Tejano Awards," *Billboard*, 27 March 1993, 35.

52. John Lannert, "Latin Notas," *Billboard*, 30 October 1993, 39.

53. "Edición XVII de Premios a la Música Tejana," *La Prensa* 5 (1997): 15; "Nominaciones del Tejano Music Awards," *Qué Onda!* 4 (1997): 10–11. Notably, a host of newspapers and magazines across Texas have been founded in recent years that cater specifically to the Mexican and Latino community. All such periodicals have distributed information not only about the Tejano Music Awards but about the Tejano music industry in general to an apparently vibrant reading audience. Typically, these publications are either bilingual or they publish material solely in English or Spanish.

54. "Edición XVII de Premios," *La Prensa,* 15; Calderón, "Tejano Music Awards Founder," 3.

55. Several Texas cities vied to become the location for the Tejano Music Hall of Fame, but the facility will be built in San Antonio at an estimated cost of $4 million. Among other activities promoted by the TTMA have been the creation of a Tejano music event in Las Vegas, the Amigos de Tejano Music Club, video production of the TMA, production of an annual cassette featuring the TMA's winning songs, recruitment of Fortune 500 corporate sponsors, creation of music scholarships for promising students, and organization of various dances and special events often held outside San Antonio. John Lannert, "Taking Another Look at Tejano Awards; Feliciano Leads Capitol Fall Contingent," *Billboard*, 19 September 1992, 33; Ramiro Burr, "Tejano Awards Persevere Despite Flap," *Billboard*, 12 December 1992, 33.

56. Ricardo E. Calderón, "Tejano Music Hall of Fame to Be Built by TTMA," *Eagle Pass Business Journal* 4 (1997): 6.

57. Ibid. Burr felt that none of the labels had "produced any evidence to substantiate their complaints." The Sony Discos statement, issued in April 1992, affirmed that the boycott applied to the artists they represented who supported the decision and further instructed the TMA not to use their names in any promotional material.

58. Lannert, "Taking Another Look," *Billboard*, 33.

59. Ibid.

60. Burr, "Tejano Awards Persevere," *Billboard*, 33. Burr and Lannert disagree on the details of the names and number of awards—new and existing ones—wrought by the Tejano Music Awards Committee's work. Twenty-three awards were presented as a result of these changes at the 1993 TMA. The total number of awards continued to expand, and at the most recent TMA edition twenty-eight were presented. See "Nominaciones del Tejano Music Awards," *Qué Onda!*, 10–11. Still, the point to notice is that the number of awards increased and the industry was given exclusive rights to nominate and vote in several distinct categories. In short, the changes sought conciliation and appeasement with the powerful major and independent labels that had called the boycott. The results of the process henceforth were independently verified and certified.

61. Capitol/EMI Latin had basically played the best hand in dominating the TMA and, in achieving as much, the Tejano music industry itself. Not much is said in the sources about the obviously intense politics involved in explaining how Capitol/EMI Latin had arrived at the position it held in La Onda Tejana, and the TMA in particular. Nonetheless, the nomination and voting process was modified to suit the labels endorsing the boycott. To his credit, Treviño made sure to keep the entire industry immediately informed as to the work and resolutions made by the TMA committee during the summer.

Despite the boycott and nomination/voting changes, in 1993 EMI Latin led the way at the TMA for the third consecutive year as EMI artists Emilio Navaira, Selena, Grupo Mazz, and David Lee Garza won eleven of thirteen categories. See Burr, "Capitol/EMI Latin Again Sizzles," *Billboard*, 35. Indeed, EMI Latin's position within the TMA was nothing but dominant. Again in 1995, the first year in which all major labels returned to the TMA, EMI Latin artists won in ten of fifteen categories. See John Lannert, "Soho's India Puts Zest Back in Salsa," *Billboard*, 25 February 1995, 39.

62. John Lannert, "Celia Cruz Puts Faith in New Album; Fonovisa, Luna Link; Iglesias in English," *Billboard*, 30 January 1993, 41; Ramiro Burr, "Selena Reigns at Tejano Awards," *Billboard*, 25 February 1995, 39. For information regarding the method for determining the popular vote portion of the award selection process, see John Lannert, "Latin Notas," *Billboard*, 5 February 1994, 32; and Ramiro Burr, "Navaira, Selena, Fandango U.S.A. Dominate TMAs," *Billboard*, 26 March 1994, 111–12.

63. Ibid.

64. Burr, "Navaira, Selena, Fandango U.S.A.," *Billboard*, 111–12.

65. John Lannert, "A New Tribute to Carmen Miranda's Music Bears Fruit," *Billboard*, 3 December 1994, 45.

66. Burr, "Grupo Mazz, Navaira Take Top," *Billboard*, 6, 89. Los Lobos won the 1989 Grammy in the Mexican American artist category.

67. Ramiro Burr, "Texas' Mazz to Wind Its Way Thru Mexico: Capitol/EMI Latin Sets Tour for Top Tejano Troupe," *Billboard*, 21 July 1990, 27.

68. Ibid. The ever-present José Behar, vice president and general manager of Capitol/EMI Latin, stood strongly behind Grupo Mazz's first Mexico tour in terms of both conceptualizing and extending technical support for the effort. Joe López, Mazz vocalist and songwriter, acknowledged as much during a press conference held to promote the tour.

69. Ibid.; also see Ramiro Burr, "Tex-Mex Act Hits the [Mexican] Road," *Billboard*, 13 October 1990, 38. La Mafia undertook road shows in Mexico, learning as they went. Already by 1990, however, their label representatives, CBS Records, and the Mexican government, in what Burr terms "a new spirit of cooperation," began to intervene for the band, and the previously prohibitive paperwork was made easier. They were also able to do this by contracting or establishing a business relationship with Servando Cano, one of Mexico's largest entertainment promoters. As a result, customs requirements were handled with greater flexibility. Also see Joseph Treviño, "Más 'grupero' que 'Tejano'," *La Opinión*, 8 May 1996, 1D, 6D. Roberto Pulido was born and raised in La Palomita, Nuevo León, but moved to Texas with his parents and currently lives in Edinburg, Texas. Norteño or conjunto is his major musical influence.

70. Burr, "The Future Looks Bright," *Billboard*.

71. John Lannert, "First Latin Music Awards Recognize Range of Talent," *Billboard*, 21 May 1994, LM-12. At *Billboard*'s first Latin Music Awards (1994), La Mafia was honored twice, in the Regional Mexican category for Song of the Year and in the Hot Latin Tracks category for Track of the Year. Three other Tejano artists were among the awardees in this first-ever *Billboard* awards event: Selena, who swept two awards (Regional Mexican category/Album of the Year and Female Artist of the Year),

Emilio Navaira (Regional Mexican/Male Artist of the Year), and Jay Pérez (Regional Mexican/New Artist of the Year). In all, twenty-four awards were presented in eight categories, with Gloria Estefan leading the pack, having netted three in the Tropical/Salsa category.

72. John Lannert, "Latin Notas," *Billboard*, 10 June 1995, 34; John Lannert, "Latin Music Conference: Award Winners Show Diversity of Latin Music," *Billboard*, 10 June 1995, L-10. The Hot Latin Tracks chart was reinstated in 1988.

73. John Lannert, "Sony Discos Mines for Gold with La Mafia's 'Vida' Set," *Billboard*, 19 February 1994, 1, 101. According to Mando Lichtenberger, La Mafia's accordionist, keyboardist, and producer, the direction of the group's music was influenced "toward slower-tempoed material," after their hit single "Me estoy enamorando" (I'm Falling in Love). Speaking in early 1994, Lichtenberger noted: "We're trying to develop a world music type of thing, and I think the ballad is one of the only [cadences] that is universal. When we first formed, we really didn't plan on doing a lot of ballads, because they're hard to do live and we like to be energetic. But lately 'Me estoy enamorando' has become the high point of our shows. . . . *Estás tocando fuego* was a turning point in every sense. We changed our musical style because we were coming in with Sony and we wanted something special. We started using a lot of different writers, which gave us a different sound." Also see John Lannert, "A Full Plate for Estefan's Crescent Moon," *Billboard*, 9 April 1994, 32; Joseph Trevino, "La Mafia va en busca de su primer Grammy," *La Opinión*, 26 February 1996, 1D; and Francisco Pérez Rivera, "La Mafia convierte en oro y platino todo lo que toca," *La Opinión*, 8 July 1996, 1D, 5D. Oscar de la Rosa, the group's singer, noted that in the beginning (1980) the band's members included himself, his brother Leonard Gonzáles, and three nephews. They elected to call themselves " 'La Mafia' to call attention [to the group]."

74. John Lannert, "Avila Prepares to Jam in Anglo, Latin Markets," *Billboard*, 3 April 1993, 36. The sales claim was reported by George Zamora, Sony Discos's vice president for marketing.

75. Burr, "The Future Looks Bright," *Billboard*.

76. Burr, "Tejano Takes Off and Labels," *Billboard*, 41. Note that the 1990 concert at Houston's Astrodome by Emilio Navaira, Roberto Pulido, and Vikki Carr drew 52,000 approving fans. In 1993, La Mafia and the Texas Tornados pulled 56,000 Tejano fans into the Astrodome, thereby setting an attendance record for the venue and, to wit, grossed a respectable $576,000. See Ramiro Burr, "Acculturation in America," *Billboard*, 46.

77. Ramiro Burr, "Groups Explore Roots While Taking Music in New Directions," *Billboard*, 20 March 1993, 44.

78. John Lannert, "Latin Notas," *Billboard*, 28 November 1992, 36; John Lannert, "Sony Had Spectacular Year in All Categories; Secada Sparkled; Polygram Revived Latin Unit," *Billboard*, 26 December 1992, 47; John Lannert, "U.S. Media Hunt the

Hot Latin Sound, While Anglo Acts Score Big South of the Border," *Billboard*, 25 December 1993, 52–53. Other notable British and American acts that performed in Mexico City in 1993 included Guns N' Roses, Paul McCartney, Michael Bolton, Duran Duran, Bon Jovi, Michael Jackson, Madonna, and Frank Sinatra. Lannert writes: "The primary attraction for such a big-name migration? Stratospheric ticket prices that often quintupled the going rate in the U.S." *Amusement Business* reported that three of the four highest-grossing concert stands in 1993 occurred in Mexico City. For details on the Tower Records move to Mexico City, see John Lannert, "Tower Moves to Mexico; ALMA Showcase Escapes Onlookers; Lucero Lights Crowd," *Billboard*, 20 March 1993, 39; John Lannert, "The Gringos Are Coming! Tours, Radio and TV Help Swell Sales of Foreign Acts," *Billboard*, 26 November 1994, 73, 76; and Ed Christman, "The Gringos Are Coming! After Junkets and Joint Ventures, U.S. Retailers' Border Crossings Get Mixed Results," *Billboard*, 26 November 1994, 73, 76, 78.

79. John Lannert, "Whoomp! Part 2; Luis Makes Tracks," *Billboard*, 24 October 1993, 46–47.

80. John Lannert, "Los Temerarios Rock the Rosemont," *Billboard*, 14 May 1994, 44.

81. John Lannert, "Latin Notas," *Billboard*, 7 January 1995, 29. Ana Gabriel records with the Sony Discos label.

82. Lannert, "Tejano Gaining Foothold in Country Market," *Billboard*, 35.

83. John Lannert, "Latin Notas," *Billboard*, 20 February 1993, 40–41.

84. Ibid.

85. John Lannert, "Rozenblat Takes Reins at WEA Latina; Palmieri Headlining N.Y. 'Festival'," *Billboard*, 24 October 1992, 40.

86. John Lannert, "Rock/Country Acts 'Partner' Up with Jiménez on Tex-Mex Set," *Billboard*, 5 September 1992, 37. Jiménez's accompanying quartet on his *Partners* album consisted of David Jiménez (drums), Joe Morales (saxophone), Oscar Téllez *(bajo sexto)*, and Rubén Valle (bass).

87. Ibid. For a discussion of the marketing and promotion problems/strategies presented by the music produced by the Texas Tornados (whom Doug Sahm referred to in jest as the "Grateful Dead of Tex-Mex" and Fender as the "Four Dorian Grays") for Warner/Nashville, which produced their third album, *Hangin' By a Thread*, see Jim Bessman, "Texas Tornados' Full-Blown Marketing Plan: Warner Sketches 'Colorful' Promo Ideas," *Billboard*, 19 December 1992, 13, 15. The Tornados are best known for their incredible live performances, which label executives felt were not matched in record sales. Among the promotional ideas was a mostly Southwest forty-stop tour sponsored by Miller Lite complete with "standups, posters, and tent cards," as well as a tour of the rodeo circuit and another focused in Texas.

88. González, "Hay 'Flaco' Jiménez 'pa' rato'," *La Opinión*, 1D, 3D. In 1990, the Texas Tornados were awarded a Grammy for their album *Soy de San Luis* (I Am from San Luis).

89. Ramiro Burr, "Coming to Country Crossroads, Tejano's Crossing Over," *Billboard,* 23 April 1994, 30, 32.

90. Ibid.

91. Ibid.

92. Ramiro Burr, "Arista Commits to Tejano's Growth," *Billboard,* 12 February 1994, 33. At the Austin press conference in January, Cameron Randle, vice president for Arista Texas, noted: "We came to Texas to promote regional music, and we feel Tejano is the most compelling music today. We want to expand Tejano [by establishing] the commercial integrity of a major label recording while maintaining the unique and genuine quality of the art form."

93. John Lannert, "Latin Notas," *Billboard,* 5 March 1994, 38.

94. John Lannert, "Latin Notas," *Billboard,* 1 October 1994, 38; John Lannert, "Liberty, EMI Latin Link to Ink Tejano Star Emilio Navaira," *Billboard,* 15 October 1994, 14, 101. In the previous three years, moreover, both Warner and Arista had "each formed a Latino subsidiary." Navaira's career by late 1994 had attracted several corporate sponsors to his name, including Wrangler, Coca-Cola, and Stetson. Further, Sears was underwriting Navaira's nonprofit organization, Tejanos for Children, which dispensed funds for children's hospitals. His benefit concerts had raised $300,000 for the purpose.

95. Ibid.

96. Joseph Treviño, "Para Emilio, Navaira o no, la vida sigue siendo buena," *La Opinión,* 15 October 1995, 5D; Lannert, "Liberty, EMI Latin Link," *Billboard,* 14, 101.

97. Lannert, "Latin Notas," *Billboard,* 5 March 1994, 38.

98. John Lannert, "Latin Accent Graces NARAS Event," *Billboard,* 12 March 1994, 38.

99. John Lannert, "SBK Signs Latin Star Selena to Worldwide Deal," *Billboard,* 20 November 1993, 1, 89.

100. "Album Reviews," *Billboard,* 2 April 1994, 52. Selena was so hot following her Grammy success that her fifth EMI album release, *Amor prohibido,* reached the number two position on the *Billboard* Latin 50 chart within two weeks of entering the chart, and stood behind only Gloria Estefan's *Mi tierra,* which had been on the charts for forty-one weeks. See, "The Billboard Latin 50," *Billboard,* 16 April 1994, 43. Meanwhile, her hit single "Dondequiera que estés," recorded with EMI labelmates, the Barrio Boyzz, sat atop *Billboard's* Hot Latin Tracks for the fifth straight week after only twelve weeks on the charts. Similarly, Selena's hit single, "Amor prohibido," on her eponymous album zoomed into the charts by scoring the highest debut of the year (1994), entering at number thirteen on the Hot Latin Tracks. See "Hot Latin Tracks," *Billboard,* 23 April 1994, 28; and John Lannert, "Orquesta de la Luz Blazes New Trail," *Billboard,* 23 April 1994, 28, 31, 39. "Amor prohibido" stood at number one on the Hot Latin Tracks for nine weeks, one week short of the record on the HLT. Four songs by other artists were tied for the ten-week record. Selena was unseated by

labelmate Jon Secada. See John Lannert, "Secada Tops Selena, Earns Fifth No. 1," *Billboard*, 13 August 1994, 29.

101. Lannert, "sвк Signs Latin Star," *Billboard*, 1, 89.

102. Ibid.

103. Ibid.

104. John Lannert, "Selena Grabs Top Spot on Latin 50," *Billboard*, 18 June 1994, 34; "Billboard Latin 50," *Billboard*, 25 June 1994, 65.

105. John Lannert and Ramiro Burr, "Label Roundup: Current Acts and Activities," *Billboard*, 26 November 1994, 66. In contrast, Gloria Estefan's record-setting 1993 album, *Mi tierra*, had sold one million units in the United States by mid-1994 and another 900,000 units in Spain, thus making it the second-highest selling album ever in that country. According to Lannert, among Latino recording artists, only Julio Iglesias in 1984 and Linda Ronstadt in 1991 had matched Estefan's achievement prior to 1994 in the U.S. market. See, "Gloria's 'Mi tierra' Enters Platinum Territory: Third Spanish-language Set to Sell One Million in U.S.," *Billboard*, 30 July 1994, 34. Recording with Epic Records, Estefan received multiplatinum honors late in 1994 for worldwide sales of two of her albums, *Mi tierra* (three million units) and her *Greatest Hits* (four million units). See John Lannert, "Latin Notas," *Billboard*, 17 September 1994, 39. By early 1995, Estefan's 1991 album, *Into the Light*, had gone over two million units sold, and her most recent album, *Hold Me, Thrill Me, Kiss Me*, had just been certified platinum. In all, the Miami-based artist had sold more than twelve million records in the United States and claimed five multiplatinum albums. See John Lannert, "Disney Christmas Album Beats Odds, Hits Big, Stones Brazil Concerts Sell Out in One Week," *Billboard*, 14 January 1995, 29.

106. John Lannert, "Latin Notas," *Billboard*, 22 October 1994, 43.

107. Lorena Escontrías, "In Memory of Selena," *Eagle Pass Business Journal* 2 (1995): 10; Luis Manuel González, "Selena asesinada en Texas," *La Opinión*, 1 April 1995, 1A, 6A; Jesse Katz and Stephanie Simon, "Latin Music Star Selena Shot, Killed in Texas Hotel," *Los Angeles Times*, 1 April 1995, A1, A21–A22; Patoski, *Selena*, 160–61.

108. Thanks to Olga A. Vásquez for her comments regarding this section in an earlier draft of this essay. Her basic points were incorporated.

109. Enrique Lopetegui, "A Crossover Dream Halted Prematurely, Tragically," *Los Angeles Times*, 8 April 1995, F1, F10.

110. Julia Prodis, "As Millions Mourn, Many Others Ask: 'Who was Selena?'," *Press-Enterprise*, 7 April 1995, A3.

111. Katz and Simon, "Latin Music," *Los Angeles Times*, A21.

112. Selena's story became the first feature-length film about an American Latina. Space considerations do not permit extensive discussion of the production of the film *Selena*. The film was released in mid-March 1997, nearly two years to the day from her tragic death. In its first week the film grossed more than $11.6 million at the box office, exceeding Warner Brothers' expectations of receipts of $8 million. All the

while, her music remained strongly popular with the buying public, who supported her posthumously by purchasing more than seven million copies of her albums by the time of the film's release. See "In the Authorized 'Selena,' She's Seen in the Best Light," *Los Angeles Times,* 21 March 1997, FI, FII.

113. For a history of conjunto music through the 1970s, see Peña, *The Texas-Mexican Conjunto*; for a history of Mexican *corridos* from the Texas-Mexican border dating from the colonial period to the 1940s, see Américo Paredes, *A Texas-Mexican Cancionero: Folksongs of the Lower Border* (Urbana: University of Illinois Press, 1976); and for a discussion of why contemporary Tejanos, especially working-class Tejanos, dance the music, perform the ritual as it were, see José E. Limón, *Dancing with the Devil: Society and Cultural Poetics in Mexican-American South Texas* (Madison: University of Wisconsin Press, 1994), 141–86.

114. Manuel Peña, *Música Tejana: The Cultural Economy of Artistic Transformation* (College Station: Texas A&M University Press, 1999), 184–217; and Ramiro Burr, *Tejano and Regional Mexican Music* (New York: Billboard Books, 1999), 7–45.

115. This paragraph is based on several press releases issued by the Tejano Entertainers and Music Association (TEMA) in 1998 and 1999.

Outside Inside—The Immigrant Workers: Creating Popular Myths, Cultural Expressions, & Personal Politics in Borderlands Southern California

JUAN GÓMEZ-QUIÑONES

*A*n immigrant student, a one-time border crosser, in a class at an immigration services center wrote the following lament anonymously on the blackboard:

Iba buscando trabajo,
Caminé por muchos lugares—
Pero como se aprovechan
De nosotros, los que se
Llaman patrones.

Los ilegales sufrimos
Mucha descriminación,
Nos persiguen agentes de inmigración.

Con cuanta tristeza escribo
Lo que sufre un ilegal
En este país, ¿Hermano,
Pero por que nos tratan mal?

Vuela, vuela palomita
Vuela, vuela sin parar

llega hasta la frontera
y dile a la migra
que nos deje de molestar.

As the immigrant penned these lines, she/he by writing, by acting, by being in the classroom in this center, challenged these conditions. The immigrant did not depend on the *palomita* but became the message and the messenger both, moving across several spaces, as have many immigrants and border crossers.

Currently the multiple movements of cross-border workers, capitalists, and merchandisers are manifestations of intensifying world interdependence.[1] These individual forces supersede the historical institutional patterns that have evolved within national cultural spheres at the borders, increasing further the multifaceted processes of internationalization. At borders, workers, women and men, challenge social structures and cultural constants as they themselves live under oppression. Crises create challenges, which in turn propel transitions. In the U.S.–Mexican border region proimmigrant artists and writers—as different as the poet Alurista from the novelist Miguel Méndez and the immigrant-inspired music of Los Tigres del Norte from Los Illegals—fashion art, voice survival, and conjure dreams. Their art reflects their views of themselves and the world and becomes emblems of resistance to the conditions they face. Indeed, the immigrant experience is exquisitely expressed in the arts. A survey of a selection of these expressions leads to certain interpretive generalizations of the immigrants' views and attitudes.

Realities

To seek humanistically and analytically a greater understanding of the cultural expressions of Mexican immigrants, it is essential to examine their identities and the myths that comprise their realities.[2] Through these works we see a reflection of the existential relations of immigrants and borders. Here, I selectively address the skill and irony used by those engaged in delimited actions to voice specific statements. This essay attempts to encompass different approaches to writing the contemporary political and cultural history of the immigrants discussed. José Ortega y Gasset in *La deshumanización del arte* refers to *"el punto de vista humano,"* which springs from *"la realidad vivida,"* arguing that experience shapes being and, presumably, experience can be decoded from the individual's messages voiced during his/her life.

The unfolding cultural practices of Mexican people in the borderlands are an expression of their political and personal experience. As expression, culture, ideals, and practices themselves have changed, they have been re-defined.[3] This redefinition supersedes the legal constraints of borders and the stereotypes of imagined traditions. Many individuals of border populations share cultural traits and characteristics of the adjoining zones and the ongoing dynamics of self-assertions (i.e., the experience of the act and actions of self-assertion, which in turn stimulate other actions). Although a word, a document, nationality, ethnic origin, or citizenship may formally ascribe identity, personal identity is more dynamic.

Downside Up

Misinformed generalizations about immigrants and immigration are plentiful in the academic literature of the United States.[4] The negatives embedded in the literature are simplistic myths. Many authors are inspired by the subtextual quest for an immigrant or border "essence" of a sort, despite the fact that to decry such characterizations is *de rigueur* in today's critical studies. Prevalent misperceptions are those that argue immigrant non-agency, i.e., immigrant workers are not proactive organizationally nor are they engaged in public self-definition. One reason advanced for this alleged passivity is that immigrants are not concerned about their absolute and relative deprivation in the United States. In fact, they are concerned—and critically so—as can be shown in immigrant contestations that are both material and ideological. Furthermore, their actions are not simply the transference of the rural and unsophisticated to the urban and cosmopolitan setting.

Immigrant women, gay men, and lesbians are underrepresented in the literature, and when they are recognized, their experiences, actions, and concerns are often distorted.[5] Commonly, male academicians present immigrant women as victims, as advocates of the conventional, and as a subgroup that is even more passive than immigrant men. When individual women are discovered to be self-directed or to have identities beyond the "mother" or "grandmother" stereotype, these male academicians are sincerely congratulatory. What they often overlook is that, in practice, many women immigrants define themselves in an ongoing process. They are conscious of greater options for themselves, but at the same time their potential is curtailed by their sense of responsibility for others. For these women, past icons or role models—although perhaps remembered respectfully—are not guides to the future. Immigrant gays and lesbians often are not included in academic literature. Where they are included, they are derogatorily sexualized as part of an exotic border life. Contrary to this marginalized presentation, gays and lesbians are active members of immigrant families and neighborhoods. Some materials indicate that immigrant gays and lesbians are, by force of circumstances, contesters of the conventional and harbingers of the future. Their cultural statements are multifaceted critiques of the realities they face. Mexican immigrants, whether heterosexual or homosexual, are noted, but their presence is denounced, and their civic or productive personas and rights are not acknowledged.

Today, though still used for rhetorical purposes, benign myths concerning "the immigrant experience" in the United States are somewhat dated.[6] The gist of these myths is that immigration is passage from a purgatory to a heaven—the passage from the homeland, Europe, to the homeland's "frontier," America. This benign assertion on immigration to the United States often explicitly omits Mexicans. When referred to in the immigration discourse, Mexicans are seen as unhappy exceptions to the vulgar metaphor of "the melting pot." Public discourse against Mexican immigration raises questions concerning Mexican suitability for assimilation or the optimum possible rate of integration into mainstream society. Mexican immigrants are particularly underrepresented in empirical studies that emphasize questionable generalizations. Consequently, immigrants are characterized as "problems" in the status quo of policy studies. These scenarios are certainly not creative dialectical projections. In these scenarios problems are to be resolved by immigrant caretakers, mechanically, somewhere outside the borders. However, the problems are to be dealt with in a not-too-brutal manner. Lurking in these tedious discussions about the Mexican immigrant is indeed a potent myth, based on fear of the Mexican: The Mexican is a separatist, a subversive overthrower of the constructed social order, a dissident. To some Mexican Americans, the immigrant is a memory best forgotten. Stereotypes also exist in Mexico, of course. In some Mexican literature the emigrant is somehow found wanting. The immigrant is a national byproduct, a defective being, but one who serves at least one purpose by sending remittances from abroad. These remittances are considered an embarrassment, as is the emigrant himself/herself. Among the privileged strata in Mexico the emigrant is a lower class—at best a prodigal daughter or son, at worst an actual or potential Cain.

More challenging than uncorrected historicism or empirical misinformation are the liberal's views of the immigrant as pathetic "victim" or the domesticated "other." Such views are more challenging because of their good intentions, their avowed humanism. These too are stereotypes, and although metaphorical, they are, in fact, dehumanizing. These patronizing and reifying reductions are the grist for the small number of writings offering literary speculations about Mexicans in U.S. society and, in particular, Mexicans in the borderlands. In these literary speculations immigrant life is pathos. Contrary to such fictional accounts, in real life the "victim" and the "other" respond and transform, but they do so within the confines of pejorative social and economic orders. As others attempt to culturally annihilate them, some immigrants challenge and affirm themselves and their surrounding order—politically and aesthetically. Immigrants' views of themselves are quite different from the pejorative ones.

Reconstructing Cultural Practices

Manifesting and documenting an evolving consciousness, borderland immigrants have dramatically maintained an expressive cultural tradition, which is often insurgent and nearly always synthesizes the individualistic with the collective. Such tradition is manifested in music, poetry, literature, theater, and graphic art.[7] Power and its denial, affirmation and defamation, suffering and revolt are pervasive themes used in the arts. Asymmetrical relations are understood and challenged. Borderlands humor is particularly rich and sharp. It draws inspiration from cultural and class situations and from borderlanders' shared consciousness. It often describes how the bottom rail becomes the top. Humor is a main mode for expressing social criticism, quite often from a clear working-person's position or from one marginalized by adverse power relations. These persons represent the judgmental perspective in such humor. They share the same perspective as their audience, a group to whom they belong. Richly meaningful street expressions are particularly dense and clever in the borderlands and among immigrants. This humor depends on multiple references, environments, and contests; can be bilingual; and is delivered in rapid-fire style. Among immigrants, formal institutions are questioned, often humorously, always critically, as are elite cultural pretensions of both societies and even the pretensions of immigrants themselves. Humor characterizes, contextually or subcontextually, immigrant cultural expressions of all kinds.

Though the Southwest border tradition on the whole is Mexican in inspiration, and the language expression is richer in Spanish than in English, Mexicans on the U.S. side are more visibly prolific in the arts than on the Mexican side. An equally ready observation is that, until recently, Mexican traditions have influenced Anglo border traditions or cultural practices much more so than the reverse. Ironically, it is so-called Anglo "majority" cultural practices on the borderlands that seem thin, forced, and incomplete in comparison to the creative resiliency of "minority" Mexican cultural practices. Arguably, the depth of cultural practices in Anglo borderlands does not compare with its Mexican counterpart nor, for that matter, with the cultural arts expression of several regions of the United States, for example, the deep South or New England. The dynamism of today's immigrant cultural expressions are layered on an existing cultural heritage from decades past. Will the strength of cultural practices of Mexican origin persist over time? Allegedly, cultural influence follows economic and political influences. If this is so, then presumably over time Anglo consumer culture may be predicted to prevail in the borderlands.

To date there is an increasing depth and richness in immigrant and border-related arts. Indeed the novels of Miguel Méndez, *Peregrinos de Aztlán* (1979), and Tomás Rivera, . . . *Y no se lo tragó la tierra* (1971), insist on social persistence, the continuation of the Mexican social community, as well as change. They are powerful aesthetic statements about immigrant workers that assert the power of peoples' cultural practices. These works reflect a growing acknowledgment of the voices and diversity of immigrants, border dwellers, and border crossers. Defiant tones are sounded by graphic artists whose pictures incorporate words. For example, the East Los Angeles mural by Carlos Almarez voices the refusal *No somos . . . esclavos* (1974), and Ester Hernández turns the Statue of Liberty into a Mesoamerican stele in *Libertad* (1976). Yolanda M. López asks, *Who Is the Illegal Alien, Pilgrim?* (1978), and Malaquías Montoya echoes *Abajo con la migra* (1979). Interspersed among these words are other phrases, some by and/or for immigrants, others directed at audiences with the hope of swaying their feelings of empathy for the immigrants or their condition.

Incantations of the seemingly weak weapons of love and pity may in fact be counterpoints to cultural annihilation and signposts on what is nominally a self-chosen journey. In the late 1960s and 1970s no poet voiced the experience of the border crossers with more beauty and defiance than the immigrant poet Alurista.[8] His words followed narrative discourses punctuated with pounded rhythms. He performed dialogues of one or several voices against visual backdrops. In his words and performances "alien" and "illegal" were words of proactive play.

Concurrent with an ethos of social assertion and self-confidence, some writers or artists have empathized with immigrants but have mistaken pity for solidarity. Consequently, self-violence, self-pathos, and even self-pity are found in some of the art that refers to immigrants by artists who are empathetic toward immigrants but who are not immigrants themselves. Expressions of pathos can be extreme but also have varying meanings depending on how such expressions are viewed. Consider Luis Humberto Crosswaite in the short story "Marcela y el rey, al fin juntos en el Paseo Costero" from *Línea quebrada* (1987). Marcela, the immigrant, and Elvis, the Mexican American, are represented as pseudointellectual noncommunicants. Both are mired in social alienation and spiritual poverty, and their ultimate redeeming act is to die together. Yet the dying together is a sign of the future, a prelude to rebirth.

Artists in the vein of José Antonio Burciaga, who proclaimed *Amor indocumentado* (Undocumented Love, 1986), ask for the pity of outsiders (e.g., they die on the *paseo*), or they are postmodern sojourners seeking shelter *(posada)*, or they ask outsiders to feel sorry for immigrants by pointing out how hard they work *("pobrecitos trabajan tanto")*, such as in Elizabeth Sisco et al.'s silkscreen, "Welcome to America's Finest Tourist Plantation" (1988). Luis Jiménez, the Texas sculptor, avoids the banality of pathos through the sheer emotional power of his compelling statues, *Crossing the Río Bravo* (1989) and *El chuco/El paso* (1993). In California, immigrants are not accorded these tenacious romanticisms. Instead, immigrants inspire macabre road signs and border markers (e.g., warning motorists that families may dart across busy freeways in their effort to avoid deportation). The pathos of the immigrants may be perceived only as a corollary to their obvious self agency. This is clear in the *retablos* of immigrants reproduced in Durand and Massey's *Miracles on the Border* (1995). In this art, immigrants express thanks to God or to saints for actions committed and pitfalls avoided. Pity does not make for strong art or strong self-assertion, and this attitude of self-assertion set off the immigrant cultural climate of the 1980s and 1990s.

In the 1980s and 1990s anger minus pathos characterized the compelling work of several border artists.[9] The immigrant Guillermo Gómez-Peña through the enactment *El mojado peligroso* (1979), altars such as *Homage to the Fallen at the Border* (1986), and performances such as *Border brujo* (1992) spoke with a unique mixture of irony and romance. Their message: The unappreciated immigrant is the salvation of the punitive host society. Concurrently Víctor Ochoa offered a particularly striking, grim (even terrifying) representation of the border and immigrants through the inversion and re-creation of a children's traditional game in the artwork *La lotería* (1986), which is a series of characterizations of the universe. In art as in life the immigrant survives the worst of life's chances, the worst of the universe. In the mid-1980s through the photography of Philip Brookman, *Border Nopal*, inspired by María and Santos Avalos, spoke of the tenacity evidenced in the immigrant will: Cactus grows through steel fences.

In the mid-1990s artists took the offensive with cruel humor directed at the dominant society and its Latino henchmen who exploited immigrant works and workers. Among these productions were the grotesque portrayals by Enrique Chagoya in his painting *The Governor's Nightmare* (1994), and Lalo Alcaraz's cartoon *Migra Mouse* (1994), the scathing critique by Lalo López and Esteban Zul in *Pocho Magazine* (1994–98, see fig. 2.1), and the video *Hispanics for Wilson* (1994). The proworker *fotonovelas* of Ruben Ortiz and Steve Callis (1996) are also quite scathingly critical. As individual artists spoke, many Chicano art centers began to host immigrant-related art activities from time to time, providing venues for expression. For example, one center that regularly offered space during the early 1990s was the free-standing El Mocambo, a social center in central Los Angeles. Here diverse artists, genres and audiences spoke emphatically. These energies resonated in part through the broad outreach provided by radio stations.

Radio

Immigrants, like other people, are surrounded by media and routinely rely on the media for information. They are affected by media, and sometimes they have an impact on media.[10] Many owners, clients, and distributors of television and print media strive for the immigrant audiences and celebrate the immigrant presence. One media outlet in particular, radio, is strongly identified with immigrants. Radio is as direct and personal as the human voice. Radio is widely heard. Inexpensive portable radios are easily available, and radio listening can occur while on the job or driving. Instructional or didactic programs directed at immigrants are excessively optimistic about

FIGURE 2.1 A page from *Pocho Magazine* (spring/summer 1997), a satirical publication that synthesizes the immigrant experience of the nineties with that of the Chicano Movement of the sixties and seventies. (Courtesy of *Pocho Magazine*, © 1997 Pocho Productions [www.pocho.com]. *La Cucaracha*, "Le Producer Bistro," © 1997 Lalo Alcaraz [www.cartoonista.com], originally appeared in the *Los Angeles Weekly*.)

the benefits of their products. Programming directed at immigrants often emphasizes humor about immigrant life, stereotypes, and opponents of the presence and rights of immigrants, and from the 1970s to the 1990s such programming increased dramatically. Undeniably, radio commentators are effective communicators among the radio-sensitive immigrant population, and a range of programming is targeted toward immigrant listeners.

In the 1970s Hugo Morales, an immigrant, developed the concept of Radio Bilingüe using a local nonprofit station in Fresno, California. It prospered in the 1980s and 1990s and eventually reached one million listeners nationally, in both urban and rural areas.[11] Radio Bilingüe emphasized accessible cultural and information formats for Spanish speakers, many of whom were immigrants. Morales initially aimed his efforts at improving the life of farmworkers, a life he shared. To do better economically, Morales's family had migrated from Oaxaca to the Santa Rosa Valley, California, when he was nine years old. Morales describes his parents as farmworkers and rural organizers who helped others. In describing his people from Oaxaca, he asserts that they were proud, intelligent, and political. He saw his future as consistent with his family's aspirations and ethics. Morales received a scholarship to Harvard, graduated, and in a sense returned to the fields. He returned not to harvest crops but to sow the seeds of civic knowledge.

In 1976, Morales organized farmworkers interested in establishing a bilingual station. Radio was a natural choice because the workers carried radios with them in the fields. Morales had some experience in radio as he had helped his older brother run a program in Spanish before. Anticipating the need for resources, he sought volunteers who would raise money for the station by organizing cultural events.

Radio Bilingüe began broadcasting in 1980, and ten years later it was producing "Latino-oriented" programs sent to twenty stations via satellite. Cultural and news programs were geared toward the interests of Mexicans, Mexican Americans, and other Latinos. Topics included civics, civil rights, history, culture, health, and education. The first sponsors of Radio Bilingüe were the Catholic Church and the Rosenburg Foundation. In 1986, the Ford Foundation funded a Radio Bilingüe series on immigration law and migrant workers, and through the 1990s, as the programming reach became national, additional sources of support followed. The civic emphasis has been consistent.

Around that same time, immigrant activists convinced KPFK, a progressive English-language noncommercial radio station in Los Angeles, to offer immigrant-oriented programs in limited time slots.[12] In fact this was one of a range of Latino programs the station was already considering. The focus here was on both information and entertainment. This programming came about not only as a result of advocacy by activists but also as a result of audience expectations, which were being reevaluated in light of changing southern California demographics. Subsequently, for several years during the 1980s, these programs were produced by a self-avowedly politicized Latino collective and addressed cultural and civic affairs in the United States and Latin America, including immigrant aspects. Presumably, Latino immigrants have been a major audience. These bilingual programs reportedly have been well received by them as judged by on-the-air callers. Certainly, they have been among the best sources of information on subjects of interest to immigrants; thus, to some extent these programs have contributed to shaping a politically sensitive immigrant sector.

Immigrants are strongly interested in learning and improving their English language skills. Marketing though commercial radio programming is widespread and profitable. Some programming efforts are conscientious, whereas others are not. An exemplary radio show that aired in the late 1980s on Los Angeles station KSKQ was *Learning English with Mario Hernández*.[13] This Sunday morning show attempted to teach English to a Spanish-speaking audience. The popular program was created by Mario Hernández, an immigrant from Guatemala who was committed to various projects emphasizing the teaching of English. Persisting in his adult schooling for eight years, Hernández attended night school and eventually moved from community college to the University of Southern California in 1982. Listeners filled the phone lines of the show with questions about English and requests to order workbooks and cassettes offered by the program. The owners and potential investors of KSKQ also shared Hernández's concern for immigrants' interests and considered a drastic change in programming and personnel to achieve greater immigrant audience appeal. In 1991 KABQ of Albuquerque reported success with a bilingual youth program that was also sensitive to immigrants.

Border radio stations from Matamoros to Tijuana developed a family-sensitive, worker-friendly approach over the years. This approach combines music with some advertising. This style of radio programming increased dramatically in the late 1980s and 1990s. One Los Angeles station, "La Equis" (KLAX), emblematized the immigrant presence. Soon after inaugurating a program format of *banda* and *ranchero* music in August 1992, KLAX introduced a different public communication format[14] addressing immigrant ways and life, including discussions of social/legal issues. The approach combined music, a call-in format, caustic immigrant slang, explicit proimmigrant views, and riotous humor often directed at political figures by charismatic disc jockeys such as Peladillo, who is an immigrant. KLAX climbed to the top of the radio ratings in Los Angeles, a major listening market. This commercial station achieved a startling 8.4 Arbitron rating, which meant that perhaps a quarter of a million listeners tuned in at peak times. Within two years, several other Spanish-language stations adopted a similar style and format, though often with a greater sexist slant than an emphasis on civics. However, indicating diversity in listening preferences among immigrants, the highly profitable KLVE-FM (Radio Amor) emphasized romantic music in 1995–96 and overtook KLAX. Eventually, other radio stations outperformed KLAX as well.

Among immigrant listeners, KVAR Variedades became a lead Los Angeles station. This station offered a wider range of music and civic issues in its news, and public affairs commentary in a smoother and lower-key Spanish format compared with La Equis.[15] Work ethic and family values were lauded, sexist commentary and contraband music were avoided. The moderately large audience was attentive and more sensitive to certain immigrant-oriented commercials and commentaries. Audiences responded at a high rate during call-in shows.

Further changes were afoot in Spanish-language radio. Listeners readily offered their views on social issues, and announcers readily responded to the interests of their callers. Advertisers also increasingly responded to immigrant listeners, and some fomented sexist commentary. This radio market attracted advertisers with a variety of messages and became increasingly commercialized beyond the parameters of the 1980s. The immigrant radio market fragmented into listening niches. Although popular programming was common, the radio market also provided an outlet for and increased its programming of an older format of immigrant communication: theater.

Teatro

Whether widely appreciated or not, theater and all its subgenres, including farce, comedy, drama, and musicals, have been intertwined with Mexican immigration since the nineteenth century.[16] For example, the pre–World War II theater groups were attentive to immigrant sensibilities. In the early 1960s political theater of the Chicano movement in part highlighted immigrant farmworkers.

In the space of a few months in 1990, theater about or by immigrants took directions more explicitly political than earlier drama. Works by Jorge

Humberto Robles Arenas, *Los desarraigados* (1953), and Luis Valdez, *I Don't Have to Show You No Stinking Badges* (1986), are examples of this trend. Nearly forty-five years after *Los desarraigados,* two plays were specifically addressed to immigrants.

Eres un sueño (You Are a Dream), aired as a radio soap opera along the border.[17] In this instance popular radio for immigrants was used to convey a somewhat instructional format through popular drama. Written by the southern California playwright Carlos Morton, *Eres un sueño* helped Mexican immigrants to the United States become familiar with their rights and obligations. This radio soap opera was produced by an office of Mexico's Ministry of Foreign Affairs, which initiated the broadcast in Mexico. The cast of the radio program included first-line actors Hector Bonilla, Rodrigo Vidal, Eric del Castillo, Evita Muñoz Chachita, and Mario Iván Martínez. Los Temerarios, a favorite group among immigrants, provided the music.

Carlos Morton confessed that he was inspired by the idea of strengthening civic bonds between Mexicans and Mexican Americans. More to the point, his inspiration came from the immigrants, as he came to know them. He has consciously provided an optimistic message for immigrant workers in the United States. Morton said, "My goal for this radio soap opera looks forward to help Mexicans not be apolitical, so they get organized into a real community, because it is the only way to fight racism." *Eres un sueño* is about the experiences of Gerardo, a young man from a ghost town in Durango, who is making an effort to improve his future. Gerardo is an undocumented person in the United States who is looking for a way to keep studying, as well as looking for his missing father. Thus the story joins the believable point of departure—the need for work and the acknowledgment of the past sacrifices of parents by a generation intent on creating a future through education. Clearly Gerardo is superseding past history.

As this radio drama succeeded, a second radio program, *Eramos seis,* and a television *novela* aptly named *La paloma* (The Dove) followed. These programs consciously sought large audiences; however, other radio dramas were aimed more directly at audiences in specific locales. The life story of the immigrant is the recurring theme.

¿DE DÓNDE?

¿De dónde? is a theater work depicting the hardships faced in 1990 by undocumented immigrants in Los Angeles.[18] It is intended for immigrants and their sympathizers and is presented in an accessible format. Produced by a

collective directed by Mary Gallagher, the play dramatizes the histories of several individuals. The title is the invariable yet seemingly mundane question that police agents often ask immigrants: Where are you from? The question may seem simple, but the answer is definitely not.

In fact several questions and answers are involved. The play focuses on the role of the U.S. Immigration and Naturalization Service (INS) in relation to undocumented workers and its deportation of undocumented immigrants. This work also highlights the role of North American reformers who for a variety of reasons help undocumented immigrants. Several vignettes consisting of different life experiences of an undocumented immigrant crossing the border attempt to raise audience awareness.

The play's main message is that the audience (i.e., society) has a responsibility to address a situation that is portrayed as inhumane for immigrants. In this view, society—or those who are civically conscious—has a responsibility toward undocumented immigrants. By revealing injustice before a North American audience, the actors cultivate a message of resistance. These dramas also remind Latinos of the level of indoctrination in support of government repression that exists among Latinos. In one example, a Mexican American INS officer is shown deporting a child. This scene clearly addresses the issue of personal/individual accountability versus lack of sensitivity toward undocumented immigrants. The message is that unmitigated authority is wrong and contrary to human sensibilities. In a strong voice this play addresses singular and collective identity, membership, and solidarity.

FRONTERAS

Fronteras, a forty-minute bilingual theater work under the direction of Susan Franklin Tanner, tells the personal histories of seven undocumented immigrants.[19] The intended audiences are individuals sensitive to the rights of workers. Sponsored by the Los Angeles County Federation of Labor, the 1990 work reveals the feelings, opinions, frustrations, and determination of these undocumented immigrants. The actors, who are themselves undocumented immigrants, speak of the hostility they receive from other workers, their fear of deportation, and the daily hardships they face because of their immigration status. They voice their feelings in response to exploitation and societal discrimination.

The actors convey several messages to their audience. They let Latinos and others know that immigrants are not alone in their circumstance and, more important, that they are "able to do something as Latinos and not just stay behind." This is a call to unity, to take pride in who they are as undocumented immigrants. The work as a series of collective statements sends a strong message of humanism, strength, unity, and hope.

This work also conveys a message to non-Latinos about undocumented immigrants. By speaking about their hardships the actors attempt to touch the hearts of audience members and convey their feelings as human beings who suffer from harsh and inhumane treatment. They appeal to the audience to be empathetic and understanding toward undocumented immigrants at a time when much anti-immigrant sentiment is being propagandized.

Donde caminan los dioses

Donde caminan los dioses dramatizes the reality of the daily lives of the undocumented street vendors who form Teatro Realidad, directed by Sally Gordon.[20] The 1990 story revolves around the suffering of street vendors as a result of police harassment and public indifference to their rights, which the vendors believe they have. Twenty Latino immigrant vendors participated in the play to assert their convictions concerning the rights they have earned and the dignities they deserve. They drew inspiration from the hours and days they had spent walking to earn a living and support a family.

Donde caminan los dioses has several obvious messages. One is that civic-minded individuals need to be aware that undocumented street vendors receive hostile treatment from the police force, but that an educated audience can be the catalyst for positive change. Characters also convey that street vendors experience rejection from people who consider them a threat to the "décor" of the city, that the dominant public ethos is antiworker and antipoor, but that this ethos can be changed. Speakers show how the society discriminates against immigrants because of their national origin and class position.

In this drama the actors are the characters and the authors of the drama. The actors convey that they are ethical, hard-working people who receive unjust treatment by the governing elite and its police force. In the play immigrants claim rights, they do not merely plead for sympathy.

R and J

Texas Chicana playwright Edit Villareal brings together and resolves the myths and conflicts in the relations between Mexican immigrants and Mexican Americans in her play *R and J*.[21] The 1991 play based in Los Angeles draws material from Anglo literature and Mexican myths. At one level it is a play about romance between a young Mexican-born Romeo and a third-generation Mexican American–born Juliet, who has a wealthy father. They fall in love but cannot publicly declare their love because Romeo is an undocumented immigrant. The drama takes place between Halloween (October 31), a North American festive day, and Día de los Muertos (Day of the Dead, November 1 and 2), when Mexicans religiously commemorate the deceased in their family. *R and J* generally follows the same story line as Shakespeare's *Romeo and Juliet;* however, important differences exist.

Unlike Shakespeare's *Romeo and Juliet,* legalized status, rather than a family dispute, is the circumstance that prevents the lovers' marriage from being socially acceptable. Villareal's play shows the bigotry and self-hate that exist among Mexican Americans who discriminate against undocumented Mexicans in the United States. This is a strong and important point. The author is able to make the audience sympathize with undocumented people through the character Calavera Benny, who acts as the audience's conscience. Throughout the play, Benny voices that the prejudices that exist against undocumented Mexicans are unjust and divisive. Calavera Benny conflicts with Calavera Tommy, who represents animosity against undocumented Mexican immigrant youth.

Shared cultural practices and beliefs are underscored in Villareal's play. Ultimately, commonalties are more important than differences. The use of Día de los Muertos as the date of the play makes a powerful statement about Mexicans' traditional views of life. Romeo and Juliet die on Día de los Muertos, which represents an entry into another life. This is made clear at the end of the play when Romeo and Juliet reunite in Mictlan, a place where no borders or exploitation exist.

Indigenous elements and concepts are included to remind the audience of the Mexican people's culture and their ties to the land. Their right to participate in society is depicted as historical. Romeo is the only character in the play who refers to indigenous culture. This suggests that immigrants from Mexico continually reinforce Mexican culture in the United States. Romeo's presence challenges Mexican Americans to remember their background and responsibility toward other Mexicans. The character Tezcatlipoca, a spirit who judges or evaluates the ethics of human beings, frequently speaks. Romeo represents a test for Mexican Americans and Anglos. Villareal includes Mesoamerican concepts, although her interpretations of Tezcatlipoca are literal and benign, avoiding an analysis of this spirit's paradoxical and complex representation in ancient Mexican culture. Through Tezcatlipoca's positive significance and representation, the audience is asked to understand the relevance of indigenous culture, and further, to understand fairly the trials of survival.

Worker life is part of the context of the play. Romeo is a painter who earns meager wages. He wears his painter's outfit to Juliet's engagement party because he is unable to buy a festive Halloween costume. He also wears it to their wedding because he does not have the money to buy a suit. However, Romeo dresses for the ceremony by wearing a Michoacán sash around his waist. The sash together with the painter's outfit bring together strands of Mexican popular culture. Juliet's love for Romeo is stronger than any class prejudices. Her acceptance of his class position is symbolic of the unity that must exist in the Mexican community in the United States among different classes of people who share Mexican origins.

The end of the play expresses hope for the Mexican youth whom it represents. Romeo and Juliet's union in Mictlan represents the eventual disappearance of borders for Mexicans and the existence of a future utopia. Mictlan as a place of rebirth symbolizes a Mexican concept of the future and not one dictated by existing society. The audience is made aware that this future is very far away. At the end of the play Calavera Benny is still chasing after Calavera Tommy. With talent and sensitivity the playwright wrote a musical version of this work, *The Language of Flowers,* with a faster pace intended for youth.

DEPORTING THE DIVAS

Among immigrants there are diverse audiences and relations. Lighter but no less subversive and didactic, *Deporting the Divas,* by Guillermo Reyes, explores romantic relations among undocumented gays and lesbians.[22] In this 1996 comedy, self-criticism and reflection are in order for all, not only the older and more privileged crowd. Here love is also subject to being seen as unlawful, a negative judgment that is refuted. Indeed humor serves to teach and to lighten the lives of people facing threats of legal persecution and illness. Discrimination and frustrated dreams are the teachers of libertarian options, not formal ideologies. These subversivenesses echo the subversiveness of yesterday and today among some immigrants (i.e., libertarian dreams are subversive to the status quo, whether in 1915 or 1995). Love here crosses several borders.

La esperanza *Mural*

Angst for personal freedom and equal respect visibly supports immigrant art. This angst is depicted in graphics, dramas, and drama-murals. In most public and commemorative Mexican/Chicano United States murals, the concepts, symbols, and ideas that comprise them are directed at several age and educational levels.[23] These works are purposely not exclusive to formal art audiences. Since the Chicano reaffirmation in the 1960s and 1970s, the purpose of Mexican/Chicano muralism has been to inspire and inform without elaborate explanation to convey message content. In fact, muralism allows multiple conceptions and understandings. People integrate their own points of view and experiences as they view a mural.

The OSIEC (One Stop Immigration and Education Center) mural, *La esperanza* or *Tome conciencia* (1987), located at an immigrant rights center on Whittier Boulevard and Esperanza Street in a predominantly immigrant neighborhood in East Los Angeles, is unapologetically political, immigrant worker—inspired, and addressed to the working people.[24] By its form, size, and content, the popular work of art is both drama and mural. Although not created by the Chicano cultural elite, nor subsidized and sanctioned by city or university administrators or even by certified educators, the mural *La esperanza* is significantly removed in scope and action from politicized murals of past decades in Mexico. Conceptually, it is an excellent and ambitious work by five young Mexican artists, three women and two men, who are temporary immigrants and border crossers from the Taller de Gráfica Monumental and the Instituto Nacional de Bellas Artes (Mexico, D.F.), which works in conjunction with immigrants at OSIEC.

Because the mural is in public view, it invites contemplation by all manner of people, irrespective of age, sex, nationality, ethnicity, ideology, language, or education. This public access facilitates contemplation interactive with individual cultural conceptions of the world, of life, and of human beings. These conceptions facilitate the individual viewer's appreciation of the vibrancy, form, and meaning of this mural. The mural has been dedicated by its artists to all Los Angeles workers, especially those who are undocumented. The work stresses consciousness as a catalyst for action. This is not the "imbibing" of culture as it spills into the drains of American society, in the manner of the *"tome cultura"* of Mexican Americans.

In *La esperanza,* the consumerist slogan is confronted and reformulated according to utopian politics. At the front of the building, at the extreme north end of the wall, on a plane where the architectural structure eliminates the corner, consumerist symbols are painted above the figure of a quasirobotic or mechanized undocumented worker who defends himself by extending his palm. Revealed in his open palm is the figure of Ollin-Tonatiuh, who symbolizes the origins of his culture. Ollin-Tonatiuh is at the center of the Aztec calendar and represents the Fifth Sun or the Age of Movement in Mesoamerican culture. The historical myth of rebirth and continuity is made contemporary.

Parody, denial, and affirmation occur in the universe depicted in this mural. At the extreme south end of the wall is the figure of a migratory worker entering this country over a border fence in front of the face of a dejected and injured mythic Statue of Liberty, above which flies a Border Patrol helicopter. The figure of the authoritarian pseudomyth Superman comes into action at one side of the Statue of Liberty, and behind the statue is the old Los Angeles City Hall, representing discredited exclusionary politics. In the center of the mural, two children holding picket signs stand out from the rest of the mural. The picket signs depict a woman's smiling face with a fist-shaped rosebud surging upward from her mouth, representing the optimism of the immigrant and the beginning of the next generation.

To the left of the children is a giant television with its picture tube exploding and exposing young Latin American demonstrators who have thrown a broken and pain-ridden figure of Superman out of the screen. From inside the screen appear the slogans *"Raza sí, migra no"* and *"Por los derechos plenos de los trabajadores indocumentados"* as well as the flag of the United Farm Workers. Above the television, as an ultimate emblematic statement of the demonstrators, is the black eagle of La Hermandad General de Trabajadores.

The scene continues with the majestic eagle's head high above, underneath which is an image of Ricardo Flores Magón, precursor of modern Mexican militancy. Inscribed behind the image of Flores Magón, who crossed the border in 1904, is "Leavenworth 1922," the name and date of the prison in Kansas to which he was sent and where he died incarcerated.

From the face of this indomitable Mexican organizer and editor of the newspaper *Regeneración,* flyers and pamphlets float forth all the way to the back of the mural. On the last of the flyers the words of Flores Magón are inscribed, *"El presente es de lucha, el futuro es nuestro,"* which are echoed in contemporary slogans of immigrant-rights activists.

The mural, set in a working-class ethnic neighborhood, announces that a contemporary movement has come forth in the city of Los Angeles. Although the ethnic origins of this movement are Mexican, the movement extends to all minority groups. It is a movement of civic ideas, a movement of popular culture, a movement of caustic art, a prolabor and neighborhood defense movement. It is a public movement, clear in aim and open to all, to claim denied rights and to confirm and consolidate the social and civic space that is due Latin Americans as an integral part of the future.

Intentionally, *La esperanza* is a conscious contribution of political, economic, cultural, and artistic meaning to the legacy of the Mexican American community of East Los Angeles, a place of work and residence. Thus, the mural is a contribution to the consciousness of those in the United States, one forged by Mexicans within the reality in which they actively participate as conscious actors. This work is dedicated to those like Flores Magón who struggle.

The mural in and of itself symbolizes the reality in which the issue of the immigrant and undocumented worker unfolds. The social content of the work tellingly unites the mythical, the historical, and the contemporary. It is based in modern times in which the authorities have recognized some of the rights acquired by the undocumented worker community through struggle.

The call for further struggle for immigrant rights based on rights already made and earned is also a subtext of some immigrant-related music. Such subtexts appear in of one of the earliest post-1848 songs still played, "El corrido de Joaquín Murrieta."

1980s and 1990s Sounds

Songs of the immigrant experience are legion and range from *corridos* to salsa, from the tragic to the comic, from the lyric to the sentimental, from the purposeful to the merely rhythmic. Immigrant and native-born music voicing immigrant concerns changed during the 1980s, at least in a few expressions.[25] In the 1980s new rock groups from East Los Angeles articulated an angrier, sarcastic, more insistent voice by immigrants raised in the United States or their children.

The Brat (founded by the gifted Teresa Covarrubias) epitomized these sentiments.[26] As The Brat stated in "The Wolf" from their 1983 album *Los Angelinos, El renacimento del Este de Los Angeles:*

A star spangled Wolf comes,
Says that
This land was made for all
So hard to grasp the logic
Foaming from its Rabid Call.

You say this democracy believes
In our equality.
You lie!

The Wolf and the Lamb
And we are the Lamb.

The country runs right through us
And it doesn't even blink an eye
Living off the poor man's labor
Sucking all our spirits dry.

We say this democracy
Is laced with Hypocrisy.
It's true!

The Wolf and the Lamb
And we are the Lamb.

Your claw of justice
Knows no boundary lines
Tell me O' Wolf of slaughter
How many peasants died?

With this one Democracy's
Atrocious foreign policy
Yeah
The Wolf and the Lamb
And we are the Lamb.

In this one song alone several conventional myths are discarded and replaced. No paradise, the United States is a harsh place, yet compelling. It is a

place of power, not justice, but then a contradiction is voiced. The immigrant is seen as victimized and yet is asserted to be the country's sustenance and salvation.

The members of another contemporary band, Los Illegals, led by the creative Willie Heron, were civil rights activists and consciously chose to be both artistic and political, and they accomplished both remarkably well.[27] In effect, the group created language and music to fit the realities of young immigrants and to echo the motivations and ethos of the more unconventional and dissident among them. Language and experience are weapons here.

Dedicating their album *Internal Exile* (1983) to undocumented workers, Los Illegals mimic the *migra* officer and the civics teacher in their song "A-95":

It's immigration
We know you're in there
Open up, If you don't
We'll kick the door in
You've been surrounded
There's no way out
We're coming thru if it's the last thing

Drop to the floor
You too, get over there
Hands behind your back
We've had enough of your kind
Coming here and trying to hide

We are the tired
We are the poor
A huddled mass
Yearning to breathe free,
Wretched refuse of the teeming shore
We are the homeless, tempest-tossed.
(Inscription on the U.S. Statue of Liberty)

Los Illegals paraded their nonconformity specifically among immigrants and eventually linked to another group favored by immigrant youth ten years later, the Spanish-language Los Angeles–based immigrant rock group

María Fatal. This group also has a tough attitude and an immigrant follow-ing. Their songs, sung in Spanish, criticize and parody nearly every social and political convention, whereas Los Illegals do the same in English.

Los Illegals do not think of themselves as "huddled masses." In their song "El Lay (L.A.)," they state that gratitude should be reserved for another day:

> Standing on the corner, got nowhere to go
> I'm here in El Lay, got no place to stay
> A man came up to me and he asked me my name
> Couldn't speak his language, so he took me away.
>
> Is this the price you have to pay
> When you come to the U.S.A.?
> We come to work, we pay our taxes
> Migra comes and then they kick us on our asses.
>
> El Lay
> He threw me on the bus, that headed one way
> I was being deported, for washing dishes in El Lay
> Looking out the window, I felt that I belonged
> A million illegals, we can't all be wrong.
>
> Is this the price you have to pay
> When you come to the U.S.A.
> I don't know why, we cannot stay
> Didn't Gronk erase the border yesterday?
>
> El Lay
> We ended at the border, hands above my head
> I told him all I wanted, was a chance to get ahead
> No future for my family, can't even get respect
> What happened to the liberty, and the justice that we get.
>
> Is this the price you have to pay
> When you come to the U.S.A.
> We came to work, we pay our taxes
> Migra comes and then they kick us on our asses.

This song springs directly from family experience, the hard-to-come-by job, and eventual deportation. In "We Don't Need a Tan" (1983) immigrants voice their own civics:

> Policia nos mandan, nos mandan
> Derechistas nos mandan, nos mandan
>
> you can't solve your problems
> by putting us down
> we've been here forever
> we've paid for this town.

The songs and groups with their titles, names, themes, and choice of language evidenced a distinct cultural and political reality. Contemporary immigrant reality, however, is distant from the stereotype of times past and present, of "modern" or "postmodern" or conventional popular arts, or for that matter, of immigrant songs of the pre-1980s decades.[28] Local rapper and activist Víctor Aldana of Aztec Generation is one artist, for example, who sang tougher and called for action, as in his song "Yo no soy ni pocho ni mojado" (1996):

> Yo no soy ni pocho ni mojado
> me quedo mas conforme
> si me dicen Mexicano.
>
> Levanta tu frente
> y siente el orgullo
> ésta es tu tierra natal.
>
> Ayúdame a pelear
> y siempre lucharé
> por el bien de mi gente.
>
> Es tiempo de unión
> defender nuestros derechos
> sin condición, demostrar la fuerza del honor.
>
> Yo me gano la vida con sudor
> yo soy obrero, mi trabajo es primero

por eso siempre digo
lo que quiero
trabajo sí, racismo no
yo defiendo mi raza de corazón,
lucha, ponte trucha.

Here and now there is self-conscious welding of the historical, the subjective, and the occupational.

In the 1990s immigrant youth and young adults promoted a broad diversity of music, and within this diversity songs associated with the *norteño*, *quebradita*, and banda sounds spoke affirmatively on many occasions.[29] Much of this music was dance music, some sentimental and humorous. Some songs explicitly addressed immigrant concerns but were quite different in attitude from the sad and sentimental "Canto del bracero" of the 1950s by the popular Pedro Infante, which concluded lovingly but inanely, "stay home." Perhaps two contrasting attitudes toward the immigrant experience of today are expressed in the differentially nostalgic but resolute "La jaula de oro" (1980), by Los Tigres del Norte, and the nostalgic but assertive "El ilegal" (1990), by Joan Sebastian. The former portrays an immigrant raising a family in the United States, and the latter underscores the pride of having an immigrant father. Nostalgia is affirmed, played with, and negated.

Among the many themes that appear in immigrant music, the difficulty of life has appeared and reappeared. "La tumba del mojado" (1988), for example, offers a sarcastic reference to the contrast between the cruel immigrant reality and some other representation of the border as a postmodern illusion, a romantic heaven. The song states that blood and roses differ. They are not only different in content, they are different in desire. Now at the beginning of the twenty-first century, place and identity are both much broader and more specific.

A gradual set of changing perceptions has occurred, including those that heralded the more active participation of immigrants during the 1980s. A sign of this perhaps has been the strong sales among immigrants of the Los Tigres del Norte album, *Gracias . . . América . . . Sin fronteras*, awarded a Grammy for the best regional Mexico–U.S. recording in 1988.[30] Another example, while on the surface one more quasinationalist lament, is the song "El otro México" (1988), which deals with proactively immigrant transformation, community-building, and earned rights in the United States. Songs about immigrants date back nearly a hundred years, but in the 1980s the

FIGURE 2.2 Los Tigres del Norte with Carlos Monsiváis (with glasses), author and prominent social critic. (Photograph courtesy of Los Tigres del Norte.)

tempo increased, and this popular genre changed. The song "El chicano" (1980), emphasized ethnic solidarity, while the song "El sueño de Bolivar" (1988), emphasized transnational achievement.

Members of the Tigres del Norte group immigrated from Sinaloa, Mexico, to seek a better livelihood, intending to return after a while (fig. 2.2). They stayed, settled in San Jose, California, and then permanently legalized their stay in 1985 (as did many in their audiences) in order to make the most of immigrant audiences and their greater access to new technology in music marketing. Their main songwriter, Enrique Franco, is an immigrant who has gone through much travail. Lyrics and emphasis are a spectrum of insights, faults, and obvious reactionary contradictions as well as progressive affirmations. Arguably the contradictions found in the group's repertoire may give greater substance to their positive affirmations. For example, some Tigres music contains lyrics touting the contraband trade and the profligacy of men, but in other songs and speech they denounce such activities before their audiences. The inspiration is local and personal, and also consciously sensitive to the immigrant market.

Some songs have explicitly somber themes yet become very popular among immigrants in the United States. Striking are the Los Tigres songs that speak to ethnic pride in contrasting ways while referring to stresses commonly shared by immigrants. They speak of being the Mexican of today as in the song "El otro México" or of being Latino as in "El sueño de Bolivar." Several Los Tigres songs address the rights due immigrants as in the songs "Vivan los mojados" or "Los hijos de Hernández." (1988). Solidarity among immigrants is stressed as in "Tres veces mojado" (1988) and "Cuando gime la raza" (1988). On behalf of immigrants, songs appear that are ideological but transpartisan, addressing identity beyond cultural distinctions, for example, "Frontera internacional" (1988), "Sin fronteras" (1988), and "América" (1988), the last of which asserts that immigrants are Americans, too.

Los Tigres's music, as well as music by other immigrants as they see themselves variously speaks of values and incidents of life that restructure equalities.[31] Once in the United States, Mexicans become aware that people from Central America also suffer many of the injustices that they do while crossing the border. "Tres veces mojado," by Los Tigres del Norte, points this out. When migrating from El Salvador, workers risk their lives to cross not only the border of the United States, but also those of Mexico and Guatemala. The mistreatment suffered in Mexico and Guatemala makes the worker think about the need for solidarity. Despite the problems that arise from the Salvadoreño's uncertain status in Mexico, the song points out that at least one mexicano named Juan helped him. This implies that while the country, be it Mexico or the United States, labels the Salvadoreño "indocumentado," some Mexican individuals are willing to help; their identity is with their fellow immigrant.

Awareness of others' perceptions can be turned to group advantage by becoming the point for arguing for equity. A song that illustrates some of the problems stemming from perceptions of Mexicans in the United States is "Los hijos de Hernández," by Los Tigres del Norte. First it underscores that detractors use immigrants as scapegoats. They blame Mexican immigrants for unemployment in the United States. When told this by an INS officer, a worker is quick to respond that Mexicans are in fact hard working. The song alludes to the fact that a disproportionate number of Mexicans have fought in the armed forces of the United States. Furthermore, Mexicans are assigned more dangerous combat positions. The worker ends by rebutting that the officer may not like Mexican last names on payroll lists but that he can also find Mexican names in the missing-in-action lists. He and his sons meet their obligations. Immigrants face their obligations.

Contrasting with Los Tigres in several ways while addressing some of the same realities is Guillermo Velázquez (and his band Los Leones). In a way, he sings about obligations, and his songs combine explicit civic defiance and self-criticism.[32] Avoiding circumlocutions, he states in "El derecho legal al trabajo" (1986) that no one should deny another person the right to work. Velázquez uses historical forms such as *décimas* to communicate, just as other groups use the commercial, innovative, or radical forms. His work draws on songs and lyrics that predate the modern *corrido* and other currently popular forms. Velázquez particularizes situations and dialogues even more than do other singers. As a result, he and his accompanists are particularly identified with by persons from specific regions. Among his most effective presentations are those featuring María Isabel Flores and him in dialogues that emphasize ethical behavior. Overlooked commercially, Velázquez is widely respected by activists, artists, and working people. He has modest sales because he is his own distributor.

For years Velázquez was a caustic political commentator living in Guanajuato, in central Mexico, his perspective influenced by workers' travails in Mexico. Eventually, the hardships and mobilizations suffered by immigrants in the United States caught Velázquez's attention. Although his songs criticize what he perceives as negative tendencies among immigrants, nevertheless some immigrants respond to his songs. Since the late 1980s, he has been touring the Southwest with messages that address labor, civics, and gender issues. He is skeptical of progress, yet supports civic rights and the struggle against injustice. His impressive collection of songs, "Los trovadores" (1982), "Me voy pa'l norte" (1986), and "México es magia pero también . . ." (1988), and the tellingly titled "Fronteras de fantasías" (1996), cover a variety of themes. The challenges of immigration and immigrants are repeatedly underscored, as well as the theme that the life of immigrants is characterized by struggle.

Presumably, some listeners would expect Mexican singers to refer to death as part of the struggle of life. In some songs immigration is indeed presented as a life-affirming act containing the possibility of death. Arguably, equality is actually the emotive gist in such songs as "El vagón de la muerte" (1987), "La tumba del mojado," and "Pasaporte a la muerte" (1994). In songs such as these, death as a central theme is an invitation to reflection. The years of work may bring death, without the bravado on the subject found in other types of Mexican popular music. Workers' concerns about death involve concerns over family and the explicit recognition of uncertainty in human affairs. Songs such as "Un puño de tierra" (Ramón Ayala

1984), "Nadie es eterno" (Lalo y Los Descalzos 1992), and "Allá nos juntamos" (Banda Móvil 1993) all stress a worker's concern for death, yet punctuate this concern with resolution. "Allá" underscores an awareness of class differences in death. However, it seems that *el pobre* is ahead of the game because he knows that in the cemetery, earth covers both rich and poor. Thus, death is the leveler, implying that life circumstances should be more equal. Acknowledging that death transcends any other material power, this and other songs nevertheless underscore class differences and the inflexibility of life. Seemingly nihilistic, the point in these songs is often that what is important is the ethics with which life is lived.

The way in which death is expressed in a song gives a sense of what survival means to Mexican immigrants. In "Mojado," by Maldita Vecindad (1990), death is macabre, yet the opportunity for defiance is through dance. Here the father dies, while the children survive to dance. The message of a song may very specifically refer to the family members of the voice in the song. Thus, for Mexicans, persistence in the struggle to negate death means survival for a family. In the song "Mis tres canciones," by Banda Vaquero from their album *Musical* (1989), we hear the voice of a man on his deathbed. He asks for his children to be taken care of, and of them he asks that they love and respect their spouses. This sentimental song conveys the importance not only of love for family but also of respect for women.

Although immigrant-focused songs and norteño, *conjunto*, and banda groups are predominantly male, women do participate in composing and performance. The songs of María Isabel Flores and her appearances with Guillermo Velázquez are a contrast to most commercial presentations. Some female singers such as Graciela Beltrán are more than regionally popular, and some of their *canciones* deal with female issues that are different from the common love song. The songs may reflect both male and female work values, because both women and men listen to the radio and request the songs. Significantly, the norteños and bandas are now trying to replace some chauvinist material with material about Mexican women's concerns and their contributions to the Mexican community. Implicitly or explicitly, women are viewed as partners. This arguably can be attributed to the *indígena* and *campesino* ties that Mexican workers hold. Even in the chauvinist song "La mojada" (1992), by Banda Móvil, the clear representation is that women are part and parcel of the immigrant work experience and that previous beliefs do not hold. "Mantenido" (1994), by Cuisillos Musical, voices the complaints of a young man who stays home, cleans, and takes care of the baby while the young woman works. In the song "Mojado desobligado" (1986), by Guillermo Velázquez and María Isabel Flores (with Los Leones), roles are explicitly reversed. The man answers to the woman, Guillermo answers to his *compañera*.

Some of the songs played over the radio not only tell us something about worker life but also relate how workers are critical of aspects of society and the problems faced by the working community. "El hijo pródigo" (1992), by Banda Móvil, presents the story of a son who leaves his family's home, implicitly rejecting the traditional duty of caring for one's family. He attributes his leaving home to lack of experience. At his return he finds his parents dead, and he ends up in jail. He then recommends that one should fulfill one's obligations to parents and family. The family is important for Mexicans, but its importance is better understood through experience, which includes denial and reaffirmation. The value of duty to family is echoed in the lyrics. Not listening to the family may produce negative conditions, as in the case of "El hijo pródigo," but in fact many immigrants have been forced to be prodigals, as expressed in the previously mentioned song "Mojado desobligado."

Because class discrimination and deprivation are part of Mexican workers' lives, these are themes that figure in some songs, particularly those of Los Tigres. Material need is often the cause cited for people to leave their pueblos. Perhaps immigrants similarly rationalize their feelings about leaving their pueblos because of the necessity for work, as voiced in the song "Mi pueblo," by Gerardo Reyes, to defeat hunger and end ignorance.

The worker may see the pueblo somewhat differently when he/she returns, realizing that changes have occurred. The changes are understood to be irrevocable. Songs do not necessarily specify what is seen, but intimate that abuse and poverty exist, perhaps more than was noticed before. Indeed memory and nostalgia are mediated by daily needs, as noted in the song "Carta de Petra" (1986), by Guillermo Velázquez and María Isabel Flores (with Los Leones).

The immigrant journey does not grind away ethnic awareness, and in some cases it may sharpen it. The song "Un indio quiere llorar," by Banda Machos in the album *Sangre de indio* (1991), incorporates an awareness of class and ethnic differences with the typical laments about unrequited love. This *indio* laments and the song emphasizes that the *dama* does not reciprocate the indio's love because they belong to different class and ethnic groups. In this very popular song we see contemporary Mexican workers openly acknowledge being Indian. Perhaps this cultural pride may be attributed to the song's appearance in 1991, a year in which indigenous nations reaffirmed their pride in being native to this land. Thus, the song documents a period in contemporary history that the workers can relate to. This song about love crossing ethnic and class boundaries is far more popular among immigrants than among Mexico's middle classes.

"Sangre de indio" (1992), by Banda Machos, is particularly telling because it refers to many of the values held by new immigrants from rural townships. This song underscores pride in being indigenous and in indigenous values. Among the song's themes are fidelity, spirituality, familism, and compassion. All these values are associated with being indio and with having a relationship to the land. A concern for children's well-being is also specified. The parents leave the sierra to offer their children a better living. The indio attributes his values to both his father and mother.

By acknowledging the mother's contributions there is an explicit affirmation of women's importance within the indígena culture. The song suggests that Mexicans believe that both men and women have important roles within the community. A few of these songs raise two difficult themes that are generally avoided in Mexican discourses, intragroup racial or ethnic animosity and female subordination or inequality. There are also clear renunciations of these themes not only in words and metaphors but in the performances and performers. The Banda Machos themselves negate the former theme, and María Isabel Flores and Graciela Beltrán negate the latter.

To be sure, songs are the products of a commercial market, and some express an awareness of immigrants as consumers who are influenced by competitive and selfish values. Yet they also highlight certain aspects of worker experiences, values, and concerns. In some cases these themes are clearly underscored. In others the emphasis is quite contradictory. Guillermo Velázquez is scathing in his song "El chupe, la tele y el futbol" (1988). Some novelty songs highlight alienation or criticize societal fragmentation by focusing on technological items that are desired yet denigrated with humor. In "Apaga la tele" (1992), by Los Tigres, a husband alleges always finding his wife in front of the television watching *telenovelas* when he arrives home from work. The husband asks his wife to turn off the imaginary world and live reality, that is, his reality. Although the song has a romantic tone, it serves to illustrate how once-desired consumer items can cause friction in a household. The song also points out that once workers leave their jobs for the day, they have to go home and deal with both emotional dilemmas and material needs. In the Los Tigres song "El celular" (1992), a working person buys a cellular phone to upgrade his/her own social appearance. What he/she bought is another anchor to a hierarchical society. Both these songs humorously discuss social change, but the change that is important is not the acquisition of items of technology, as in the song "Mojado desobligado," but the questioning of values and conventions.

Immigrant energies emerge in other music-related phenomena that explicitly question acquiescence. The dance phase of the early 1990s known as "la quebradita" celebrated assertion and pride, as voiced in Banda Arkangel R15's song "De dónde es la quebradita" (1993): *"La Quebradita es un baile que baila toda la gente. / Se oye bonito su ritmo, tiene sabor diferente. / ¿De dónde viene éste ritmo? aquí pregunta la gente."* This norteño music is more from California immigrants than from rural workers in Nuevo León or Chihuahua. The music is driving, playful, and aggressive all at once. During the 1990s norteño fashions became popular among youthful immigrants; they began to wear vaquero hats, shirts, boots, belts with hanging leather straps, and scarves. Perhaps thirty thousand youth were involved in clubs that promoted organized activity centered on the quebradita trend celebrated by Graciela Beltrán in her 1989 song "Pochita de Sinaloa": *"Yo soy pochita Californiana. / De Sinaloa (Nayarit y Jalisco) mis padres son. / Y mis costumbres son mexicanas, / mi sangre es brava y le canto al amor."*

Both the dance and style consciously made statements. As immigrant mobilization heightened, one commercial album appeared that compiled the most popular proimmigrant songs, *Americas sin fronteras, el canto de los inmigrantes,* by the Piratas del Norte (1996). This was a group that was willing to play any songs popular with listeners but that preferred the more socially conscious popular songs.

As the audiences for norteño, quebradita, and banda music increased, a less predominantly immigrant dance movement, Danza Azteca and its scores of subgroups, grew in the 1990s.[33] These groups embraced indigenous dance as a means of approaching Native American culture and spirituality to be sure, but not from an academic perspective. They approached it as feeling, caring persons who asserted pride in the indigenous way of living. More generally, immigrant music interprets and judges immigrant binational or transnational situations in the context of harsh economies. Through song, immigrants also express their own political interest in a transnational political context. "El otro México" is indeed ideologized by Los Tigres del Norte as a constructed homeland.

In this song immigrants speak of their citizenship, their civic belonging, and their civic virtues. This citizenship is not merely consciousness of exploitation or infatuation with a dance hall trend but is expressed in direct political mobilizations and repeated public cultural affirmations. Immigrant activists emphasize the need for civil rights to be both universalized and validated by some force or some one. To be sure, this commitment synthesizes personal belief and self-will. More to the point are immigrant personal justifications that recall Herbert Marcuse's radical assertion that substantive culture springs from the dissenting classes because they give life to the validity of democratic values such as freedom, equality, and justice. According to him, these values have authenticity only in resistance to established conformities and constraints.[34]

Conclusion

Identity or being is too often treated as a ready-made label or a "platonic essence" (the philosophical notion that ideas are real). In everyday life, identity is rooted in practices and myths that are fundamental to individual social reaffirmations and cultural reproductions. Identity is created from the actions of existence, not academic abstractions. Symbols of the practices and beliefs of a community are reference points in the participatory processes that give some cohesion to the ongoing genesis of contemporary society. At any given moment social identity is the tension rooted in practice between change and continuity. In fact in the Mexican borderlands, identities are social rather than parochially territorial or formalistically pseudopopular, and they are subject to alteration. They may subsume, supersede, or be corollary to several identities, including ethnic, national, or regional identities, as well as gender and sexual ones.

Of course personal dreams, fears, and beliefs—our very own myths—at one level are expressions of identity. More than simply "illusions," myths are invoked ideals or potent appeals to ourselves and those immediately around us. At one colloquial level "myth" is a description for a counterfeit or counterfactual statement. (This is but one use of the word "myth" in the historiography. Not much is gained by saying that falsehoods are false.) Here myth is used in the oppositional, radical sense of what ought to be. Positive or negative symbolic messages, myths explain, they rationalize. They may be the individual standard for judging self. Myths are maps and depictions of social relations that reside in the mind's eye of an individual, private yet intended to be shared. Some myths are inherited from elders, some are devised in the present, some are wholly invention, some are partially based on historic facts. Although myths may vary, they relate to social needs in both a personal and a public sense. For example, publicly voiced reasons of groups endorsing specific popular expressions, or state-promoting histories, have myths as part of their content. Both are conventional validations, justified by rationalization of selected memories usually in the name of survival, ethics, and progress. In contrast, personal myths are specific to individual aspirations in specific contexts.

Diverse, even contradictory, Mexican immigrant myths are personal and public references to ourselves in relation to others and to others in relation to ourselves. As shared beliefs, myths provide identity and order; myths are expressed by individuals in word and action. They are internalized designs that code the parameters of social relations evaluated and performed in a particular time and space. Among immigrants in the borderlands, the circumstances derived from life in Mexico and the United States have inspired myths that meet, converge, and finally dissipate as other myths emerge.

Immigrants live bilingually in many aspects of their lives. Mexican immigrant identity expressed in Spanish conveys an ongoing process—*soy, somos.* Their English-language counterpart conveys constancy—I am, we are. Arguably the language difference hinting at process is but a small connotative hint of significant denotative cultural distinctions involved, but also distinctions that are synthesized. Indeed identity is singular and collective, stable one minute, changing the next. Being involves both the personal and the shared, the fated and the chosen, the conventional and the innovative. The material affirmation of self in real life is survival, and this occurs within the context of gender, family, personal relations, and economic activity. These interactions produce and reproduce customs as delimited social processes that shape immigrant identity, give voice to myths, and impart reason to chosen cultural practices and their ongoing changes.

"Culture" in daily life is not reducible to a personified, much less a generalized, abstraction. Neither is it reducible to simplistic polarities supposedly documented in government forms. Indeed, individuals may and do practice nearly all specific parts of the intellectual qualities shared by a group and reproduce cultural materials associated with these qualities. Yet cultural practice is an individual choice within a group phenomenon. Cultural practices are social-ideological conglomerations, time-determined and space-associated, a genesis and a cultivation. Borderland Mexican cultural expressions are continually transforming themselves. The transformation is nourished by historical memories and impelled by social conditions and needs, but it is not limited to these. Through renovation and innovation, cultural practice redefines what one is and what one believes. Although cultural practice subsumes both being and myth, it is dependent on them. The three are in interactive transformation in precise specifics voiced in longings and actions: Who am I? What do I want? These in turn may lead to the question: Of what am I a part? In other words, group identification by an individual is preceded by an individual or personal (I am) existential affirmation.

In viewing the U.S.–Mexico borderlands, some critics have emphasized the poverty and the culturally "discordant" side of the United States relative to the rest of the country, and the "dependency" status and the emulative posture of the Mexican side of the boundary. Some have underscored the subversive or retrogressive "threat" that each side of the border represents to the other country. Others have emphasized their mutual "complimentary regionalization." Persistently devoted believers of a "national essence," whether in Washington, D.C., or Mexico, D.F., or simply out-of-date pundits denounce the perceived loss of a mythical monolithic perennial "national culture." Supposedly this phenomenon is particularly noticeable at the border. Perhaps some pessimists and cynics may doubt that substantive civic consciousness or civic identity is authentically possible for immigrants or border dwellers—if they are Mexicans. This is obviously negated by immigrant activities. To urban planners, statistically, the borderland Mexican populations convey social and economic patterns calling for policies, not liberties. However, numerical analyses fail to convey the drama of real life, the singularity of the neighborhoods for the resident individuals, the vibrancy of diverse borderland cultural practices, and the vigor of individual lives as expressed in popular arts.

As cultural practices of individuals evolve, these adapt and change. Today, for the moment, achieving civil rights for Mexican immigrants is interactive not only with cultural practices but also with cultural changes and civic assertions. Proimmigrant rights activities are part of the postindustrial context of the United States, no less social than family relations, no less "cultural" than "artistic" expressions, no less political than diplomatic relations. The manifestations of self-validated proimmigrant rights are visible in daily living and in conscious efforts at communicating personal experiences and public needs. These manifestations are multifaceted and dynamic, resulting in new fusions.

The fusion is salient in expressive cultural practices that are simultaneously historical and contemporary, conventional and radical. Contemporary popular cultural expressions in the Mexican borderland draw from a
rich heritage, one fashioned by hispanicized Indians, mestizos, mulattos,
farmers, workers, and artisans. Many immigrant artists consciously draw
from this heritage. Over time the arts encompass modern literature, drama,
music, and crafts, but they still draw from the popular culture common to
the early settlers and often from Indian groups, especially their designs,
ceremonies, dances, and ideological metaphors. Sources range from the ver-
bal and visual traditions of the late nineteenth and early and mid-twentieth
centuries to the analogous expressions of today. Newspapers and informal
performance have been recurrently important to artistic expression and
continuance, but electronic technology has energized border arts dramatically in the last twenty years. Mexican border writers, artists, and musicians—men and women of the twenty-first century—are talented and diverse. Artistic richness and diversity across the different arts and within a
single art form are indeed demonstrations of a continuing social dynamism
of change and vitality rooted in the multifaceted society and economy of the
United States today.

Notes

1. For this essay on contemporary cultural expression, art materials, videos, cds,
newspapers, interviews, and some direct participation and observation in immigrant cultural activities are important. Published contemporary sources consulted
were *La Opinión*, the *Los Angeles Times*, *Nuestro Tiempo*, the *New York Times*, the
Sacramento Bee, *Hispanic Link*, and *Hispanic Business*, as well as several irregular
publications and print materials. Several persons were interviewed, including ten
immigrant workers following a simple open-ended questionnaire emphasizing perceptions and opinions. I participated in several presentations on art projects or
discussed such projects with participants. I thank Minnie Ferguson and Marcos
Aguilar for assistance at the early stages of this research project. Selected sources
pertinent to immigrants and the border are as follows: for empirical portraits, see
David E. Hayes Bautista, "Latino Immigrants in Los Angeles, A Portrait from the
1990 Census" (Los Angeles: Alta California Policy Research Center, 1994); Frank D.
Bean et al., "Post-irca Changes in the Volume and Composition of Unauthorized
Migration to the United States, An Assessment Based on Apprehension Data," in

Unauthorized Migration to California, eds. F. D. Bean et al. (Washington, D.C.: Urban Institute Press, 1990); Thomas Muller, *The Fourth Wave: California's Newest Immigrants* (Washington, D.C.: The Urban Institute Press, 1984). For information on Mexican immigrant characteristics and immigration currents during the 1980s, see Wayne Cornelius, "Los migrantes de la crisis," *Federalismo y Desarrollo* 20 (marzo-abril 1990). For life stories, read Merilyn P. Davis, *Mexican Voices, American Dreams: An Oral History* (New York: Henry Holt and Company, 1990). For overall Mexico–U.S. interdependence, see the innovative María Esther Schumacher et al., *Mitos en las relaciones México–Estados Unidos* (México, D.F.: Secretaría de Relaciones Exteriores/Fondo de Cultura Económica, 1994); and for labor arrangements, see Jorge A. Bustamante et al., *United States–Mexico Relations: Labor Market Interdependence* (Stanford: Stanford University Press, 1992). See also Julian L. Simon, *The Economic Consequences of Immigration* (Cambridge, Mass.: Basil Blackwell, 1989). On demography and the quality of border-life statistics in past decades, see Peter Reich, ed., *Statistical Abstract of the United States–Mexican Borderlands* (Los Angeles: University of California/Latin American Center Publications, 1984); David E. Lorey, ed., *United States–Mexico Border Statistics, 1990 Update* (Los Angeles: University of California/Latin American Center Publications, 1991); Niles Hansen, *The Border Economy: Regional Development in the Southwest* (Austin: University of Texas Press, 1981); and E. R. Stoddard, *Patterns of Poverty along the U.S.–Mexico Border* (El Paso: University of Texas at El Paso, Center for Inter-American Studies and the Organization of United States Border Cities, 1978). For ethnographic views of California immigrant and border life in the 1980s and 1990s, see Leo Chávez, *Shadowed Lives: Undocumented Immigration in American Society* (Fort Worth: Harcourt, Brace, Jovanovich, 1992); Luis Alberto Urrea, *Across the Wire: Hard Times on the Mexican Border* (New York: Anchor Books, 1993); and Ramón "Tianguis" Pérez, *Diary of an Undocumented Immigrant* (Houston: Arte Público Press, 1991). For how immigrants are viewed, see the sensitive account by Arturo Madrid-Barela, "Alambristas, braceros, mojados, norteños . . ." *Aztlán* 6 (1975); and Arturo Islas, "On the Bridge, at the Border: Migrants and Immigrants" (Ernesto Galarza Commemorative Lecture, Stanford University, 1990). The novels of Arturo Islas are compassionate insights into border Mexican American and Mexican immigrant memories: see *The Rain God* (Palo Alto: Alexandrian Press, 1984) and *Migrant Souls* (New York: Morrow, 1990). Insightful also is the novel by Alfredo Véa, *The Silver Cloud Cafe* (New York: Dutton, 1996). For discussions of culture and citizenship, see Thomas Bridges, *The Culture of Citizenship: Inventing Postmodern Civic Culture* (New York: State University of New York Press, 1994); and Ronald Beiner, ed., *Theorizing Citizenship* (New York: State University of New York Press, 1995).

2. For the evolution and function of borders, see Paul Guichonnet and Claude Raffestin, *La geographie des frontieres* (Paris: Presses Universitaires de France, 1974);

and Owen Lattimore, "The Frontier in History," in *Theory in Anthropology,* eds. Robert A. Manners and David Kaplaw (Chicago: Aldine, 1968). For characteristics of the Mexico–U.S. border in the 1970s, see Romeo Flores Caballero, *La frontera entre México y los Estados Unidos, desarrollo histórico* (Monterrey, N.L.: Universidad Autónoma de Nuevo León, 1976); and Joaquín Xirau Icaza and Miguel Díaz, *Nuestra dependencia fronteriza* (México, D.F.: Fondo de Cultura Económica, 1976). For basic information on the borderlands, see E. Stoddard et al., *Borderlands Sourcebook: A Guide to the Literature* (Norman: The University of Oklahoma Press, 1983); and Peter Reich, ed., *Statistical Abstract of the United States–Mexico Borderlands.* For analysis of the border area in the 1980s as a system, see John W. House, *Frontier on the Rio Grande* (Oxford: Clarendon Press, 1982). For excellent contributions to analysis of the 1990s public policy issues, see John R. Week et al., *Demographic Dynamics of the United States–Mexico Border* (El Paso: University of Texas at El Paso, 1992); and Abraham F. Lowenthal, *The California-Mexico Connection* (Stanford: Stanford University Press, 1993). For a basic advisory overview for studies of the border, see Jorge Bustamante, "Frontera México–Estados Unidos: reflexiones para un marco teórico," *Estudios sobre las culturas contemporáneas* 11 (1991). For a striking visual presentation on border life, see Alan Weisman and Jay Dusard, *La Frontera: The United States Border with Mexico* (New York: Harcourt, Brace, Jovanovich, 1986).

3. For reflections on border and Mexican American culture, change, and conflict, see Juan Gómez-Quiñones, "Hacia un concepto de cultura," in *A través de la frontera,* ed. Ida Rodríguez Prampolini (México, D.F.: CEEST/IIE-UNAM, 1983); also see the sections on culture in the following collections: *Estudios fronterizos* (México, D.F.: ANUIES, 1981); Roque González Salazar, ed., *La frontera del norte* (México, D.F.: El Colegio de México, 1981); Mario Miranda Pacheco and James W. Wilkie, *Reglas del juego y juego sin reglas en la vida fronteriza* (México, D.F.: ANUIES, 1985); and the special issue of *New Scholar* 9 (1984). For Mexican transborder cultural similarities in the 1970s, see Américo Paredes, "The Problem of Identity in a Changing Culture: Popular Expression of Culture Conflict along the Lower Rio Grande Border," in *Views across the Border, the United States and Mexico,* ed. S. R. Ross (Albuquerque: University of New Mexico Press, 1978). For what the border signifies for some Chicanas and Chicanos, see José David Saldívar, *The Dialectics of Our America: Genealogy, Cultural Critique, and Literary History* (Durham: Duke University Press, 1991), 149–53; and Alfred Arteaga, "An Other Tongue," in his collection of essays *An Other Tongue: Nation and Ethnicity in the Linguistic Borderlands* (Durham: Duke University Press, 1994), 9–33.

4. For a review of literature on Mexican immigrants, see Jorge Durand and Douglas S. Massey, "Mexican Migration to the United States: A Critical Review," *Latin American Research Review* 27 (1992). For Mexican academic views of immigrants, see some of the essays in María Esther Schumacher et al., *Mitos en las relaciones.* For Mexican

cinematic views on immigrants, see David Maciel, "Los pochos y otros extremos en el cine mexicano, el cine mexicano se va de bracero," *Pantalla* 16 (primavera 1992). On Mexican American views, see David Gutiérrez, *Walls and Mirrors* (Berkeley: University of California Press, 1995). For an informed assessment of numbers, costs, and benefits in the United States at this time, see *Fiscal Impact of Undocumented Aliens* (Washington, D.C.: Urban Institute, 1994). For informed economic effects in California specifically, see Kevin F. McCarthy and Robert Burciaga Valdez, *Current and Future Effects of Mexican Immigration in California* (Santa Monica: The Rand Corporation, 1984). For an overview of immigration, see Juan Gómez Quiñones and David R. Maciel, "What Goes Around, Comes Around—Political Practice and Cultural Response 1890–1990," in *Culture Across Borders*, eds. David R. Maciel and María Herrera-Sobek (Tucson: University of Arizona Press, 1998).

5. For sensitive studies with special attention to women, see Pierrette Hondagneu-Sotelo, *Gendered Transitions, Mexican Experiences of Immigration* (Berkeley: University of California Press, 1994); and Silvia Pedraza, "Women and Migration: The Social Consequences of Gender," *Annual Review of Sociology* 17 (1991). For expositions on the condition of women workers, see Lourdes Arguelles, "Undocumented Female Labor in the United States Southwest: An Essay on Migration, Consciousness, Oppression, and Struggle," in *Between Borders: Essays on Mexicana/Chicana History*, ed. Adelaida R. Del Castillo (Encino: Floricanto Press, 1990); and Patricia Fernández Kelly, *For We Are Sold, I and My People, Women and Industry in Mexico's Frontier* (Albany: State University of New York at Albany, 1983). Also on female workers, see Vickie L. Ruiz and Susan Tiano, eds., *Women on the U.S.–Mexico Border, Responses to Change* (Boston: Allen and Unwin, 1987); Patricia Zavella, "The Impact of Sun Belt Industrialization on Chicanas," *Frontiers* 8 (1984); and Margarita Melville, "Mexican Women Adapt to Migration," *International Migration Review* 12 (1978). Gloria Anzaldúa speaks in a strong border feminist voice in *Borderlands/La Frontera: The New Mestiza* (San Francisco: Spinsters/Aunt Lute, 1987). For sensitive portrayals of women, see Estela Portillo Trambley, *Trini* (Binghamton: Bilingual Press, 1986); Sandra Cisneros, *Woman Hollering Creek and Other Stories* (New York: Random House, 1991); and Norma Iglesias, *La flor más bella de la maquila* (México, D.F.: Secretaria de Educación Pública 1985).

6. For views of the alleged "general" immigrant experience, see John Higham, *Strangers in the Land: Patterns of American Nativism 1860–1925* (New York: Atheneum, 1963); David H. Bennett, *The Party of Fear: From Nativist Movements to the New Right in American History* (Chapel Hill: University of North Carolina Press, 1988), 159–237; Thomas J. Archdeacon, *Becoming American: An Ethnic History* (New York: Free Press, 1983), 143–72; and Roger Daniels, *Coming to America: A History of Immigration and Ethnicity in American Life* (New York: Harper Collins, 1990), 265–84. For a harsher view, see Peter Brimelow, *Alien Nation: Common Sense about*

America's Immigration Disaster (New York: Random House, 1995). For a survey of policies, see "Immigration: History of U.S. Policy," in *Harvard Encyclopedia of American Ethnic Groups*, ed. Stephan Thernstrom (Cambridge, Mass.: Harvard University Press, 1980), 491–92.

7. For a discussion on border culture, myth, and identity, see the essays in José Manuel Valenzuela Arce, ed., *Entre la magia y la historia* (México, D.F.: Programa Cultural de las Fronteras/El Colegio de la Frontera Norte, 1992). For an analysis of popular culture in the 1970s, see Carlos Monsiváis, "La cultura de la frontera," in *Views Across the Border*, ed. Stanley R. Ross (Albuquerque: University of New Mexico Press, 1978). For an analysis of popular culture in the 1980s, see José Manuel Valenzuela Arce, *A la brava ése* (Tijuana: El Colegio de la Frontera Norte, 1988). For overviews on border art, see two publications by Ida Rodríguez Prampolini, *A través de la frontera*; and "Un arte sin fronteras," *Memoria de Papel* (April 1992). For historical music and arts on the border, see Américo Paredes, *A Texas-Mexican Cancionero, Folk Songs of the Lower Border* (Urbana: University of Illinois Press, 1976); and Jacinto Quirarte, *Mexican American Artists* (Austin: University of Texas Press, 1973); and for some historical writings, see *The Texas Humanist* 6 (March-April 1984). For the work of one acclaimed sculptor, see Ellen J. Landis et al., *Man on Fire, Luis Jiménez* (Albuquerque: The Albuquerque Museum, 1994). For recent developments in popular graphics, see José Manuel Valenzuela Arce, "Expresión gráfica, mural, placaso y tatu" (Tijuana: Colegio de la Frontera Norte, unpublished paper, 1985); and for monoprint images, see *Imágenes de la frontera: monotipia* (Tijuana: Festival Internacional de la Raza, 1992). For a range of arts, see Christopher Knight, "Exploring the Border Experience," *Los Angeles Times*, 13 March 1993; Jeff Kelley, ed., *The Border Art Workshop* (BAW/TAF) 1984–1989: A Documentation of Five Years of Interdisciplinary Art Projects Dealing with U.S.–Mexico Border Issues (A Binational Perspective) (San Diego: Border Arts Workshop, 1991); Kathryn Kanjo et al., *La Frontera/The Border: Art about the Mexico/United States Border Experience* (San Diego: Centro Cultural de la Raza and Museum of Contemporary Art, 1993); and for commentary on border art, see Victor A. Sorell, "Citings from a Brave New World: The Art of the Other México," *New Art Examiner (The Independent Voice of the Visual Arts)* 21, no. 9 (May 1994): 28–32 and 56–57. For art practiced by immigrants themselves (in contrast to that of showcase artists), see Jorge Durand and Douglas Massey, *Miracles on the Border—Retablos of Mexican Migrants* (Tucson: University of Arizona Press, 1995). For the intertwining of the political with the artistic in public representations, see James C. Scott, *Domination and the Arts of Resistance: Hidden Transcripts* (New Haven: Yale University Press, 1990).

For a discussion of border life related in some novels, see Armando Miguelez, *An Analysis of the Border as a Literary Setting* (El Paso: The University of Texas at El Paso, 1983). For critical evaluations of border-related literature, see Hector Calderón and José David Saldívar, *Criticism in the Borderlands: Studies in Chicano Literature, Cul-*

ture and Ideology (Durham: Duke University Press, 1991); and Teresa McKenna, *Migrant Song: Politics and Process in Contemporary Chicano Literature* (Austin: University of Texas Press, 1997). For commentary on a variety of writings on humor, see Ricardo Aguilar Melantzon, *La frontera México–USA, novela, cuento y chiste* (El Paso: The University of Texas at El Paso, 1990); José Reyna, *Raza Humor: Chicano Joke Tradition in Texas* (San Antonio: Penca Books, 1980); and Américo Paredes, *Uncle Remus con chile* (Houston: Arte Público Press, 1993). For examples of writings on and from the border, see *Literatura fronteriza: antología del Primer Festival, San Diego–Tijuana, Mayo 1981* (San Diego: Maize Press, 1982); and the centennial issue on "Texas Literary Tradition," *Discovery* 8 (Winter 1983); for Baja California in particular, see the excellent anthology, Gabriel Trujillo Muñoz, ed., *Lecturas de Baja California* (Mexicali: Instituto Nacional para la Educación de los Adultos, 1990). Also see the periodicals *Esquina baja* (1992), *Cultura norte* (1992), and *Rutas* (1993), and the earlier periodicals *Maize* (1986) and *La línea quebrada* (1986–87). Some of these have telling photographs. In a satirical vein with immigrant and border materials, see *Pocho Magazine* (1994–98). Ruben Ortiz Torres and Steve Callis appropriated the *fotonovelas* avidly read by many immigrants and turned the format into readable, compelling, proworker, pro-union arguments; see *Bienvenidos al hotel California* (Salem, Oregon: John Brown Books/State Employees International Union, 1998).

8. For Alurista, see statements such as "Poem in Lieu of Preface," in *Aztlán: Chicano Journal of the Social Sciences and the Arts* 1 (1970); and the collections, *Floricanto en Aztlán* (Los Angeles: Chicano Studies Center Publications, University of California, 1971), *Nationchild Plumaroja* (San Diego: Toltecas en Aztlán, Centro Cultural de la Raza, 1972), and *Timespace Huracán* (Albuquerque: Pajarito Publications, 1976). In line with these views but with a difference, see poetry by Santiago Baca, *Immigrants in Our Own Land* (Baton Rouge: Louisiana State University Press, 1979); or the writings of Jose Antonio Burciaga *Undocumented Love/Amor indocumentado: A Personal Anthology of Poetry* (San Jose: Chusma House Publications, 1992).

9. See Guillermo Gómez-Peña, *Warrior for Gringostroika* (St. Paul: Greywolf Press, 1993); Guillermo Gómez-Peña, *The New World Border: Prophecies, Poems, and Loqueras for the End of the Century* (San Francisco: City Lights, 1996); and "A New Artistic Continent," *High Performance* (1986). In the polemic "The Multi-cultural Paradigm . . . ," *High Performance* 12 (Fall 1989), Guillermo Gómez-Peña argues that the positive multiplication of criteria in the arts is concurrent with the fuller citizenship of all individuals in society.

10. Luís Manuel González, "Radio a la medida," *La Opinión*, 2 February 1993; Henry Muñoz Villalta, "Música de banda acapara audiencia de la radio en el Sur de California," *La Opinión*, 30 April 1993; Margy Rochlin, "Loud and Proud," *New York Times*, 25 July 1993; Cristine González, "Banda Rides Wave of Hispanic Pride," *Wall Street Journal*, 4 October 1993; Joan Easley, "Strike up the Banda," *Los Angeles Times Supplement*, 29 October 1993; Maria Zate, "Don't Touch That Dial!" *Hispanic Business* 16

(1994): 47; Rick Mendoza, "Back from the Brink," *Hispanic Business* 16 (1994); Jerry Adler and Tim Padgett, "MexAmerica: Selena Country," *Newsweek,* 23 October 1995; and Claudi Armann, "The Audience Is Listening," *Hispanic Business* 17 (1995).

11. Radio Bilingüe archives, 1992–1993.

12. KPFK archives, 1992–1993.

13. KSKQ archives, 1992–1993.

14. KLAX archives, 1992–1993.

15. KVAR archives, 1994 [format and ownership changed during 1997].

16. For theater, see Nicolás Kanellos, *Mexican American Theater: Then and Now* (Houston: Arte Público Press, 1983).

17. Carlos Morton, *Eres un sueño* (1996), typescript (Spanish).

18. *¿De dónde?* (1990), typescript (English with some Spanish).

19. *Fronteras* (1990), typescript (bilingual).

20. *Donde caminan los dioses* (1990), typescript (bilingual).

21. Edit Villareal, *R and J* (1991), typescript (English with some Spanish).

22. Guillermo Reyes, *Deporting the Divas* (1996), typescript (English with some Spanish).

23. For a discussion of Chicano public art, see Shifra M. Goldman, *Dimensions of the Americas: Art and Social Change in Latin America and the United States* (Chicago: University of Chicago Press, 1994), 245–312.

24. *La esperanza* or *Tome conciencia* by Norma Urenda, Isela Guerrero, Ester Cimet, Eduardo Juárez, and Mauricio Gómez (1987). See Carlos Alberto González, "Develan mural de la esperanza en este de L.A.," *La Opinión,* 25 Septiembre 1987.

25. On music, see Steven Loza, *Barrio Rhythm: Mexican American Music in Los Angeles* (Urbana: University of Illinois Press, 1993).

26. The Brat, *Los Angelinos, El renacimento del Este de Los Angeles* (1983).

27. See the album *Internal Exile* by Los Illegals (1983), and tapes by María Fatal. Also apropos are the albums by Aztlán Nation, Kid Frost, Lighter Shade of Brown, and Latin Alliance (in particular their song "What Is an American"), all from the late 1980s and early 1990s. Immigrant-related innovative rock groups from the late 1980s that deserve artistic appreciation are Eclipse, Los Sagitarios, and Los Humildes.

28. Víctor Aldana (i.e., his tape *Generación Azteca,* 1996).

29. Songs selected for comment were identified by listening to call-ins and music requested at KLAX and KVAR, as well as popularity charts maintained by the radio stations; programming staff were helpful, as were listings in music radio publications. Richard Salazar at EMI on several occasions provided information from their state-of-the-art files as well as material; helpful also were Nogales and Associates, a media investment firm at Century City. See also Carlos Haro and Steven Loza, "The Evolution of Banda Music and the Current Banda Movement in Los Angeles," *Selected Reports in Ethnomusicology* X (1994). Some insights applicable to music and considered here were gleaned from Kathleen Steward, "Nostalgia—A Polemic," in

Reading Cultural Anthropology, ed. G. E. Marcus (Durham: Duke University Press, 1992); and Scotty Dupree, "Know What the People Want," *Media Week* 3 (1993). For a study of immigrants and popular music, see María Herrera-Sobek, *The Mexican Immigrant Experience in Ballad and Song* (Bloomington: Indiana University Press, 1993). For helpful interpretive cues in examining music, see Timothy Rice, "Toward the Remodeling of Ethnomusicology," *Ethnomusicology* 13 (1981); and Thomas Turino, *Moving Away from Silence: Music of the Peruvian Altiplano and the Experience of Urban Migration* (Chicago and London: University of Chicago Press, 1993).

30. For twenty years Los Tigres del Norte have been a barometer of the negatives and positives of immigrant-identified music; listen to *Gracias . . . América . . . Sin fronteras* (1988). See Jesús Martínez Saldaña, "Los Tigres del Norte en Silicon Valley," *Nexos,* November 1993.

31. More than fifty recordings were identified and surveyed, and the knowledgeable Dr. Carlos Haro was interviewed (6 November 1992). See Elena Oumano and Enrique Lopetegui, "The Hottest Sound in L.A. Is Banda," *Los Angeles Times,* 1 May 1993; "Agusto con la quebradita," *La Opinión,* 12 agosto 1993; and "En lugar de pelear," *Nuestro Tiempo,* 10 February 1994. For a postmodern takeoff on the genuinely popular music trend, see Rubén Martínez, "The Shock of the News," *Los Angeles Times Magazine,* 30 January 1994.

32. "Guillermo Velázquez y los Leones de la Sierra de Xichu," unpublished typescript provided by Paula Ramírez (January 1998).

33. For the contemporary interest in indigenous dance, see Guillermo García-Duarte, "La danza Azteca, una tradición espiritual," *La Opinión,* 9 agosto 1995; and Juan Ríos, "Indigenismo in the Urban Environment: A Discussion with Paztel Mireles, Aztec Dance Elder, Los Angeles, 1994," *Raíces* 1 (1995).

34. Herbert Marcuse, *One Dimensional Man* (Boston: Beacon Press, 1964).

"Yo soy chicano":
The Turbulent and Heroic Life of Chicanas/os in Cinema and Television

DAVID R. MACIEL AND SUSAN RACHO

*A*mericans live in an audiovisual world. According to a recent study, "the average American by the age of eighteen will stockpile nearly 17,000 hours of viewing experience."[1] And that figure is rising every day. Children clearly are reading less and viewing more. In fact, mass media in the United States now transcend socioeconomic status, because even the less affluent have considerable access to television and film. Close to 97 percent of all homes in the United States are estimated to own a television set.[2] Thus, media have become among the most, if not the most, influential elements in the life of North Americans. As one recent observer noted, "Americans eat, dress, sleep, converse, court, play and even propagate to the rhythms of commercial mass media."[3]

Yet, these media forms are far from neutral.[4] Multinational corporations own, regulate, and fabricate the mass media.[5] Obviously, these organizations wield enormous influence on public perceptions of public policy issues, culture, and values. To a large degree, they mold the American mind. The gatekeepers of the media industry strive to maintain ideological hegemony, legitimizing the status quo. They do so by providing programming that entertains more than it questions and that offers escapism more than social commentary. This is not to imply that the mass media make no positive or educational contributions whatsoever; however, they do so only on rare occasions.

According to one study, mass media in America contribute to several negative developments.[6] For Chicanas/os and other minorities, however, the negative influence is even worse. Besides experiencing the usual detrimental effects of mass media, minorities have consistently encountered institutionalized racism and constant discriminatory actions.[7] The practice of prejudice directed at Chicanas/os in the media follows Albert Memmi's definition of racism postulates. He defined racism as "the generalized and final assigning of values to real or imaginary differences, to the accuser's benefit and at his victim's expense, in order to justify the former's own privilege or aggression."[8] At least four major expressions of institutionalized racism by U.S. mass media have had an impact on Chicanas/os. These are stereotyping, borrowing from and distorting their culture, outright exclusion of their presence in the media, and obstruction of their artistic projects.

This chapter will elaborate these concerns and discuss Chicana/o efforts to confront complex media issues. The development and trends of Chicana/o cinematic productions are analyzed. A discussion of the Chicana/o struggle for representation in television programming is included. And finally, critical reflections on the current and future perspectives of Chicanas/os in visual media are postulated.

Screen Images of the Chicana/o

Chicana/o media representations have a lengthy history in U.S. cinema and television. In films, Chicana/o characters appeared almost simultaneously with the birth of initial productions.[9] Yet, since those early years at the turn of the century, they have become victimized by the institutionalization of certain stereotypical screen images.[10] In numerous films and later television programs, the Chicano has been portrayed as the greaser, the convenient villain, the perpetual *bandolero,* the buffoon, the Latin lover, and the *peón.* Chicanas, for the most part, have fared no better. They have been repeatedly cast as the "female clown" (such as in the films of Lupe Vélez and Carmen Miranda), the dark lady, the prostitute, or the maid.[11]

Recently, Chicana/o portrayals have varied somewhat, but not for the better. In contemporary Hollywood, Chicanos have become major protagonists as drug users/dealers or as urban gang members. Such productions as

The Three Amigos (1987), *Colors* (1988), *Predator 2* (1990), *Bound by Honor* (1992), *Mi vida loca* (My Crazy Life, 1994), and *187* (1997) illustrate the return of the greaser and clearly reveal that commercial cinema clings to the traditional formula of casting Chicanas/os as perpetual villains. With few exceptions, Hollywood as well as U.S. commercial television programs convey only one-dimensional aspects of the Chicana/o experience: crime and drugs.

The demeaning portrayals of Chicanas/os carry major societal implications. By stereotyping the Chicana/o in such a manner, the injustice and discriminatory actions directed at their community by the dominant society are more easily justified. The victim, rather than the oppressive elements of the system, is blamed for the overall condition of the Chicana/o.

Stereotypes reinforce people's beliefs and prejudices and can prove harmful to the victimized community. If these slanted views are frequently heard and often observed, minorities themselves might be prone to incorporate them at least as half-truths. Stereotyping and prejudicial representations have clearly helped spawn negative self-images among Chicana/o youth.[12]

Another major trend in Hollywood films is the near-invisibility of the Chicana/o community. In mainstream films, even those that take place in highly Chicano-populated areas (such as *Grand Canyon* or *Volcano,* both of which take place in Los Angeles), Chicanas/os are invisible. In fact, almost no major Chicana/o actor appeared in a central role in any of the most acclaimed commercial (non-Chicano–produced) films of the 1980s and early 1990s.[13] Such invisibility also exists behind the camera. A 1992 study released by the Directors Guild of America reported that of its 9,759 members, which include directors, associate directors, and unit production managers, only 167, or 1.7 percent, had Spanish surnames.[14] Such reports convey that Chicanos and Latinos are the most underrepresented ethnic group in film and television.

The Struggle for Resources and Space

For many years, the Chicano community voiced indignation about these negative media images, with some success. However, it would not be until the Chicano Movement of the late sixties that major changes would come about. As a result of years of Chicano activism, media organizational advocacy, and civil rights and women's movements, federal regulations against discriminatory practices were established by the Equal Employment and Opportunity Commission. Also, increasing numbers of Chicanos were recruited by college and university film schools and television stations. Thus, a first generation of Chicana/o filmmakers and other media specialists emerged in the early seventies.

In search of resources to practice their craft, experience to build a resume, and a job to pay daily expenses, many of these prospective Chicana/o filmmakers sought employment in television as a stepping-stone to feature-film production. Establishing credibility and creative worth within the "good old boy" studio network of exclusive guilds and unions has always been extremely difficult for aspiring filmmakers. In the case of Chicanas/os, decades of exclusion had created barriers in the form of institutionalized racism, sexism, and ageism, barriers that persist in the industry.

The major obstacle, the "catch-22," in acquiring substantial studio financing is the casting hurdle. Given a good script and a proven director, studios or production companies will insist on casting "stars" to complete the package. According to the studios, except for Edward James Olmos, few Chicana/o superstars currently exist, and only a select group of "bankable" Latino stars are regularly hired. This very small group includes Andy García (Cuban), Rosie Pérez (Puerto Rican), and more recently, Jennifer Lopez (Puerto Rican) and Salma Hayek (Mexican). Latinas have been cast in so few major roles in recent decades that no Latina actress is considered to be of star status—with the possible exception of Puerto Rican Rosie Pérez.

The media-related opportunities for Chicanas/os that emerged in the seventies were short-lived. As the years passed, media access for the Chicano community decreased. Undoubtedly, institutions had acted in response to activist pressures, and when those pressures waned, the outlets that included Chicano artistic expression began to disappear.

The 1980s, advertised as the "Decade of the Hispanics," was ironically a period of growing conservatism and "white backlash" with regard to affirmative action employment practices in film and television. Even the Corporation for Public Broadcasting (CPB), the funding arm of the Public Broadcasting Service (PBS), reflected this conservative trend, despite past programming that had included several Chicano cinema projects such as *Seguín, The Ballad of Gregorio Cortés, El norte,* and *Stand and Deliver.* The study, "Balance and Diversity in PBS Documentaries," found that although the representation in television of racial minorities increased for most minority groups from 1978 to 1987, the numbers of Latinos involved actually fell by one third. The study concluded: "The visibility of most minority groups on PBS documentaries was roughly proportional to their representation in the general population. Only Hispanics were conspicuously underrepresented."[15]

As a result of conservative Republican administrative appointments, the National Endowment for the Arts (NEA) and the National Endowment for the Humanities (NEH) were also increasingly unresponsive, even hostile, to proposals submitted by members of the Chicano community. Almost no Chicana/o projects received support from these foundations during the 1980s and early 1990s. When proposals were submitted, they were invariably rejected. Because PBS and NEA/NEH are major cultural foundations for the support of cinematic initiatives in the United States, their decisions proved most detrimental to the development of Chicano narrative cinema and television programs.

With the ascent of Bill Clinton to the presidency, and his re-election, the situation has taken a turn for the better. NEH and NEA once again have made diversity a strength, and subsequently, select Chicana/o productions—mainly documentaries—have received critical financial support. At the same time, however, film and television industries have remained unwilling to abandon their racist, sexist, and ageist employment practices. Thus in the 1990s, as relative newcomers to the industry, the small number of Chicanas/os striving to succeed in the profession have been at a clear disadvantage in this very competitive job market. An acute shortage of Chicanas and Chicanos exists in all areas and at all employment levels in front of and behind the camera; this shortage is especially acute at the decision-making level. Although few staff positions are currently held by Chicanas/os at major studios and television stations, work in the film and television industries is available on a limited freelance or independently contracted basis, especially at select creative levels.

The nearly constant on-screen invisibility of Chicanas/os in film and television translates into very few opportunities for Chicana/o actors to practice their craft. This is especially true for Chicanas. Over the last twenty years, more than 80 percent of all film screenwriters and more than 70 percent of television writers have been Anglo men. As of 1991, working minority writers comprised only 4 percent of the Writers Guild's active members.[16] Producers, directors, and casting agents tend to audition Chicana/o actors only if a script expressly calls for a "Latin type." Not surprisingly, Chicano actors are often forced to accept stereotypical, negative roles if they want to work at all.

Because of this atmosphere, Chicana/o filmmakers increasingly have realized that they must produce their films independently, that is, outside the confines of the major studios. This has meant securing the financing for the projects themselves in order to tell their stories without compromising style, script, or cast. Yet, even if all the obstacles are successfully overcome and the production is completed, other issues remain. The production of a film is only half the issue. Once made, a film must be distributed, and distribution can be a daunting task. In the past two decades theater ownership has become increasingly monopolized by corporations that work closely with studios to package films. These packages are sold to the theater chains. Thus, the studios are in a position to exert substantial control over production, from the filming and publicity process to the distribution and exhibition of movies.

One alternative to overcoming this monopoly for Chicano filmmakers has been to screen their films at a number of Chicano/Latino film festivals. For example, the Guadalupe Cultural Center in San Antonio holds its Cine-Festival on an annual basis. Cine Acción in San Francisco has recently sponsored the annual Festival Cine Latino.

Another alternative means of distribution for Chicana/o films has been through public television broadcasts. Although Chicano filmmakers and producers have criticized PBS for not providing as much funding for Chicana/o programming as has been expected or desired, PBS has nonetheless funded or broadcast more than half of all Chicano feature films made to date. For instance, producers of the feature *Break of Dawn* were unable to find a theatrical distributor in the United States. Fortunately, the film was shown to a national public television audience through the efforts of the National Latino Communications Center on PBS. Because of the popularity of its two leading stars, *Break of Dawn* is exhibited periodically in Mexico.

On another front, Chicana/o directors and producers have explored coproductions with their Mexican counterparts. In pursuit of this goal, a select group of Chicanos met with Mexican filmmakers in 1990 and 1993 to explore a potential collaboration on creative matters, financing, production, and distribution. These conferences were held in Mexico City and were referred to as "Chicanos Noventas." However, mirroring the "good-old-boy network" of the U.S. film industry, Mexican hosts invited only male Chicanos from the United States to participate in the first conference of Chicanos Noventas. The rationale given was that only Chicanos had produced or directed feature-length narrative films. Because of this exclusion, Chicanas and Mexicanas planned and convened their own conference—called the "Encuentro de Mujeres Cineastas y Videastas Latinas: Mexico–Estados Unidos"—in late 1990 at the Colegio de la Frontera Norte in Tijuana. Thirty-five women filmmakers were invited from the United States and Mexico to share their work and to begin their own dialogue.[17]

In 1993, another Encuentro took place in Mexico City between Chicano filmmakers and their counterparts in Mexico. This group, made up of both Chicanas and Chicanos, discussed their current and future projects. Two filmmakers, Luis Valdez and Moctezuma Esparza, were able to formulate several agreements. Valdez, for example, received a commitment from the Mexican Film Institute (IMCINE) for partial funding of his proposed film, *The Two Fridas*.[18]

A Cinematic Reconquest? The First Steps: Chicana/o Documentaries

Many Chicano filmmakers began their careers in documentary production, working on one or more of the unprecedented number of Chicano television specials and public affairs and documentary series of the early seventies. These early programs, broadcast during prime time on commercial and public television, included *Acción chicano, Impacto, Reflecciones, Realidades,* and *Unidos.* These productions and others were shown primarily in California, although some aired in other Southwest and Midwest cities such as San Antonio and Chicago. *Realidades* was also broadcast nationally through PBS.

The opportunities that emerged in the seventies fostered an important genre, the Chicano documentary. Generally, documentary production was an affordable and particularly appealing format to this first generation of idealistic, activist-bred filmmakers (see fig. 3.1). Motivated by an urgent Chicano Movement agenda, these hard-edged political, cultural, and historically revisionist documentaries quickly proliferated. Their ranks include Jesús Treviño's *Yo soy chicano* (I am Chicano), Luis Valdez's *I Am Joaquín,* Moctezuma Esparza's *Cinco vidas* (Five Lives), Sylvia Morales's *Chicana,* and José Luis Ruíz's *The Unwanted.*

By 1990 more than 100 documentaries (including television documentaries) had been completed and exhibited. Among them are *Huelga* (Strike, 1965), *Yo soy Joaquín* (I Am Joaquín, 1967), *Tijerina* (1968), *Los compadres* (Old Friends, 1971), *La Raza Series* (including "Celebración," "A Political Renaissance," "A Working People," and "Quo Vadis"), *América tropical*

FIGURE 3.1 Raul Ruiz, Raza Unida leader from California, addresses a general assembly at the Raza Unida National Convention in El Paso, Texas. The convention, held in September 1972, was the topic of a film report on Accion Chicano, KCET's Chicano affairs program.

(Tropical America, 1971), *Chicano Moratorium* (about the Chicano protests against the war in Vietnam, 1971), *Chicano* (1971), *Nosotros venceremos* (We Will Overcome, 1971), *Requiem-29* (1971), *Soledad* (Solitude, 1971), *Cinco vidas* (Five Lives, 1972), *Los vendidos* (The Sell-Outs, 1972), *Raza unida* (The People United, 1972), *Strangers in Their Own Land—The Chicanos* (1972), *Yo soy chicano* (I Am Chicano, 1972), *A la brava: Prison and Beyond* (A Call to Action: Prison and Beyond, 1973), *La vida* (Life, 1973), *Sí se puede* (Yes You Can, 1973), *Somos uno* (We Are One, 1973), *Cristal* (1975), *The Unwanted* (1975), *Chulas fronteras* (Pretty Borders, 1976), *Guadalupe* (1976), *El corrido: la carpa de los rascuachis* (The Ballad: The Tent Show of the Rascuachis, 1976), *Agueda Martínez* (1977), *La morenita* (The Little Brown One, 1977), *Chicana* (1979), *Del mero corazón* (Truly from the Heart, 1979), *Lowrider* (1976), *Murals of East Los Angeles* (1976), *The Ballad of the Unsung Hero* (1980), *The Lemon Grove Incident* (1980), *Soy chicano* (I Am Chicano, 1980),

La onda chicana (The Chicano Wave, 1981), *Luisa Torres* (1981), *Decision at Delano* (1982), *Barrio Murals* (1983), *Through the Eyes of the Tiger* (1983), *Una mujer* (A Woman, 1984), *Royalty in Exile* (1986), *Corridos! Tales of Passion and Revolution* (1987), *Cholo Murals . . . y bien firmes* (Cholo Murals . . . and Solidly Standing, 1987), *Eye-Witness Report: A Call to Arms* (1987), *Folklórico* (1987), *El corrido de Juan Chacón* (The Ballad of Juan Chacón, 1987), *Vaquero: The Forgotten Cowboy* (1987), *Chicano Park* (1988), *Gangs* (1988), *Los carperos* (The Tent Show Performers, 1990), *Los mineros: The Miners* (1990), *My Filmmaking, My Life* (1990), *Perdidos* (Lost, 1990), *The New Tijuana* (1990), *Chicano: History of the Mexican-American Civil Rights Movement* (1996), and *The Struggle in the Fields* (1997).

As the titles of these Chicana/o documentaries reveal, this genre has been diverse in themes and techniques. Thematically, Chicano documentaries have addressed such varied issues as civil rights; the Chicano Movement; education; health concerns; La Chicana; labor struggles; Mexican immigration; the U.S.–Mexican border; and other social, cultural, and community issues. The tone and course set by *Yo soy Joaquín* and *Yo soy chicano* were followed by numerous other documentaries. Jesús Salvador Treviño, director of *Yo soy chicano,* clearly articulated the relationship between the artist and La Causa: "Chicano film art must be clear in its denunciation of past and present brutalities and must go further: It must attend to the necessities of the community, reflect the beauty of our way of life, point out our road for the future, [and] unite with the common cause. Ours must be an art of defense and support."[19]

Subsequently, many other documentaries would follow the constraints dictated by the social movements, as well as those established by the perspectives of their leaders.[20]

As documentary production increased, various Chicana filmmakers excelled in their endeavors to depict the specific issues of the Chicana. The first generation of such filmmakers included Sylvia Morales, Lourdes Portillo, and Esperanza Vázquez. Later to the scene were Elvia Alvarado, Olivia Chumacero, Salomé España, and Osa Hidalgo de la Riva. Betty Maldonado and Beverly Sánchez-Padilla also made important contributions to Chicana films. Collectively, their documentaries have created a feminist thematic discourse in their depictions of the major concerns and the legacy of the Chicana experience. Their work was accomplished despite obstacles that impeded dissemination and recognition.[21]

One subject that has been particularly salient in the Chicana/o documentary is Mexican immigration to the United States. Chicano immigration documentaries have addressed critical aspects of the Mexican immigrant experience in all its complexity with unmatched sensibility and advocacy. Unlike the great majority of U.S. media pieces on Mexican immigration, the Chicano documentaries have been based upon sound research and analysis. Through their art, Chicana/o documentary filmmakers have not only contributed imaginative, important, and artistic documentary films on this policy issue, but have been a powerful lobby group for social justice for immigrants.

Besides specific Chicano themes, Chicana/o documentary filmmakers have dealt with broader Mexican and Latin American historic and contemporary topics in such films as Lourdes Portillo's *Las madres de la Plaza de Mayo* (The Mothers of the Plaza de Mayo) and *Después del terremoto* (After the Earthquake), Héctor Galán's *Stand-off in Mexico* and *The Hunt for Pancho Villa*, Jesús Salvador Treviño's *Neighbors and the U.S. and Mexico*, and Paul Espinoza's *The New Tijuana*. These documentaries clearly reflect a Chicano/a appreciation and sensitivity in addressing Mexican and Latin American realities and issues.

Alongside the extensive production of documentaries, other film genres have also been promoted by Chicanas/os. They include commercials, animated films, films for governmental agencies, short fiction films, and videos. For example, Moctezuma Esparza won an award for his one-minute commercial for the National Alcoholism and Drug Council. In the field of animated films, Severo Pérez has made impressive productions with the support of the National Institutes of Health.

Many important and interesting works are found among the films made by Chicanos under the auspices of federal agencies. These include *Our Children's Children* (1976) and *Real Reality* (1977) by José Luis Ruíz with the support of the U.S. Department of Health, Education, and Welfare and the U.S. Department of Housing and Urban Development, respectively. In these films the visions of the sponsors somewhat predominate over the artistic talent of the creators. Nevertheless, there is no doubt that with the resources provided, these filmmakers have been able to realize technical innovations that have subsequently been utilized by authors of other films.

Short fiction films have also shown promise in Chicano cinema. Among these films are Esperanza Vázquez's *Tabla rasa* (Tabula Rasa, 1973), Lourdes Portillo's *Después del terremoto* (After the Earthquake, 1979), Luis Reyes's *Los*

Álvarez (The Alvarez Family, 1981), and Juan Garza's *The Trouble with Tonia* (1991). More recently, the video industry has opened new avenues for the artistic expression of Chicano filmmakers. Important efforts in this area have been made by Ernie Palomino, Juan Salazar, Daniel Salazar, Harry Gamboa, and Willie Varela. In addition, other Chicano film directors have made important contributions in video, although some contributions have not been well received. In Francis Salomé's *Ánima* (1989) and *Mujería: The Olmeca Rap* (1990), the predominance of an exclusively masculine vision of Chicano nationalism has been criticized.

The mid-1990s rekindled the theme of the Chicano Movement in two of the most accomplished documentary projects ever undertaken: *Chicano* and *The Fight in the Fields*. In April 1996, *Chicano: History of the Mexican-American Civil Rights Movement*, a four-hour miniseries premiered nationally on PBS. To date this documentary series is the single most accomplished and ambitious Chicana/o documentary. The series powerfully and artistically captures the story of a proud people in search of social justice, respect, and a national identity. The series narrates and critically analyzes the tumultuous decade between 1965 and 1975, examining the social and political activism that was pivotal in uniting Mexican Americans to stand up and be counted as legitimate citizens of the United States. The four-part production united many leading Chicana/o filmmakers—José Luis Ruíz, Jesús Salvador Treviño, Héctor Galán, Susan Racho, Sylvia Morales, and Mylene Moreno—who contributed their considerable talents to the writing, filming, and editing of this memorable series.

Equally powerful in its message and just as well crafted artistically is *The Fight in the Fields*, written and produced by Rick Tejada Flores. This excellent documentary vividly traces the exemplary life of César Chávez and his courageous struggle with the farmworkers against exploitation, overwhelming odds, and societal indifference toward their plight. Sensitively written, *The Fight in the Fields* uses solid narrative, interviews, and actual footage of key events to capture that gallant collective moment that changed the lives of so many of the most forgotten and oppressed workers in America. In 1999, Lourdes Portillo's informative and sensitive documentary *Corpus: A Home Movie for Selena* aired on PBS. The film offers a moving and complex view of the legendary singer.

Overall, the documentary is still the dominant cinematic genre for Chicano and especially Chicana filmmakers. It is a format that clearly reflects their major cinematic contributions, past and present. The documentary is not the only film genre, however, in which Chicanas and Chicanos have made contributions.

Chicano Narrative Cinema

Chicano narrative cinema is a very recent development in the century-old business of U.S. movie-making. Director Jesús Salvador Treviño reflects on this time, "Although I'm an American citizen, I had to go to Mexico to direct my first feature. I found more sympathetic ears than here."[22] Creatively self-determined full-length narrative features written, directed, or produced by Chicanos first received wide theatrical distribution in the early eighties. Chicano narrative cinema has developed aesthetically through increasingly compelling stories, strong characters, varied genres, and original and innovative narrative styles. Its evolution in focus and style has reflected the times in which the works were produced. The small handful of male Chicano directors, writers, and producers is largely perceived by the industry as a marginal, creative community with a high-risk, unmarketable product. Not surprisingly, as minorities in two aspects, Chicana filmmakers have been less successful at establishing themselves as key creative players in feature-length narrative cinema than their male counterparts.

Thematically, Chicano narrative films of the 1970s and later have shared certain trends. Historical revision of key events in the Chicana/o experience has predominated in feature films. Mexican/Latino immigration to the United States is a key issue. In narrative cinema another major source of inspiration for filmmakers has been the rich literary expression of recent Chicana/o writers. Family and traditions have been dominant elements in Chicano feature films. In addition, drama has clearly overshadowed all other cinematic genres. Comedy has been sporadic but important in Chicano films.

Most Chicano narrative cinema to date has been produced as independent films. *Alambrista, Once in a Lifetime, Break of Dawn, El mariachi*, and *Tierra* are among the most prominent examples of Chicano independent productions. In a select number of cases, such as *El norte, The Ballad of Gregorio Cortés*, and *El mariachi*, corporate studios eventually incorporated them in their film distribution packages. A few Chicano cinematic productions were produced from the onset by a leading studio *(Zoot Suit, Born in East L.A., La Bamba, American Me, Mi familia, Selena*, and *Desperado)* or were realized, as in the case of *El norte, Ballad of Gregorio Cortés,* and *Stand and Deliver,* as television productions sponsored by PBS. Only *Raíces de sangre* (Roots of Blood) was a Mexican state–produced Chicano film.

Full-length narrative cinema by Chicanos had a peculiar beginning. In the early and mid-seventies, an enigmatic and unconventional young man from San Antonio, Efraín Gutiérrez, wrote, coproduced, directed, and starred in a dark trilogy of the Chicano experience: *Please Don't Bury Me Alive, Chicano Love Is Forever, Junkie/Tecato Run.* Originally shot in 16 mm and later converted to 35 mm, these movies narrate stories of Chicano youth on the fringes of society, facing life that offers only despair, alienation, conflict, and solitude. In Gutiérrez's films, the characters and narrative discourse attempt to construct a powerful individual—perhaps autobiographical—statement regarding those Chicanas/os who either self-destruct or are crushed by the institutions and society around them.[23]

In 1976, Jesús Salvador Treviño received an invitation from the Mexican government's film-producing company, CONACINE, to write, cast, and direct his script, *Raíces de sangre,* in Mexico with full government financial backing. Although the film was entirely produced and distributed by Mexican governmental agencies, more than half the cast, the script, and the direction were Chicano. The overly ambitious plot focuses upon community and labor organizing against the *maquiladoras* (in-bond industries), which divide and exploit the Mexican-origin communities on both sides of the border. As Jesús Treviño said of his film:

> *Raíces de sangre* es una película de ficción en la realidad de los chicanos y los mexicanos que viven en la frontera. Los hechos principales de la película, huelgas obreras en compañías multinacionales, ataques por parte de los policías, la discriminacion y la vida hogareña y peligrosa que han ocurrido y que ocurren actualmente. Espero que *Raíces de sangre* pueda concientizar un poco y ayudar a que las cosas cambien y mejoren para los chicanos y los mexicanos que viven en la zona fronteriza.[24]

The movie has generally received positive reviews in Mexico, the United States, and abroad. The theme clearly is the solidarity of the communities of Mexican origin in their struggle against imperialism. The political statement does not, however, detract from the movie's artistic value.

Unfortunately, *Raíces de sangre* was completed at the end of the Echeverría years. As a result of the change in the cultural policies of the next administration, it received poor distribution within Mexico. In fact, *Raíces de sangre* has had a greater impact in the United States than in Mexico.[25]

Jesús Salvador Treviño followed his earlier directorial debut with a pilot short film, *Seguín*. This movie was the initial episode of a projected historical epic of ten parts dealing with the Chicano community from the nineteenth century to the present. *Seguín* attempted a revisionist interpretation of the events and protagonists in the Texas rebellion of 1836. *Seguín* received mixed reviews. Although the film's interpretation was considered noteworthy, the uneven construction of characters and its unclear ideological and political message lessened its achievements.

Alejandro Gratian's *Once in a Lifetime* was a personal endeavor. It attempts to provide a character study of a middle-aged Chicano artist as he struggles to reconstruct his life after the loss of his wife. Through the film, existential individual questions are merged with barrio issues and artistic expression. Despite these positive features, the movie enjoyed neither commercial success nor critical acclaim. In fact, *Once in a Lifetime* has had a very limited distribution.

Conversely, *Alambrista* (1979), written and directed by Robert Young, was a landmark narrative film in the evolution of Chicano cinema. This sensitive feature relates the odyssey of a Mexican undocumented worker, Roberto, from his native village in rural Mexico to the agricultural fields in California. The film powerfully captures the harsh and precarious nature of the immigrant work experience of Mexicans in the United States. It vividly reflects how migration to the north is undertaken as a last resort because of grave economic necessity and the lack of opportunities in Mexico.

The next crucial film in Chicano narrative cinema was Luis Valdez's *Zoot Suit*. This movie, adapted from his successful play of the same name, recounts one of the most dramatic episodes in Chicana/o history: the Sleepy Lagoon incident in Los Angeles in the early 1940s. This film successfully combines theater and film techniques. *Zoot Suit* masterfully recreates the ambiance of the period and portrays a vital segment of the Chicano community in the 1940s.[26] The principal male characters are well developed and characterized, especially "El Pachuco," played with true inspiration by Edward James Olmos. The energy and creativity of the choreography and the musical score are exceptional. As a political statement and an artistic film, *Zoot Suit* (fig. 3.2) is certainly one of the landmark achievements of Chicano narrative cinema.

In the initial phase of Chicano narrative cinema, the dominant tradi-

FIGURE 3.2 Della (Rose Portillo), Henry (Daniel Valdez), and friends flash back to re-create a dance before the Judge (upper right, played by John Anderson) and the mythical El Pachuco (upper left, played by Edward James Olmos) in *Zoot Suit*. (© 1981 Universal City Studios, Inc.)

tion combined artistic qualities with social and political commentary. Representative of this film tradition is *The Ballad of Gregorio Cortés* (1981), directed by Robert Young and starring Edward James Olmos (fig. 3.3).[27] The feature narrates the tragic circumstance by which the title character becomes a popular Chicano hero and a symbol of the plight of Mexicans in south Texas at the turn of the century.[28] The story and the characters vividly reconstruct a society characterized by class interests and racial inequalities. The performances, photography, and direction merit special recognition.[29] As with other films of Robert Young, the characters never fall into stereotypes but instead reveal the full complexity of human nature. In a well-performed role, Edward James Olmos moved one step closer to becoming the one bona fide Chicano superstar.

Two years later, director and screenwriter Gregory Nava made his screen debut with *El norte* (1983). This independent film, originally produced and planned for the PBS series *American Playhouse* became one of the most successful independent films of recent times. *El norte* depicts the complex and often tragic drama of Central American immigration to the United

FIGURE 3.3 Edward James Olmos (right) portrays Gregorio Cortés, a Mexican cowhand accused of murdering a Texas sheriff, and Victoria Plata plays his wife, Carmen, in *The Ballad of Gregorio Cortés,* shown on PBS. The teleplay is based on an actual event that took place in south Texas in 1901. (© Esparza/Katz Productions.)

States.[30] The film traces the plight of a Guatemalan brother and sister (beautifully played by David Villalpando and Zaide Silvia Gutiérrez) who, out of fear of being killed by the military as their parents were, are forced to flee their native country and seek refuge in the United States.

El norte does seem to highlight certain values and character portrayals toward which American audiences would be sympathetic. Rosa and Enrique display traits of goodness and purity and have no faults or serious weaknesses. The main characters are shown as naturalist heroes, victims of cir-

FIGURE 3.4 *El Norte* stars David Villalpando and Zaide Silvia Gutierrez as two oppressed Guatemalan teenagers who escape to freedom in the United States. The film, by Gregory Nava and Anna Thomas, was nominated for an Academy Award and aired on the PBS series, *American Playhouse*. (© 1983 Cinecom International Films.)

cumstance, who have little or no chance to control their own destinies. The film also plays on the empathy of the viewer through the tragic outcome of the story. Despite these aspects, the film's characters, structure, and subtle political message made *El norte* (fig. 3.4) one of the most successful and best contemporary Chicano films in the United States. The film clearly displays the talents of director Gregory Nava.

In 1983, producer/director Frank Zúñiga completed the independent film, *Heartbreaker*. This little-known and uninspired production focuses upon the life and situation of an East Los Angeles Chicano low-rider, played by Mexican actor Fernando Allende. The story deals with the tribulations of the central character, his *compañeros*, his rivals, and his Anglo girlfriend. The attempt to recreate a distinct Chicano cultural experience and the complex dimensions of an interethnic romance is lost.

Born in East L.A. (1985) once again addresses the theme of immigration, but does so from a strikingly original perspective. Combining parody with social satire, director, writer, and star, Cheech Marin, takes direct aim at various U.S. and Mexican institutions, character types, and perceptions.[31] Inasmuch as *Born in East L.A.* was the first narrative comedy of Chicano cinema, it enjoyed critical acclaim and respectable box-office success. The social satire and message of the film are effective and well-narrated. The talent of Cheech Marin is most evident. The direction, characterization, acting, and musical score are solid. This movie received first prize at the Havana Film Festival of 1988 because of its many artistic merits. However, the film is not without its detractors.

Certain film critics, particularly feminist ones, have expressed their concerns regarding the representation of women in *Born in East L.A.* Particularly problematic to them is the fact that certain of the female characters exhibit titillating dress styles and manners. In addition, women are indeed the least developed characters in the film.[32] Nonetheless, *Born in East L.A.* is one of the most accomplished and effective Chicano films to date.

Two important and very diverse Chicano narrative films were exhibited in 1987, *Break of Dawn* and *La Bamba*. Written and directed by Isaac Artenstein and produced by Jude Eberhard, *Break of Dawn* is based upon the life of Pedro J. González, who became the first Spanish-language radio celebrity in the United States in the late 1920s. He also became a political and community activist on behalf of the rights of the Mexican-origin population during the late twenties and the thirties. As a consequence of his struggles on behalf of his people, González fell victim to injustice. He was falsely accused of rape and, ultimately, was imprisoned for six years in San Quentin. The film masterfully traces all these events and concludes with his release from prison.

The script of *Break of Dawn* (fig. 3.5) clearly reveals a deep sympathy and understanding of the story and the events. History and film are seldom combined with such outstanding results. This film is an important and creative production and has been the recipient of well-deserved praise. However, the lack of an adequate production budget as well as the fact that no major U.S. studio would distribute it seriously limited its audience and popularity.[33] The inability to secure a major distributor shows just how difficult is the producer's job of selling a Chicano-theme film with a Mexican-origin cast to studios and networks that are culturally insensitive or simply uninterested in the Chicana/o experience. Fortunately, the film was exhibited nationally by PBS, thus assuring at least one national audience.

La Bamba is a significant chapter in the evolution of Chicano narrative cinema. This impressive box-office and critical success greatly enhanced the directorial career of Luis Valdez. More than any other Chicano film to date, *La Bamba* carried an ethnic theme to receptive mainstream audiences both within and outside the United States.[34] The linear narration of *La Bamba*

FIGURE 3.5 Oscar Chávez as Pedro J. González in *Break of Dawn*. (© 1988 Cinewest Productions.)

traces the rise of Ricardo Valenzuela (alias Richie Valens) in his quest to become a rock-and-roll celebrity. His short-lived stardom came to a tragic end when an airplane accident took his very promising life. The film, however, is much more than a simple musical biography. Ideologically, *La Bamba* embraces a certain controversial thesis that only through accommodation or near assimilation does Richie Valens achieve his goal of attaining the "American Dream." The insistence on this theme in *La Bamba* is its most questionable aspect.[35] The degree of the protagonist's characterization (including his supposed inability to speak Spanish) does not seem at all realistic for a working-class Chicano from the barrio and the agricultural fields of California. In addition, the conception of the U.S.–Mexico border and the delineation of various Chicano characters repeat traditional stereotypes. The film also takes a great deal of artistic license with certain biographical facts of Richie Valens's life.

Notwithstanding these observations, on an artistic level *La Bamba* is a notable and important film. Luis Valdez is unquestionably a creative talent who has mastered the tasks and challenges of directing commercial cinema. The combination of a success story, a rock-and-roll fable, the musical score performed by Los Lobos, and a sympathetic hero made for a sure screen

success. In fact, by box-office returns, *La Bamba* has been the most successful Chicano film to date.

The inspiring *Stand and Deliver* (1988) continued the genre of effective
portrayals of real-life heroic figures. On an elementary level, the film narrates the efforts and tribulations of mentor/math teacher Jaime Escalante
(played by Edward James Olmos) in bringing about social change through
education to Chicano youth. He not only instills pride and self-worth to his
students but also manages to inculcate interest and excellence in mathemati-
cal and technological skills. Through character study and moving situations,
themes of alienation, institutionalized racism, and ethnic consciousness are
skillfully addressed and well developed. On a deeper perspective, *Stand and
Deliver* pays homage to the triumph of the spirit and the will to struggle
against discrimination, indifference, and fatalism. This movie achieved a
modest box-office success. More important, it obtained overall high acclaim
and an Oscar nomination for Edward James Olmos for best performance by
an actor that year.

The artistic and financial success of this body of narrative Chicano
cinema brought about the expectation that perhaps the so-called "Decade of
the Hispanics" could resonate in the film industry.[36] Chicana/o filmmakers
anticipated that major production companies would now acknowledge the
significantly larger audiences that were responding to Chicano/Latino film
themes and stars and that such new film projects would be sought out and
supported. They were wrong. Mainstream Hollywood continued its previous policy on Chicanas/os, stereotyping them—usually as villains or pros-
titutes—or outright ignoring them.

Several years passed before the next narrative feature premiered, *American Me* (1992). This individualistic, highly charged effort is an intense and
disturbing portrayal of Chicano gang/prison life. Edward James Olmos
served as director, coscreenwriter, coproducer, and star (fig. 3.6). In this
nihilistic character study, Olmos attempted a didactic, anticrime social message aimed at Chicano youths. The morality tale fictionalizes the rise and fall
of the so-called prison-based Mexican mafia. The odyssey begins with the
brutal violence directed at Chicanos during the zoot-suit riots and continues
to a destructive end.

Intended to "scare straight" its young male audience, the film instead
conveys a message of hopelessness in breaking the cycle of violence and
revenge.[37] The narrative also reinforces the charge that Chicanos fault Hollywood for making films that depict only one aspect of the Chicano ex-

FIGURE 3.6 Edward James Olmos makes his feature film directing debut and stars as Santana, a powerful crime lord who has spent half his life in penal institutions in the film *American Me*. (© 1992 Universal City Studios, Inc.)

perience—gangs. Although *American Me* did not gain the economic remuneration it expected, critics and viewers applauded its courage, artistic experimentation, and strength of narrative. The effort also increased the star power of Edward James Olmos.

The Waterdance (1992), written and codirected by Neal Jiménez, represents the advent of a second generation of Chicano filmmakers.[38] Unlike the generation of the Chicano Movement era, in which directors emphasized political over other issues, this later generation displays clear differences with the past. Attuned to a more general audience acceptance and themes of wider interest, these most recent filmmakers are striving to merge Chicano topics and/or characters with mainstream cinematic appeal.

With a great deal of sensitivity, *The Waterdance* focuses on three paraplegic men. The movie narrates their life stories through their interactions with each other and their reactions to their plight. Unlike other films that deal with physical disabilities, *The Waterdance* approaches this issue with compassion, humor, complexity, and optimism.[39]

The first narrative film directed by a Chicana was *The Devil Never Sleeps,* by Estela Portillo. This work is an imaginative personal thriller that reads and is structured on a number of levels and dimensions. The plot follows the main character as she searches for her legacy and past while attempting to resolve unanswered questions about her uncle's death in Mexico. In the search for truth, though interviews and flashbacks, the Chicana comes to terms with her homeland, her forgotten family roots, and ultimately, herself. No easy answers are offered, only questions and complex possible interpretations and resolutions by the audience. *The Devil Never Sleeps* was the first step in the distinguished career of Estela Portillo.

A less successful directorial debut is Marcus de León's flawed *Kiss Me a Killer* (1992). This is a weak and lifeless remake of the classic, *The Postman Always Rings Twice,* although the action switches to the barrio of East Los Angeles. The plot focuses on a romantic triangle that leads to lust, murder, and a predictable doom for the illicit lovers.

A different and much better production is the impressive debut film of Robert Rodríguez, *El mariachi* (1993) (fig. 3.7). This action/adventure story features a lone mariachi who is falsely mistaken for an infamous hit man, because both wear black and carry a guitar case. The well-narrated story has all the ingredients of the best classic genre: continuous action, romance, humor, well-defined characters, and crisp dialogue. The narrative never falters, and the film more than delivers all its objectives.

Notably, *El mariachi* was a one-person show from beginning to end and was originally produced with a budget of a mere $7,000. Director Rodríguez was also the scriptwriter, cinematographer, sound person, editor, and producer. Rodríguez stated that "I shot every scene in one take . . . I just fed the actors the line and moved on . . ."[40] Spoken entirely in Spanish and set in the border towns of Ciudad Acuña, Coahuila, and Del Río, Texas, *El mariachi* is one of the most remarkable debuts of a Chicano director.

The success of *El mariachi* propelled Robert Rodríguez into the fore-

FIGURE 3.7 Carlos Gallardo plays the title character in and coproduces Robert Rodríguez's *El mariachi*. (© 1992 Columbia Pictures Industries, Inc.)

front of sought-after directors. He signed a three-film contract under the
most generous terms with Columbia Pictures. The studio executives picked
up on the fact that Rodríguez displayed a clear talent as a skilled technician
and action narrator. Notoriety drew new friends and associates, such as
Quentin Tarantino. The stage was set for his follow-up film. Although Rodríguez originally planned a trilogy to narrate the adventures of *El mariachi*,
he opted instead for a large-scale remake with *Desperado*. Armed with the
necessary budget for a mainstream action film, he cast established box-office

attractions Antonio Banderas, Cheech Marin, Joaquin de Almeida, Quentin Tarantino, and rising Mexican star Salma Hayek. There are some notable aspects to the film: certain strikingly choreographed scenes, exceptional chemistry between Banderas and Hayek, solid performances by the cast, particularly by Antonio Banderas (who in the opinion of many had delivered his best work since *The Mambo Kings*), artistic photography by Mexican Guillermo Navarro, and the musical score by Los Lobos. Yet, even such attributes do not hide its serious problems. *Desperado* did not reflect the freshness nor the blend of humor and action that *El mariachi* developed so well.

Riding high on the fanfare of *Desperado,* Rodríguez teamed up with soul-mate Tarantino to film *From Dawn to Dusk.* With the talent of a top-draw cast, with George Clooney, Harvey Keitel, and Quentin Tarantino in the lead roles, the allegorical narrative traces two bank-robber brothers fleeing to Mexico in their attempt to evade justice. In the typical Tarantino/Rodríguez style, the film proceeds with nonstop action, excessive gore, choreographed killings in every conceivable manner, and the antihero triumphing over evil.

Although *From Dawn to Dusk* is certainly not Chicano cinema in theme or cast, the fact that Chicano director Robert Rodríguez directed and had a good deal of artistic control over it makes this film a significant contribution to and raises the question of future trends in Chicano mainstream narrative cinema. Rodríguez is currently one of the most visible Chicano directors in mainstream Hollywood cinema.

La carpa (The Tent, 1993) is a one-hour movie that was produced for PBS and broadcast on *American Playhouse.* A promising young director of this second generation of Chicano filmmakers, Carlos Avila, made his professional debut as director and cowriter of this film. Interestingly, all Chicana/o characters speak their dialogue in Spanish.

Set in Depression-era California, *La carpa* is the bittersweet story of a young, shy, hard-working Mexican field laborer whose life is transformed when a raucous, ragged traveling *carpa* (vaudeville) troupe comes to town. As a very subtle form of social history, the film portrays la carpa as a unique mediating force for exploring the political and social problems experienced by small rural communities of that era.

In 1994, after a ten-year hiatus since directing his first film, Luis Valdez teamed up with producer Moctezuma Esparza and media entrepreneur Ted Turner to film a contemporary remake of the classic western character, *The Cisco Kid.* This version has Jimmy Smits (the Cisco Kid) and Cheech Marin

(Pancho) caught up in Mexico during the 1860s and fighting on the side of President Benito Juárez against French imperialism. This light-hearted action/comedy succeeds on the purely entertainment level of a movie made for television. Notably, the film's impressive musical score was composed by Joseph Julian Gonzales, a highly accomplished young Chicano musician who also wrote the score for the Quentin Tarantino film, *Curdled*. A careful reading of *The Cisco Kid*, however, reveals a flawed script, uneven performances, and a not-so-successful Chicano interpretation of Mexican traditions, history, and folklore.

Tierra (The Earth, 1994), directed by Severo Pérez, is faithfully based upon the classic novel, . . . *Y no se lo tragó la tierra* (. . . And the Earth Did Not Part), by Tomás Rivera. The narrative is told through the eyes of the son of the protagonist family. It recounts the exploitative working conditions and the lives of Chicana/o agricultural laborers in Texas and the Midwest. The film succeeds in powerfully capturing the hardships and meager existence of the migrant Chicana/o farmworkers prior to the Chicano Movement years. This production, however, has several flaws, including its narration. *Tierra* suffers from a too rigid tone in its discursive structure.

My Family/Mi familia (1995), the third feature film by writer/director Gregory Nava, returns to one of his earlier favorite themes, immigration, although he now expands this with other issues. As the title indicates, the narrative traces various generations of one Chicano family in Los Angeles. The narrative opens with an immigrant from Michoacán migrating and settling in Los Angeles. He subsequently marries and has a family. With the passing of years and maturing of the children, their joys, sorrows, aspirations, and successes are interwoven in the film. Family values, discrimination, ethnic consciousness, binational links of Latinos with their homelands, and the evolution of the Chicana/o community as observed through the eyes and actions of one family are the principal themes and constructs of the film. Even though many characters are introduced and an ambitious historical period is covered by the narrative, for the most part the film succeeds on all levels and more than meets its goals.

The spiritual bonds that resonate in the characters' common experiences and values of the family members are the strengths of *Mi familia*. The solid cast includes Edward James Olmos, Eduardo López Rojas, Esai Morales, Elpidia Carrillo, Jimmy Smits, and Jennifer Lopez (fig. 3.8). The film was well received by the critics and general public. Clearly *Mi familia* solidified the career and artistry of Gregory Nava.

FIGURE 3.8 Jimmy (Jimmy Smits) and Isabel (Elpidia Carrillo) fall in love dancing in the street in New Line Cinema's epic drama, *My Family/Mi familia*. (© 1995 New Line Productions, Inc. [Photograph by Rico Torres.])

FIGURE 3.9 Jennifer Lopez in the memorable role of the legendary Selena in the film of the same name. Shown here are Selena (Jennifer Lopez) and Chris Lopez (Jon Seda). (© 1997 Warner Bros.)

Selena (1997), written and directed by Gregory Nava and produced by Moctezuma Esparza, is the most recent Chicano narrative film exhibited (fig. 3.9). After a great deal of hype and publicity, the production was shot in record time. Receiving the full endorsement and cooperation of Selena's family, director/writer Nava crafted a chronologically linear script tracing the childhood, adolescence, early years of fame, and the tragic death of the legendary Selena, the Tex-Mex musical icon. The narrative is by all accounts an homage to the fallen star, her impressive musical talent, and her legacy.

The film offers few surprises or original twists. Little new material on the life of Selena Quintanilla-Pérez or her family is revealed. The focus of the entire plot is on the Selena character, masterfully acted by Jennifer Lopez, and her father, also impressively performed by Edward James Olmos. All other characters in the film are secondary to the point of invisibility. *Selena* is a film structured not on character study or intricate discursive elements but on the traditional Hollywood formula of a success story. Selena's rise to superstardom, her exceptional charisma, her ability as a singer and performer, her family values, and the aspect of Chicano musical culture make up the essence of the film.

Skillfully choreographed and acted by the two leading actors, *Selena* had a respectable showing at the box office in the United States and abroad. Overwhelming support for the film, however, has come from the Chicano/Latino community. As much as it attempted to be a crossover film, it did not achieve this end to the degree hoped.

The film's strengths are clearly its musical numbers and the inspiring, sensitive, and moving performance by star Jennifer Lopez, who ably captured the charm, electrifying presence, and talent of Selena. The narrative and its ideological contrasts, however, are at times problematic. There is an excessively conscious attempt to accommodate Selena's character to American values and tastes. All the dialogue is in English, as are most of the musical numbers, even though in reality it was only in the last years of Selena's career that she interpreted songs bilingually or in English.

Moreover, Nava continues to express ambivalent and at times negative attitudes toward Mexico, as do other Chicano directors. Various scenes and dialogue clearly reflect such attitudes. Nonetheless, *Selena* is a well-crafted film and a major artistic achievement for all those who made it possible.

Luminarias, written by Evelina Fernández and directed by Jose Luis Valenzuela, is a comedy/drama of the lives and friendship of four Chicanas. Through character development and dialogue the film reveals a humorous and at times serious look at four unique professional Chicanas/Latinas who meet and share secrets and feelings about their careers, family, relationships, expectations, and sex.

Narrated with humor and sensitivity, *Luminarias* challenges cultural stereotypes by creating successful, intelligent, and complex women characters. For once, the leads are not only Chicanas but ones that are assertive.

The Hostile Tube: Commercial and Public Television

Certain changes took place regarding Chicanas/os and commercial television as a consequence of the Chicano Movement. The Los Angeles–based organization, Justicia, empowered by federal regulations to challenge television license renewals, paved a clear way to greater media access in the form of public affairs and documentary programming as well as employment opportunities behind and in front of the camera.[41] Justicia, headed by Ray Andrade, began in 1968 as the Committee for Motion Pictures and Television under the aegis of the Mexican American Political Association. It evolved into CARISMA and then into Justicia in 1969. The name of the organization was suggested by the late Rubén Salazar, a reporter for the *Los Angeles Times* and KMEX-TV who was killed during the Chicano Moratorium of 1970. Though Justicia is more concerned with Chicano media image than employment issues, its work directly resulted in an increased presence of Chicano actors, on-camera news reporters, and behind-the-scene technicians in both the film and television industries.[42] An alternative to the militant Justicia, the Nosotros organization (whose members were primarily actors concerned with employment issues) was created shortly thereafter under the guidance of the Association of Motion Picture and Television Producers and officials of Los Angeles Mayor Yorty's office. Its early leadership was provided by such veteran actors as Ricardo Montalbán.[43]

In U.S. commercial television, the issue has not only been one of negative and persistent stereotyping or employment opportunities, it has been one of gross neglect as well. Chicanos and Chicanas have been practically invisible on the small screen for the past twenty years. Moreover, a 1993 survey commissioned by the Screen Actors Guild and the American Federation of Television and Radio Artists found that Latinos, who make up more than 9 percent of the U.S. population, are cast in less than 1 percent of prime-time television roles. Of all television shows made in 1992, Latinos represented a mere 3 percent of performers employed.[44] The most recent study released by the National Council of La Raza "found that Hispanics represented only about 1 percent of all characters on TV and that they tend to be seen in either criminal or stereotypical roles."[45]

Whereas African Americans are included in a number of prime-time and daytime series and even have their own starting shows, currently Chicanos rarely appear on network television. Expressing utter frustration at the continued exclusion of Chicanos and Latinos from mainstream television programming, about 1,130 Chicano/Latino organizations launched a nationwide protest and boycott against ABC in 1995 as a first step. The groups protested that the network had no Latino-themed programs on prime time—but then neither did NBC, CBS, United Paramount Network, or Warner Brothers.

The action did have an effect. ABC subsequently created *Common Law* and added it to the 1996 fall schedule. The series, however, lasted for less than one season. *Latin Heat* reported that thirty-two contracted Chicano/Latino actors appeared on major television shows in the autumn of 1995, compared with only six in 1993. The new 1996 fall season included thirty-nine new dramas and comedies, five of which featured Chicano/Latino actors in leading roles. The situation even got worse. In the autumn of 1999 new television shows were previewed by the four major networks. None of the new series had one actor of color in a leading role.

It remains to be seen, however, whether shows that include Chicano/Latino characters and themes will employ other Chicanas/os as writers or directors or in other creative capacities. Certain individuals remain skeptical. One Chicana producer stated, "we aren't really there yet. Most of us still have to struggle to get our projects made."[46]

A Chicana/o presence is still more evident in film than in narrative television. Chicana/o executives are still absent from studios and television networks. The Chicano community as an audience has also been ignored. The television industry (and its programming decisions) is largely ruled by Nielsen and Arbitron audience rating systems. Both companies continue to base their reports on electronic rating boxes that are kept at predominantly Anglo households.

The single area where Chicanas/os have seen some progress in commercial television is in local and certain national news programs. This is likely due in large part to the advocacy efforts of media organizations such as the National Hispanic Media Coalition, which petitions to deny license renewals to television stations that do not hire minorities. Under the current Federal Communications Commission rules, a station must employ a minority group at the rate of at least half the level of those employed within its reporting area. For example, if Latinos make up 36 percent of Los Angeles's total work force, then stations would be required to have a minimum of 18 percent of Latinos on its payroll. Considering the amount of Chicana/o talent and experience available throughout the Southwest and elsewhere, the lack of Chicano representation is even more glaring. The pattern of invisibility and/or neglect is most evident in national television news. Because the Chicano community has few spokespersons in national or even local television news programs, stories and reports on Chicano issues are seldom featured. This clearly reflects societal attitudes and prejudices toward the Chicana/o community.

In the public television arena, Chicanas/os continue to struggle for public funding from sources such as the NEH, NEA, CPB, the recently created

Independent Television Service (ITVS), and various foundations that support media projects. In early 1993 an unprecedented congressional inquiry was prompted by the National Latino Communications Center and the Congressional Hispanic Caucus to investigate the CPB's decreasing level of support for Latino programming. A request was made by the Hispanic Caucus to defer approval of CPB's 1997–99 license renewal until it provided an appropriate level of support for Latino programming.

Spanish-Language Television

Spanish-language television in the United States has grown considerably in the last decade. Three major networks now exist—Univisión, Telemundo, and Galavisión—that cover the entire country. Potentially, these networks could provide outlets and employment opportunities for Chicanas/os. Unfortunately, nothing could be further from the truth. Since their creation, network management has displayed no interest whatsoever in hiring Chicanas/os in major positions. The only exception occurred in 1997 when Henry Cisneros was hired to preside over Univisión in Los Angeles.

The network's programs in Spanish television are more than 50 percent foreign. The programming content is largely characterized by numerous soap operas, principally from Mexico, Venezuela, and Brazil (dubbed into Spanish); variety shows; films, mostly from Mexico and Argentina; news programs; and talk shows. The great majority of the owners as well as the hosts, newscasters, and reporters are Cuban American, Mexican, or of other Latin American origin. Although much of the three stations' efforts are directly aimed at the entire Latino community, including Mexican Americans, direct Chicano involvement has been insignificant. A recent study has even argued that Spanish-language television has displaced Chicanos in U.S. society "by not promoting their sociocultural and ethnolinguistic identity."[47]

The lack of Chicano involvement in Spanish television has resulted in controversy and Chicano activism aimed at modifying the existing condition. For example, in 1989 in Los Angeles, the Chicano community held protests against Telemundo for the firing of Frank Cruz, the only Chicano in a managerial position at the time. The departure of Cruz highlighted other issues adverse to a Chicano agenda.[48] Chicano pressure groups have not had much success in forcing these networks to comply with a more positive policy toward hiring Chicanas/os. Thus, as with other media systems, Spanish-language television has been one more arena of conflict and

closed opportunity for the Chicano community. The one positive consequence of the emergence and development of Spanish-language networks is
that their news programs pay considerably more attention to information
on issues of concern to Chicanas/os such as immigration, bilingual education, and affirmative action, than does mainstream television. Also, their
coverage of the U.S. Latino community is much more comprehensive and
informative than English-language local or national news programs.

Future Perspectives

It is an acknowledged fact that Chicanos are the fastest growing minority in
the United States; in less than a decade, they will be the largest ethnic group
in this country. Among them exists a recognizable and influential leadership,
a growing professional class, and a recent surge of activists. Moreover, the
Chicano cultural renaissance has captured the imagination and awareness of
specialists and the general public by contributing great artistry and commitment to such genres as literature, theater, art, folklore, and media, as well as
contributing to academic studies and research.

Clearly, Chicana/o filmmakers have already achieved modest commercial success and have contributed significant cinematic films and television
programs. Recently, a second generation of Chicana/o film directors has
begun to make strides in breaking the resistance to Chicanas/os in the
media. At the same time, veteran Chicano filmmakers are building on past
experiences and accomplishments to seek alternative directions. Even with
the "hostile tube," small windows of opportunity have been opened, at least
in terms of employment. News programs at the local and national levels have
reluctantly hired some Latinos but few members of the Chicano community,
especially women.

Such is not the case, however, for program content. Chicanas/os continue to be a largely invisible minority in both daytime and prime-time
television programs in English. When Chicanas/os do appear on the screen,
the portrayals still seem to convey only the negative aspects of the Chicano
experience: crime and drugs. As the National Council of La Raza president,
Raúl Yzaguirre, stated, "What we are seeing here is a systematic slander of
the entire Hispanic community. The entire [television] industry is propagat-
ing a big lie when it comes to Hispanics."[49]

The future of Chicanas/os in cinema and television is uncertain, at
best. The major movie studios and television networks still do not believe in

the economic viability of Chicana/o thematic programs. Unlike the recent flowering of African American filmmaking and of Native American themes, no such interest for Chicana/o filmmakers or themes is evident in Hollywood or mainstream television networks. Opportunities are occasionally offered to Chicano directors, but only when they agree to surrender all artistic control and film the project as dictated by others.

In addition, the "catch-22" in securing financial backing from a major Hollywood studio or television network is the casting hurdle. If a producer packages a good script with a proven, creative director, he/she will invariably want stars to complete the package, but at present, few established Chicana/o stars exist.

To avoid submitting creatively to Hollywood's industrial whims, Chicano narrative cinema to date has often been produced independently, which means finding alternative ways to raise financing and seeking alternative distribution outlets. The problem with that model is that if Chicano filmmakers pursue only the independent route, then budget, exhibition, and distribution opportunities for their productions will be limited.

Chicanas/os continue to struggle for public funding from sources such as the NEH, CPB, PBS, and ITVS. One positive change was the naming of respected actress, Jane Alexander, as head of the NEA in the first Clinton administration. In this capacity she has been an advocate of diversity and multicultural programs. She recently announced her retirement from the position, however, and it remains to be seen whether the next administration will favor Chicana/o themes and projects.

To significantly improve the status of Chicanas/os in cinema and television, several changes must occur. First, a much larger number of Chicanas/os must establish themselves as key players—screenwriters, production executives, directors, and decision makers—at the studios and networks. Until they do, creative opportunities for Chicanos in film and television will not increase. Training and talent, combined with perseverance and luck, are key factors in achieving this first goal. It cannot be achieved, however, without aggressive affirmative action to improve Chicana/o employment at policy and decision-making levels as well as at creative, performance, technical, and administrative ones. Although not an easy task, it is a vital one. If affirmative action fails to achieve diversity at all industry levels, the economic clout of the substantial Latino market might be the only incentive to bring about change.

Second, compelling Chicana/o stories will not be told until a significant number of writers and established producers have emerged. Producers need to be well versed in all aspects—development, packaging, financing, deal-making, production, postproduction, distribution, promotion, and marketing—of the business of films. Currently, far more Chicana/o directors and actors (albeit underemployed) exist than producers or writers.

Third, the distribution of Chicana/o films needs to be pursued more aggressively. The festival, art, and university circuits as well as independent distributors might offer important outlets.

Fourth, other outlets for Chicana/o films and television programs, such as cable television networks, must continue to be developed. Many recently created national cable networks are striving to break new ground and supersede major networks. Some have shown interest in using Chicano thematic agenda as one alternative direction in programming. For instance, HBO, Showtime, TNT, and TBS have already expressed an interest in and provided funding for Chicano-theme productions.

After a dismal year in 1999, in which there was not one single Chicano film of any sort, some positive developments and changes may occur in the near future. Among such prospects are the following: New Latin Pictures will release and distribute the film *Luminarias* in early 2000. Director Gregory Nava is scheduled to begin shooting the first of various films that he will direct for New Line Cinema. Artisan Entertainment will release *El norte* in 2000. Actor John Leguizamo's Lower Side Films is set to produce a film biography of Mexican composer Juan Garcia Esquivel. Esparza/Katz Productions is finishing the preparations for the shooting of *Price of Glory,* a film with a boxing theme involving a Chicano family. In 1999, more than 23,000 people attended the Los Angeles Latino International Film Festival, a major increase from 1998. Various of its showings, in fact, were sold out.

It does seem inevitable that Hollywood and television executives will finally realize that Latinos are the fastest-growing segment of the movie-going audience in the United States. In Los Angeles, for example, 45 percent of the prime film audience is Chicano/Latino. And those trends will only increase in the future.

There is, however, one slight bright spot in the representation of the Chicano in American films: independent cinema. Two recent productions are a welcome departure from the traditional Hollywood view of the Chicano. *Lonestar,* written and directed by the noted director John Sayles, is an imaginative narrative situated on the Texas-Mexico border. The drama focuses on a number of Chicano and Anglo characters and life stories from south Texas. Unlike other Hollywood productions, *Lonestar's* characters include Chicanos/as as principal protagonists of the narrative. The film also accurately captures aspects of the society and the essence of the Texas-Mexico border. As usual, John Sayles has delivered a film that is well crafted, with an interesting and complex story line and characters. *Lonestar* is certainly one of the few American films that, although not devoid of traditional stereotypes, is nonetheless a solid cinematic achievement.

A second major achievement is *The City/La ciudad* (1999), written and directed by David Riker. This remarkable documentary-style drama exposes the lives and experiences of Mexican/Latino immigrants to New York. Employing no professional actors, but rather immigrants themselves, and shot over a period of five years, *The City* powerfully, and with the stark realism of past neorealistic films, traces the oppressive and hopeless lives of a significant portion of the underclass and labor pool of American capitalism. Although each of the four stories can be read as distinct, their commonality is the marked contrast between those who have access to the riches and comforts of New York, and these immigrants, who labor long and hard with little chance at survival or hope for the future. Tragic and dark, the stories reflect struggle and the will to survive. These key elements of Latino life are accurately captured by the film. Above all else, *The City* reveals a portrait of America seldom seen or addressed by U.S. films. Also important is the choice of New York, a city not usually associated with Latino experiences other than that of the Puerto Ricans. Yet, the Latino experiences narrated by *The City* will only become more evident in the future.

These changes will hopefully translate into more visibility and influence for Chicanas/os in cinema and television. Perhaps in the near future, Chicana/o media images will be determined to a major degree by Chicanas/os themselves and not by outsiders. When this happens, the screen portrayal of Chicanas/os as the "convenient villain" or the perpetual "dark señorita" will finally be replaced with a more accurate picture of Chicanas/os as a vibrant complex community.

Notes

1. Randall M. Miller, *Ethnic Images in American Film and Television* (Philadelphia: Balch Institute, 1978), xiii.
2. George Comstock, *Television in America* (Newbury Park: Sage Publications, 1991).

3. Miller, *Ethnic Images*, xiii.

4. Amos Vogel, *Film as a Subversive Art* (London: Weidenfeld and Nichols, 1974).

5. See the excellent study on this aspect by Herbert I. Schiller, *Communication and Cultural Domination* (White Plains, N.Y.: International Arts and Sciences Press, 1976).

6. Michael R. Real, *Mass-Mediated Culture* (Englewood Cliffs, N.J.: Prentice Hall, 1977), 20–21.

7. The pioneer monograph by Clinton Wilson and Félix Gutiérrez, *Minorities and Media* (Beverly Hills: Sage Publications, 1985), is an insightful overview of Chicanos and media in the United States.

8. Albert Memmi, *Dominated Man* (New York: Orion Press, 1968), 186.

9. The standard works on Chicano images in cinema are Arthur Pettit, *Images of the Mexican-American in Fiction and Film* (College Station: Texas A&M University Press, 1980); and Allen Woll, *The Latin Image in American Film* (Los Angeles: University of California/Latin American Center Publications, 1985). More recent comparative analyses of Chicana/o cinematic images are found in David Maciel, *El Bandolero, el pocho y la raza: imágenes cinematográficas del chicano* (México: UNAM, 1994); and Carlos Cortés, "The History of Ethnic Images in Film: The Search for a Methodology," *MELUS* 11 (Winter 1984): 63–77.

10. Pettit, *Images of the Mexican-American;* and Woll, *The Latin Image.*

11. Charles Ramírez-Berg, "Stereotyping in Films in General and of Hispanics in Particular," *The Howard Journal of Communications* 2 (1990); and Luis Torres, "The Chicano Image in Film," *Caminos* (1982). Both are informative and interpretative overviews.

12. On this point, see the insightful chapter by Goeham Kindem and Charles Teddlie, "Film Effects and Ethnicity," in *Film Culture: Explorations of Cinema in Its Social Context,* ed. Sari Thomas (Metuchen, N.J.: Scarecrow Press, 1982), 195–209.

13. The recent collection edited by Clara E. Rodríguez, *Latin Looks: Images of Latinas and Latinos in the U.S. Media* (Boulder: Westview Press, 1997), contains various important studies that document Latino images in television and cinema.

14. William and Denise Bielby, *The 1993 Hollywood Writers Report* (Santa Barbara: n.p., 1993), 4–12, contains important statistical materials and figures on Chicanos/as in media.

15. Cited in *Center for Media and Public Affairs* (Washington, D.C.: n.p., 1992).

16. William and Denise Bielby, *The 1993 Hollywood,* 16.

17. Interview with Norma Iglesias, Tijuana, Mexico, 18 June 1991.

18. Interview with Ignacio Durán Loera, Mexico City, 24 July 1993.

19. Jesús Salvador Treviño, "Presencia del cine chicano," in *A través de la frontera,* ed. Ida Rodríguez Prampolini (México: Centro de Estudios Económicos y Sociales del Tercer Mundo, 1983), 198–99.

20. Chon A. Noriega, ed., *Chicanos and Film. Essays on Chicano Representation and Resistance* (New York: Garland Publishing, Inc., 1992), 159–88.

21. Rosa Linda Fregoso's *The Bronze Screen* (Minneapolis: University of Minnesota Press, 1993) is a most authoritative discussion of the participation and contribution of Chicanas in film.

22. Interview with Jesús Salvador Treviño. Los Angeles, California, 12 June 1990.

23. Gregg Barrios, "Efraín Gutiérrez y el nuevo cine chicano," *La Opinión*, 18 August 1985, 3. This is one of the few notes on the cinematic works of Efraín Gutiérrez.

24. Jim Miller, "Chicano Cinema: An Interview with Jesús Salvador Treviño," *Cineaste* VIII (1978): 38–41; and Jesús Salvador Treviño, "*Raíces de sangre*. First Feature Film Directed by a Chicano," *Somos* (1978): 17, are two informative published interviews with Treviño.

25. David R. Maciel, "La reconquista cinematográfica," *Fronteras* III (invierno 1998): 27.

26. Katherine Díaz, "Luis Valdez. The Making of *Zoot Suit*," *Caminos*, 7–9 September 1981.

27. Michael Healy, "*Gregorio Cortés*, Superbly Crafted Small Film," *Denver Post*, 31 August 1984, E-9.

28. See Américo Paredes, "*With His Pistol in His Hands*": *A Border Ballad and Its Hero* (Austin: University of Texas Press, 1958). This publication forms the basis of the narrative story of the film.

29. "Edward James Olmos and Robert Young with Twenty-one Reasons Why You Should See *The Ballad of Gregorio Cortés*," *Caminos* (1982): 26–27.

30. Vincent Canby, "*El norte*: A Fine Movie Fueled by Injustice," *New York Times*, 22 January 1984, H-17; and Jane Maslin, "Film: *El norte* Promised Land for Guatemalans," *New York Times*, 11 January 1984, 15.

31. Chon Noriega, "Café Órale: Narrative Structure in *Born in East L.A.*," *Tonantzin* (1991): 17–18.

32. Rosa Linda Fregoso's "*Born in East L.A.* and the Politics of Representation," *Cultural Studies* IV (1990), addresses critical issues of sexism and gender representation.

33. David R. Maciel, "Cine chicano: entrevista con Isaac Artenstein," *Dicine* (1989): 6–10.

34. Susana Cato, "El cine chicano impone su imagen en la pantalla norteamericana," *Proceso*, 19 September 1987, 12–14.

35. Yolanda Broyles-González, "What Price Mainstream/Luis Valdez' *Corridos* on Stage and Film," *Cultural Studies* IV (1990): 35–48.

36. Victor Valle, "The Latino Wave," *Los Angeles Times*, 2 April 1988, 1, 11.

37. Nelson Caro's "Entrevista con Edward James Olmos," *Dicine* (Mexico City), November 1992, 20–22, is an insightful review of Olmos's stated purpose and design of *American Me*.

38. The exact significance of the title apparently alludes to "the miraculous self-assurance of these paraplegics if they are to survive and keep their sanity: It is like dancing on water." Vincent Canby, "Heroism and Humor as Paraplegics Learn," *New York Times,* 13 May 1992, C-13.

39. Brian D. Johnson, "Redefining Manhood," *Maclean's,* 8 June 1992, 49.

40. Terrence Rafferty, "Have Guitar Will Travel?" *The New Yorker,* 22 February 1993, 169–70; and Robert Rodríguez, *Rebel without a Crew, or, How a 23-year-old Film-maker with $7,000 became a Hollywood Player* (New York: Penguin Books, 1995). Filmmaker Robert Rodríguez narrated the background and handled the day-to-day shooting and the distribution of *El Mariachi.*

41. Chon Noriega, "In Aztlán: The Films of the Chicano Movement, 1969–79," in *New American Film and Video Series 56* (New York: Whitney Museum of American Art, January 1991), 1–4.

42. These and other organizational Chicano movement efforts are discussed in Francisco J. Lewels, Jr., *The Uses of the Media by the Chicano Movement* (New York: Praeger 1974), 98–125.

43. Ibid., 99.

44. George Gerbner, *SAG and AFTRA Report* (Philadelphia: n.p., 1993).

45. Cited in Marc Gunther, "La Raza Says TV Slanders Hispanics," *Albuquerque Journal,* 10 September 1994, B-2.

46. Quoted in Anna Maria Arias, "Fitting the Gap," *Hispanic,* November 1991, 20.

47. Adalberto Aguirre and Diana Bustamante, "Critical Notes Regarding the Dislocation of Chicanos by the Spanish Language Industry in the U.S." *Ethnic and Racial Studies* 16 (1993): 21.

48. Arias, "Fitting the Gap," 20.

49. Gunther, "La Raza Says," B-2.

The Politics of Chicano Representation in the Media

VIRGINIA ESCALANTE

I think that I shall never see
any Chicanos on TV
It seems as though we don't exist
and we're not even missed
and yet we buy and buy their wares
but no Chicanos anywhere.

We need more color on TV
'Cause black and white is all you see.
I'd like to see a shade of brown,
In real life we're all around.
All kinds of TV shows abound,
but no Chicanos can be found.

There are Chicanos in real life,
Doctors, lawyers, husbands, wives.
But all they show us on TV
Are illegal aliens as they flee
Or some poor cholo that they bust,
flat on his face, he's eating dust.

Script writers never write for us.
I think it's time we raised a fuss!
Casting directors never call,

they never think of us at all.
Edward James Olmos and Montalbán
that's all we've got, son of a gun!

Don't buy the product, if you see,
no Chicanos on TV
Huggies has its three babies,
White and black and Japanese.
Chicano babies also pee,
but they don't show them on TV.

—"No Chicanos on TV,"
Song by Lalo Guerrero

*W*hen he laments the absence of culturally relevant images on television, recording artist Lalo Guerrero[1] articulates a consciousness
not only about the relationship between advertising and audiences, but also
about the role of media in the politics of identity and the definition of social
reality. Embedded in Guerrero's lyrics are questions about who controls or
participates in cultural production, who is visible and who is not, and who
symbolically constructs—or annihilates—a group's existence. The guitarist
prompts us to ask who decides what worlds are significant, how they should
be represented, and who is depicted in what way, why, and to what effect.
Furthermore, Guerrero not only challenges the symbolic ways in which Chicano identities are negated or twisted, but also offers an alternative discourse
in which he gives voice and meaning to more positive constructions.

In contrast to journalists who may be unfamiliar with his culture and
thus more susceptible to misrepresenting it, Guerrero, who is seventy-nine,
is a Chicano cultural worker and icon. He began singing in Arizona desert
towns in the 1930s and recorded songs such as "Marijuana Boogie" and
"Pachuco Stomp" in the 1950s. He has continued to record since then. In the
1990s he produced a children's compact disc, featuring the rock group Los
Lobos, which was nominated for a Grammy Award. In 1996 he was recognized for his many contributions when he was awarded the National Medal
of Arts by President Clinton. With a voice that resonates even when he
speaks, the musician uses his art to create oppositional images that more

closely resemble the people he knows than those depicted as undesirable by the dominant media. Moreover, through his song Guerrero advocates Chicano resistance to cultural domination when he calls for a product boycott "if you see no Chicanos on TV."

The cultural icon thus addresses several significant issues, including the role of media in society; the political economy and social structure that shape cultural productions; the position of Chicanos and other Latinos[2] in the social hierarchy; and the struggle of Chicanos and other Latinos for cultural empowerment. Within this context, this chapter seeks an understanding of the developments created by a proliferation of what has been labeled "Hispanic" or "Latino"[3] media, a trend that has gained momentum in the 1980s and continues in this decade.

The growth of "Latino" media constitutes a development of several dimensions. First, Chicanos/Latinos have undertaken media production to achieve a voice and to construct alternative identities, often contesting the silencing, invisibility, and negative portrayals encountered in hegemonic communications. Second, mainstream media, which have traditionally excluded or stereotyped Chicanos/Latinos, are launching their own Spanish-language or bilingual productions, maintaining hegemonic ideologies, images, and messages in one language while, hypothetically, negating them to some degree in another. Third, some Chicanos/Latinos who have undertaken media production are mimicking the formats of the hegemonic models, raising questions about the actual alternative character of the projects. Given the constraints of this essay, I will focus on the first two aspects, with a discussion of the third point limited to economic considerations.

I suggest that the proliferation of "Latino" media constitutes a struggle for representation arising from the conflict between images and messages that are externally imposed and those that are internally constructed, as well as from economic imperatives in the communications arena. However, the boundaries may not be as clear-cut or absolute as they may seem, nor is this communications trend without its contradictions. In terms of representation, for example, mainstream media may include positive images of minority populations. Similarly, Spanish-language and bilingual media owned by Anglo Americans may offer culturally relevant or accurate representations, a reminder that ownership is not necessarily causal in image-making. Nonetheless, ownership does play a crucial role in cultural productions because it can, and usually does, set the parameters for expression.

Thus, although I focus my discussion on the struggle for cultural representation as a legacy of conquest and contestation manifested in the media, I do not merely describe a tension between hegemonic and alternative images and messages. I also consider how the distribution of resources affects cultural productions. I therefore situate the struggle for representation within the context of the political economy and the racialized social structure of the United States, both of which operate in conjunction with one another.

I will use Omi and Winant's[4] theoretical framework, which focuses on racial formation in the United States, to guide my analysis. The assumptions in this work rest on the notion that "we are indeed inserted into a comprehensively racialized social structure," through and in which the economic system operates. As sites of ideological production and as arenas where the struggle for representation is played out, mainstream media consist of racially oriented works that link social structure to cultural representation. What this means is that the media may not only support and perpetuate hegemony, they can resist it as well. Therefore, in its treatment of Chicanos/Latinos as subjects, audiences, and participants in cultural production, the dominant media system supports, legitimates, and reproduces the social hierarchy in which Chicanos are subjected to invisibility or negative representation. However, this domination has not gone uncontested. Contemporary resistance is manifested in opportunities for representation in mainstream media productions and in alternative cultural productions; boycotts, lawsuits, and other forms of political action; and in community newspapers, such as *El Sol de San Diego,* which will be used as a local example for the discussion.

El Sol, a bilingual newspaper, was founded in 1986 by a Chicana photojournalist who was denied employment by mainstream newspapers in San Diego. Although more research is needed, I suggest that publications such as *El Sol* serve as a challenge to the hegemonic communications system in the United States. The introduction of such publications thereby constitutes an appropriation of resources, meager as they may often be, that facilitate representation and the construction of alternative or oppositional identities and ideologies.[5] By creating a platform for shared experiences and the creation of meaning, such publications enable Chicanos/Latinos to organize, politicize, and engage in social action. In the long run and in a broader context, these small-scale media contribute to the national discourse about what constitutes "an" American identity, contradicting the notion that such an identity is singular, one-dimensional, or Eurocentric.

Dominant Media Constitute Racial Projects

When we examine the role of dominant media in Chicano/Latino communities, we find a set of "racial projects," what Omi and Winant[6] call those social institutions, policies, practices, and cultural forms that connect social structure to cultural representation. Dominant media embody the unequal distribution of information resources, which restricts Chicano/Latino access to ownership and control of media as well as their participation in cultural productions in either mainstream or alternative media. They also reinforce the social hierarchy by relegating Chicano/Latino subjects, audiences, and participants to subordinate positions in media coverage, through discriminatory employment practices, and through oppressive newsroom policies. Although there are exceptions, in terms of cultural representation, mainstream media tend to negate the existence of Chicanos/Latinos; to produce racist constructions of identity; and to construct and commercialize identities that further the interests of a capitalist media industry, as the "Latino" media boom indicates.

Ownership Determines Expression

If media ownership were equitably available, Chicanos/Latinos might simply fulfill the need for self-expression and counter the negative portrayal and invisibility found in majority-owned media with their own communication vehicles. Instead, the unequal distribution of wealth and power in a capitalist system provides abundant resources to mainstream media, whereas Chicano/Latino-owned media must often struggle and make do with far fewer resources. The power differential, drawn along the lines of race, class, and gender, means that the control of mass communications is in the hands of largely Anglo-dominated corporations. In 1983, for instance, about fifty corporations controlled 25,000 major media outlets; by 1996 that concentration had dramatically increased.[7] That is, fewer corporations controlled a greater number of communications entities. A media map or diagram in the June 3, 1996, issue of *The Nation*, for example, outlines this media convergence in which General Electric, Time Warner, and Disney/Capital Cities control not only the four major television news divisions—NBC, ABC, CBS, and CNN—but also satellite systems; cable, movie, and television programming and production; radio stations; and book and magazine publishing, to name but a few. Two of the corporate giants are also defense contractors involved in nuclear production.[8] This affects not only Chicanos/Latinos but all Americans and, increasingly, international communities as well. Consistent with Schiller's argument, such domination constitutes the corporate takeover of public expression and the intensification of a commercialized culture.[9] Along similar lines, Calabrese and Burke[10] argue that media corporations comprise individuals who enjoy "meaningful rights of self expression," a privilege of those with wealth and power, and who, "whether by design or default," play a key role in the construction of an American nationalism that subordinates the representation of culturally diverse groups.

The distribution of resources along racial lines means that ownership and control of presses on a grand scale are virtually out of reach for Chicanos/Latinos. Such economic constraints mean that the creation of weekly magazines and daily newspapers, for example, is prohibitive for the primarily working-class Chicano/Latino population. The start-up costs for magazines may run at least $100 million, whereas a newspaper plant may cost at least half a billion dollars.

Coverage

Because social, political, and economic power has been concentrated in the hands of white men since colonial times, it is not surprising that the values upheld in the communications industry are those of white, upper-middle-class men. This propensity and its outcomes are well documented. In 1968, for example, the Kerner Commission found that the media tended to present the news through a white viewpoint.[11] Three decades later, subsequent research reveals that little has changed. In fact, stereotyping, which is designed to "neutralize white apprehension of people of color while accommodating their presence," has actually increased since the Kerner Commission's report, Wilson and Gutiérrez argue.[12] They also found that stories featuring people of color tended to portray them as welfare recipients; as lacking in educational, job, and linguistic skills; as residents of crime-ridden neighborhoods; as "illegal aliens"; and as a people who cause problems for society.[13]

In 1992, an analysis over a two-month period of 4,000 articles in seven daily newspapers and three news magazines, including *USA Today,* the *Chicago Tribune, New York Times, Time,* and *Newsweek,* found that the national media do not provide sufficient daily coverage of Latinos and that they report from a white male perspective.[14] In addition, the analysis found that there was no coverage of political priorities for Latinos but that most articles during national presidential elections tended to focus on presidential candidates trying to win Latino voters. Stories in which Latinos were portrayed ranged from social events to gang tensions, while coverage for the most part failed to include the positive contributions to society by Latinos. Instead, the study reported, the press tended to perpetuate social polarization with simplified analyses of news events. In its analysis of news coverage of the Los Angeles riots that year, the project also found that coverage was divisive, stressing tensions between Latinos and blacks rather than cooperative efforts toward positive goals. It concluded that "The media fanned the flames of racial and ethnic unrest between blacks and whites, blacks and Latinos, and other groups by reducing complex events to short phrases which were repeated again and again in news stories. These phrases or key descriptions were often misleading."[15]

Similarly, another analysis of more than 800 news articles published in the *Los Angeles Times, New York Times, Washington Post, USA Today, Wall Street Journal,* and *Christian Science Monitor* also found coverage of the Latino community during the riots to be absent or negative.[16] The study found that although Latinos comprised 45 percent of the population in south central Los Angeles, owned almost 40 percent of the businesses damaged by the riots, and comprised 28 percent of the fatalities during this time, they were identified in only 11 percent of more than 6,000 articles containing racial and ethnic references. The analysis also indicated that the coverage failed to address the impact of the riot on Latinos and that there was a lack of in-depth coverage of Latino issues in general.

In television, recent research regarding Latino images supports Lalo Guerrero's doubts that he will ever see Chicanos on TV. While they were not entirely absent, Latinos accounted for only 2 percent of all characters depicted in prime-time series during the 1994–95 television season, up from 1 percent in 1992–93 and down from 3 percent in 1955, according to the Center for Media and Public Affairs, an independent media research group in Washington, D.C.[17] The study, commissioned by the National Council of La Raza, found that the majority of Latino characters appeared in only two series on Fox, *New York Undercover* and *House of Buggin'*, which was cancelled. Latino portrayals were "still largely stereotypical," with few portrayed as "prosperous, well-educated, authoritative characters," the report indicated. Although the number of Latinos portrayed as criminals fell from 16 percent of all Latino characters in 1992 to 6 percent in 1994–95, the figure exceeded that of 4 percent of white characters and 2 percent of African Americans shown as criminals.[18]

These findings are echoed in other research studies regarding the portrayal of minorities in the media. George Gerbner, for example, found that Latinos rarely make up more than 1 percent of characters in any programming other than game shows, where they appear only as contestants. According to Gerbner's analysis of programming from the 1982–83 to the 1991–92 seasons, for every 100 major Latino male characters, sixty were depicted as failures or ineffectual. In contrast, the ratio for Anglos was thirty-seven failures for every 100 characters.[19]

In keeping with the Cultural Indicators project begun in 1967, Gerbner also found that 63 percent of Latino characters—in observations of more than 3,000 programs and 36,000 characters—were involved in violence, either as perpetrators or as victims. In Gerbner's words, "being Latino/Hispanic or lower class means bad trouble: They are the most likely to kill and be killed. Being poor, old, Hispanic or a woman of color means double trouble, a disproportionate chance of being killed."[20]

Educational Inequality Limits Chicano Participation

As in other forms of media where the imbalance in resource distribution is evident, the inequality in the nation's communication systems is also related to educational institutions that help maintain the status quo. In 1968, the Kerner Commission drew that correlation when it called for increased media training for people of color at all levels of education, with efforts to be intensified in higher education. Implicit in the Commission's recommendations was the assumption that media and educational systems are powerful institutions that are inextricably linked in the social structure and that conjointly operate as mechanisms to uphold, reproduce, and legitimate that structure. When social structures that set standards and influence conduct in areas such as education, employment, housing, and government limit the opportunities available to people on the basis of race, the process of discrimination occurs, according to the U.S. Commission on Civil Rights. Links between those structural areas, including education and media, reproduce cycles of discrimination in what sociologists and the Commission of Civil Rights identify as "structural discrimination."[21]

In the symbolic arena, structural discrimination occurs when racial inequalities in the educational system influence similar outcomes in mainstream media. Persell argues that educational institutions reproduce the social hierarchy through tracking, expectations, values, and practices that prepare some students for leadership positions and others for labor.[22] This stratification feeds a dual market that favors the ruling class over the working class and Anglo males over people of color and women.[23] By steering members of nonwhite racial groups toward vocational goals rather than higher education, where journalism and communications training occurs, educational institutions stratify student populations. Various racial groups are thus excluded from cultural production as well as from other areas of study and employment.

The structural links between education and media are clearly demonstrated by statistics concerning the academic background that most journalists have for entrance into the field and by newsroom demographics. More than 86 percent of those hired in the newsroom are journalism majors, and 87 percent of the journalism majors are Anglo.[24] When we consider that journalism schools provide the labor pool for the media industry and that the majority of those in this pool are Anglo, the number of prospective journalists of color is predictably and exceedingly low.[25] In 1993, for example, the number of Latinos in college or university journalism departments accounted for only 5.5 percent of the total enrolled in those programs, according to a 1994 study at the Ohio State University School of Journalism.[26]

Journalism faculties also reflect that composition. About 90 percent of the journalism academy is white, a profile that is unlikely to change soon because of existing educational inequalities and university resistance to change. Moreover, the Accrediting Council in Education in Journalism and Mass Communication, which sets standards and certifies journalism units in colleges and universities, continues to grant accreditation even when schools fail to meet guidelines for achieving diversity. The Accrediting Council, established in 1978, requires journalism departments or schools to undertake efforts to hire and recruit diverse faculty, enroll students of color, and implement a multicultural curriculum. However, in failing to enforce the standard, the Council helps maintain the status quo.[27]

Lack of Representation in Employment

Aware of the inequality and incongruity between the way it represents minorities and actual social realities, the communications industry has acknowledged its own failures by setting minority employment goals and creating links with minority-affiliated professional organizations and educational institutions. In its discourse, the industry agreed that one of the functions of media is to provide a "representative picture of the constituent groups of a society," as the Hutchins Commission, organized by Henry Luce, emphasized in its investigative report about the media in 1947.[28] Because it assumes that diverse viewpoints and voices cannot be presented or heard without hiring members from different segments of the population, the American Society of Newspaper Editors in 1978 set the year 2000 as the deadline for meeting parity in the newsroom. In efforts to meet that goal, newspapers, journalism schools, and media organizations and associations have created training programs, internships, and scholarships for ethnic high school and college students as well as for journalists of color, although few minority journalists currently exist.[29] Furthermore, in an effort to change negative news reporting with regard to nonwhite communities, some newspapers have during the past decade enlisted consultants to sensitize their staffs to the information needs of these diverse populations.

Despite these varied efforts, however, progress toward achieving racial equality in the newsroom has not only been slow but has actually declined in the 1990s. Relegated largely to service and clerical areas, Chicanos/Latinos are excluded from professional positions in journalism. In 1978, 3.95 percent of print journalists were minorities, with that number growing to only 10.49 percent of an estimated 53,700 newsroom labor force by 1994.[30] In 1993, Latinos totaled 552—3.6 percent—of minority journalists working at the nation's top 100 newspapers, a significant drop from 634 in 1992. The number of Latino photographers declined 25 percent between 1992 and 1993.[31]

In 1994, the number of people of color employed at all newspapers also fell because the percentage of newspapers with a circulation of 50,000 to 100,000 and with at least one minority journalist dropped from 94 to 91 percent that year.[32] In 1994, the yearly employment survey conducted by the American Society of Newspaper Editors (ASNE)[33] found that Latinos totaled 1,667—3 percent—of the newsroom labor force nationwide. That number differs from that of the National Association of Hispanic Journalists (NAHJ) because the number of dailies in these surveys varied; but the percentages for Latinos in the two studies were nonetheless consistent. In 1994 the absence of Latinos from print media was so pronounced that of 1,492 newspapers in the United States, 71 percent had no Latinos in their newsrooms. Forty-five percent of American dailies had no people of color on their staffs that same year.[34] Although employment at major newspapers grew by 7 percent in 1992, two thirds of the people hired were Anglo.

The numbers for Latinas are even more dismal. In a patriarchal society, women are relegated to secondary status. For Latinas, the degree of exclusion in the media is magnified: The ratio of Latinos to Latinas in journalism is three to one.[35]

The pattern of inequality found in print media extends to the broadcasting industry as well. In 1993, Latinos made up 5.3 percent of 24,500 people in the television workforce and 3.6 percent of 15,000 in radio news, according to Vernon Stone, who conducts yearly employment surveys of the broadcast industry. The percentage in television reflects a decrease since 1992, when Latinos were 6 percent of the television workforce.[36]

Few Chicanos in Positions of Power

While the representation of Chicanos and other minorities in the field of journalism is minimal or nil, their absence in positions of power is even more conspicuous. The ASNE and NAHJ studies, for example, show that the overwhelming number of ethnic media workers are reporters and that few hold decision-making posts that allow them to set the tone and policy of the newsroom; to reinforce or sanction coverage of particular subjects; or, through the power to hire and fire, to shape participation in media production. At least 53 percent of Latinos were reporters, whereas only 17 percent were copy editors, and 13 percent were photographers, ASNE's findings indicated.[37] In contrast, the ASNE survey also determined that 97 percent of 12,144 supervisors and 91 percent of 8,122 copy editors were Anglo.[38]

Despite its designation as "public," National Public Radio demonstrated an equally inadequate minority representation. Echoing the aforementioned research, FAIR (Fairness and Accuracy in Reporting, a media watchdog group), in its four-month analysis of National Public Radio, found that the network was also "too white, too male, and too friendly with Washington insiders."[39] The analysis indicated that twenty-three of twenty-seven news commentators were men and that all but one were white.

As with newspapers, Chicanos/Latinos are not well represented in electronic media management. In television, thirty-one of 740 news directors—4.2 percent—in 1993 were Latino, including those who worked for affiliates of Univisión and Telemundo, the two Spanish-language networks in the

United States. In radio, the number of Latino news directors for that same year totaled 135 of 5,520—2.4 percent—a drop from 2.7 percent the previous year.[40]

Newsroom Policies as Mechanisms of Control

When Chicanos/Latinos and other people of color gain entry into mainstream journalism, they often encounter the racial and psychological oppression that is evident in other institutions. Conditions for Chicanos/Latinos in dominant media are getting worse, and the struggle to persevere has intensified to such an extent that they are being driven out in what appear to be record numbers. In a 1990 survey, for example, 60 percent of Latino journalists in California indicated that they intended to leave their profession within ten years,[41] with most of them citing a lack of advancement opportunities as the reason for leaving. In yet another poll of 1,400 journalists conducted by the Freedom Forum, the number of dissatisfied white professionals planning to leave doubled from 10 percent in 1982–83 to 20 percent in 1992.[42] However, in contrast to people of color, who usually cite racism for their departure, Anglos attributed their dissatisfaction to boredom or poor wages.[43]

When five Latino anchors and reporters at KNBC-TV in Los Angeles resigned in 1994, they cited discrimination for their departure. They were among eight Latinos who left within eleven months after a new news director was appointed. The last five who resigned charged that under the new director, white male reporters received preferential treatment in the form of better story assignments, better work schedules, and more career incentives, whereas Chicano/Latino journalists received less important assignments and were relegated to morning and weekend shifts. The conditions were so oppressive that they opted to leave without plans for alternative employment.[44]

When Chicano/Latino journalists articulate the cause of their dissatisfaction or disillusionment as a lack of upward mobility, discrimination, or disrespect for their communities, they underscore the fact that racial politics, whether hidden or overt, lie at the heart of their oppression. Racial ideologies influence the kind of and the importance accorded to contributions made by Chicano/Latino reporters, the amount of coverage provided for minority groups, and the way in which news stories about minorities are framed.

Newsroom Ideologies as a Form of Subordination

Mainstream journalists and editors describe themselves as liberals and believe themselves to be free of ideologies in keeping with notions of objectivity and professionalism.[45] These beliefs are themselves ideological constructs, however, which may be influenced by convictions about race that permeate newsroom policies and practices. For example, it is common practice in mainstream newsrooms to ask Chicano reporters if they are Chicanos first and reporters second or vice versa. This practice demonstrates the suspicion that journalists of color cannot be objective and therefore are not as qualified as other reporters if they cover their own communities. In contrast, Anglo reporters who write about the dominant culture are not asked "Are you white or a reporter first?" If their objectivity is questioned, it is usually not linked to race. Thus, the assumption that race is linked to objectivity and expertise when such a question is posed to Chicanos/Latinos is itself a racist ideology resulting in unwarranted scrutiny and the implication that they are inferior to their white counterparts.

Journalists of color are quite aware of how these racial ideologies manifest themselves in the newsroom in terms of coverage and professional equality. One study, as reported by Wilson and Gutiérrez, found that 71 percent of nonwhite journalists said their newspapers cover issues of concern to their racial constituency marginally or poorly; in contrast, only 50 percent of white journalists agreed. Journalists of color (63 percent) were twice as likely as their white colleagues (31 percent) to believe that race plays a role in newsroom assignments, promotions, and advancement. Seventy-two percent of nonwhites and 35 percent of whites said that newsroom managers and supervisors doubt the ability of journalists of color to perform their jobs adequately.[46]

While all racial groups are dissatisfied with the way the press covers their populations, one of the surveys included in the NAHJ report indicated that Latinos were the most critical about how their communities are portrayed, with 70 percent rating coverage of their racial groups as poor or very poor. They pointed to stereotypical reporting and a "narrow view of American society" as earmarks of misportrayal. Reporters and editors of color tend to agree that assigning people of color to report on racial and ethnic communities is one solution to improving coverage. Nearly 75 percent of African Americans, 68 percent of Latinos, and 63 percent of Asians indicated that such endeavors made a great deal or a moderate amount of difference. In contrast, only 10 percent of whites said that assigning ethnic reporters to cover racial groups made a great deal of difference, whereas 33 percent said that it would improve coverage moderately.[47]

Social Control of the Newsroom

An explanation of how and why these practices and their underlying ideologies continue to be perpetuated lies in the dynamics of social control wielded in the newsroom. Newsroom policies are crucial in defining the norms and values of the profession, Breed argues; they constitute what is defined as standard procedure to which journalists must conform. "[N]ew reporters are not told what [the] policy is, but they all know what [the] policy is," Breed asserts.[48] Thus, policies constitute an unwritten code of behavior, which journalists learn by participating in the story conference, where assignments or proposed stories are discussed; by observing which stories are printed in the paper and the kind of attention they are given; and by hearing through the grapevine how editors reinforce or sanction stories. They also discover what is considered deviant when editors reprimand them, withhold positive feedback, and cut stories, or edit certain elements out of them, and which journalists are deemed as "safe," Breed indicates.[49] Columns and editorials also serve as a guide to existing policies, and thus reporters model stories after those that are published, Breed states.[50] Through this socialization process, reporters "discover and internalize the rights and obligations of their status and its norms and values," what management's prejudices, biases, or preferences are (including those on race; parenthetical comment mine), and thus they learn to anticipate what is expected of them in order to reap rewards, Breed argues. Otherwise, journalists stand to be punished through sanctions, reprimands, assignment to a less desirable beat, negative treatment of stories, and blocks to upward mobility. These methods serve as an effective means of control, of enforcing newsroom policy.[51]

Through this process journalists also learn how different social groups are perceived, what race means, how race-related stories are received, and how much space such stories will be allotted.[52] As Breed states, "a southern reporter notes that Republicans are treated in a 'different' way in his paper's news columns than Democrats. The news about whites and Negroes is also of a distinct sort. Should he then write about one of these groups, his story will tend to reflect what he has come to define as standard procedure."[53]

Wilson and Gutiérrez point out that a special series on one racial group or another only highlights the ongoing neglect of established policy to provide the general audience with a complete surveillance of the social landscape.[54] The word "complete" should be coupled with "accurate," because coverage of the landscape may be inclusive but may still yield a derogatory view. On July 12, 1981, for example, a *Los Angeles Times* story headlined "Marauders from Inner City Prey on L.A.'s Suburbs." Anglo reporters depicted black people and Latinos as "desperate for money . . . marauding out of the heart of Los Angeles to prey upon the suburban middle and upper classes, sometimes with senseless savagery."[55] The story prompted black journalists to protest and to request a series they produced about their own people. Latinos followed suit with their own series, which won a Pulitzer Prize in 1983.[56]

Like other reporters, nonwhite reporters value the esteem of their peers and want to achieve upward mobility, to fulfill their employment obligations, and to protect their jobs. Because ethnic reporters are affected by sanctions as much as their white counterparts, they may accept distorted perspectives as the "standard operating procedure" to which Breed refers. In fact, contrary to the assumption that a more diverse staff would yield diversity in coverage, ethnic reporters may avoid covering their own communities—a frequent occurrence I found during my career as a journalist. Reporters who fall into this category tend to state that they do not want to be "typecast" or "pigeonholed." Or they are unwilling, understandably so, to cover minority stories because of the psychological as well as the professional consequences. Víctor Valle, former writer for the "Calendar" (arts and entertainment) section of the *Los Angeles Times*, for instance, wrote from a cultural perspective that resulted in stories that were "sat on" and thus were too late to run or that received negative comments from editors who said they didn't "understand" his articles—precisely the kinds of punishments, sanctions, or reprimands to which Breed refers.[57] Valle recalls adhering to the "dollars and screens" approach, which focuses on the profits films make, to which his editors were partial, and of omitting his own reading of Aztec symbolism in his story about Luis Valdez's film, *La Bamba:*

> I knew that night in July, when I first saw *La Bamba*, that I'd have a
> hard time selling a mythic take on this film. To write such a story
> would risk raising questions that existed outside the experience of
> my editors, answers my editors were likely to interpret as exotic,

esoteric, and pretentiously academic. This wasn't the first or last time I'd face such a quandary. It happened whenever I trusted my deepest instincts to describe the world as I saw it, and not as my editors were accustomed to seeing it. . . . These experiences were not uniquely mine . . . But I believe it is exaggerated for minority reporters, especially those few who are thoroughly bilingual and biliterate. At least that was my experience. My cultural otherness was a guest who could not overstay his welcome.[58]

Valle, like other ethnic reporters, had learned what race or cultural difference means and what survival in the newsroom entails. Given these conditions, ethnic reporters may therefore not deviate from the norm, helping to maintain the policies and practices that generate misrepresentation, under-representation, or invisibility. Thus, the "cultural patterns of the newsroom produce results insufficient for wider democratic needs," Breed asserts.[59]

Power and Representation

What is the solution? In more than 175 interviews for a *Los Angeles Times* series on media and ethnic populations, minority journalists indicated that regardless of how enlightened or well-intentioned Anglo editors are, fundamental changes in coverage of ethnic communities cannot occur without the inclusion of people of color in the decision-making process.[60] In the words of David Bartlett, president of the Radio-Television News Directors Association (RTNDA), "Management is who pulls the trigger, who makes judgments with respect to news coverage, with respect to overall approaches, with respect to assignments, with respect to hiring and subsequent firing. If management is diverse, then the staff is diverse."[61]

The assumption here, too, is that diversity can make a difference in the actual images and messages produced, a fact further illustrated by Shaw's documentation of the experiences of Thomas Greer, managing editor of the *Cleveland Plain Dealer,* who is an African American. According to Shaw, Greer achieved quick results when he threatened to fire sports photographers who repeatedly came back with photos of only white fans at the Cleveland Browns football games—a startling situation, considering Cleveland was more than 40 percent black.[62]

Whiteness Is the Norm

Although various industry leaders acknowledge and are attempting to address the inequality of the newsroom, other media professionals do not or cannot acknowledge the existence of white privilege, place blame on the victims, or resist or resent endeavors that would improve race relations. Some media industry leaders, for example, attribute the ongoing, negative conditions to the fact that efforts to change them have come long after the pipeline was created and will thus take longer to accomplish. Others often point to the dearth of "qualified" ethnic journalists, revealing the construct of inferiority they place on the "other" as well as an inability or refusal to explain the social and economic reasons for the low numbers of nonwhite people in the field in the first place. In contrast, media managers who want to bring about change cite hostility they encounter when they try to integrate their news organizations.[63]

For Latinos, the oppressive conditions mean they must continue to struggle in the industry, leave it, or embrace it at the cost of assimilation in order to survive. Although some Latino journalists are involved in organizations that monitor media performance and are exerting pressure for change, others have internalized the racism to which they are subjected. They have done so to such an extent that they employ a form of cultural deficit theory to explain the lack of progress, by characterizing their own people as shy and in need of improving self-promotion skills, of adjusting to corporate culture, or of devoting too much energy to overcoming stereotypes of minority journalists as less capable than white reporters.[64] What most of the people who hold these viewpoints tend to overlook, fail to acknowledge, or fail to articulate is the fact that the social structure has not undergone the fundamental changes needed to alleviate the previously discussed inequalities. Instead, the structure and its institutions continue to produce, reproduce, and sustain the ideologies and social relations upon which domination depends.

Chicanos Resist

The hegemonic system may not be as monolithic as it appears; nor, given the cultural terrain discussed above, is it confined to economic and political forms of control. Conflicts, disruptions, and contradictions are part of the counterhegemonic process and occur in the sphere of cultural production as well, underscoring vulnerability within the system and thereby challenging the notions of domination as stable and of culture as unchanging or closed. Instead, as Lowe argues, hegemony is neither absolute nor conclusive. Rather, "the general social terrain of culture is open, plural, and dynamic."[65]

That variability and the potential for counter-hegemonic reconfiguration in the communication landscape is strikingly exemplified by the proliferation of media that appeal to the cultural background and consumer behaviors of Chicanos/Latinos in this decade. Ironically, the very Chicano/Latino populations who had previously been ignored by Madison Avenue and major communication outlets are now a prime target of ongoing marketing studies, intensified advertising, and the new mass media created as vehicles for them. The forms of communication range from small Chicano/Latino–owned newspapers, such as *El Sol*, to television networks that are owned and controlled by transnational corporations categorized under the rubric of "Hispanic" or "Latino" media. I use quotes because these terms imply minority ownership, even though few *major* communication outlets are actually owned or controlled by Chicanos/Latinos. I emphasize "major" to denote the wide, daily dissemination that media corporations enjoy as opposed to the limited reach and scope of smaller outlets that nevertheless meet the criteria of "mass communications."

The pursuit of Chicano/Latino audiences by small and major media outlets gained momentum in the 1980s, as the demographics changed dramatically in this nation. The Latino population—65 percent of which is of Mexican descent—rose to 14.6 million in 1980, is currently estimated to be 27 million, and is projected to be 36 million by the year 2005, according to the U.S. Census Bureau. These statistics do not include 1.2 million Latinos who were identified but nevertheless excluded in the Census's 1991 Post-Enumeration Survey, an undercount that numerous cities throughout the country unsuccessfully challenged with lawsuits because of the negative impact on political representation and apportionment.[66]

When advertisers and dominant media in search of untapped markets became aware of what some mainstream journalists called the "browning" or "Latinization" of America, advertising budgets in the communications industry escalated, as did the number of vehicles designed to reach what became defined as a viable consumer group or marketing niche. While they may be in low-paying jobs and thus may not be affluent individuals, collectively, Latinos spend an estimated $190 billion to $200 billion a year.[67]

For Chicanos/Latinos, whose efforts at media production have been a constant economic struggle, the growing population and its potential support meant that community-oriented communication outlets might be more feasible and that existing media could at least survive and perhaps even flourish. The demographic growth generated more advertising revenue, which spurred the creation of specialized media to the extent that the number of newspapers and magazines labeled as "Hispanic" had risen from 200 in 1970 to 350 in 1989.[68] In May of 1994, one analyst estimated the number of newspapers aimed at Latino readers to be 330, including 176 Spanish-language, 117 bilingual, and thirty-seven English-language newspapers.[69] Another study of Hispanic publications, which included newsletters and quarterly books, placed the number of publications at 436. Of these publications, 54 percent were printed in Spanish; 87 percent of the content was devoted to Latino social issues; and 66 percent targeted readers of all Latino backgrounds.[70] Especially significant is the fact that 60 percent were owned by Latinos, according to the study. Seven percent began publishing before 1939; 12 percent from 1940 to 1959; and 81 percent from 1960 to 1991.[71]

Many community newspapers have come and gone, but the number of failures has not been tallied, although the failure rate for English-language magazines with Latino audiences is estimated at 80 percent.[72] During the 1980s, magazines published in both an English-language and a Spanish-language format included *Hispanic, Hispanic Business, Puntos, Que Pasa, Saludaos Hispanos,* the now-defunct *Más, La Familia de Hoy, Imagen, Americas 2000,* and *Caminos.* Despite the high failure rate, new magazines have continued to spring up in this decade, including *Latina, Moderna, Latina Style, Latin Beat, Sí, ¡Qué Linda!,* and most recently *Newsweek en Español.*

Similarly and more dramatically, the media boom targeting Chicanos/Latinos continues to expand and reverberate not only locally and nationally but also internationally in broadcasting. In the late 1980s, the number of radio stations targeting Latino audiences skyrocketed to 400, with 190 of them broadcasting full time in Spanish—up from thirty-two of 203 stations that devoted an entire day to a Spanish format in 1985. The first Latino FM station went on the air in 1988. In 1995, Latinos were granted thirty-four—0.6 percent—FM licenses, whereas Anglos obtained 5,167, or 97.8 percent, of licenses in that category. In 1992, Latinos controlled only fifty-five of 9,070 radio stations in the nation, with about 75 percent of those being owned by Chicanos.[73]

Altogether, Chicanos/Latinos owned only 1 percent of the nation's 11,412 radio and television stations in 1995.[74] The number of Spanish-language television stations was forty-nine at the beginning of this decade, according to the 1991 *Broadcasting Yearbook*. Currently, the two major Spanish-language television networks, Telemundo and Univisión, own twenty-eight affiliates and 700 cable affiliates.[75] These networks are in the hands of Mexican and South American media moguls rather than U.S. Chicano/Latino citizens. Overall, electronic media are overwhelmingly in the hands of non-ethnic, transnational corporations. For the past ten years, these entities have intensified their acquisitions through either new media they have created, buy-outs, mergers with other Spanish-language radio and television groups, or joint ventures via cable or satellite that reach millions of people in Latin America and other parts of the world. The details of this trend are too extensive for the purposes of this paper.

To understand this media proliferation, as well as the tensions between corporate media and local journalism in Chicano/Latino communities, it will be helpful to consider the difficult relationship between economics and communications, between viewing communication through the "prism of the market" and through the "prism of community," two distinctive perspectives, as Carey argues.[76] Similarly, Hallin ascribes a "dual social identity" to media, defining them as economic as well as cultural institutions, as "profit-making business[es] and at the same time a[s] producer[s] of meaning, a[s] creator[s] of social consciousness."[77] This dichotomy will be useful in deliberating the differences and similarities between cultural production undertaken by media corporations and that undertaken by ethnic communities.

The way in which the role of media is viewed depends on who's in charge. For those who control major media outlets, who have not only a monetary advantage but a cultural advantage as well, the primary concern tends to be profit. In contrast, Chicanos/Latinos, who must rely on minimal resources, often launch their media projects out of a need for self-expression and representation of their communities. This is not to say that dominant media do not offer community-oriented projects or agendas that they define as beneficial to the public interest, nor does it mean that cultural productions by Chicanos/Latinos are never driven by profit motives. Economic considerations are paramount for all forms of media production, whether they appeal to Chicano/Latino audiences or not.

For Carey, the difference between commercial and community imperative in communication constitutes a clash between economics and communications in both theory and practice. Because economics and communications have different goals, they tend to be what Carey calls "mutually exclusive activities." The contradictions that they create can be reconciled, according to Carey, only by:

> [a]n evacuation of the resources of meaning in the service of profit and power. Therefore, the only useful relationship between communications and economics is a countervailing one both at the level of theory and practice. Communications and economics derive from different motivational structures and produce incommensurably alternative pictures of human action and social life. They can cancel or neutralize one another; they can check off each others' biases, but otherwise they will be fiercely resistant to any form of integration. They constitute a contradictory order of things: their root meanings and consequences are opposed in theory and practice.[78]

Although Carey draws an uncompromising line between the two, allowing for no middle ground, which some scholars may find troublesome, what is significant here is how the understanding of communication through the prism of the market or of community affects the role of media in Chicano/ Latino communities and therefore their content, quality, accessibility, and longevity. The contrast in "root meanings" and "consequences" is illustrated in publications such as *Nuestro Tiempo,* which was market-driven, and *El Sol,* which was not. The former, a bilingual weekly broadsheet launched by the *Los Angeles Times* in 1989, enjoyed the advantages of monetary and technological support, as evidenced by its reporting and translation staff, ample space, color photography, sophisticated graphics, and wide distribution (400,000) within a short time.[79] In 1993, the *Los Angeles Times* expanded the supplement, transforming it from a bilingual monthly to a weekly, 90 percent of which was published in Spanish.[80] *Nuestro Tiempo,* however, ceased publication in August of 1995 as part of the Times Mirror Company's economic cutbacks in the face of skyrocketing newsprint costs and reportedly diminishing profit margins[81] (which are nevertheless gains, not losses). In doing so, the company laid off most of its Chicano/Latino staff and left the Chicano/ Latino community without the coverage it had been promised. In contrast, *El Sol,* despite its meager capital, technological limitations, and comparatively small circulation (31,000), has enabled its owner, Julie Rocha, a Latina, to engage in media production and has served as a site for the expression of marginalized ideas and images. In contrast to publications produced by the *Los Angeles Times* that are aimed at minority populations, *El Sol* continues to be published at the start of the millennium.

Through the Prism of the Market

In the desire for a balance between commercial interests and community needs, Tony Marcano, the former editor of *City Times*, wonders whether the two must be incompatible.[82] An inner-city edition published by the *Los Angeles Times* in the aftermath of the 1992 Los Angeles riots, the *City Times* sought to provide coverage for mostly ethnic communities that the press has traditionally overlooked. Instead, along with *Nuestro Tiempo*, the *City Times* was also closed down in 1995. "At what point does the bottom line supersede the tenets of good journalism, which includes thorough and accurate coverage of the whole community?" asks Marcano, who views the role of communications through prisms of both market and community. Whereas Carey argues that articulating an ideal is impossible, Marcano wonders whether "the tasks of making money and nurturing credibility [are] mutually exclusive?"[83] The answer varies, but the elimination of the two Times-Mirror editions seems to indicate that if the issue is whether monetary gains are more important, the answer is "yes." This conclusion is based on the fact that the profit margin for Times Mirror in 1995 rose to 10 percent, an increase of 6.1 percent from 1994, for a gain of $204,733,000.[84]

Although it is true that publishing is costly as evidenced by newsprint prices, which comprise 60 percent of a newspaper's cost and which soared 40 percent during the past year,[85] the dominant presses continue to claim that they are losing money, even as they realize substantial revenues and encroach on the ethnic press to augment their gains. Compared with other industries where profit margins average 5 to 6 percent, profit margins in the newspaper business are high, averaging in the mid-teens and perhaps running into the twenties, reports Sally Lehrman, a former journalist at the *San Francisco Examiner* and Stanford journalism fellow.[86] The *Buffalo News*, owned by billionaire Warren Buffet, for example, in 1995 realized a profit margin of 29.9 percent—$46.3 million; the McClatchy chain realized 12 percent—$64.7 million; and Knight-Ridder, 12.5 percent—$281.2 million.[87]

The commercial appetites of media giants, however, are never satisfied, and these corporations have been launching their own editions or supplements or buying established Spanish-language or bilingual presses in order to maintain their economic and cultural dominance. By 1992, five main-stream newspapers in California had created their own Spanish-language editions, including *El Económico,* published by the *Press-Telegram* in Long Beach; *Excelsior,* by Freedom Newspapers Inc., which publishes *The Orange County Register* and owns twenty-six other dailies in nine states; *El Nuevo Tiempo,* by *The New York Times* Company in Santa Barbara, where it also publishes the *Santa Barbara News-Press;* and *Vecinos del Valle,* by the *Daily News,* Woodland Hills.[88] In 1990, the *Los Angeles Daily News* began publishing a Spanish-language weekly named *Vecinos del Valle* (Valley Neighbors), and the McClatchy chain, which publishes the *Fresno Bee,* created *Vida en el Valle* (Life in the Valley). Originally published weekly, the latter publication became a biweekly in 1991 because of the high cost of production and distribution.[89]

Other major newspapers that began publishing editions aimed at Latino readers included the *Rocky Mountain News, Denver Post, Chicago Tribune,* and *Fort Worth Star-Telegram.* In addition, as the result of a joint venture, the *Chicago Sun-Times* and *La Raza,* the leading Latino newspaper in that city, were considering the publication of a Sunday magazine. In addition to its Santa Barbara publication, the *New York Times* in 1993 also made plans for multilingual supplements to newspapers in the New York area, beginning with a Spanish-language section in eighteen newspapers, with advertising pages costing $20,000 each.[90] Other newspapers had already heeded the trend. Faced with white flight and the realization that the potential readership had changed, the *Miami Herald,* for example, in 1987 revamped its Spanish-language supplement, renaming it *El Nuevo Herald* and printing it as a daily.[91] Reactionary and heavily anti-Castro in its coverage, *El Nuevo Herald* appeals to the predominantly Cuban community in that city.

As part of the acquisition strategy, the *Los Angeles Times* in 1989 acquired 50 percent interest in *La Opinión.* The oldest Spanish-language daily, *La Opinión* has been published since 1926. The *Los Angeles Times* acquired this daily with good reason. Between 1981 and 1991, the paper's circulation grew 155 percent, with its advertising revenue skyrocketing by 600 percent, *The Quill* reports.[92] In addition, after closing *Nuestro Tiempo* and *City Times,* Times Mirror in October 1995 started another bilingual paper in cooperation with *La Opinión* called *Para Ti,* which ceased publication on December 29, 1999. The Thompson Newspaper Corporation, which publishes three dailies in the San Gabriel Valley in California and in 1995 enjoyed a 17.3 percent profit margin of $216 million, is currently exploring the acquisition of *Vida Nueva,* the Spanish-language newspaper of the Los Angeles Roman Catholic Archdiocese.

Other major newspapers involved in acquisition attempts include the *San Diego Union Tribune,* which had turned Julie Rocha, the owner of *El Sol,* away nine years ago but was sufficiently impressed by the publication's reputation and potential to begin negotiations for a buy-out. The deal fell through in 1995 after nineteen months of talks. However, in 1998 the *Union Tribune* began publishing its own Spanish-language supplement, *The Union Tribune en Español,* whose title it changed to *Enlace* in 1999. It hired a former freelance journalist and advertising salesman for *Excelsior,* published by the *Orange County Register,* as well as a former reporter for *El Sol.*

The convergence and competition seen in the newspaper business are also found in the magazine industry. In 1990, Time Warner acquired 27 percent interest in *Vista Magazine,* which was originally owned and published by Latinos and inserted in twenty-seven English-language newspapers.[93] Time Warner also created *La Familia de Hoy* (Today's Family), a Spanish-language magazine targeting Latin immigrant women, which was discontinued.

People magazine discovered the market potential of the Latino population after its commemorative issue on the late Tex-Mex singer, Selena, sold one million copies in 1994.[94] In the spring of 1996, the publication issued its first Spanish-language edition with an issue on "The Diana Years," devoted to the English princess. A commercial success, *People* continues to appear in Spanish.

The magazine trade targets 9.5 million Chicanos/Latinos with annual household incomes of $20,000 to $30,000, a segment that comprises nearly half that group's population and that constitutes a growing middle class.[95] Chicano/Latino households with annual incomes exceeding $25,000, for example, grew 38 percent between 1984 and 1992, whereas those with incomes over $50,000 grew by 112 percent.[96] Chicanos/Latinos are not naïve about the marketing rationale for the new publications, and people such as Julie Rocha resent the exploitation.

The Market Commodifies the Citizen

The market or economic perspective clearly demands that Chicanos/Latinos and others be viewed through the commercial lens, and thus audiences are constructed as commodities that must render a profit. That is, the product that a medium delivers is not the printed news story nor the television program but rather the audience. Ettema and Whitney define audience-making as the process in which the receivers "[a]re constituted or reconstituted as *institutionally effective audiences* that have social meaning and/or economic value within the system. These include *measured audiences* that are generated by research services, sold by media channels, and bought by advertisers."[97]

Readers, viewers, or listeners are thereby converted into a consuming entity rather than a citizenry, a market rather than an audience in the traditional sense of the word. As Carey argues, not only is culture privately manufactured and privately distributed, but its audience is conceived as statistically concentrated individuals or members of segmented transnational groups rather than as citizens of a common polity or participants in a common tradition.[98] Paul Adams, vice president of CNN, exemplifies that development quite well. In describing the target for Noticiero Telemundo/CNN, the Spanish language counterpart of CNN, which began broadcasting in Latin America with the Moscow summit in 1988, he gloated, "Three hundred million Spanish-speaking viewers are, for Ted Turner, a finger-licking, lip-smacking good audience."[99] (The news program airs on eighteen U.S. Spanish-language stations owned by or affiliated with Telemundo Group Inc., a Miami-based network that went on the air in 1987 and has eleven markets in Latin America.)[100] Rodríguez suggests that this kind of marketing knowledge was made possible only after the Latino population in the United States was conceptualized as a national, abstract entity that could be created, recreated, and sold by the cultural industry, including advertising and marketing firms. In what she identifies as the "re-mapping of Latino audiences," Rodríguez argues that this reconfiguration of a historically ignored group by mainstream media occurred because of market research that permitted the quantification of consumer group actions and made Latinos a commodity.[101] This national market research targeting Latino consumers, the first of which Rodríguez credits to the former Spanish International Network in 1978, legitimated, produced, and delineated them as a profitable audience. This made Latinos intelligible to mainstream advertisers, who were largely ignorant about them and rarely had any contact with them.[102]

Chicanos as a Commodity

Now that it viewed Chicanos/Latinos as a viable audience, and in its efforts to increase consumption, the media industry spent $628.2 million in 1993 on advertising aimed at Latinos, as stated in the *Hispanic Link Weekly Report*.[103] That amount rose to $952.8 million in 1994, but the totals for both years pale in comparison to the estimated $130 billion spent on all advertising in 1991.[104] When Guerrero sings that "Chicano babies also pee, but they don't show them on TV," he understandably is suggesting that Chicanos at the very least be included in advertising; but the current exploitation of Chicano audiences as a commodity may be more than he and others bargained for. Now Chicanos/Latinos are being bombarded by commercial messages, many of which are detrimental to their health. Others are a downright affront to their culture, as some of the advertising gaffes demonstrate. In 1987, Braniff promoted its leather seats, saying that a passenger could fly *"sentado en cuero,"* which intended to convey that passengers could sit in leather seats but was more akin to saying that the passengers could fly naked.[105] In 1988, a slogan advertising chicken, "It takes a tough man to make a tender chicken," ended up in Spanish as "It takes a sexually excited man to make a chicken affectionate."[106] In 1991, a *Newsday* headline for a story about competition between Pepsi and Coke read, "Pepsi, Coke Pitch Thirsty Latinos: Mi Cola es Su Cola"—my tail is your tail.[107]

Through the Prism of Community: Resistance and Contestation

Viewed through the prism of community, culturally based media productions embody more than a market rationality. Through this different lens, media become the site for alternative voices and formats. Lowe's reading of Gamsci reminds us that the hegemonic process not only presumes a dominant group, but also "subaltern" groups who resist or contest the power structure.[108] Thus, although the subordinate group may appear to be passive and consenting, especially because their discourses are missing from traditional channels of communication, they routinely engage in alternative constructs that go against the grain, albeit in ordinary ways. As Scott stresses, social and economic limitations may not make collective action on a grand revolutionary scale possible, but seemingly mundane individual actions need not be brushed off as trivial or inconsequential and outside the pursuit of resistance.[109] As we have already seen, Lalo Guerrero uses his voice, guitar, and social consciousness to not only name and protest the inequalities of representation but also to issue a call for action. "Script writers never write for us," he sings. "I think it's time we raised a fuss." Over the years, Chicanos/Latinos have done just that and continue to do so. In contesting the dominant media structure, they have used a variety of tactics.

In the 1960s, opposition to stereotypes resulted in the elimination of the mustachioed, *pistola*-toting Frito Bandido commercials. Opposition in this era included filing FCC license challenges and conducting television boycotts. By 1990, for instance, groups such as LULAC (League of United Latin American Citizens), together with the NAACP and the National Hispanic Media and National Black Media coalitions, had filed challenges asking the FCC to revoke the licenses of 204 television and radio stations that had not hired Latinos or provided better coverage of Latino issues. Sometimes the groups were successful.[110] In 1993, for example, LULAC entered into negotiations with five television stations to increase hiring of Latinos and to improve coverage of their communities, after filing petitions against fourteen stations in Arizona, Nevada, and New Mexico. It also filed complaints against another sixteen stations in Texas that year, with six of them resulting in success.[111] In 1995, the dearth of Latino representation at ABC prompted more than 130 Latino organizations to launch a national boycott to force the network to provide programs with Latino themes,[112] but as a television "brown out" asking Latinos to turn their sets off for two weeks in September of 1999 indicates, that strategy was not effective.[113]

History of Alternative Production

Ultimately, Chicanos/Latinos have created their own alternative strategies to counter hegemonic media barriers. Because of limited capital, Chicano/Latino ownership and production are heavily concentrated in print media, the most economically feasible communications arena, but not necessarily the most preferable, given the reach of electronic media. The current explosion of "Latino" media is part of a journalistic tradition dating to the 1800s, when Spanish-language and bilingual newspapers were a component of hegemonic media as well as of alternative media production. In the last century, commercially oriented bilingual and Spanish-language publications, many of which were Anglo-owned, tended to function as vehicles for advertising, whereas those that were part of the partisan press, regardless of ownership, focused on generating political support from Spanish or Mexican constituencies.[114]

The journalistic arena, however, was not monopolized by Anglos.

Mexicans, too, owned and published their own newspapers, with that number totaling 380 between 1848 and 1958, 132 of which were founded before 1900.[115] As a form of cultural resistance, the Mexicano/Chicano-owned press sought to give voice to an indigenous people who were subjected to the Anglo invasion and conquest achieved with expansionism and the U.S.–Mexican War of 1846–48. During the 1800s, Mexicanos/Chicanos, like their contemporary counterparts, coped with the unending social, political, economic, and cultural consequences of domination partly by communicating through their own publications. Although Anglo-owned newspapers offered clips from other papers or military orders as news or launched blatantly racist attacks on the Latino population as their editorial fare, Mexicanos looked to the press not only as a form of cultural or literary expression but also as a form of political communication, as an avenue of resistance. As with other newspapers of the period, the Mexicano press was a form of what Hallin describes as "politically committed journalism" that invited readers to "participate in political debate or action."[116]

By existing side by side with their competitors and serving as a vehicle for preserving Mexicano culture and the Spanish language, these papers filled the criteria for alternative cultural forms. But Mexicanos/Chicanos also sought to change their oppressive conditions by articulating their discontent or outrage, thus using the press in oppositional ways. For example, in Los Angeles, Francisco Ramirez, a seventeen-year-old former editor of the Spanish section of the *Los Angeles Star,* founded *El Clamor Público* in 1855 and used the paper to decry various injustices such as lynching, vigilante raids, and other forms of violence against "Mexican-Americans," as Chicanos were called.[117] Debating the impact of statehood on their civil rights in their various newspapers, Mexicanos/Chicanos delayed California's statehood for several decades until they could be assured that their rights, such as the preservation of their language as provided in the Treaty of Guadalupe Hidalgo, would be protected. In addition, throughout its history, the Mexican/Chicano press has challenged stereotyping in dominant media. *El Boletín Popular* in New Mexico, for example, protested the characterization of New Mexico natives by Anglo government officials as being of low moral standards and superstitious and of New Mexico as a state that was overrun by Catholic priests and ineligible for statehood.[118]

With the Mexican Revolution of 1910, the number of immigrants from Mexico continued to grow and so did the number of Spanish-language publications. Between 1901 and 1920, 239 newspapers appealing to people from Mexico, Spain, and Central and South America began publication, with 178 ceasing within the same period, Park's study of the immigrant press shows.[119] Despite the number of Spanish-language papers that failed during the period covered by Park, a substantial number were introduced in the 1930s. In 1938, *La Prensa* (whose owner was also the founder of *La Opinión*) published a list of 451 Spanish-language periodicals that had been published in the United States, evidence that the Latino press continued to grow after Park's analysis. According to Gutiérrez, sociologist John Burma predicted that the Spanish-language press would die by the 1970s.[120]

The Chicano press, however, experienced a resurgence during the Chicano Movement of the 1960s in the form of activist newspapers, with some of them such as *El Tecolote,* in San Francisco, continuing to the present day. In 1965–66, more than 200 Chicano-oriented periodicals were published throughout the Southwest and Midwest, representing the "new sentinels of *chicanismo,*" which meant they "tended to be heavy on the rhetoric and light on digging for the facts," asserts Armando Rendón in his study of the Chicano press.[121] Many of these publications also fell by the wayside, but Rendón argues, publications that survived were "those periodicals which balanced a strong sense for dealing with injustices and inequalities which Chicanos experience, with a solid factual base. . . ."[122]

El Sol *as a Local Cultural Site*

Like other specialized publications that fill the ethnic news gap left by metropolitan newspapers,[123] *El Sol* creates an identity specific to the Chicano/ Latino community on a national—albeit limited—as well as local level. In her study of Univisión, Rodríguez posits that the Spanish-language television network constructs or imagines a largely immigrant audience unified through a "deep horizontal comradeship" through the use of a standardized or "accentless" Spanish; programming that focuses on the diverse Latino population in the United States; and Latino journalists who, by telling stories to Latinos about Latinos, maintain cultural unity.[124] The concept of a deep horizontal comradeship assumes that the various groups that come under the rubric of "Latino" or "Hispanic" are interested in news about one another. In its coverage of news of interest to the various cultures along the border (e.g., Mexican Independence Day), Univisión thus constructs a homogeneous, or what Rodríguez calls a "denationalized, panethnic," community. As Rodríguez asserts, and despite evidence to the contrary, the "community is conceived of as united by the Spanish language, immigrant history, and their residence in the United States."[125] Media such as Univisión "encourage ethnic cohesion and cultural maintenance as they simultaneously contribute to their audiences' acculturation by responding to their . . . demands for knowledge about their adopted country."[126]

With its limited resources and reach, and in its role as a community newspaper, *El Sol* cannot construct or appeal to a national audience as does Univisión, but it relies on many of the same assumptions to provide information for immigrant readers. Like Univisión, *El Sol* assumes a solidarity or deep horizontal comradeship among its readers, both U.S.–born and foreign-born. In grouping them as "Latinos" or "Hispanics" *El Sol* constructs a panethnic identity through stories, such as those about governmental or educational policies, that stand to affect the entire Latino population, regardless of nationality. It strays from that construct by specifying subgroups when appropriate (e.g., a meeting of the Chicano Federation).

El Sol assumes that Latino immigrants, regardless of nationality, need information in their native language that will help them adapt to their new surroundings (e.g., a series on the citizenship process, obtaining credit, and health care issues). Like Univisión, *El Sol* also adheres to a standardized Spanish to appeal to all its Latino readers, using no idiomatic expressions peculiar to, say, a Chicano or Puerto Rican dialect, except in direct quotes.

El Sol, with its limited resources, does not have a full-time staff that functions as a typical media entity, with a hierarchical structure that reaches out to the community. Instead Rocha and her partner, Lynn Johansen, although they often report and write for the newspaper themselves, rely heavily on members from the Latino community, including college and elementary school students (the latter of which have their own children's page), members of their advisory board, national and local leaders, activists, professors, and writers, to collectively organize and co-construct a diverse Chicano/Latino community. *El Sol* presumes more than one audience, immigrant as well as native-born readers, and monolingual as well as bilingual and bicultural readers. Overlap of interest by these various audiences is expected to occur when, say, legislation or local events may affect all readers, or when Chicanos, for example, wish to compare stories in both English and Spanish or to read stories that appear in only one language. Despite its duality, however, *El Sol* attracts mostly a U.S.–born, largely Chicano, readership and constructs a bicultural, bilingual, or monolingual (English-speaking) audience through its use of English and Spanish; through its coverage of community issues, events, and personalities; and through the use of contributing writers and reporters drawn from the San Diego area.

In contrast with Univisión, *El Sol* constructs its local identity in keeping with Kaniss's observation that newspapers must overcome the problem of a "splintered identity" created by urbanization; decentralization; and differences in the class, culture, and ethnicity of readers.[127] As Kaniss points out, the success of newspapers depends on their ability to "link their audiences to a common bond of local identity."[128]

A content analysis of *El Sol* reveals that the newspaper not only articulates different definitions of identity more appropriate to the racial consciousness and self-image of Chicanos/Latinos but also provides news coverage that resonates with their social realities. The newspaper *El Sol* also provides an avenue for the community to organize itself; serves as a forum for multiple voices and perspectives; and includes other genres such as historical accounts, fiction, and poetry. *El Sol* provides a platform for ideologies that are oppositional to those perpetuated in mainstream publications, and their articulation may encompass a battle over representation.

Conclusion

In this informal survey of changes in the communications terrain, what emerges is the imposition of an increasingly commercialized culture that eclipses alternative or oppositional cultural forms. Because of the success of competing media that target previously untapped minority audiences, mainstream media have begun to create Spanish-language or bilingual productions. How this incorporation mediates definitions of Chicano/Latino identity must be examined, but a more important question is whether, having absorbed the alternative or oppositional competition, these special editions can address the problems inherent in mainstream media. That is, do their primary English-language editions continue to provide negative portrayals or to avoid coverage of Chicano/Latino groups, to consider them as commodities, and to exclude Chicano/Latino journalists? In effect, racial and class-based groups may be isolated from one another as mainstream media separate their audiences to exploit the economic ends that market segmentation promises.

Alternative forms of media may appear to "ghettoize" their audiences, thus perpetuating a type of segregation and subordination that helps uphold the status quo. However, these kinds of culturally relevant media are necessary for constructing racial consciousness by providing images and voices that counter the detrimental representations encountered in the hegemonic press. There are other important issues to consider as well. The scope and effectiveness of alternative media in the public sphere may be curtailed because limited resources may greatly affect their professional quality, audience reach, and longevity. Although they may claim to be arenas for the democratization of cultural expression, some of the new publications mimic dominant publications or are produced by the mainstream industry itself, giving rise to cultural and political contradictions. Some Chicano/Latino groups pretend to provide an alternative or oppositional media form by presenting Chicano/Latino subjects and/or publishing in Spanish. Such publications, however, may emphasize sports or entertainment at the expense of more substantial issues, thus failing to address profound political and social problems. Similarly, mainstream newspapers that implement Spanish-language or bilingual editions may provide representation of a racial group they had previously ignored, but these supplements do not address or solve the inequalities that continue to be the earmarks of their English-language mainstays. Although economic considerations are paramount for all media, I conclude that market-driven mainstream media maintain their dominance by purchasing alternative newspapers and, by doing so, threaten or inhibit the production of popular culture. In addition, the emphasis on consumerism and reliance on economic forces discourages dissent. Nevertheless, I also suggest that seizing opportunities to utilize available communication forms is necessary if Chicanos are to achieve an equitable redistribution of information resources, a more democratic media system, and thus, cultural empowerment.

Notes

1. Lalo Guerrero, "Chicanos on TV," from the album *Folklyric* (Arhoolie Records, El Cerrito, Calif., 1978).

2. I use "Chicano" to refer to people of Mexican descent born and raised in the United States, and I use "Mexicano" to refer to inhabitants of the U.S. southwestern lands that belonged to Mexico prior to the Mexican War of 1846 and to people currently living in Mexico. Although I recognize that Latinos are heterogeneous, for

convenience, I use "Latino" to refer to diverse groups, including Chicanos and other people with roots in Latin America and the Caribbean residing in the United States. I rely on "Chicanos/Latinos" to indicate that my statements may apply not only to Chicanos but also to various other groups from Latin America or the Caribbean.

3. I place the terms "Hispanic" and "Latino" in quotation marks because they imply Chicano/Latino ownership and control, which is not necessarily the case; convenience forces me to use "Latino."

4. Michael Omi and Howard Winant, *Racial Formation in the United States* (London: Routledge, 1994), 60.

5. I use "alternative" to denote those publications or individual news articles which offer different constructions of Latino identity and reality, and "oppositional" to designate those which, as publications or individual messages, challenge the social structure or dominant ideology regarding Latinos.

6. Omi and Winant, *Racial Formation,* 60.

7. Ben Bakdikian, *The Media Monopoly* (Boston: Beacon Press, 1987), xxii.

8. Mark Crispin Miller, "Free the Media," *The Nation* 262 (1996): 9–15.

9. Herb Schiller, *Culture Inc.* (New York: Oxford University Press, 1989); and idem, *Information Inequality* (New York: Routledge, 1996).

10. Andrew Calabrese and Barbara Ruth Burke, "American Identities: Nationalism, the Media, and the Public Sphere," *Journal of Communication Inquiry* 6 (1992): 52–73.

11. National Advisory Commission on Civil Disorders, *U.S. Riot Commission Report* (New York: Bantam Books, Inc., 1968), 366–86.

12. Clint C. Wilson II and Félix Gutiérrez, *Race, Multiculturalism and the Media* (Thousand Oaks: Sage Publications, 1995), 161.

13. Ibid., 157–58.

14. "Media Report," *Hispanic Link Weekly Report,* 26 October 1992, 10. Commissioned by Women, Men, and the Media at New York University, this study was funded primarily by the Freedom Forum and conducted by Unabridged Communications.

15. Ibid.

16. "Media Report," *Hispanic Link Weekly Report,* 15 April 1993, 1. This study was conducted by the National Association of Latino Elected and Appointed Officials Educational Fund in Washington, D.C., and released in April 1993.

17. Greg Braxton, "Latinos on TV: Mixed Findings, Progress," *Los Angeles Times,* 16 April 1996, F1.

18. Ibid.

19. "Media Report," *Hispanic Link Weekly Report,* 4 October 1993, 10.

20. George Gerbner, "Television Violence: The Power and the Peril," in *Gender, Race and Class in Media,* eds. Gail Dines and Jean M. Humez (Thousand Oaks: Sage Publications, 1995), 552–56.

21. U.S. Commission on Civil Rights, *Promises and Perceptions: Federal Efforts to Eliminate Employment Discrimination through Affirmative Action* (Washington D.C.: U.S. Civil Rights Commission, 1981).

22. Caroline Hodges Persell, *Education and Inequality: The Roots and Results of Stratification in America's Schools* (New York: The Free Press, 1977), 5–13.

23. Ibid.

24. Ron Smith, "In the Search for Minority Journalists: The Quest Begins before College," *The Quill* (1991): 25.

25. Mercedes Lynn de Uriarte, "The Annual Ying-Yang Rituals of Latinos in the Newsroom," *Hispanic Link Weekly Report*, 29 May 1995, 3.

26. Unpublished study by Lee B. Becker and Gerald M. Kosick cited in Inés Pinto Alicia, "No Headlines, No Headway," *National Association of Hispanic Journalists, 1995–1996 Report* (1996): 20.

27. Wilson and Gutiérrez, *Race, Multiculturalism*, 209–10.

28. Hutchins Commission, *A Free and Responsible Press* (Chicago: The University of Chicago Press, 1974), 26–27.

29. Wilson and Gutiérrez, *Race, Multiculturalism*, 211.

30. William Glaberson, "Hiring of Minority Journalists Has Slowed, Survey Says," *New York Times*, 15 April 1994, A18.

31. National Association of Hispanic Journalists, *No Headlines, No Headway: Hispanics in the News and Media Losing Ground: A 1994–95 Report* (Washington D.C.: National Association of Hispanic Journalists, 1995), 1.

32. Glaberson, "Hiring of Minority Journalists," A18.

33. American Society of Newspaper Editors 1994 Annual Survey, cited in *Hispanic Link Weekly Report* 13, no. 16 (17 April 1995).

34. "Media Report," *Hispanic Link Weekly Report*, 17 April 1995, 8.

35. National Association of Hispanic Journalists, *No Headlines*, 1.

36. Vernon Stone, "1994 Radio Television News Directors Foundations Study, University of Missouri," cited in National Association of Hispanic Journalists, *No Headlines*, 17–18; and "Media Report," *Hispanic Link Weekly Report*, 7 April 1992, 7.

37. National Association of Hispanic Journalists, *No Headlines*, 15.

38. Christian R. González, "Latino Newsroom Presence Rises Slightly for Fourth Year in a Row," *Hispanic Link Weekly Report*, 18 April 1994, 2.

39. "Media Report," *Hispanic Link Weekly Report*, 3 May 1993, 7.

40. National Association of Hispanic Journalists, *No Headlines*, 12–18.

41. David Shaw, "What's the News? White Editors Make the Call," *Los Angeles Times*, 13 December 1990, A37.

42. National Association of Hispanic Journalists, *No Headlines*, 5–8.

43. Shaw, "What's the News?" A37.

44. Greg Braxton, "What's Behind Latino Exodus at KNBC News?" *Los Angeles Times*, 3 February 1994, F1.

45. Herbert J. Gans, *Deciding What's News: A Study of CBS Evening News, NBC Nightly News, Newsweek and Time* (New York: Vintage Books, 1980).

46. Wilson and Gutiérrez, *Race, Multiculturalism*, 210.

47. National Association of Hispanic Journalists, *No Headlines*, 6.

48. Warren Breed, "Social Control in the Newsroom," *Social Forces*, May 1955, 335.

49. Ibid., 328–35.

50. Ibid., 328.

51. Ibid., 328–35.

52. Wilson and Gutiérrez, *Race, Multiculturalism*, 161–62.

53. Breed, "Social Control in the Newsroom," 329.

54. Wilson and Gutiérrez, *Race, Multiculturalism*, 163.

55. Richard Meyer and Mike Goodman, "Marauders from Inner City Prey on L.A.'s Suburbs," *Los Angeles Times*, 12 July 1981, A1.

56. *Southern California's Latino Community* (Los Angeles: Times Mirror Publishing Company, 1984).

57. Víctor Valle, "Chicano Reporter in 'Hispanic Hollywood'," in *Chicanos and Film: Essays on Representation and Resistance*, ed. Chon Noriega (New York: Garland Publishing Company, 1992), 261–72.

58. Ibid., 263.

59. Breed, "Social Control in the Newsroom," 335.

60. Shaw, "What's the News?" A36–A37.

61. National Association of Hispanic Journalists, *No Headlines*, 20–21.

62. Shaw, "What's the News?" A1.

63. Ibid., A36.

64. National Association of Hispanic Journalists, *No Headlines*, 3–4.

65. Lisa Lowe, *Critical Terrains: French and British Orientalisms* (Ithaca: Cornell University Press, 1991), 1–5.

66. U.S. Department of Commerce, Economics and Statistics Administration, Bureau of the Census, "Post-Enumeration Survey," 13 June 1991; and *Hispanic Americans Today* (Washington, D.C.: U.S. Government Printing Office, 1993).

67. "Media Report," *Hispanic Link Weekly Report*, 13 December 1993, 12; and M. L. Stein, "Hispanic Publishers Take Aim at Mainstream Press," *Editor and Publisher*, 12 February 1994, 11–13.

68. Félix Gutiérrez, "Latinos and the Media," in *Readings in Mass Communication*, eds. Michael Emery and Ted Curtis Smythe (Dubuque, Iowa: Wm. C. Brown Co. Publishers, 1983), 171; and Rudolph G. Penner and William Lilley III, *Economic and Social Impacts of Media Advertising* (New York: Leadership Council on Advertising Issues, 1990), 19–29.

69. Margaret G. Carter, "Latin Lessons: Spanish-Language Newspapers Add Salsa to One of the Nation's Most Competitive Media Markets," *Presstime* (1994): 40.

70. "Media Report," *Hispanic Link Weekly Report*, 22 February 1993, 8.

71. Ibid.

72. Danilo Alfaro, "Magazines Forge on Despite Odds," *Hispanic Link Weekly Report,* 17 April 1989, 1–2.

73. "Radio Serves a Smorgasbord to Latino Listeners," *Television and Radio Age,* 23 November 1987, A16–A26; Enrique Loza, "Business, Amigo? No! Amigo Business? Sí!," *Public Relations Journal* (1988): 8–10; and "Hispanic Radio Stations Grow to 400; Half Strictly Spanish," *Variety* (1988): 102.

74. "Media Report," *Hispanic Link Weekly Report,* 8 July 1996, 8.

75. "Publishers Tap Latino Market," *San Diego Union-Tribune,* 23 June 1996, 8.

76. James W. Carey, in *Communications and Economics,* ed. Robert E. Babe (Boston: Kluwer Publishers, 1994), 334.

77. Daniel Hallin, "The American News Media: A Critical Theory Perspective," in *Critical Theory and Public Life* (Cambridge, Mass.: Massachusetts Institute of Technology Press, 1985), 16.

78. Carey, *Communications and Economics,* 321–27.

79. "Media Report," *Hispanic Link Weekly Report,* 6 November 1995, 8.

80. "Media Report," *Hispanic Link Weekly Report,* 20 September 1993, 8.

81. Sally Lehrman, "Cutting Out the Heart and Soul of Newspapers," *Outlook* 8 (1996): 6.

82. Tony Marcano, "*City Times,* A Victim of the Bottom Line?" *Outlook* 8 (1996): 5–6.

83. Ibid.

84. Telephone interview with John Morton, head of Morton Research, Inc., and media analyst at Lynch, Jones and Ryan, Boca Raton, Florida, 17 May 1996.

85. Morton Research Inc., *Newspaper Segment Data* (Boca Raton, Florida), Table B, 1996.

86. Telephone interview with Sally Lehrman, 17 May 1996.

87. Morton Research Inc., *Newspaper Segment Data.*

88. Carter, "Latin Lessons," 39; and idem, "Media Report," in *Hispanic Weekly Report,* 15 June 1992, 6.

89. Virginia Escalante, "In Pursuit of Latino Audiences: The Media and Latinos," *Renato Rosaldo Lecture Series Monograph,* vol. 7, series 1989–90 (Tucson: Mexican American Studies and Research Center, University of Arizona, 1991): 32.

90. "Media Report," in *Hispanic Link Weekly Report,* 12 April 1993.

91. Escalante, "In Pursuit of Latino Audiences," 32.

92. Ron Chepesiuk, "Hitting Home, Cashing In: The Hispanic Press Finds Gold in Service to its Communities," *The Quill* (1993): 48.

93. Escalante, "In Pursuit of Latino Audiences," 29–53.

94. "Media Report," *Hispanic Link Weekly Report,* 6 May 1996, 8; and Marcano, "*City Times,*" 8–9.

95. Kathryn Jones, "Some New English-Language Magazines Are Aimed at Hispanic Readers Earning More Than $30,000," *The New York Times,* 20 November 1995, A1.

96. "Publishers Tap Latino Market," 1-1.

97. James S. Ettema and D. Charles Whitney, eds., *Audience Making: How the Media Create the Audience* (Thousand Oaks, Calif.: Sage, 1994), 5.

98. Carey, *Communications and Economics*, 324.

99. Ettema and Whitney, *Audience Making*, 5

100. Escalante, "In Pursuit of Latino Audiences," 31.

101. America Rodríguez, "Creating an Audience and Remapping a Nation: A Brief History of U.S. Spanish Language Broadcasting 1930–1980," *Quarterly Review of Film and Video* 16, no. 3–4 (July 1995): 1–23.

102. Ibid.

103. "Media Report," *Hispanic Link Weekly Report*, 13 December 1993, 12.

104. Joseph Wells, "The Hispanic Market's Leading Indicators," *Hispanic Business* 12 (1990): 32–34; and M. L. Stein, "Advertisers Still Ignoring Hispanic Media," *Editor & Publisher* 1 (1992): 20.

105. "Braniff Inc.'s Spanish Ad Bears Cause for Laughter," *The Wall Street Journal*, 9 February 1987, A5.

106. "Advertisers Learn Spanish the Hard Way," *Television and Radio Age* 35 (1988): A3.

107. Ivan Cintron, "Pepsi, Coke Pitch Thirsty Latinos: Mi Cola Es Su Cola," *Newsday*, 22 April 1991, 33.

108. Lowe, *Critical Terrains*, 29.

109. James C. Scott, *Domination and the Arts of Resistance: Hidden Transcripts* (New Haven: Yale University Press, 1990), 120.

110. Escalante, "In Pursuit of Latino Audiences," 41.

111. "Media Report," *Hispanic Link Weekly Report*, 28 October 1993, 6.

112. Margarita Contín, "130 Latino Organizations Launch Boycott of ABC-TV," *Hispanic Link Weekly Report*, 1 May 1995, 1.

113. Roberto Rodríguez and Patricia Gonzáles, "Television Brown Out Protests Further Whitening of Media," *Universal Press Syndicate*, 10 September 1999.

114. Edward Kemble and Helen Bretnor, *A History of California Newspapers 1846–1858* (Los Gatos, Calif.: The Talisman Press, 1962), 234–35.

115. Félix Gutiérrez, "Spanish-Language Media in America: Background, Resources, History," *Journalism History*, 4 (1977): 38–39.

116. Hallin, "The American News Media."

117. Gutiérrez, "Spanish-Language Media," 41.

118. Porter A. Stratton, *The Territorial Press of New Mexico* (Albuquerque: University of New Mexico Press, 1969), 106.

119. Robert Park, *The Immigrant Press and Its Control* (New York: Harper & Brothers Publishers, 1992), 317.

120. Gutiérrez, "Spanish-Language Media."

121. Armando Rendón, *The Chicano Press: A Status Report on the Needs and Trends in Chicano Journalism* (Washington D.C.: The Chicano Press Association, 1974), 3, 49.

122. Ibid., 49.

123. Phyllis Kaniss, *Making Local News* (Chicago: The University of Chicago Press, 1991), 1–4.

124. America Rodríguez, "Made in the USA: The Construction of Univisión News" (PH.D. dissertation, University of California, San Diego, 1993).

125. Ibid., 6.

126. Ibid., 4–10.

127. Kaniss, *Making Local News,* 1–4.

128. Ibid., 4.

Chicana/o and Latina/o Gazing: Audiences of the Mass Media

DIANA I. RÍOS

*T*he eighties and nineties have been an era of inconsistent recognition of Latinas/os[1] as a general population group within many realms, including communication studies. The eighties were allegedly the "decade of the Hispanic,"[2] yet, as that decade has come and gone and as the nineties are nearly over, Latinas/os have not achieved a more equitable sociopolitical status in our society. Hollywood did not usher forth substantially more Latina/o television and movie characters, personalities, or themes in the late eighties, contrary to the trends critics and producers had predicted after the commercial successes of the movies *La Bamba* (1987) and *Stand and Deliver* (1988). In communication studies, Latina/o issues were largely overlooked in theories on the audience, whether spectator or reader. If professional communication caucuses and conference panels can be used as one gauge of Chicanas/os coming of age in the field of communication, then it is clear that minority involvement and Chicana/o issues are still relatively new. Recent evidence that minorities are beginning to be addressed in communication issues includes the Minorities and Communication division of the nationally recognized Association for Education in Journalism and Mass Communication, La Raza Caucus of the National Communication Association, and panels consisting of women of color at the international meetings of "Consoling Passions: Television, Video and Feminism."

Theories on the audience within mass communication research and cultural studies have indeed been developed during recent decades, however, Latinas/os in general and Chicanas/os (people of Mexican heritage born and living in the United States) in particular remain at the margins of this discourse. Theoretical development of the role of minority audiences in the field of communication is important to the Chicana/o community for practical and academic reasons. Practically speaking, Chicanas/os use a substantial amount of English and Spanish media forms, and theoreticians, public policy–makers dealing with the media, and marketers alike need to know more than ever how to better serve this rapidly growing consumer group. Ignoring or belatedly and inadequately addressing these issues will only delay fulfillment of minority needs for representation and further disappoint and anger the brown people who are currently being excluded.

I focus my concern on the paucity of theories in academia to describe the intricate relationship that Chicana/o audiences have with popular media forms. I will also call attention to the well-documented absence of Chicana/o representation in popular media such as television, cinema, and newspaper texts. Moreover, I ask: Is there an adequate model, theory, or framework to address the precarious connection that Chicanas/os have with mass media? Is there an approach that can adequately explain the attraction and pleasure that Chicanas/os may derive from popular media as well as explain the repulsion and dissatisfaction that they may experience with the same media? Currently, few theories can adequately explain the ties that Chicana/o audiences have had with media during the eighties and nineties— decades when Hispanic issues were supposed to be the focus of national deliberation and attention. I will present some building blocks and issues that describe the Chicana/o experience with communication messages. I hope that these building blocks will comprise part of the foundation for those working on more practical solutions to the problem of reaching the public, that is, at a grassroots level.

The path toward a framework that better explains Chicana/o links with media during the last two decades lies in the integration of three areas of research involving the audience experience with media: 1) Chicana/o audience exposure to analyze how much time is spent with different forms of media; 2) functional media use and gratification to determine what rewards viewers obtain from media exposure; and 3) feminist popular culture theories to determine the relationship that female audiences have with media. Audience exposure studies tell us *what* media Chicana/o audiences are using and for *how long* they use each form. Functional media studies use models to tell us *why* Chicanas/os are using certain media. Feminist popular culture theories on audiences attempt to avoid textual determination common in cultural studies and tell us what is unique about women's experiences with media. A careful look at the contributions and limitations of these three components is crucial to uncovering the "richness and contradictions"[3] of Chicana/o "gazing," or ways of engaging with mass media.

This essay will also discuss media content that continues to both impede and facilitate Chicana/o participation. Although the emphasis of this essay is on audience rather than content, the audience cannot be understood without consideration of text (see David Maciel and Susan Racho's chapter on media content). Four important aspects to consider when analyzing the connections between Chicana/o audiences and media are: 1) Chicana/o-Latina/o characters are usually absent in the mass media; 2) Chicana/o audiences often find media representation of their culture to be negative; 3) Chicana/o audiences might see reflections of themselves in positive or acceptable contexts, but may not recognize Chicana/o or Latina/o actors because members of La Raza come in many colors; and 4) Chicana/o audiences may be pleased to see themselves reflected in positive contexts but maintain a guarded stance because of decades of exclusion from media.

Overall, I believe that an understanding of the Chicana/o experience with mass media will strengthen the Chicana/o voice in theories that describe them and will subsequently have some practical impact on the media that serve them.

Chicana/o Audiences and Patterns of Mass Media Use

A variety of studies have been conducted on Chicana/o and Latina/o audiences because these populations have become identifiable in the public eye and therefore constitute viable topics for funded research. Media exposure research gives baseline data on how much time people are spending with media. Baseline research is primarily descriptive in nature and complements research conducted within a theoretical or interpretive framework. Especially since the 1970s, investigations on "Spanish-speaking," "Chicano," "Mexican American," "Hispanic," and "Latino" print and broadcast audiences have considered demographic characteristics, English- and Spanish-language media exposure patterns, attitudes and opinions about mainstream and ethnic media, and media utility. Although uneven in measurement, design, and sophistication, these descriptive studies have revealed some important results.[4]

A comparison of older with more recent baseline studies indicates some consistent media exposure patterns from Chicanas/os and Latinas/os across the country. López and Enos[5] studied Spanish-language television viewing habits, attitudes, and viewer characteristics in a cross section of Latina/o adults in Los Angeles County, California. Valenzuela[6] focused on the general media habits and preferences of Chicanas/os in selected southwestern cities. Guernica[7] provided specific information on ethnic and mainstream media and consumer products, giving insights into how to better serve various Hispanic markets. Yankelovich, Skelly, and White[8] focused on demographic aspects of the Spanish-speaking market in relation to social values, outlooks, and consumer orientations. Veciana-Suárez[9] provided overviews of the media outlets that cater to various Latina/o population markets. Greenberg, Burgoon, Burgoon, and Korzenny[10] provided the most comprehensive study on Mexican Americans and mass media in the Southwest. The data collection and analysis for this project were conducted in the late seventies and early eighties, which certainly dates the research. However, such documentation is still valuable for summarizing Chicana/o behavior, attitudes, and opinions regarding media usage. Currently no other published research can rival this landmark study.

Some generalizations can be made from these and other descriptive studies. Overall, Chicana/o media users tend to favor broadcast media such as radio and television over print media such as newspapers and magazines. Researchers, advertisers, and newspaper and magazine publishers have speculated as to why broadcast media may be favored over print media in Spanish-speaking communities. One reason is that the various forms of broadcast media are more easily available and easier and more flexible to use than print media. So, one can be doing multiple things at home, work, or recreation while using broadcast media. Use of print media requires more reading skills (in both English and Spanish) and monopolizes an individual's time. One cannot as easily engage in multiple tasks while concentrating on reading the newspaper. Chicanas/os also favor broadcast over print media because of a dearth of culturally relevant print media from which to choose. Recently, in response to demand, new Spanish-language magazines for women and men have appeared in cities with high concentrations of Latinas/os. Spanish-language imports from Spain, Mexico, or other parts of Latin America do not cater to the full spectrum of U.S.–born Chicanas/os who may want to read bilingual articles or see news topics relevant to their communities covered. Complicating the common Chicana/o audience profiles further, broadcast media are more often used by lower socioeconomic classes and print media are more often used by those in higher class positions. This finding mirrors national U.S. trends in broadcast and print media use, whereby print media use tends to positively correspond with education and income.

The media language of choice may be determined by a number of variables. Language preference may be determined by generational proximity to a Spanish-speaking country, whereby earlier generations in the United States favor the Spanish-language media and later generations shift toward bilingual media use or move completely to English-language media use. Media language of choice may also be determined by socioeconomic class as defined by education and occupation, whereby Spanish-language media are more often used by lower socioeconomic classes and English-language media are more often used by those in higher class positions. Of course there are exceptions to these trends. For example, a well-traveled Latina/o immigrant with a college degree who feels more comfortable with Spanish-language media and a second-generation U.S.–born Chicana/o dentist who minored in Spanish-language Chicana/o literature might favor Spanish-language media. However, most immigrants from Latin America and most early-generation Chicanas/os in the United States have less formal education than the average Anglo American, are workers of poor to middle-class status, and are Spanish-language dominant.

The exposure patterns described above have proved to be somewhat enigmatic to ethnic and mainstream media professionals trying to reach the wide spectrum of Chicana/o and other Latina/o groups, from those who have been culturally assimilated to those recent immigrants from Mexico who live in cities closer to the U.S.–Mexican border. In addition, pockets of regionally distinct Spanish-speaking subgroups (such as those in Kansas City and Chicago) are not an uncommon phenomenon in the United States and pose a theoretical and practical research challenge. If public-policy makers or health campaign planners are trying to identify ideal strategies to inform communities about voter registration, population enumeration, or better health practices, they will need to understand the unique characteristics of these communities in order to reach them in an effective and respectful manner.

More theoretically rigorous media studies on Chicanas/os and Latinas/os have been conducted recently. These studies get closer to the cultural processes involved in the audience-media dynamic. Results indicate that Chicanas/os and Latinas/os have particular sociocultural connections with mass media during exposure. Subervi-Vélez's[11] "dual media function" research examined ethnic and mainstream media use and the assimilationist and pluralistic effects across groups of Cubans, Mexican Americans, and Puerto Ricans in the Midwest. He found that media impact varies by type of medium, language of medium, and Latina/o group. His results support the idea of differential cultural impact and heterogeneity among Latina/o communities.

A study by Ríos and two studies by Ríos and Gaines examined mainstream and ethnic media exposure and functions among people of Mexican and Spanish heritage[12] in Texas and New Mexico, using Ríos's Chicana/o "media uses and gratifications" model. Generally, this model explains that people use media to "get something out of it" (gratifications). All three studies integrate the concept of "audience activity," which asserts that viewers, listeners, and readers use sociocultural tools to negotiate media impact. This position contrasts with the defunct assumption that media has all-powerful effects on audiences. These studies also address how audiences use English- and Spanish-language media for two cultural goals, cultural maintenance and cultural and structural assimilation. Ríos[13] identifies three audience subgroups with distinct cultural orientations and distinct ways of utilizing mass media for cultural goals. The value of this study of uses and gratifications is at least twofold. First, this model is the only culture-specific model currently under development for Chicana/o and Latina/o audiences in the United States. Practically speaking, the information gleaned from this type of research gives media planners a more complete understanding of the cultural needs of Chicana/o communities. This research is quite revealing about the role of Chicana/o audience ethnicity and culture in media use; however, Ríos does not examine the role of gender in the media use process as do the subsequent two studies.

Of particular interest are the Ríos and Gaines analyses of audience data from Texas and New Mexico. Ríos and Gaines[14] tested the assumption that women play the key role of cultural mainstay in Chicana/o communities. The authors expected a clear "Chicana advantage" in the degree to which female audiences would be able to exploit English- and Spanish-language media for cultural maintenance. However, the gender of Chicana/o audiences and the degree to which they found mainstream and ethnic-oriented media useful presented a more complex picture in the gender-media utility dynamic than expected. Women and men held different kinds of advantages, based on language and media type, with regard to cultural maintenance.

Overall, women did not necessarily have the upper hand by scoring higher in cultural maintenance with mass media; they favored different media than men did for cultural maintenance purposes. Among other findings, the Chicana realm tended to be oriented more toward television and Spanish-language media, and the Chicano realm tended to be oriented more toward newspaper and English-language media. The replication research by Ríos and Gaines[15] also indicates that women and men hold different kinds of advantages in using mainstream and ethnic media for cultural maintenance. The significance of these studies is that the Chicana/o audience–mass media relationship must be understood in conjunction with ethnicity, culture, and gender. These main characteristics in combination are important when trying to comprehend what contemporary women and men are getting out of media. To reach a specific gender group for public service, educational, and entertainment programming, media professionals need to recognize the pattern of heterogeneity across Latina/o groups.

Research on Fans, Spectators, and Readers, or, This Popcorn Is Good but It Needs Chile

Starting in the eighties a variety of feminist projects on women and media have blossomed. Audiences are referred to as "fans," "spectators," or "readers," depending on the research. Some look at the text (i.e., the television program itself, the movie, etc.) and the audience (the actual people who are watching), others look at the text only and an implied audience (the researcher's informed construction about people who watch), and still others focus mostly on the audience. Among the many important qualities of these projects is the fact that women's gender identity is not subsumed beneath a generic masculine audience norm. The gender quality of implied and real audiences has been acknowledged in women's encounters with media. For the projects that deal with real women, the idea of "audience selectivity" with media versus "audience gullibility" is also a key theoretical constituent. One daunting problem among the feminist media projects, however, is the fact that ethnicity and race issues are still rarely addressed.[16] The scarcity of discourse on race and ethnicity permits behaviors of major portions of the U.S. multicultural audience to remain unexplained. Also, Chicana/o media projects focusing on Chicana/o gender issues (the "chile on the popcorn") are requisite as we enter the twenty-first century, because girls, boys, women, and men deserve more relevant and culturally sensitive programming.

Radway[17] and Bobo[18] have conducted notable projects on real women who use popular media. These projects have some limitations, but other scholars can use these studies to supplement their own research on Chicana/o audiences. Radway used textual analysis of romance fiction and interviews with fans of this genre to explain why women read romance novels and what they are getting out of them. Bobo analyzed data relating to textual subjects (black women audiences implied by the film) and the oppositional stance of social subjects (real black women audiences) with regard to the controversial film *The Color Purple* (1985). She also considered black men's reactions to the movie.

Among her results, Radway found that midwestern Anglo women from "Smithton" were selective in their genre reading. One aspect of selectivity was avoidance of "bad novels" that contained violent or oppressive behavior by male characters. On the other hand, women were drawn to pieces that uplifted sensitive, intelligent, and strong female protagonists and promised a loving mate. Furthermore, Smithton women negotiated patriarchal thematic structures from romance novels and used reading activity to protect personal time. Overall, Radway seems to see romance novels as a double-edged sword for fans because they can use reading as a feminist tool, but they seem to keep within safe fictional and real-life boundaries that do not endanger patriarchy.

A limitation of Radway's research is that she does not address the issues of ethnicity or race. A Chicana researcher is compelled to ask, "What role does Anglo ethnicity or whiteness play with regard to gender in the practices held by the Smithton women? And, how would an Anglo woman's choice and interpretation of reading materials be different from that of a Chicana? Ethnicity certainly has a great deal to bear on the interpretation of romance novels, which are written for mainstream Anglo American women. Ethnicity in reader-response projects has not been well addressed for various reasons. First, audience-response research is still developing, and relatively few projects exist. Second, I speculate that Anglo feminist scholars may not yet know how to ask critical questions about the majority white culture to which they belong. Third, Anglo feminist scholars might feel that, by addressing ethnicity, they are intruding upon women of color's research agendas.

When reading romance novels, the Chicana reader must negotiate meaning through her experiences as a woman of color and as a member of a proud yet disenfranchised culture in the context of the United States. For the novels to make sense to her and for her to retain a sense of dignity, she would need to re-make the novel using her Chicana sociocultural tools of understanding. She could also understand these novels from a careful distance, maybe only partially identifying herself with transcendent womanly aspects of the main female character. A possible deleterious outcome for the Chicana would be that she would find herself lacking European American values or traits when attempting to identify with the female characters. Consciously or unconsciously, a Chicana could find the difference between herself and European American characters to be disconcerting, thus causing her to consider her *chicanidad* (Chicana-ness) to be backward and her olive complexion to be ugly.

Bobo's research in the black community regarding differential reception of the film *The Color Purple* is a small landmark study of ethnic minority audiences, gender, and media reception. This study has implications for other people of color such as Chicanas/os and for the gender differences that exist in the interpretation of media. Bobo's project was spurred by the debate among women and men in the community. Bobo states, "The film . . . has incited a face-off between [b]lack feminist critics and [b]lack male reviewers."[19] Bobo describes that, on one hand, black men perceived that the film, packaged for the mainstream audience and directed by a white male (Stephen Spielberg), launched racist attacks on black men and on the black community. On the other hand, many black women found their voice in the experiences of the main character, Ciele, and the other black female characters. Black women viewers were taken by Ciele's eventual triumph after much suffering and heartache. Women in the community were "decoding" the film in a much different manner than their brothers, based on their feminine histories and experiences.

Bobo asserts that women of color (here, black women) and other marginalized groups reject popular media and thereby hold an oppositional stance when engaging with mainstream popular culture. "Out of habit, as readers of mainstream texts, we have learned to ferret out the beneficial and put up blinders against the rest."[20] Overall, armed with highly sophisticated reception skills honed by decades of gender and racial oppression, black women were able to find something useful that spoke to them in a mainstream Hollywood film. Bobo's observations can certainly be extended to the gender reception modes in the Chicana/o community. Chicanas, for example may find particular kinds of media and content more useful for their needs than would Chicano males.

Fregoso[21] presents a compelling selection of essays on Chicana/o film, with excellent insights on several film texts and the implied Chicana/o audience. In one essay on gendered subjectivity, the author discusses how Chicanas and Latinas have been portrayed as central narrative subjects in a few productions. For example, a rebellious teenage Chicana plays a central role in the public television production of *The Pastorela: A Shepherd's Play* (1991). In this made-for-television movie, the young Chicana may be the main character, but she is not the speaking subject.[22] In the end, her rebellion is placed in check, within the limits of Chicano-defined familial order. In short, the film does speak to Chicana audiences, but in a way that potentially stifles independence and mature feminine self-realization. Furthermore, Fregoso discusses "tactical subjectivity" as a U.S. action exercised through films such as *Después del terremoto* (1979). She describes how some films offer the Chicana audience an opportunity for "tactical positioning," which is a slippery and astute type of spectator gazing. The phenomenon of tactical positioning can also be understood as clever and critical ways of engagement. Fregoso's analysis of the Chicana spectator is mainly determined by the content of the film text, but it is still an important contribution to a framework that explains Chicana/o viewing in relation to Chicana/o and Latina/o productions. An important point that I derive from Fregoso regarding media productions is that even though a production may be ethnic group–specific, this quality does not guarantee that all segments of that ethnic group will be satisfied or uplifted upon viewing the production.

Press's[23] ethnographic study of mostly Anglo women sheds light on the ways in which women of younger and older generations and of the working and middle classes actively receive prime-time television. In contrast, the pilot qualitative reception study by Ríos[24] and colleagues of the Mexican film *Like Water for Chocolate* explains some ways in which younger- and older-generation Chicana/Latina women receive an international Mexican film. Through individual interviews with women in various parts of the United States, Press has found that women who came of age in the 1950s tend to identify less with television characters than do women who came of age in later decades. Television socialization is less evident in women of older generations than in women of younger generations. Also, some middle-class women tend to be more skeptical than working-class women about television realism. Although Press's research does not deal with ethnicity across her Anglo respondents (with the exception of one Chicana), her work has led the way for audience response studies on women of color, such as the pilot study undertaken by Ríos.

Ríos conducts audience-response research using the film *Like Water for Chocolate,* which is the first project of its kind to study U.S. Chicana/Latina audiences. In the context of the film's critical and commercial success in the United States (it was the highest grossing international film in Hollywood history), a key goal in this project was to document the cross-cultural reception of a Mexican-made film among U.S. Chicanas/Latinas. These women's viewing lenses have been tempered by different experiences with Anglo American culture and by Chicana/o and Latina/o group values and customs. The research questions asked: What makes this foreign film successful with U.S. Chicanas/Latinas? What ingredients within the film are hailing them? What ingredients are they rejecting? Preliminary results have shown that the generation level in the United States and the age of the respondents may explain different reactions to the film among the women. Middle-aged women tended to have more compassion and understanding for the female characters and whether they were following or rejecting Mexican cultural traditions. Their life experiences with marriage, divorce, child-rearing, and work gave them a more mature lens with which to view the film. Younger women, in their late teens and early twenties, tended to voice cultural connections as well but did not have the same compassion for the characters, such as the matriarch of the film, Mamá Elena, or the sister, Rosaura. Older women particularly regarded the ending, where Tita and Pedro consummate their love, die, and go into the next life, to be "stupid" because they felt that Tita was not adequately rewarded for her generosity and suffering. Younger women tended to see the ending as a sweet, romantic "fairy tale ending," where Tita and Pedro would live happily ever after in the next life. Most Chicana/Latina women from all generations seemed to think that the film spoke to them in a special way because of their cultural background and their gender, but added that the film also offered something to women of other cultural backgrounds in the United States and abroad. Most Chicanas in the study were impressed by the excellent quality of the film and the fact that finally a film had been made that depicted women of a cultural background similar to their own.

More of these projects are urgently needed to enable further development of a Chicana/o framework of media reception. Theoretically, communication research must clarify the specific Chicana/Latina audience experience. Perhaps producers, directors, and writers would then be better informed about the cultural and gender identification needs of Chicanas/os and Latinas/os who are watching domestic and Latin American–made films. Overall, my rough analytical framework should allow a more refined insight into Chicana/o audience reception, at least during the past two decades, and into how Chicanas/os are likely to use future forms of mainstream, ethnic, and internationally imported mass media.

Intervening Factors for Chicana/o Audiences

In addition to research that can be used to build a framework toward Chicana/o audience studies, several intervening content variables in Chicana/o media use have appeared during the eighties and nineties. Chicanas/os have developed a particular way of selectively perceiving mass media. The Chicana/o audience perspective, or gaze, is necessarily accommodating, conflicting, contradictory, discriminating, traditional, new age, survivalist, vulnerable, protective, suspicious, impatient, accepting, and rejecting. This perspective is unique because it is culture- and ethnic group–specific. Personal, social, and regional histories guide Chicana/o audiences in sifting through a barrage of film, print, and audio images and messages. Specific characters and themes that Chicanas/os have grown to expect in popular texts have also been part of audiences' relational development. Although audiences are pleased to see themselves reflected in positive contexts, they may be slow to accept the message because of decades of receiving no gratification from media.

As previously mentioned, there are four important aspects or interventions to consider when analyzing the effects of media on Chicana/o audiences. The first two interventions I will address are 1) Chicana/o and Latina/o characters are usually absent in the mass media; and 2) when they are represented, the representation is often negative. Scholars have documented the lack of representation and type of representation of Chicanas/os and other ethnic minorities[25] and women[26] portrayed on television, in cinema, and in broadcast and print news (also see Virginia Escalante's chapter for a discussion on print media). The lack of representation in the media text probably has a negative impact on the self-esteem of ethnic minority peoples because they have been essentially declared nonexistent. Exclusion from screen and print may tell a people that they are not important, not worthy, not beautiful, not brave, and not talented enough to be portrayed.

During the last two decades, Chicana/o and Latina/o representation has been embarrassingly sparse. Their presence on television and in cinema has not been in proportion to national demographics. In the same vein, when representation occurs, it is often unfavorable. Although some mainstream city newspapers have attempted to improve their news content by hiring minority journalists, featuring community news sections in the main sections of the newspaper, and using Chicana/o and Latina/o bimonthly inserts such as *Vista*, Chicana/o and Latina/o regular and casual readers still complain that the media form does not represent them (see field research by Ríos[27]). Grassroots Chicana/o and Latina/o papers such as *La Prensa* of San Antonio and Austin, Texas, *El Hispano* of Albuquerque, New Mexico, and *El Extra News* of Hartford, Connecticut, fulfill important cultural needs in these communities by focusing on the Raza community, but they do not have the circulation or the print space to compete with a big city newspaper.

Researchers of audience trends, such as Bobo and Ríos, have discussed the potential for people of color to contest and subvert media content for their own ends. Research by these scholars indicates that people of color, because of absence and poor representation in the media, have developed highly sophisticated spectator tools that allow them to extract or "ferret out" those ideas that they find acceptable or useful. Those ideas which are not useful to the spectator as determined by gender, ethnicity, and other individual differences may be discarded or revised. The negation potential for Chicanas/os may be considered by some to be overly optimistic, given the lack of media attention. Obviously, the media in the United States *do not* adequately serve Chicana/o and Latina/o communities. However, the "magic bullet theory" (that messages go magically into one's head to influence one instantly) of media has long been defunct in mass communication research, and a multifaceted perspective of Chicana/o audiences is a more reasonable way to describe why Chicanas/os continue to use mainstream and ethnic-oriented media that may not adequately fulfill their needs. An example of how a multifaceted perspective can work for Chicana/o audiences using mainstream media is seen in the case of two prime-time television hits, *Dallas* and *Miami Vice*.

During the 1980s the television show *Dallas* featured no starring Chicana/o actors but did show Chicana/o maids, nannies, and butlers. This show was popular with people across the United States, and certainly many Chicana/o families watched this serial religiously every week (as did my family and extended family in California). How can the popularity of this program with Chicanas/os be explained except through the process of selectivity? I recall watching the Chicana nanny caring for the Ewing heir, John Ross; a cook announcing a meal; or a tall, dark Chicano butler telling one of the Mrs. Ewings that her car was ready. We met these menial representations with guffaws and criticism about why Hollywood could do no better with such a successful show set in Texas, where so many people of Mexican heritage lived. We speculated that some of the brown help would have the last laugh after they saved their money from serving the Ewings and finished advanced college degrees. After we had subverted the text and confirmed our opinions to one another, we would quiet down quickly so as not to miss the dialogue. We rejected Chicana/o stereotypes from the episodes, and we sought other acceptable qualities from the show's characters in order for the show about rich Anglo *patrones* to be palatable. We admired Miss Ellie's strength and her compassion toward her family, Pam's endurance, and Bobby's honesty.

Another top-rated 1980s show that I watched with other Chicanas/os was the highly stylized *Miami Vice*. Each week the program showed detectives from the Miami police department outwitting slick Central and South American drug lords. The stereotyping of Latinas/os was tiresome, and we, like other Chicana/o and Latina/o audiences, probably took solace periodically by focusing on the few Latina/o good guys.

The third intervention is that Chicana/o audiences might see reflections of themselves in positive or acceptable contexts, but may not recognize Chicana/o or Latina/o actors because members of La Raza come in many colors and play various roles. The problem that audiences have with recognizing Chicana/o and Latinas/os makes gratifications derived from media more difficult. For example, in the prime time 1980s hit, *Falcon Crest,* Lorenzo Lamas, son of classic Hollywood's Fernando Lamas (a Latino), plays a very assimilated Italian American named Lance Cumson, who is part of a wine-making family in northern California. Ana Alicia, also of Latina heritage, plays Lance's Italian American wife in the early part of the series. César Romero, a Latino who made his mark during the Golden Age of cinema, makes several guest appearances as a long-lost Italian love interest of the wine family's matriarch. In other 1980s programs, actress Saundra Santiago plays an ambiguous, sometimes Italian, sometimes Latina, detective in the show *Miami Vice.* In a more recent syndicated television series, still on the air in the late 1990s, Lorenzo Lamas plays a former police officer named Reno in *Renegade.* The renegade cop's ethnicity has not been a point of dialogue nor has it been incorporated into the story line, although the audience is led to believe that he is of Anglo descent. Also, closet Latina actress Daphne Zuniga of the scandalous television serial *Melrose Place,* a top show during 1995, plays a mainstream Anglo character.

The difficulty that Chicana/o audiences have in finding bronze people on screen is itself a negative intervention. Chicana/o uses and gratifications research has indicated that audiences can use mainstream media for cultural maintenance goals but that this task could be made easier if actors could extend themselves to Raza viewers. If writers and directors would avoid stereotyping actors of Latina/o heritage and allow them opportunities to play well-rounded Chicana/o and Latina/o characters, then Chicana/o audiences could more easily identify Chicanas/os in the media. Furthermore, Chicana/o and Latina/o actors who prefer to hide their heritage contribute to the problem of absence in the media. Although ethnic identification of characters may not seem so important to directors or to some actors, ethnicity muddling is at minimum counterproductive to reversing the racist reputation that Hollywood has built for itself.

The fourth intervention states that when Chicana/o audiences do find themselves represented in positive or acceptable contexts, they may be pleased and relieved. However, after decades of mediated cultural dissonance, Chicanas/os cannot help but maintain a guarded stance toward the characters and the stories in which the characters appear. One example of positive Chicana/o characters on television is Edward James Olmos's powerful lieutenant on *Miami Vice.* This character provided a much-needed positive balance to the droves of Latino crooks that appeared weekly. Jimmy Smits won accolades for his role as a Chicano attorney on Emmy award–winning *L.A. Law.* For several seasons, Jimmy Smits played the strong Latino detective, Simone, on *NYPD Blue.* For a number of seasons, Roxanna Biggs-Dawson, a Puerto Rican, played a forthright B' Elanna Torres in *Star Trek: Voyager.* B' Elanna's character is a half-Latina, half-Klingon character on the multicultural Federation starship team. This character has been dimensionally filled out and developed and is frequently featured on the program. I see this character as part of U.S. Latina television history because she is positive, intelligent, and among the very few Latinas on mainstream television. Hector Elizondo as Dr. Phillip Watters in *Chicago Hope* slowly revealed his Latino identity during the 1994–95 season as his Spanish-language skills and cultural knowledge were called upon to assist patients. These images have been well received among Chicana/o television-viewing audiences, but as a result of the more abundant negative stereotypes of Spanish-speaking people in popular media, audiences certainly wait for the positive image to ultimately become flawed or for the program to be canceled. This is not a pessimistic perspective on behalf of audiences but rather a guarded perspective that permits minority audiences to conditionally enjoy and more effectively negotiate with media.

A Chicana/o Audience Framework for the Contemporary Era

The purpose of this section is to present composite audience profiles based on the research components needed for a relevant audience framework. Audience exposure, Chicana/o media uses and gratifications, feminist popular culture theory on audiences, and finally media-content interventions will be illustrated. These areas of research plus media-based interventions should be considerations in the study of audience-media experience.

Audience exposure studies are among the most common media studies in the arena of communication research because marketers as well as academics want to know who is watching what and for how long. For example, here is a profile of a southwestern Mexicana named "Ramona,"[28] who was born in the United States and raised in predominantly Spanish-speaking communities. She is a working-class senior citizen and prefers Spanish for interpersonal communication. She also prefers Spanish broadcast media such as radio and television. One reason for her broadcast preference is that her literacy skills are poor. She is fortunate to be residing in one of the most concentrated areas of Mexican population in the country, and so Spanish-language media are readily available. She spends time listening to Radio Bilingüe for several hours each day. In the evening, she watches Spanish television for a few hours. She watches the *noticias* (news) from the local television stations and then watches one *novela* (soap opera), if it's a good new one or a very good repeat.

Here is a baseline profile of a southwestern woman named Elena. Elena is a Chicana, born in Mexico and raised in the United States. She is middle-aged and middle class and communicates and reads in both English and Spanish. She does not spend a tremendous amount of time using mass media, but the ten to fifteen hours per week that she does spend with media are preferably with Spanish-language broadcasts such as television (*telenovelas* on Telemundo and Univisión such as *Marimar, Dos mujeres un camino,* and

María la del barrio and talk shows such as *Cristina*) and Latina/o music on the radio.

Here is a baseline description of a "Generation X" Chicana, "Miriam," in her early twenties. Miriam's family has been in the United States for several generations. She has some relatives in Mexico, but does not know them well. She speaks English and Spanish, but feels much more comfortable using English. She comes from a mixed working- and professional-class family background. She has a college degree. She listens to top ten radio and some Chicana/o stations for many hours during her workday at a computer chip—manufacturing company, but she prefers listening to music from her compact disc collection when she is at home. Her personal collection contains rock, soul, Tejana/o, and Latina/o music. Her favorite television programs include the *X-Files, Rosie O'Donnell,* and *Xena: Warrior Princess.* She does not have much time to watch a lot of television, but she loves to relax in the evenings and weekends with certain shows. Her favorite media are television and recorded music.

These simple descriptions give us a basic understanding of the Chicana/o audience. Although media exposure research can tell us how long people are spending with a certain kind of medium, it cannot address *why* people may be using various kinds of media or repeating their particular kind of media use. The next conceptual level in understanding the Chicana/o audience is to determine whether the audience is "active." The idea of audience activity for Chicanas/os means that they seek out media for social and cultural needs.

To what degree do certain media fulfill or fail to fulfill sociocultural goals of active Chicana audiences? Chicana/o media uses and gratifications research reveals to what degree media are most useful for personal intentions. For example, Ramona has practical motivations, based on social class and education, for using broadcast media, in addition to cultural motivations for media preference. Broadcast media allow Ramona to move around freely, answer telephone calls, and cater to friends and family. Ramona spends time with Radio Bilingüe because she enjoys the *ranchera* music format and the local Mexicano style that the announcers use when they speak directly to the audience over the airwaves and when they speak to each other. This radio station reflects her background and is culturally fulfilling. No English-language radio station could compete. In the evening, she watches Spanish-language television for a few hours. She watches the noticias from the local television stations, and then she watches one novela, if it's a good new one or a very good repeat. She wants to see news from Mexico because she still has family there. She also wants news about the local Mexican American community. Economic and immigration news is especially important to her because these issues have direct impact on her friends and relatives living nearby. Will economic conditions have a negative impact on finding a job and paying the rent? Is the *migra* (Immigration and Naturalization Service) cracking down again on people who look like they do not have proper documents? The mainstream network news will not give her the specific information she needs regarding the issues facing her community. Her choice of novela depends on whether it is about *la vida real* (real life). She does not like the weird, fantastic tales that come up periodically. U.S. English-language soap operas, which she has watched, are only superficially fulfilling compared with the novelas.

Elena's professional job has her working all day in an Anglo-dominated environment; she prefers Spanish-language media at home to relax and recharge her batteries, so to speak. Spanish-language media also offer her a connection to her culture. Imported telenovelas and domestic and international music in Spanish help Elena maintain her culture and her identity as a woman of Mexican heritage. By using these media, she affirms her connections to Mexico and her membership in the U.S. Chicana/o community. Another point about Elena and other Chicana audience members is that they do not simply absorb whatever is in front of them, be it a magazine, newspaper, movie, or television program. Chicanas/os are discerning audiences who consciously and subconsciously have goals in mind when selecting Spanish- or English-mediated communication. These fuller profiles show how media works for active Chicana audiences; however, additional depth is still needed. For example, what role does gender play in the manner in which a Chicana uses media?

Feminist theories on popular culture help complete these Chicana profiles. Ramona, Elena, and Miriam use television, which for the last few decades has been considered by advertisers and academics to be a woman's medium. For example, Ramona enjoys certain novelas because she feels that they allow her to reflect on past interpersonal relations and that they allow her to learn about younger Mexicana/o and Chicana/o generations. For example, when a rotten stepmother appears in a novela series, she remembers the pain that her own stepmother inflicted upon her when she was growing up. Out of respect, she had to tolerate and obey her stepmother. Out of respect and a strong sense of values, she helped raise her younger siblings. Her personal experiences and recollections as a girl and as a young woman give her a basis for connection to certain female characters in the novelas. The novelas remind her never to repeat certain oppressive behaviors with her young female relatives. As a senior citizen without much contact with young folks, the contemporary issues about careers, love, marriage, adultery, divorce, and betrayal are educational for Ramona. The novelas provide her with information about family struggles over love, relationships, and social-class power. She is sometimes reminded of the struggles she has had in her personal life as well as those of Spanish-speaking women and women of other ethnic groups whom she has known. At other times, she is simply entertained by the antics of supporting characters and the outrageous twists of the story. She may wonder, "How could someone be that wicked?!"

Elena's gaze is not one that is whole-heartedly accepting of everything depicted in a novela. Her gaze is selective. She is sometimes critical of Mexico's class structure and the novelas' persistent portrayals of a highly Europeanized, successful Mexican elite and the noble poor. Sometimes she is simply taken by the rich and luxurious lifestyles of the families depicted, wishing that she could someday have some of the same luxuries. She hates it when an obviously bright woman accepts patriarchy by giving in to a *pendejo* (idiot) male character who repeats his mistakes. She may exclaim, on behalf of the main female character, to the television set itself and to her friends gathered around the television, "Forget that dork!"

Miriam is very proud of her heritage and sticks up for her community when she feels challenged at work by coworkers who believe stereotypes about her people. She has a strong Chicana identity. Her choice of music reflects her multicultural experiences in the United States and abroad. She is highly aware that her life is much different from her female relatives from generations past. She has had many more opportunities in education and profession. She does not have Chicana programs to watch that present images of women like herself, so she adapts to the English-language shows. She picks out those things that she as a Chicana can use and identify with to some degree. For example, the female character Scully is a medical doctor on the *X-Files*. Miriam can identify with the issues of being a professional woman in the sciences and also with the personal struggles of being an intelligent woman with a degree in an Anglo male–dominated environment. She likes Scully and believes that no one can pull one over on her. The Xena character, although in a cheesy show, is a tough woman who does not wait to be rescued by a man. Xena can "kick major butt" on her show. Xena is a compassionate leader, much like Miriam sees herself.

Final Remarks

This essay has been ambitious in suggesting theoretical remedies for gaps in communication studies pertaining to Chicana/o and Latina/o audiences. Practical solutions were also discussed. Components for a contemporary Chicana/o audience framework consist of audience exposure studies, Chicana/o uses and gratifications research, and a feminist popular culture theory on audience. Exposure studies are the most easily obtainable for academic researchers and media professionals who want to know basic media behavior patterns in Chicana/o communities. Uses and gratifications research, based on the Ríos model for Chicana/o populations, reveals what women and men are obtaining from media and some motivations behind media selection. Media-related intervening variables were also discussed. So, when we look at what media Chicanas/os are using and why they are using them in conjunction with "media-based gaze interventions," a complex portrait appears for our consideration. As we enter the twenty-first century and as great strides are taken by professionals to improve media service to Chicanas/os, the relationship that Chicanas/os have with media may improve. However, given the current state of social politics and the reactionary backlash against immigrants and ethnic Americans, I cannot realistically envision radically improved multicultural television, film, and print media appearing nationwide. I can realistically see only that subversive and guarded qualities of the Chicana/o gaze would intensify if media remain unresponsive to the issues raised in this chapter.

Notes

1. The masculine gender is indicated by the "o" in terms such as "Chicano" or "Latino." Unfortunately, the feminine gender is obfuscated in this so-called "gender-neutral" practice. In this essay I use the suffix "a/o" for the purpose of gender equity.
2. "Hispanic" is a term imposed by the U.S. Census Bureau. I prefer to use the term

"Latina/o" when I refer to Spanish-speaking groups of various origins. For a discussion of ethnic identifiers, see Gerardo Marín and Barbara V. Marín, *Research with Hispanic Populations* (Newbury Park: Sage, 1991).

3. This phrase belongs to Jacqui Roach and Petal Felix, "Black Looks," in *The Female Gaze: Women as Viewers of Popular Culture,* eds. Lorraine Gamman and Margaret Marshment (Seattle: Real Comet Press, 1989).

4. No individual study holds the ultimate truth about Chicana/o-Latina/o audiences. Although some results from one study to the next may in fact be contradictory, results from many studies examined as a whole allow a sensible understanding about Chicana/o audiences and their media consumption. This paper discusses selected works.

5. R. W. López and D. D. Enos, "Spanish-Language–Only Television in Los Angeles County," *Aztlán* (1974): 283–313.

6. Nicolas A. Valenzuela, *Media Habits and Attitudes: Surveys in Austin and San Antonio* (Austin: University of Texas Center for Communication Research, 1973).

7. Antonio Guernica, *Reaching the Hispanic Market Effectively: The Media, the Market, the Methods* (New York: McGraw-Hill, 1982).

8. Yankelovich, Skelly, and White, Inc., *Spanish USA: A Study of the Hispanic Market* (New York: Yankelovich, Skelly, and White, 1984).

9. Ana Veciana-Suárez, *Hispanic Media: Impact and Influence* (Washington, D.C.: Media Institute, 1990).

10. Bradley Greenberg, Michael Burgoon, Judee Burgoon, and Felipe Korzenny, *Mexican Americans and Mass Media* (Norwood, N.J.: Ablex, 1986).

11. Federico A. Subervi-Vélez, "Hispanics, the Mass Media, and Politics: Assimilation versus Pluralism" (doctoral dissertation, University of Wisconsin, Madison, 1984).

12. In Texas, respondents identified themselves as being of Mexican heritage to participate in the research. In New Mexico, where the politics of ethnic identity differ, respondents identified themselves as either of Mexican or Spanish heritage in order to participate. For the sake of facility in this essay, all respondents will be called Chicanas/os.

13. Diana I. Ríos, "Mexican American Audiences: A Qualitative and Quantitative Study of Ethnic Subgroup Uses for Mass Media" (doctoral dissertation, University of Texas at Austin, 1993).

14. Diana I. Ríos and Stanley O. Gaines, Jr., "Impact of Gender and Ethnic Subgroup Membership on Mexican Americans' Use of Mass Media for Cultural Maintenance," *Howard Journal of Communication* (1997): 197–216.

15. Diana I. Ríos and Stanley O. Gaines, "Latino Media Use for Cultural Maintenance," *Journalism and Mass Communication Quarterly* (1998): 746–61.

16. See Jane Rhodes, "Falling through the Cracks: Studying Women of Color in Mass

Communication," in *Women in Mass Communication,* ed. 2, ed. Pamela J. Creedon (Newbury Park, Calif.: Sage, 1993).

17. Janice Radway, *Reading the Romance: Women, Patriarchy and Popular Literature* (Chapel Hill: University of North Carolina Press, 1984).

18. Jacqueline Bobo, "*The Color Purple:* Black Women as Cultural Readers," in *Female Spectators: Looking at Film and Television,* ed. Diedre Pribram (New York: Verso, 1988).

19. Bobo, "*The Color Purple,*" 90.

20. Bobo, "*The Color Purple,*" 96.

21. Rosa Linda Fregoso, *The Bronze Screen: Chicana and Chicano Film Culture* (Minneapolis: University of Minnesota Press, 1993).

22. Rosa Linda Fregoso, *The Bronze Screen,* 95.

23. Andrea L. Press, *Women Watching Television: Gender, Class, and Generation in the American Television Experience* (Philadelphia: University of Pennsylvania Press, 1991).

24. Diana I. Ríos, Ofelia Barrios, Mark J. Gilboard, Patricia González, and Tatiana Jaramillo, "The Intercultural Reception of the Mexican Film *Like Water for Chocolate* among Mexican/Spanish American and Anglo American Women in New Mexico" (unpublished pilot study, 1995).

25. Clint Wilson and Félix Gutiérrez, *Race, Multiculturalism, and the Media: From Mass to Class Communication* (Newbury Park, Calif.: Sage, 1995).

26. Maurine H. Beasley, "Newspapers: Is There a New Majority Defining the News?" in *Women in Mass Communication;* Marilyn E. Gist, "Through the Looking Glass: Diversity and Reflected Appraisals of the Self in Mass Media" in *Women in Mass Communication;* and Sue A. Lafky, "The Progress of Women and People of Color in the U.S. Journalistic Workforce: A Long, Slow Journey" in *Women in Mass Communication.*

27. Diana I. Ríos, "Chicano Cultural Resistance with Mass Media," in *Chicanos in Contemporary Society,* ed. Roberto M. DeAnda (New York: Allyn and Bacon, 1995); and Diana I. Ríos, "Latino Cultural Experiences with Mass Media," *Our Voices* (Los Angeles: Roxbury, 2000).

28. The names of audience members are fictitious. The details in the audience profile are composite qualities of women of Mexican heritage whom I interviewed formally and spoke with informally in Texas, New Mexico, and California.

A Historical Overview/Update on the State of Chicano Art

GEORGE VARGAS

Chicano Art as North American Art

Whether of a political or an art-for-art's-sake intent, Chicano art is a visual manifestation of Chicano society, serving the Chicano community and, increasingly, the broader American culture. It represents an American expression born from the unique social and political conditions that have motivated and confined Chicanos in their struggle to become accepted as Americans while maintaining allegiance to their sense of Mexicanness. Though commonly perceived as mural or protest art, Chicano art reflects a great range of techniques, media, and content. Today, Chicano artists communicate both political and personal statements, utilizing traditional artistic expressions, as well as new vehicles such as conceptual/performance art, film/video, and installation art.

Despite denial and prejudice, Chicano art does exist, as do Chicanos who increasingly are cultivating the arts to validate their dual identities as Americans who are proud of their Mexican heritage. José Narezo (art teacher/muralist/painter from Grand Rapids, Michigan), who migrated with his family from Anáhuac, Mexico, to work in the fields and factories of Michigan, embraces both Mexican and Chicano/American cultural identities. "I have been interested in the customs and traditions of my homeland. I feel that an artist must be aware of his roots in order to be more profound in making a visual statement."[1] Many of the most talented Chicano artists are unknown outside their communities. Their art will become more recognized when Chicanos themselves become accepted as a people and as Americans in the United States. Until that transformation occurs, Chicano art will not be accepted or understood in the mainstream art market.

This chapter organizes Chicano art into categories relating to role and purpose: art as a visual document or text, art as a political vehicle, and art as personal expression. (Remember that some artists may defy categorization, and this is true for Chicano artists, too.) It then looks at the history of Chicano art, underscoring the importance of the individual artist's creativity by exploring the lives, works, and ideas of seven contemporary Chicano artists who have diversely participated in the history of Chicano art. Thus, the present state of Chicano art will be examined, as well as speculation regarding its future.

This chapter hopes to stimulate dialogue, if not answer questions, regarding the development of Chicano art within a historical framework. What is the new face of Chicano art, and how is it different from its original identity? Why has Chicano creativity increased when the Chicano movement is practically nonexistent? Can revolutionary art exist without patronage to a political movement? What is the future of Chicano art? These are questions that both the artists and the community help the historian answer.

A Study of Chicano Art

New scholars in various fields have made recent contributions to our knowledge of the Chicano experience, beginning with the Spanish conquest through the Chicano Movimiento (a political civil rights movement born in the 1960s, in which the production of art was dedicated to the Chicano ideology of political resistance and cultural affirmation) and into recent years. With the inevitable crossover of Chicano culture into American popular culture, there is a need to further investigate and document Chicano creative expression. As we gain a visual literacy of the Chicano experience, we come to know the struggles and successes of Chicanos as Americans and to learn more about the rich tapestry of the greater American experience.

The present Chicano experience of American culture is rich and broad, often transcending a strict political perspective and appealing to a more diverse audience. Chicano artists have evolved, along with the Chicano community-at-large (largely blue-collar and white-collar urban dwellers), interpreting American history and constructing a new frontier through unique artistic forms that reflect their cultural reality of struggle, resistance, and change. Chicano art as a visual metaphor describes the continuity and change in the very nature of Chicano consciousness.

Chicanos represent a great and imminent change in the racial/ethnic balance of the United States. Demographic studies indicate that Mexican/Chicano people, as the largest Latin(o) American population subgroup in the United States, soon will become a majority population, dramatically changing the face of U.S. society. By examining Chicano visual art, we can gain insight into the physical and psychological forces at play in the evolution of Chicano consciousness. We can then begin to get a personal portrait of a cultural environment that is regularly affected by both the United States and Mexico.

Chicano Art as Visual Text

Art can serve as a visual text or document for historians when other expressions of material culture are limited or yet undiscovered. As such, artworks are signposts of consciousness that reveal the condition of humanity in a particular culture at a particular time. In the case of Chicano history, the exhibition and preservation of Chicano art is critical because it represents one of the few accessible visual records documenting the Chicano presence in American history.

Chicano art speaks in a visual language that incorporates signs and symbols derived from the ancient civilizations of Mesoamerica and the more recent Mexican Mural Movement (which combined images of indigenous cultures with the political rhetoric of postrevolutionary Mexico) to create visual texts that portray the history, cultural heritage, memories, and visions of a contemporary Chicano culture. The artist constantly innovates or (re)invents meaning and form for traditional images by adding accents of his or her contemporary environment. Carlos Díaz (photographer/college teacher from Pontiac, Michigan) explains, "Through the photographic document [that pertains] to the common man/woman, my choice is to engage the issues rather than escape them. . . . Visual symbols and words serve as clues or signals offering a means by which the viewer can be a participant. The contents of these [cityscape photos] not only reflect upon the people who are its occupants but also speak about our species as a whole."[2]

Abstract thoughts and ideas come to life as creative expression through the artist, and in the case of Chicano art, its artists speak specifically from a Chicano perspective to address a specific Chicano state of mind or psychology. As cultural workers, Chicano artists facilitate the social production of art, constructing signposts in the form of murals, sculptures, and other visual expressions for the beautification and enlightenment of the local, national, and international community.

As one of the most accessible popular expressions, the murals of the Chicano art movement have their own fluid language of visual environmental communication that must integrate with the architectural environment as well as communicate its message. Murals give us information about the people who live and work in that environment, how they interact or communicate, and what they think. Some neighborhoods and regions have developed distinct mural styles or approaches that can be easily identified by the knowing eye.

Chicano Art as Political Art

Many Chicano artists of the sixties and seventies supported the Chicano Movimiento by creating posters and murals dealing with issues such as inequality in education and employment. Also a vital component of the People's Art Movement (a grassroots movement composed largely of women and people of color), Chicano art of this period interpreted the Chicano experience with a radical or militant political perspective. Many Chicano artists identified with the revolutionary art of France and Russia and especially with the great art movement of social realism and intellectual expression of postrevolutionary Mexico. The posters and murals of this period portray popular Mexican and Chicano revolutionary heroes such as Emiliano Zapata and César Chávez and well-known Mexican icons such as Quetzalcoatl and the Virgen de Guadalupe, but the message was meant for Indians, *mestizos*[3] (meaning "mixed blood," which characterizes the racial/ethnic profile of Chicanos as well as Mexican and other Latin American populations), and poor and working class Americans of all colors.

Today, Chicano art no longer serves a formal political ideology, but it persists as a cultural agent of social change, especially in the continued production of mural art. The unresolved issues challenged by artists in the People's Art Movement and the Movimiento are still questioned by many Chicano artists who continue to speak out against persisting social injustice. San Francisco painter Ester Hernández supports using the arts to promote activism: "As a Xicana-Azteca, I feel we must continue to use our creative skills to give strength to our political, cultural, and spiritual struggle. We must make visible our resistance to deception and the celebration of genocide."[4]

Chicano Art as Personal Expression

Chicano art, fortunately, also acts as a popular vehicle for self-expression and can be examined within the context of an emerging Chicano aesthetic that is independent of the Chicano political ideology associated with the sixties and seventies. A personal expression of the Chicano experience may have social or emotional impact without engaging in the polemics that accompany political art. Regarding a pure Chicano art of emotional appeal, José Narezo contends, "I believe that art needs to be pure in the sense that it comes from the emotions within."[5]

Personal expression in Chicano art is complex in style and iconography, serving as a mirror for the nature and condition of Chicano artists, reflecting their hopes, fears, political concerns, achievements, and aspirations. The diversity found in Chicano art can be traced to the growing range of Chicano artists, either trained or self taught, who are exploring individual expression with innovative techniques and styles. Many Chicano artists possess a sharp universal sensibility, comparing their human ideas and feelings with other artists throughout the world.

A History of Chicano Art

Chicano visual art intertwines Mexican and American history into a unique historical perspective that, by its very nature, is political and therefore provocative because it challenges our preconceived notions about Chicanos. It chronicles the evolution of Chicano consciousness in a people who have had to survive as second-class citizens, outsiders living inside a rapidly changing American society. It interprets the life story of real Mexicans and Chicanos who, having lost land, language, and culture as consequences of the conquest, the U.S.–Mexican War, and the Mexican Revolution, nevertheless prevailed in American society. Chicano art portrays a people's cultural history within the context of a new American history.

Historical Background

In the 1960s Chicano art mass-communicated its unique perspective primarily through mural art, posters, and graffiti. It has since expanded its boundaries into virtually all forms of artistic expression. Regardless of style or time frame, Chicano artists draw from their *mestizaje*[6] (mixed culture or multicultural) experiences in synthesizing ideas and making artistic forms. Santa Barraza (painter/feminist living in Kingsville, Texas) exalts the mestizo as a powerful symbol of the people's revolution, liberation, and duality, representing a new hybrid:

> Chicanos identified with the peón mestizo of the Revolutionary Mexico of 1910 not only because of biological heritage, but also because of similar economic, working-class social status and political experience. The Chicanos utilized experiences from their history and art to create a unique culture of liberation, through which a language of expression resulting from the symbiosis of mainstream United States culture and traditional mestizo values was developed. . . . The mestizo is a manifestation of the merger of opposite forces, a duality. Allegorically, this new hybrid is the embodiment of the east and west, the conqueror and the conquered, the Christian and the pagan, capable of creating a pathway to equality and social justice for the world.[7]

Throughout its history, Chicano art has remained Chicano-oriented and people-oriented, affirming the existence of the Chicano culture and providing purpose and identity for the Chicano artist. No matter the decade, the concept of Chicano art has been balanced between political commentary, social content, and personal expressiveness.

Murals

Ideologically linked to the broader People's Art Movement, Chicano mural art was inspired by the Mexican Mural Movement (1920–30) that followed the Mexican Revolution (1910–17), and especially by Los Tres Grandes (The Big Three Mexican modernists, José Clemente Orozco, Diego Rivera, and David Alfaro Siqueiros, all of whom executed controversial murals in the United States). Themes of the government-sponsored Mexican murals (mostly painted in a traditional fresco medium) focused on a common people's historical perspective rather than a glorified perspective of the elite and rich. Associated with the school of social realism, the Mexican murals used a visual language of symbols and images easily read by the general public. No longer exclusive or academic, Mexican art was enlivened by a special accent of *mexicanidad,* celebrating the Mexican-ness of the people. These early Mexican muralists stimulated the creation of the Public Works of Art Project (Franklin D. Roosevelt's New Deal program initiated in 1933), which provided work for countless unemployed American artists while recording the idealism of the New Deal era on the walls of public buildings. Prior to this, mural art in the United States primarily had been controlled by private interests. The People's Art Movement of the 1960s revived America's interest in public art, but now it was more accessible and demystified a people's expression.

The creation of Chicano murals in the 1960s involved the active and eager participation of neighborhood artists and residents. They took political and social issues to the streets by painting their history and culture on public walls, thus reclaiming their immediate environment. Many of the earliest murals were produced on a shoestring budget independent of governmental funds, underscoring their revolutionary intent. Painted mostly in urban centers, such as Chicago, Denver, Detroit, El Paso, Los Angeles, San Antonio, San Diego, San Francisco, and Santa Fe, Chicano murals were invigorated by the civil rights, student, and women's rights movements; Chicano labor and politics; and the counterculture. Creativity became a metaphor for the freedom of personal and group expression guaranteed to all Americans, but often denied to women and people of color.

Early Chicano murals communicated contemporary themes of race, class, and ethnicity[8] that spoke specifically to the diverse Chicano experience, while addressing issues relevant to poor and working-class Americans of all colors. Depending heavily on figurative and representational painting styles easily read by the masses, Chicano muralists often combined visual elements found in early Mesoamerican history (to underscore indigenousness) with images of controversial figures from popular culture to represent current issues. In one of the earliest documented Chicano murals, Antonio Bernal's 1968 *Untitled* mural (located on the front of Teatro Campesino's office in Del Rey, California) adopted the recognizable narrative style of Mayan art (directly borrowing from the Mayan Bonampak mural cycle [c. 800 A.D.]) to portray a victory procession of symbolic Mexican revolutionary figures (La Adelita, Francisco Villa, and Emiliano Zapata) alongside American and Chicano civil rights leaders (Martin Luther King, Jr., and César Chávez). In 1975, José Gamaliel González led youth of Westtown, Chicago, in painting *Raza de Oro* (Race of Gold), which also utilized the form of a Mayan relief lintel (725 A.D.) from Yaxchilón to create a vision of the plumed serpent, symbolizing the common struggle of Chicanos as an emerging golden race, a new "people of the sun."

Like the early Mexican muralists, early Chicano artists symbolically repossessed the original home of the Mexico/Nahua Indians, Aztlán (the birthplace of the Aztecs, "People of the Sun"). The Indian became the symbol of the oppressed and of social consciousness, drawing diverse elements in the community to a common cause or shared American heritage. By painting their people's symbolic exodus, they hoped to reclaim a place of honor in the American landscape on behalf of dispossessed Mexicans and Chicanos, who at one time dominated much of the Mexican territory now known as the U.S. Southwest. In 1978, Martín Moreno's *Vibrations of a New Awakening* (Adrian, Michigan) combined Michigan state history with Aztec mythology to depict agricultural and industrial workers crucified and stripped of individual identity to the point of becoming androids. Upon "awakening," some workers escape exploitation and climb onto the back of the feathered serpent Quetzalcoatl, symbolizing a rebirth of consciousness for Indian and Chicano mestizo alike and a return to a common origin or land base.

Some Chicano artists (many from the working class) assumed the role of cultural worker, devoting their art to the Movimiento and the enlightenment and education of Chicano workers in recognition of their contributions to the economic development of American enterprise and industry. Chicano civil rights leaders and labor groups invited artists to support the Chicano revolution by creating a people's art that was reflective of *chicanismo* cultural values and the principles of self-identification and self-determination. Chicano murals and posters became the popular vehicles of mass communication that appealed to a ready-made audience created by the revolution. Muralists such as Moreno (who now lives in Phoenix, Arizona, where he creates murals, sculpture, and paintings) stressed the organic creative process rather than the end product, inviting the community to participate with neighborhood artists: "The creation of murals has become a national artistic phenomenon. Thus . . . the creation of the mural is not a simple matter of applying paint to a dreary wall. But it is instead a process by which a muralist and the community are guided into communication with each other by the experience of working together. By leaving reflections of the community, [artists] are leaving a small part of themselves."[9]

As Chicano muralists began to study more varied forms of expression in world art, such as Renaissance and Byzantine mural art, more sophisticated and contemporary styles began to appear, such as classical representation, photo realism, expressionism, and abstraction. They also began to discover more permanent paint materials and advanced design and technologies.

Art Groups

Soon, Chicano art became a cause unto itself, an art movimiento calling for cultural equality for Chicano artists and urging mainstream artists to create works that were reflective of nonwestern styles using Mexican and Chicano sources.[10] Fortunately, the early history of Chicano art was being documented by emerging scholars of the time, such as Jacinto Quirarte and Raymond Barrio.[11]

Chicano murals appeared in urban centers throughout the United States during the late sixties and well into the seventies. In the early days, many artists were consumed with the immediate message in mural art and were not worried about receiving public funding or specialized art training. As time went by, artists began consolidating their efforts by organizing into mural groups that could provide training for aspiring young artists as well as seek local and federal funding for more ambitious projects. Additionally, some artists introduced the portable mural (moveable panels innovated by the Mexican muralists) to carry the visual message into otherwise-restricted or new spaces.

In the 1970s Chicano art groups arose throughout the nation to formalize various art theories and to concentrate their creative activities by working in mural groups or collectives such as Artes Guadalupanos de Aztlán in New Mexico; Mujeres Muralistas in San Francisco (one of the earliest Chicana mural groups); ASCO and Los Four (Charles Almaraz, Robert de la Rocha, Gilbert Luján, and Frank Romero) in California; Con Safo in San Antonio, Texas; Raza Art/Media Collective in Ann Arbor, Michigan; and the Association of Hispanic Arts in New York City. In addition, the Royal Chicano Air Force in Sacramento, Galería de la Raza in San Francisco, La Raza Graphic Center in San Antonio, and Self Help Graphics in Los Angeles promoted poster art/printmaking and its production. In the late 1970s, a network of these individual art groups came together in a national coalition of Hispanic organizations to encourage funding of minority arts by federal and state governments.

One of the most significant of the Chicano alternative art groups was ASCO (Spanish for "nausea" or "disgust"). Founded in 1972 in Los Angeles by

FIGURE 6.1 ASCO members with *The Walking Mural*. From left: Patssi Valdez, Gronk, and Willie Herrón. Los Angeles, California, December 24, 1972. (Photograph by Harry Gamboa, Jr.)

Willie Herrón, Harry Gamboa, Jr., Gronk (born Gluglio Gronk Nicandro), and Patssi Valdez, the vanguard group experimented with numerous radical styles and new media, including visually striking social-commentary murals executed in abstract and expressionistic styles; alternative murals; street theater; film and video; and multimedia conceptual, performance, and installation art. Their murals extracted unlikely popular cultural elements from an urban environment to create new images and forms, ranging from the 1972 *Walking Mural* (a performance/alternative mural worn in public by ASCO members, see fig. 6.1) to the 1979 *Black and White Mural* (which incorporated graffiti painted into the design by neighborhood youth). Despite harsh criticism, ASCO's daring brand of art was a sharp knife that cut boldly to create new Chicano urban expressions to delight new tastes in neosurrealism and vanguard art. According to Gronk, "That urban sensibility gave a hard core to our work. We did our work despite what some people said, 'It's [the] worst thing being done,' or '[T]hat's ugly!' But we continued our work. That was gumption. . . . We were not passive."[12]

Chicano artists in Chicago eventually aligned with non-Chicano artists, forming mural collectives or syndicates to expedite the support and production of murals through citywide mural projects. Murals most often were produced by multicultural community-oriented arts organizations, such as the Public Arts Workshop directed by Mark Rogovin and the Chicago Mural Group founded by Bill Walker (an African American artist who painted the earliest community murals in Chicago) and John Weber. Movimiento Artístico Chicano, a group of Chicano muralists, graphic artists, filmmakers, educators, and photographers, joined citywide efforts to celebrate art, not only in the Chicano community but throughout the city as well.

Posters and Prints as Graphic Art

The satirical newspaper illustrations of José Guadalupe Posada and Manuel Manilla, popular turn-of-the-century Mexican printmakers, inspired a long-standing tradition in Mexican graphic art and later Chicano graphic art. In 1937 the Taller de Gráfica Popular was formed by Leopoldo Méndez, Luis Arenal, and Pablo O'Higgins, a graphic arts collective whose purpose was to produce art devoted to social realism and to teach graphic techniques, both traditional and new. (Some members also were in the Mexican Mural Movement.) Borrowing directly from Posada, Diego Rivera, and Mexican photographer Agustín Casasola, Chicano artists reproduced Mexican revolutionary figures to serve as heroes of the Chicano movement as well. For instance, Casasola's famous photograph of Zapata was copied by the United Farm Workers (UFW) Graphic Center in a 1970 poster, with the declaration, "Viva la Revolución."

Early Chicano posters also were influenced by the bold, bright, and "flat" design characteristics of Cuban posters of the 1960s. In 1964, the Cuban postrevolutionary government began employing its artists to create posters of Castro and Ché Guevara as a form of popular propaganda. Later, when the government-owned film industry employed them to make movie posters, the artists began to experiment with psychedelic colors and designs found in the hippie movement, creating some of their most interesting work. America's walls and kiosks were thickly layered with Cuban-influenced posters containing images of heroes of the New Left counterculture such as Ché, Bob Dylan, Malcolm X, and Zapata.[13]

Printmaking is still a powerful medium because good-quality multiple copies can be produced at a reasonable cost, making it possible to get a visually striking message across to masses of people. Posters, usually linoleum-cut or wood-cut, silk-screen, or lithographic prints, allowed Chicano artists of the sixties and seventies to mass-produce affordable, portable art for an eager Chicano audience. Chicano posters and flyers announced important exhibitions, mural unveilings, and rallies, and were distributed free or at a nominal charge.

Graffiti Art

Sharing the stage of public expression with murals and graphic arts, graffiti utilize a special sign language that resembles mysterious cult symbols or ancient petroglyphs. Historically, Chicano graffiti are linked to the *pachucos* (the Mexican American "zoot-suiters" of the 1930s and 1940s). Their *placa* (a distinctive calligraphic writing style), unusual tattoos, hand signs, and fashions reflected an alternative lifestyle of intense Mexican ethnic pride, whose influence still can be seen in contemporary gang graffiti. As part of the signage found in the urban landscape, graffiti act as pictographs, unique pictures representing a word, an idea, or a record in hieroglyphic symbols. Modernists such as Pablo Picasso and Jean Dubuffet were inspired by graffiti, as are Chicano artists such as Charles "Chaz" Bojórquez, John Valadez, José Galvez, Antonio Pérez, and members of ASCO.

To those outside Chicano street culture, graffiti may appear as indecipherable scribbling at best, vandalism at worst. To insiders, graffiti are seen as individual acts of pride or protest, gang declarations of territory or challenge, and weapons in a class war. Regardless of the issue of "Is it art?" graffiti are a cheap medium that provide instant public communication for those in society who perceive themselves as powerless. For many rebellious elements in Chicano culture, graffiti are the only accessible medium to communicate with in the urban forum.

In the 1960s Chicano graffiti artists joined other youths in a visual assault against authority figures and slumlords. "Taggers" scrawled their spray-painted nicknames or "tags" on buildings, police cars, and subways as a demonstration of their bravado and anger. In the 1970s taggers began combining felt-tip markers with their spray-paint techniques, creating a bold new calligraphy affected by *cholo* (new Chicano street culture), hip-hop, and rap cultures. Latino culture crossed over into the black American experience, producing cultural hybrids in music, film, and public art and inspiring new voices in both cultures.

The Emergence of Chicana Art

With Chicano art heavily male-dominated, the emergence of a women's or Chicana art was nothing short of a miracle. Chicanas defined positive cultural identities that embraced the traditional elements in the Chicano community while asserting their womanhood with figures denoting empowerment, independence, and unity.

Early women artists who broke into a previously exclusive Chicano mural scene include Judith Baca, who organized the monumental historical project *The Great Wall of Los Angeles* (1976–84), and Yolanda M. López, who guided high-school girls in painting one of the first murals created by women at Chicano Park in San Diego, a "people's park" that was heavily decorated with mural art throughout the 1970s.

Chicanas used graphic art to focus on feminist concerns, perhaps because they could easily access printmaking to speak their minds with more artistic freedom than they could in the more male-dominated public mural arena. Chicanas produced challenging, exciting images of women that could be easily packaged and distributed to an emerging women's market and to other interested consumers. In 1979 Isabel Castro (Santa Monica, California) made a series of color photocopies entitled "Women Under Fire," which places a young Latina in the cross-hairs of a rifle's telescope to symbolize those Mexicanas/Chicanas who were involuntarily sterilized while undergoing childbirth at a Los Angeles hospital.

Many Chicanas, including Amalia Mesa-Bains (known for her altars), Carmen Lomas Garza (painter/printmaker), and Yreina Cervántez (muralist/painter), explored heroines such as the Virgen de Guadalupe, La Malinche (Hernán Cortés's Mexican Indian mistress and translator), and Frida Kahlo and used their images to illustrate a feminist perspective in Chicano history and contemporary culture. Artists Patssi Valdez (ASCO) and Kathy Vargas (Con Safo) experimented with multimedia installation, performance art, photo-collage, and other approaches to create new images of women in traditional and innovative spaces.

Individual Chicanas, struggling to gain greater exposure in a male-controlled art world, formed their own groups to produce art and promote feminist causes. Following the lead of Mujeres Muralistas in San Francisco, Las Mujeres Muralistas del Valle was organized in Fresno in the mid-1970s to paint community murals using a women's perspective. In 1977, Chicanas founded Mujeres Artísticas del Suroeste in Austin to represent Chicanas and

Latinas from Austin, San Antonio, Laredo, and other cities in central and south Texas.

1980s: Expansion into the Contemporary Art Movement

By the 1980s, the features of Chicano art changed with the emerging "new" Chicanos, who were no longer largely poor or working class, but middle class, educated, economically mobile, and recognized consumers. Chicano artists expanded into new territories, investigating other artistic theories and media and organizing groups to address issues affecting the United States and Mexico as well as Latin American and Third/Fourth World countries. Chicano art in its new and often avant-garde forms was labeled "Nueva Onda" (New Wave art) and included conceptual and performance art, mixed-media sculpture and assemblage, video and filmmaking (rapidly becoming a popular medium of mass communication), and anti-art, to name a few of the more contemporary expressions. Houston photographer Guillermo Pulido documented his ritualized initiation into Incan Indian culture in an installation work. Gloria Maya (Oakland, California) ritualized her family's Christmas dinner in an assemblage of sculptures consisting of turkey bones, which acknowledge life by accepting death. Meanwhile, Chicana video/filmmakers Sylvia Morales, Lourdes Portillo, and Susan Racho were breaking into that male-dominated medium.

Artists continued using mural art as a popular medium of communication to the community and the larger society to promote Chicano culture, to correct cultural ignorance about Chicanos, and simply to beautify neighborhoods. For some artists the struggle to make murals turned into a struggle against institutional censorship. In the case of Los Angeles artist Barbara Carrasco, her *L.A. History–A Mexican Perspective* (a portable 16-by-80-foot mural that features the face of the artist, her braids interwoven with historical scenes and images of women and people of color, see fig. 6.2) was censored by officials of the 1984 Summer Olympics in Los Angeles. They had charged that scenes depicting the internment of Japanese Americans during World War II and a mass lynching of Chinese workers in the late 1800s would insult Asian visitors. Even though Carrasco received letters from Asian Americans supporting her interpretation of their history, the officials would not budge, insisting that she whitewash the "offensive" areas of the work. Rather than compromise her mural, Carrasco found an alternative site to display her work.[14] She compared her mural controversy with that experi-

FIGURE 6.2 Barbara Carrasco, *L. A. History—A Mexican Perspective* (1981–83). Mural located in Los Angeles, California. (Photograph by Barbara Carrasco.)

enced by David Alfaro Siqueiros when he painted his fresco mural *Tropical America* (1932) in Los Angeles's Sonora Town (so-called because of its large Mexican population). It was whitewashed by city fathers, who were upset by an image of a crucified Mexican Indian/peon.[15]

At this time, Chicano art recognized (and sometimes rejected) the canons of postmodernism and yet supported the radical aspect of the vanguard, not refuting history, but (re)discovering it by inventing and constructing new art for a new society. While maintaining self-discovery and community contact with Chicano culture, Chicano artists tore down the stereotypical images of Chicano separatist rhetoric of the Movimiento in order to create space for new cultural images of Chicanos as Americans alive with new attitudes about themselves and their struggles. With the bonfire of protest from the sixties and seventies still smoldering, Chicano artists in the 1980s celebrated contemporary life (despite the setbacks suffered by women and people of color, the poor, and the middle-class during the years of the Reagan administration), proudly affirming their Mexican roots while embracing their new American identity.

Chicano artists started crossing over into new commercial art markets. Ester Hernández had her popular 1982 "Sun Mad Raisins" silk-screen (an image of a skeleton "Sun Maid" wearing a sun bonnet and holding a basket of grapes) printed on postcards and T-shirts in an effort to educate a larger audience (especially targeting children and women) about the inherent dangers of chemical insecticides to both farmworkers and consumers. In 1986, painter Nora Mendoza (born in Texas, currently living in Michigan) was commissioned by César Chávez to produce a series of colorful greeting cards honoring migrant workers and their families that later were exhibited at the George Meaney Labor Center in Silver Springs, Maryland.

After the heyday of Chicano politics in the sixties and seventies, Chicano graphic artists were implementing new visions without compromising the ongoing Chicano struggle. In 1988–89, the Wight Gallery at UCLA, along with Self Help Graphics of Los Angeles, organized the National Chicano Screenprint Taller (funded by the Metropolitan Life Foundation). The collection of silk-screen prints displays unexpected humor, along with typical commentary. The common thread of the complex Chicano experience can easily be discovered in this collection of contemporary works. Larry Yáñez's "Cocina Jaiteca" indulges the false pride of many Latina housewives: a "high-tech" *cocina* (kitchen) with an old-fashioned refrigerator, stove, etc. Ester Hernández underscores feminist pride in "La Ofrenda," which pictures a tattoo of the Virgen de Guadalupe on the bare back of a confident young Chicana with a radical short hairstyle. Carlotta Espinoza demonstrates against institutionalized racism and oppression in "Broken Treaties," symbolized by a nude Chicana who is trapped in a web made of barbed wire and her own hair. She holds a dove in her hand (like a Greek kore statue), while behind her, the colors of the U.S. flag run and fade away.

Chicano art also became connected with a healthy trend toward pluralism/multiculturalism in American art. Chicano artists began a dialogue with other American artists of color and immigrants from Latin America and Asia, many of whom were in exile from tyranny in their native lands.[16] Chicano artists increasingly related to the experience of Latin American artists, who were also searching for a new identity and a renewed sense of historical presence in their American environment. In 1981 the Museum of Modern Art at the Institute of Fine Arts in Mexico City published a special issue of *Artes Visuales* that reported an update of Chicano visual arts as represented by artists who were "exploring new possibilities, trying to escape imposed cliches . . . to produce art at the margin of what is officially acceptable."[17] The Mexican publication also stressed the continuation of a dialogue between Chicano artists and those from Latin America to better conceptualize "the role of art in politics, and politics in art."[18]

Individual Chicano artists who exemplified the spirit of a new wave or neo-Chicano art included performance/installation artist and photographer Jerry Dreva (Los Angeles), who organized a series of performance events (including tattooing his body) to celebrate the two-hundredth anniversary of the founding of Los Angeles; performance/body artist Sylvia Salazar Simpson (born in Santa Fe), who wore a headdress of living green plants and flowers populated by earthworms in her piece entitled "Antes/ Before"; computer/video artist René Yáñez (San Francisco), who explored three-dimensional animation in hologram art in "Pachuco," about a young girl flirting with a *pachuco;* multimedia artist Jack Vargas (born in Santa Paula, California), who, in *Breakfast with Evaristo Altamirano,* projects video images alongside text, inventing new "Chicano-speak" words such as "Jiffy Beanzales" and "Mexi-Queen."

Although many new artists appeared on the scene, some drifted away and others matured, moving into new avenues. The founding members of ASCO, for example, headed down different artistic paths. By 1987, they no longer worked together as a group, leaving a prominent gap in Chicano art. Looking historically at the face of Chicano art, ASCO was the "jawline, because we could take the punches!"[19] Gronk explains. With ASCO now dismantled, according to Gamboa, "[t]here was no oasis in the urban desert."[20]

1990s: The Era of New Chicano Art

That Chicano art has survived into the 1990s should not be a surprise, given the increase in the Chicano population and its marked socioeconomic impact on the United States. As America rediscovers itself, it also discovers new Chicano art, despite its limited inclusion in museums. In the 1960s Chicano art primarily was aimed at Chicanos and other oppressed people, but in the 1990s its appeal extended to the broader American audience. Chicano artists who once condemned or boycotted the consumption of grapes, lettuce, and wine have crossed over into the mainstream graphic arts/advertising industry. Carmen Lomas Garza's popular illustrations of Chicano family life now appear in full-page magazine advertisements sponsored by Anheuser-Busch and Budweiser beer distributors. A photographic image by Gronk has been reproduced in an advertisement for the California State Lottery. The crossover of some Chicano artists into the corporate business world is significant, underscoring the acceptance of Chicanos in mainstream society.

New Chicano art signifies a new reality for Chicanos. Performance artist Ruben Guevara represents the new Chicano orientation of reality:

> I am born of magic, fire, water, earth, wind, bullets, blood, and betrayal: Grandson of Hernán Cortés and Malintzin, La Malinche un hijo de la chingada a child of Conquest. . . . My name is Xicanoatl. . . . I am a post-quincentennial cultural anti-hero— a Chicano Xicano concept: An intergalactic, interdimensional, intercultural, interdisciplinary, performance Mestizo. A powerful

blend Arabian-Spain, with the mystery of Africa and Asia, fused with the mysticism of Native America. Indigenous mysticism merging with modern technology, creating a new man, a new woman, a new reality.[21]

Contemporary Chicano art mirrors the new Chicano psychology. Yes, racism and prejudice still exist, yet Chicanos themselves must invent a new paradigm of empowerment to liberate both themselves and the oppressor. As facilitators and mediators, Chicano artists today offer a new mirror of creative transformation to replace the old mirror of oppression. Without a doubt, Chicano art is still grounded in the traditions of social commentary, thriving in Chicano urban centers as an art of conscience and activism; but now when Americans see contemporary Chicano art, they appreciate it as a new American expression without disputing the quality,[22] intent, or market value of the work. More fluid, organic, multifaceted, and multicultural, Chicano art today describes a fresh worldview of unlimited possibilities and is less strictly nationalistic.

Still defined by a history and an urban iconography that are distinctly Chicano in spirit and content, Chicano art also represents American popular art. It is infused with a strong sense of pluralism, speaking to a broader cross-section of American culture as Chicanos themselves discover the shared American dream and legacy. Increasingly, Chicano art also is becoming an important part of multicultural education as more Chicano teachers and students expect to see a reflection of their presence in U.S. society. Artists/teachers such as Diana Alva (mixed-media artist from Detroit, Michigan) depend on art to educate, enlighten, and empower Chicano children. Alva asserts, "When a child learns that he or she can transform a piece of paper into something beautiful, or mold a mound of clay into an object of his/her choice, then that child can learn to have control over even bigger things, such as one's life."[23] Currently, this new model in Chicano art is open and ready for a new definition, role, and purpose to be applied by individual artists and their communities. However, this open model is inevitably tied to the Chicano's dual cultural identity as it cultivates a universal sensibility or cosmic view. In the words of painter/ceramist Gloria Osuna Pérez (El Paso), "The reality of Mexican and Chicano communities, wherever they may be, is the theme for my work. I show people and their lives, emphasizing the positive, seeking the external reality, enlarging the reality into a universal scale that invites a participation with the details. From a particular individual I fictionalize an abstract image that reaches into the heart of the viewer. My supra portraits attempt to transcend the impersonal anonymity of humanity, to invite the outsider to come and partake of our humanity."[24]

Chicano artists in the vanguard continually innovate ways to communicate with their old and new audiences. Ingenious video artists such as Gamboa and Juan Garza are inventing new visual texts to interpret the new Chicano reality by experimenting with film, video, and computer technologies for mass communication.

Today's Chicano graphic art is more sophisticated and is being produced by both established and emerging artists. Posters include familiar subjects, new images of the contemporary Chicano lifestyle, and crossovers of pop cultural influences such as graffiti art and street culture. A spectrum of technologies is used, from the traditional to more recent innovations such as photo silk-screen, photocopy, and computer graphics. Despite technological advancements that encourage individual expression, collectives or workshops are still in popular demand, perpetuating the communal spirit of the Mexican graphic art tradition. As in the past, Chicano posters and prints are affordable for individuals, private collectors, and museums alike, and can be easily stored and exhibited.

Certainly, printmaking in the 1990s prospers under mature artists such as Rupert García, Luis Jiménez, Carmen Lomas Garza, Martín Moreno, José Narezo, and Patssi Valdez. The 1995 touring exhibition "Chicano Connection" presented a group vision of diverse and unfolding identities in the Chicano community and the world.[25] The collection of silk-screen prints addresses varied artistic interests and themes. Pat Gómez's "War Stories" places a family narrative in a thematic setting, beautifully framing it with roses and sacred hearts. Mario Calvano's "Portrait with Text" presents a human figure with indirect references to Columbus and the conquest, forcing the viewer to read between the lines regarding personal and political realities.

According to purists, graffiti art in the 1990s is distinguished by the exclusive use of cans of spray paint, although some graffiti artists also explore the use of spray guns and air compressors. Graffiti artists (many of whom are former taggers) have attempted to elevate graffiti, also known as aerosol art or "spray-fiti," to a popular and valid creative expression by channeling antisocial behavior into positive architectural decoration and community comment. New graffiti artists utilize fast-drying, longer-lasting paint and brighter colors to create vivid images protesting street gangs and other social ills, paying tribute to murdered or lost youth or just inventing tags for fun. Disavowing "studio graffiti" and destructive tagging, new graffiti artists organize competitions to encourage the "good stuff"—a controlled, tight, and original script that identifies the artist's character, community, and even region. Today, some graffiti artists enter public mural competitions.

With Chicanos slowly entering into mainstream art, the overall acceptance of Chicano art in the 1990s has only slightly improved. Currently, only a handful of galleries, collectors, historians, and museums accept it as a vital part of contemporary expression. Nonetheless, the success of the touring "Chicano Art: Resistance and Affirmation" (CARA) exhibition indicates the American public's growing interest in Chicano art. New attendance records were set during the 1990–93 tour at the sponsoring museums in Albuquerque, Denver, El Paso, Fresno, Los Angeles, New York City, San Antonio, and Tucson. Excited crowds viewed a kaleidoscopic survey of Chicano art from 1965–85, displayed within a historical framework.[26] The volume and diversity of the collection were awesome, with works including paintings, graphic prints, photographs, sculptures, installations, *altarcitos* (altar installations), graffiti-inspired art, and hologram art by a multitude of artists from all walks of life. According to Gaspar Enríquez (El Paso artist included in the exhibit who was instrumental in bringing it to El Paso), CARA's success was based on the fact that such a display of Chicano art and history never had been assembled before and that community involvement was emphasized at all exhibition sites.

In El Paso, CARA was introduced to new audiences (many of whom lived in the city but had never set foot in the El Paso Art Museum) by a parade (that included mariachi bands, low-riders, high-school bands, Chicano labor groups, and Mexican immigration support organizations) and by a series of community events (lectures, films, and museum tours, for example) on Chicano art. For some viewers, the art depicted the familiar, for others, the unfamiliar and fantastic, but it was all reflective of the Chicano experience and was stimulating for all viewers, regardless of their artistic or cultural orientation.

Speaking for a major ethnic group that has been marginalized in society and ignored in cultural institutions, CARA's high impact across the country was twofold: CARA validated Chicano history and culture for many Chicanos, confirming a sense of group identity while inspiring youth to rediscover their roots; and it enlightened other Americans about Chicanos

through a sampling of their art, unveiling a rich, diverse, and often spontaneous American expression.

The popularity of CARA with the U.S. museum establishment demonstrated this group's interest in Chicano art as well. The community's intense
involvement in CARA underscored the emerging role of museums in educational outreach to a community that increasingly wants to see exhibits that
reflect its racial/ethnic makeup. For some museum staffs, CARA proved to be
both a rich learning process and a challenging professional experience, from
mounting the show to organizing the numerous tours and educational programs. Additionally, placing Chicano art within a museum environment
made it more palatable for some critics to digest and made it easier to
dismiss the intense messages of social protest as outdated issues. If the huge
success rates at sponsoring museums are indicators of CARA's social acceptance, Chicano art has indeed "arrived."

Although Chicano art means street culture or community expression
for many artists, for others it stands for vanguard thought and form, con-
fronting old ideas with a cutting-edge visual art. Brief biographies on seven
such cutting-edge artists who have experienced and participated in the Chicano art movement from different vantage points follows. These selected
artists often use interdisciplinary, multicultural approaches that cross over
into indigenous and world cultures, expanding the definition of "community." The mixing of ethnic groups and crossover influences often results in
never-before-seen forms and symbols that defy conventional description.
These artists are part of the vanguard in Chicano and American art, representing the hybridization of new Chicano ideas and forms and their commitment to the continued development of a people's art.

Gaspar Enríquez

A Bowie High School art teacher, Gaspar Enríquez has dedicated his life to
the El Paso community, where he was born in 1942. With a degree in arts
education and a master's degree in metalwork, he has exhibited throughout
the United States. Enríquez promotes Latino culture through his public
art projects and community involvement. For more than twenty years he
has provided young artists with scholarships and dozens of mural projects
throughout the city. Drawing identity and artistic inspiration for his murals
from the best elements of his bicultural background, Enríquez declares, "I
am an American with a Mexican (Chicano) culture. . . . The form of my

creations and their execution integrate both cultures. I do not abandon either culture completely; I just reorder and use them in new ways, and sometimes I transform them."[27] He believes that the unique experience of life on the border gives border artists a singular artistic perspective, but finds it hard to define, "I live with it every day, and take it for granted, using these special images in my art."

His murals and metalwork are sophisticated and technically complex, with an emphasis on permanence and excellence in public art. Enríquez feels that new technologies have not been fully explored by Chicano artists, including himself, especially computer technology, which is rapidly becoming a more accessible and desirable medium or tool. He credits Luis Jiménez for bringing Chicano art into the arena of more "permanent statements" with his fiber-glass sculptural creations. He also admires Jiménez's professional integrity and vision, which have endured despite continuous criticism surrounding his public works. (In June of 1995 the city of El Paso finally dedicated a fiber-glass sculpture-fountain, *Plaza de los Lagartos,* by Luis Jiménez after years of bureaucratic shuffling and community controversy.)

In his mural *History of the Mission Valley* (1994) Enríquez focused on the Salt War of 1877,[28] one of the darkest chapters in Texas history, offering a (re)interpretation of the bloody rebellion in El Paso, which is usually blamed on Mexicans. Painted with the help of five University of Texas, El Paso, students[29] on an old silo (32 feet in circumference by 47 feet high) near a Big-8 Supermarket (the sponsor), the mural was executed in sign painter's paint, using both paintbrush and spray gun (fig. 6.3). The pre-Columbian history of the area is introduced with stenciled images of ancient petroglyphs (a thunderbird and a feathered serpent) and painted images of corn. The Spanish discovery is represented by conquistadors' helmets. El Paso's three missions (Ysleta, Socorro, and San Elizario) wrap around the upper portion of the silo. American settlers in wagons are pictured above bales of cotton. The flags of Mexico, the United States, and Texas signify the complex, and often violent, political history of El Paso.

In his recent mixed-media installation *La Rosa Dolorosa* (1995, his first mixed-media installation), Enríquez presents a realistic portrait of a young Chicana Madonna holding a single rose and radiating love and compassion to a dying Chicano youth and his girlfriend below. Sharing the title with a poem by Chicano poet Juan Contreras, written expressly for this sculpture, Enríquez stirs our human emotions and spiritual or inner self. We see the Madonna offering solace to the "Bronzed Barrio Warrior fallen by a

FIGURE 6.3 Gaspar Enríquez, *History of the Mission Valley* (1994). Mural painted on a silo near a Big-8 Supermarket in El Paso, Texas. (Photograph by George Vargas.)

drive-by,"[30] who grasps a rose in his right hand, while his girlfriend cradles his upper body in a scene resembling Michelangelo's *Pietà*. The two human figures are two-dimensional, or flat, black-and-white cutouts mounted on foam board, whereas the young Mother Goddess is brilliantly painted and illuminated to create a three-dimensionality that is further enhanced by the Mexican baroque-like altar and columns. In this bittersweet vignette, the artist instructs and enlightens Chicanos and others about our common culture and destiny without preaching to us.

> Now, let us see,
> un nuevo amanecer/a new awakening,
> envision a tomorrow
> minus life's tragedies
> and afflictions, minus years of tears,
> minus the rain of pain,
> where we can love one another . . .[31]

Harry Gamboa, Jr.

Balancing on the razor's edge of Chicano avant-garde, Harry Gamboa, Jr., observes the tragic side of humanity and satirizes its predicaments and pratfalls. Born in 1951 in Los Angeles, the self-taught artist calls himself an "intermedia artist," whose body of work includes essays, poems, film/video, photography, performance/installation art, conceptual art, and anti-art. He revels in the ridiculous, absurd, and dark side of Chicano urban life, and mocks our contemporary cultural icons. "I like those who ridicule reality, or make reality ridiculous," he states simply.

Obsessed with the invisible "fallen angels" of Los Angeles, Gamboa dissects the stark contradictions of America's so-called city of the future—diverse and cosmopolitan, yet possessing the largest Chicano barrio in the United States. He points to social issues affecting Mexicans/Chicanos who, despite their great historical presence in California, are generally perceived as the "phantom culture,"[32] according to Gamboa. He served as both ideologue and documenter for ASCO, whose members collectively attempted to relate to the violence and tragedy in Los Angeles by creating new art that broke away from the paralyzing stereotypes of Chicanos and other Americans. The group also satirized American pop culture and "safe" or "no-risk" artists, receiving harsh criticism but eventually universal praise for their neodadaist/neosurrealist works.

During the last two decades, Gamboa has practiced his pure art, gaining critical attention in the form of major grants, fellowships, and commissions for his individual films/videos and literary works/plays. As a videographer, Gamboa has created new video texts for the 1990s, such as his *Vis-a-Vid* (1991–92) series, which won the "Premio Mesquite for Best Experimental Work" at the San Antonio Cinefestival in 1992. The series also was shown as an example of a "video mural" at the first Contemporary Latino Mural Conference at the University of Texas at El Paso. It reveals the changing nature of Chicanos and their relationships with humanity. Shown in both the United States and Mexico, Gamboa's work involves the latest video techniques and Day-Glo colors to paint intriguing vignettes of Chicanos as real people living in a contemporary world. *Cold Java* depicts an angst-ridden Latino man who, while staring into a cup of coffee, realizes that his life, like his coffee, has grown cold. "Something is wrong with the coffee. . . . I can't drink. I can't think," he complains. *Disconnected* features Barbara Carrasco, who is being chased by a real or imagined stalker (or an angry lover?) in an eerie Los Angeles cityscape that resembles the lonely emptiness of Godard's *Alphaville*. Produced by Dr. Eloy Rodríguez (Biological Sciences at Cornell University), Gamboa's next episode, *Fire Medicine*, presents a humorous and scientific view of the Mexican/Chicano culture's fascination with chile peppers. Using relatives, friends (such as Los Angeles artist John Valadez), and the "man on the street," Gamboa gives Chicanos a chance to laugh at themselves (a man tells us about a chile pepper seed stuck in his eye), while teaching others about the strange culinary delights of the Chicano culture. In the episode *El Mundo L.A.*, actor Humberto Sandoval's character rants and raves the psychobabble of one suffering from "burnout." Yet like truths blurted out by drunks and madmen, the musings by Everyman/Sandoval about Los Angeles and the Chicano movement sound almost reasonable. Like a Chicano Travis Bickle (from the movie *Taxi Driver*), who loathes the filth and disintegration of Chicano culture, he blames the disorientation of Chicanos on L.A.'s lack of Mexican pyramids and accuses blacks of not "sharing the pie," thus denying him the "good life." The viewer prays that Everyman's fate is not ours and that he is a liar, but we fear otherwise.

Although ASCO no longer exists, the spirit of bold experimentation and intense social protest survives in the Chicano neodadaist Gamboa, whose works prophesied the present decade of social alienation, violent upheaval, and cataclysmic change that confronts humanity's future.

Margarita "Mago" Gandara

A highly trained artist (she studied under Urbici Soler, Spanish master sculptor and friend of Picasso) and teacher (with a master's degree in bicultural arts education), Margarita "Mago" Gandara was born of Spanish/Mexican parents in El Paso, Texas, in 1929. Resembling a Mexicanized Georgia O'Keeffe, she currently resides and works on both sides of the El Paso/Juárez border. Since 1973, she has been producing monumental mosaic murals for a bicultural, international community.[33]

As a young artist, wife, and mother in California, Mago lived a "hidden life," raising five children, all the while making art without the approval of her husband. Newly divorced, in 1973 she returned to El Paso to complete her degree and create murals, paintings, and sculptures. She also designed and built her adobe studio in Mexico. Calling herself an art warrior, Mago (appropriately nicknamed the "Magician") especially speaks to people who feel dispossessed of homeland and heritage. The powerful beings in her murals (always executed with the help of young apprentices whom she pays) are benevolent guardians (Mexican mythical figures and traditional icons) that protect people who are overwhelmed with survival on the physical plane and that remind them of their spiritual life.

In 1992, a blend of fate and coincidence brought Mago to her most ambitious, and best-received, mosaic mural commission, *La Niña Cósmica/ The Cosmic Child* (fig. 6.4), which is mounted above the entrance to the student cafeteria at Frederick Douglass Elementary School in El Paso (on a wall measuring 12 feet in height by 72 feet in length). A modest materials budget allowed Mago to use store-bought pieces of colored tile, stained glass, and mirror instead of her usual recycled materials, giving her the pleasure of a full range of color and texture.

She wanted the semiabstract mural to be about the Great Mother, manifest as Coatlicue, a mythical figure present throughout Aztec history who symbolizes life, death, and regeneration. The mural scene depicts a brown-skinned goddess dancing through cosmic space, her mantle of stars and serpents billowing around her. She lovingly holds her own creations, the sun (Huitzilopochtli) and moon (Coyolxuahqui), in her outspread hands.

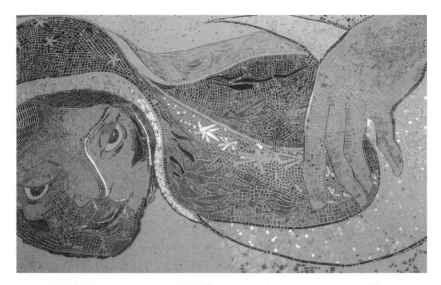

FIGURE 6.4 Mago Gandara, *La Niña Cósmica/The Cosmic Child* (1992–93). Mosaic located at Frederick Douglass Elementary School, El Paso, Texas. (Photograph by George Vargas.)

As the mural progressed, Mago frequently told stories of Coatlicue to the children and their parents, school officials, teachers, and staff. All became part of Mago's world as she labored day after day, at first spreading out the giant mural on the floor inside the cafeteria, and later working outside on scaffolding above its entrance.

To organize this masterfully executed mosaic, Mago utilized the sensuous "S-curve," a technique used to organize ancient Teotihuacán architecture and murals and found in the works of Praxiteles and Diego Rivera, who called it the "wave."[34] The curving motion of *La Niña's* undulating mantle and her graceful limbs bring an organizing rhythm to the vast space. These flowing, serpentine lines hold the artist's dazzling palette of colored glass and tile. The occasional use of bits of mirror in *La Niña's* halo and mantle of stars bring glittering movement to the mural's surface, as each piece independently reflects the trees blowing in the wind or the movement of passersby. Mago found herself wanting others to participate in the creative process, incorporating ideas from her assistants, visiting friends, Girl Scouts who came to help, and mothers and teachers passing through the school. "Mosaic mural [art] is exciting to me because it is cooperative in nature. It is not just a great 'I AM' . . . everyone has a chance to express [themselves] within the structure of the original design—not hodgepodge, not paint thrown on a wall. . . . We need to involve the public, always [remembering that] the artist is the prime soul of the design."[35]

On November 24, 1993, Mago finally celebrated *La Niña Cósmica's* completion with a community festival. More than 1,000 people packed the cafeteria to inaugurate or baptize the mural. Mago appeared in a long black dress decorated with colorful ribbons, a purple scarf artfully wrapped around her flowing long hair. When the festivities were over, Mago was filled with a sense of serenity and peace because her project had clearly brought spiritual unity and joy to the neighborhood for which it was created.

Overcoming the inevitable obstacles that materialize while making giant public works, Mago persisted in her vision, demonstrating to observers that anyone (especially the "hidden individual") can be a warrior or hero/heroine. Art, she believes, is central to the process of cultivating a unified border community, with a shared culture and common values, utilizing ideas that are universal. "We look down on a new order like astronauts. We are greeting spiritual liberation in quantum leaps." On a feminist level, Mago's murals act as implicit metaphors to illustrate her own journey: a woman's unique life experience at the border, "having to be brave, bold, and courageous in a society that does not necessarily nurture women."[36]

Nora Mendoza

Currently living in Michigan, Nora Mendoza was born in Westlaco, Texas, in 1932. She matured as an artist in Michigan after moving to Detroit in 1953 with her husband, who was completing his medical internship. While raising two children and serving in the role of doctor's wife, Mendoza still made time to study art. In the early 1970s she trained individually under respected Michigan abstract artists Richard Koslow and Ljubo Biro. When she divorced in 1975, determined to succeed as both a single mother and a working artist, she began selling her paintings in local malls, eventually gaining attention in galleries.

When necessary, Mendoza labels herself an abstract impressionist. Infused with rich color and hidden images, her paintings are now sold in galleries throughout the nation and abroad, and they decorate both private homes (such as Aretha Franklin's) and corporate offices (Ford, Rockefeller). She has been commissioned by various Chicano groups and individuals, including former UFW leader César Chávez, University of Minnesota Chicano historian Dennis Nodin Valdés, and Michigan State University linguist and Latin American historian Lucia Fox Lockert.

FIGURE 6.5 Nora Mendoza, from the *Spirits of the Fourth World* series (1992). Acrylic and mixed-media painting, 20 inches by 24 inches. (Photograph by Nora Mendoza.)

A Chicana feminist, Mendoza helped found early key Latino arts organizations such as Nuestras Artes de Michigan (an umbrella arts organization) and its offshoot, the Michigan Hispanic Cultural/Art Association (MHCAA). She also has served as consultant and advisor for New Detroit, Inc., and the Michigan Council for the Arts, helping to initiate vital support for minority artists and community organizations.

Having spent time in Nicaragua, Hawaii, and most recently Germany, Mendoza finds it exciting to cross over into other cultures in exhibiting her paintings and community murals. Following the 1992–95 touring exhibition "Crossing Bridges," which was organized by the MHCAA and featured seventeen Latino artists, Mendoza visited most of the nine German cities that the exhibit traveled to.[37] She was asked to return to Herrlingen, Germany, to produce an acrylic-on-wood portable mural with the help of local youth. As a certified elder member of Kanto de la Tierra/Medicine Eagles Gathering (a nonprofit intertribal council that brings people from many Indian Nations together to pray for the Earth's healing), she taught the German students about America's indigenous family, including Chicanos.

Her most recent work, *Spirits of the Fourth World* (fig. 6.5), combines

Chicano images and symbols with those of indigenous people. In this way, Mendoza celebrates her own Indian heritage as a Chicana. This series proudly speaks of Indian culture, protests the ongoing political trials and tribulations of Indians around the Fourth World, and captures the struggles of and changes made by Mexicans and Chicanos. Her new works serve to heal her wounds of depression and pain while acknowledging the guilt and pain experienced by other Chicanos. She believes that many youths hurt themselves and others because, "[If] you've been lied to for so many years, there's a lot of hurt, pain, and anger."[38] She believes that art can heal the pain, empowering us to improve our own lives and to help others.

From the beginning of her career as a Chicana artist to the present, Mendoza has always aimed to be true to her artistic and feminist identity. To better involve the viewer and call attention to social issues, she explains, "I have tried to express my deepest inner feelings and my own reality, which include the issues and struggles of our people, particularly women."[39]

Martín Moreno

Adept at both sculpture and mural painting (over his career he has directed more than eighty public art projects), Phoenix artist/art teacher Martín Moreno devotes much of his time to public service through community arts. Born in Adrian, Michigan (a predominantly Latino-populated farming and manufacturing community), in 1951, he was raised in Sunnyside, a Mexican/Chicano barrio, attended local schools and colleges, and worked in the fields and factories. His working-class background provides him with special memories and inspiration that are still visible in his work today. "My earliest memories are [those] of the fields—sitting in the back of a pickup truck with my family watching row upon row of corn and tomatoes form a visual pattern of rhythm," Moreno recalls. "Realities of superstition told by the elders, stories of La Llorona, the Earth, my glorious past—all the images come to life in stone, paint, and canvas, and walls."[40]

Moreno (whose works were included in the CARA exhibition) organizes public art projects in Phoenix, Tucson, and other cities in Arizona, specializing in working with youth. The CBS television network commissioned Moreno to paint a mural titled *In the Killing Fields of America* as a companion piece to a 1994 documentary of the same name, about the plague of violence that is destroying our youth and neighborhoods. Moreno led a dozen Phoenix-area children, who painted simple portraits of ten Americans who have died in "inner-city wars," including a two-year-old girl from Phoenix, above the U.S. stars and stripes on the wall of a local YMCA. Moreno insisted that all participants read short biographies of the people they were portraying. "We were all brought to tears,"[41] admits Moreno with sadness. A mural, according to Moreno, must be designed and executed with the community, because the finished product will become public property and part of that community's environment. The art form must reflect the character of the community and, through architectonics, complement the cultural and architectural environment.

Moreno most recently has received a major commission in Phoenix to sculpt a memorial monument to César Chávez (to date untitled). Two other professionals will also be working on the project, which is currently in the planning stage.[42] Mexican architect Dalinda Jimenez will design the landscape and a structure that will contain a larger-than-life-size romanticized portrait of the UFW leader by Chicano artist Zarco Guerrero (mask-maker, sculptor, and muralist living in Mesa, Arizona). Moreno will decorate the wall enclosure with relief work. The $100,000 public artwork (to be dedicated in April to coincide with Chávez's birthday) will further demonstrate the proficiency and inventiveness of Chicano artists who increasingly work in permanent public art. According to Moreno, this new opportunity represents a great honor to participate in the movement to immortalize Chávez and his accomplishments and a "chance to articulate my artistic perspective in permanent monumental sculpture."

Moreno continues to cross boundaries into new fields and to experiment with new media. For example, he has produced a series of "borderland" prints that were exchanged with Mexican artists in an effort to promote goodwill between the United States and Mexico and to explore the influence of borderland culture on both Chicano and Mexican artists. He recognizes and nurtures the ability of Chicano art to heal and inspire Chicanos and other Americans, offering optimism to both participants in his projects and to the viewers who "activate" his art by seeing a true reflection of themselves in his murals and sculpture.

Gluglio Gronk Nicandro

Born Gluglio Gronk Nicandro in 1954 in Los Angeles, Gronk is an internationally recognized Chicano artist who, without formal training, excels in casel painting, performance art, and installation art.[43] He initially gained

FIGURE 6.6 Gronk's site-specific installation *Fascinating Slippers No. 3* (1992). Painted at the University of Texas at El Paso. This photograph was taken during an early stage of the artwork's creation. (Photograph by George Vargas.)

notoriety through his work with ASCO. Often satirical, his present work reflects his long-time fascination with mass media, the results of juxtaposing images of high culture with low culture, and the constant shift of linear time from present to past. Gronk's installations are destroyed after their completion to demystify the art object by stressing the impermanence of the physical material. He welcomes visitors at his work site to participate in the creative process while he constructs his installation, encouraging personal interaction to humanize the artist and enhance a feeling of community involvement.

Above all, Gronk treasures the process of making art for and with the community, wherever that community may be. His 1992 piece, *Fascinating Slippers No. 3* (an installation that was painted at the University of Texas at El Paso over a five-day period, see fig. 6.6), was important to the artist for two reasons: It drew countless university students and community members who engaged with the artist in the creative process, thus stimulating interesting artistic and personal dialogue, and it evolved into other pieces for the artist.

> This was the first time that I had done a landscape painting. I did a landscape that wrapped around the walls like the mountains that wrap around El Paso. I also painted in lungs in the middle, because you have ASARCO [a local smelting industry] spewing all those gases into the air. The lungs unify the painting with all the

land. After all, what are wars fought about? Usually land. What do people return to? Land. You have all these issues about land. What is Chiapas [the agrarian rebellion in Mexico] all about? The row of K-Mart plastic buckets [in front of the main painted wall] symbolizes the borderland and the Rio Grande, and the water inside them speak[s] to the universal issue of water. All those kind[s] of ideas of connection come from this piece in El Paso, some of this has gone out to other pieces that I've worked on.[44]

Gronk contends that the artist needs to invent and reinvent him/herself over and over again to avoid mediocrity and stagnation. Change is necessary in the creation of new art.

My work has changed and transformed. I talk with other artists, and I think that there's a younger generation of artists who don't have to repeat things from the past. Looking at Diego Rivera many say, "Oh, look at what he did, he brought the Indians to the attention of the people!" I think that if he were alive today, he would be doing CD-ROM or videos. He wouldn't necessarily be doing murals. You utilize what is around, and you try different possibilities of communication.[45]

Consequently, Gronk represents the cutting edge of contemporary expression, never looking back but constructing ambitious installations, prints, and paintings, all seemingly taking different routes to reach new ways to define Chicano art. This diverse range in expression characterizes Gronk's work, which is all interrelated. Gronk elaborated on his new mixed-media projects in an interview with this author.

For myself, I do a diversity of projects, experimenting with painting and other media, perhaps such as music. In the piece done with Kronos String Quartet ["Tormenta Cantata," performed at UCLA, May 14, 1995, and dedicated to Gronk's dark-haired heroine who appears in some of his major work] . . . you have a string quartet trained in classical music, a soprano, and an artist with a paintbrush amplified for sound . . . and you create a visual element to a musical entity. This is opening up new possibilities for me as an artist. I learn from collaboration with different artists, different groups. I've been doing a lot of music projects. An opera [*Journey to Córdova*, performed at Dorothy Chandler Pavilion,

Los Angeles, 1995], this string quartet piece, and the Disney movie. I'm working on *Fantasia,* part two, on Beethoven's Fifth using computer animation. Very advanced stuff in the state-of-the-art. I take from that experience and incorporate it into my own work. I don't have a set of ideas [or know] where it's leading to. I research and include all that is in my journey, in my exploration.[46]

Pointing to the limited success of Chicano art in mainstream art, he appreciates that academics have documented its progress but notes that the majority of galleries and museums do not exhibit minority artists and do not have minorities employed as staff.[47] In defining where Chicano artists are now, Gronk downplays his own notable success in the mainstream because he is more concerned with the art-making process over the end product. He feels that he will be fully accepted when Chicano artists as a group are accepted and recognized within mainstream art. Commenting on Chicano art's role as avant-garde or vanguard expression:

> I consider myself more a part of the vanguard. I can't give myself that label "avant-garde." But I do think that if you're doing art on the cutting edge that doesn't quite fit, that challenges notions as to what is or should be, to me that's avant-garde. *Avant* means "front" in French. For every front, there must also be a rear! . . . The rear is the conservatism in the arts today. I feel that avant-garde means an artist who has stayed to work in the community, to make a real change in the community where he's producing art. To me that's avant, not necessarily what you read in books, not what you see in a museum or gallery.[48]

José "Match" Fernández

Attempting to correct society's misconception about graffiti, El Paso artist José "Match" Fernández uses graffiti as a vehicle of social commentary infused with fresh street culture and comic-book imagery. Born in 1955 in Ciudad Juárez, Mexico, Match moved to El Paso, where he attended Bowie High School and was instructed in art by Gaspar Enríquez.[49] He remembers being influenced by Grateful Dead posters when he moved to California and later by El Paso's *placa,* though he never was a tagger himself. A former sign painter who considers himself a street artist and border artist, Match treasures the process or public "show" of making a graffiti mural, which temporarily beautifies the environment, but eventually is painted over. Faithfully every Christmas, Match and other graffiti artists collaborate to create a special holiday mural for the El Paso community.

Since 1989, Match, Frank Molina, and others have created a graffiti mural that changes every month on the wall of El Paso's old Pershing Theater. With the permission of the building's owner, they invite emerging young graffiti artists to move away from gang vandalism and drug abuse by exploring alternative mural art with them. In 1992, the Pershing mural (at the time called *Stop the Killing*) received support from Los Murales (a Junior League–sponsored project dedicated to the proliferation and preservation of El Paso's murals), marking their first contribution to graffiti art.

However, Match's proudest community achievement was his participation in the *Gene K. Wilson Memorial Mural* project in 1994. Using only black and white spray paint, he painted a huge permanent portrait of Wilson, a popular local artist/activist, on the wall of the Goeting Clinic/ Planned Parenthood Center. Because the realistic painting faithfully captures the spirit of Wilson, many viewers are amazed that the portrait was done solely with spray cans.

Match predicts that computer/digital technology and graphics software will become a greater presence in graffiti art. Computer-generated designs and lettering are emerging influences among the youth, who, for example, now use "slice and shift" digitized lettering instead of the once-popular balloon letters or the "wild style." Finally, he believes that the future of Chicano art will be discovered in the street, where youth and other members of the Chicano community congregate and celebrate their uniqueness

Conclusion: The Future

Challenging in theme and content, with styles uniquely Chicano and yet often urbane, international, even chic, Chicano art still is intertwined with the Chicano experience of U.S. society within the context of American history. It inevitably changes as American society changes, while maintaining a link to its Mexican roots. No matter its intent, the very nature of Chicano art is cultivated from a historical continuity of diverse artistic traditions and cultural rituals that flow from a deep communal well of creativity.

Many of the artists from the early Chicano Movimiento now are established artists, art teachers, and community leaders. They have moved from making immediate neighborhood art, often with recycled and impermanent materials, to making permanent monumental public art and exploring new media such as computer technologies. Whereas the artists of the 1960s looked toward Mexico for inspiration, today's young Chicano artists have role models living and working right in their own neighborhoods. Many of these young artists are producing murals, still the most accessible vehicle of visual communication, while others explore new avenues of expression. Additionally, as the women's liberation movement left its imprint on American society, the number of Chicanas entering the art scene has increased, bringing provocative feminine visions into the limelight.

Chicano art, for better or worse, is synonymous with social movement and artistic change. Chicano artists still encounter resistance to their ideas because they are the messengers of progressive change, a message often met with resistance, as it apparently is human nature to fear that which we do not understand. Nonetheless, Chicanos represent the inevitable movement of people of color into the U.S. mainstream, much like outsiders and immigrants of previous times, and reflect the ethnic diversity that binds all Americans together. The formal influences to be discovered in Chicano art are derived from North American, Latin American, and European art movements, testifying to the migration of a people that continues between Mexico and the United States and creating local neighborhoods in a global community. Chicano artists and Latin American artists increasingly are drawn to each other's art in their shared Latin(o) American search for a new identity in the American landscape. Chicano art and Latin American art serve as reference points on a cultural bridge that spans the new world and the old one.

Today, political commentary still is quite popular in Chicano art, sometimes overshadowing the newer, more personal, expressions simply because many still expect Chicano art to be polemic, maybe even confrontational, by nature. Growing numbers of scholars and laypersons have documented, interpreted, and repeatedly interconnected Chicano art at multiple levels to broader art and political movements. Chicano art historians such as Amalia Mesa-Bains, Chon Noriega, Víctor Sorell, and Tomás Ybarra-Frausto join other scholars in deciphering the language of Chicano art to help us better understand its unfolding nature.

In earlier times there were few publications on Chicano artists and their artworks, and even fewer art historians in the field to document, research, and analyze the role and meaning of Chicano art. Many early

Chicano historians met the same resistance that confronted the artists. Even today, they continue to receive criticism for their academic studies. The general public has expressed a greater interest in Chicano culture than before, including a growing number of Chicanos who want to see their history and culture on display. Adopting a no risk attitude, most museums and galleries give Chicano art little or no attention. Denied traditional spaces, Chicano artists often turn to alternative spaces such as community centers and churches to exhibit their work. Specialized museums such as the Mexican Art Museum in San Francisco and the Mexican Art Center in Chicago have been created, directed, and staffed by professionals who generally are knowledgeable in both the Western aesthetic and the Latino aesthetic.

The future of Chicano art will continue to relate to the historical condition of the Chicano people as an emerging ethnic population inside an American sociopolitical system. Like jazz and abstract expressionism, Chicano art increasingly will be accepted as an American cultural product, as more Chicano artists cross over into mainstream society. Chicano art also will become recognized internationally as Chicanos themselves traverse international borders. Because of the increasing importance of the trade between Mexico and the United States, cities located on or near the U.S.–Mexico border, such as El Paso, Phoenix, San Diego, and Tucson, are becoming more important, as are the expressions of contemporary Mexican/Chicano culture that characterize most border towns. Ironically, once ignored by the business sector, Chicano art now is gradually being displayed alongside cowboy art and Indian art throughout the Southwest in an attempt to commercialize the unique cultures of North America's last frontier.

Just like any other transformative art, Chicano art can help unify us. How we read the messages will be increasingly interrelated to the destiny of Chicano Americans in the information age, and to their interrelationship with other Americans and the rest of the world. To better understand the state of Chicano art is to better comprehend the changes in the Chicano mind as it searches for a new identity and renewed family and societal associations. Like visionaries, Chicano artists at the cutting edge connect with the present by recalling the past while peering into the future. Chicano art in this sense is a consciousness-raising expression that has the power to enlighten, liberate, and heal while advancing the precious American ideal of individual freedom and creative liberty. Chicano art provides a practical framework of cultural reality for a people's America of the future. As such, the new open model of Chicano art increasingly will serve as a visual mirror of change and popular culture in a new American frontier.

Notes

1. Ursula R. Murray, ed., *Latino Artists: Michigan. U.S.A., Crossing Bridges* (Detroit: Michigan Hispanic Cultural/Art Association, 1991).

2. Murray, *Latino Artists*.

3. The racial/ethnic trunk of the Americas also is distinctly *mestizo*, constituting the majority of the American population. Edmund Stephen Urbanski, *Hispanic America and Its Civilizations* (Norman, Okla.: University of Oklahoma Press, 1978), 84–85.

4. Armando Durón et al., "Ester Hernández," in *Encuentro: Invasion of the Americas and the Making of the Mestizo* (Venice, Calif.: Social and Public Art Resource Center, 1991), 19.

5. Murray, *Latino Artists*.

6. The immediate cultural reality for artists in the United States, especially in the borderlands, is truly mestizo, not exclusively Mexican or Chicano. "*Mestizaje,* not *Chicanismo,* is the reality of our lives," declares feminist writer Gloria Anzaldúa. "We bleed in mestizaje, we eat, sweat, and cry in mestizaje." Gloria Anzaldúa, "Chicana Artists," NACLA *Report on the Americas* 27, no. 1 (1993): 40.

7. Durón et al., *Encuentro,* 14.

8. Shifra M. Goldman, "The Iconography of Chicano Self-Determination: Race, Ethnicity, and Class," in *Dimensions of the Americas: Art and Social Change in the Americas* (Chicago: University of Chicago Press, 1994), 398–408. For a summary on early Chicano murals, see also Goldman, "Resistance and Identity: Street Murals of Aztlán," in *Dimensions of the Americas,* 118–22; and Eva Cockcroft and John Weber, *Toward a People's Art: The Contemporary Mural Movement* (New York: E. P. Dutton & Company, 1977). Also, for an update on California mural art and Chicanas, see Eva Sperling Cockcroft and Holly Barnet-Sánchez, eds., *Signs from the Heart: California Chicano Murals* (Venice, Calif.: Social and Public Art Resource Center, 1990; also published by University of New Mexico Press, 1993 and 1996).

9. *National Council of La Raza/*NCLR *Exhibition* (Detroit: National Council of La Raza, 1993).

10. One of the first reports on Chicano art as an art movement was Manuel J. Martínez's "The Art of the Chicano Movement and the Movement of Chicano Art" (1972), reprinted in *Speaking for Ourselves: American Ethnic Writing,* ed. Lillian Faderman (Glenview, Ill.: Scott, Foresman and Company, 1975), 314–16. Mildred Monteverde was one of the first historians to contextualize Chicano art within a Chicano aesthetic and an historical chronology. See Mildred Monteverde, "Contem-

porary Chicano Art" (1972), reprinted in *Chicano Art History: A Book of Selected Readings*, ed. Jacinto Quirarte (San Antonio: Research Center for the Arts and Humanities, University of Texas at San Antonio, 1984), 80–83.

11. The first books on Chicano art history were authored by Jacinto Quirarte, *Mexican American Artists* (Austin: University of Texas Press, 1973); and Raymond Barrio, *Mexico's Art and Chicano Art* (Sunnyvale, Calif.: Ventura Press, 1975). Additionally, Quirarte documented the beginnings of Chicano art, including writings by artists, activists, and scholars on Chicano identity, Chicano manifestos, and the roles of Chicano art in *Chicano Art History: A Book of Selected Writings* (San Antonio: University of Texas, San Antonio, 1984).

12. Gronk, tape-recorded interview by George Vargas, El Paso, Texas, June 11, 1995.

13. For a review of posters as revolutionary art and its relationship to the New Left, read Eva Cockcroft's chapter on "The United States and Socially Concerned Latin American Art 1920–1970," in *The Latin American: Art and Artists in the United States*, eds. Luis Cancel, Jacinto Quirarte, et al. (New York: Harry N. Abrams, Inc., 1988), 184 221.

14. Víctor Valle, "Chicano Art: An Emerging Generation," in *Southern California's Latino Community*, eds. George Ramos et al. (Los Angeles: *Los Angeles Times*, 1983), 94–97. Also, note the reproduction of Carrasco's mural that includes a portrait of David Alfaro Siqueiros's painting *Tropical America*, in Shifra M. Goldman's article, "How, Why, Where, and When It All Happened: Chicano Murals of California," in *Signs from the Heart*, 32.

15. Mario Micheli, *Siqueiros* (Milan, Italy: Secretaría de Educación Pública, 1968), 5– 51. Also see Shifra M. Goldman, "Siqueiros and Three Early Murals in Los Angeles," (1974), reprinted in Quirarte, *Chicano Art History*, 56–63.

16. Installation/performance/earthbody artist Ana Mendieta, who was separated from her parents during Castro's revolution and sent to the United States, identified with Chicanos and other Latinos searching for their roots. (She returned to Cuba in 1980 to reclaim her roots through new works, but she tragically died in 1985.) "The condition of all Latin American artists that live in the United States is similar, although this condition is not one of my preoccupations, I recognize that, through it, a kind of search—a collision—of our roots is imposed [on] us, a search that is not necessarily the same for each one nor requires the same channels." Carla Stellweg et al., eds., *Artes Visuales* (Mexico City, Mexico: Museum of Modern Art, 1981), 69.

17. Roberto Gil de Montes, "Presentation," in *Artes Visuales*, 9.

18. Gil de Montes, "Presentation." For more information on multiculturalism and the conduits existing between Chicano and Latino American artists, see Lucy R. Lippard, *Mixed Blessings: New Art in a Multicultural America* (New York: Pantheon Books, 1990).

19. Gronk interview (1995).

20. Harry Gamboa, Jr., "In the City of Angels, Chameleons, and Phantoms: ASCO, A Case of Chicano Art in Urban Tones (or ASCO was a Four-Member Word)," in *Chicano Art: Resistance and Affirmation/CARA,* eds. Richard Griswold del Castillo et al. (Los Angeles: Wight Art Gallery, UCLA, 1991), 129. Also see S. Zaneta Kosiba-Vargas, "Harry Gamboa and ASCO: The Emergence and Development of a Chicano Art Group, 1971–1987" (Ph.D. dissertation, University of Michigan, 1988).

21. Durón et al., eds., *Encuentro,* 18.

22. Lippard argues that, unfortunately, the element of quality in art "is identifiable only by those in power . . . [caretakers] overwhelmingly white, middle-class, and—in the upper echelons—usually male." According to this "lofty view, racism has nothing to do with it. . . . Quality will transcend boundaries and prevail; so-called minorities just haven't got it yet." Artists of color and women dedicated to revising the notion of quality have been turned away at the gates of mainstream art "by this garlic-and-cross strategy." Lippard, *Mixed Blessings,* 7.

23. Murray, *Latino Artists.*

24. Gloria Osuna Pérez, *Rethinking La Malinche* (Austin, Tex.: Mixec-Arte Museum, 1995).

25. "Chicano Connection" is a touring collection of prints by Self Help Graphics (a collective/gallery in East Los Angeles) curated by the Salt River Artistic Movement (alternative art space in Phoenix) and funded by the Arizona Commission on the Arts.

26. For more detailed information on the artists, their works, and the history of Chicano art, see Griswold del Castillo et al., *Chicano Art.*

27. Griswold del Castillo et al., *Chicano Art,* 348.

28. For a complete account of the Salt War, see C. L. Sonnichsen, *The El Paso Salt War of 1877* (El Paso: Texas Western Press, 1961). See also Arnoldo de León, *They Called Them Greasers* (Austin: University of Texas Press, 1983), 99–101.

29. University of Texas, El Paso, students who worked on the silo mural include Diana Capital, Donna Haynes, Mauricio Olague, Steve Salazar, and Alfonso Valenzuela.

30. Juan Contreras, "La Rosa Dolorosa," reproduced in "La Rosa Dolorosa Exhibition" gallery sheet, El Paso Museum of Art, 1995.

31. Contreras, "La Rosa Dolorosa."

32. See Max Benavídez, "A Battle of Wills," *Los Angeles Times,* 9 June 1991. Also see his article "Latino Dada: Savage Satire from Harry Gamboa, Jr.," *L.A. Weekly,* 16–22 May 1986.

33. Summarized from an article by George Vargas, "Mago Gandara: A Woman Artist at the Border" (El Paso: Center for Inter-American Border Studies, 1995).

34. Diego Rivera, "Dynamic Detroit—An Interpretation," *Creative Artist,* April 1933, 289.

35. Mago Gandara, videotaped interviews by George Vargas, El Paso, Texas, 1993.

36. Gandara interview (1993).

37. "Crossing Bridges" successfully toured Germany (part of which at that time was still under Communism), extending its initial schedule because of its popularity with large European audiences. Latino artists from Michigan were offered low fares by the German airline, Lufthansa, to encourage them to attend the exhibition's numerous receptions in order to provide informal talks to curious yet sincere audiences.

38. Linda Ann Chomin, "Her Canvases Exude Her Indian Heritage," *The Observer* (Livonia, Michigan), 6 September 1995.

39. Nora Mendoza, letter to George Vargas, 16 September 1995.

40. *National Council of La Raza/NCLR Exhibition* (Detroit: National Council of La Raza, 1993).

41. Alita Corcos, "Portraits of the City," *Phoenix Magazine,* August 1995, 102.

42. Martín Moreno, telephone interview by George Vargas, El Paso, Texas, 17 September 1995.

43. For more background information on Gronk and ASCO, see Lippard, *Mixed Blessings,* 29, 227–29.

44. Gronk interview (1995).

45. Ibid.

46. Ibid.

47. Ibid. Regarding the noticeable lack of minority artists and staff in major museums, see David Ross et al., *Race, Ethnicity and Culture in the Visual Arts* (New York: American Council for the Arts, 1992).

48. Gronk interview (1995).

49. José "Match" Fernández, taped interview by George Vargas, El Paso, Texas, 23 August 1995.

Contemporary Chicano Theater

ARTURO RAMÍREZ

*C*ontemporary Chicano theater continues to develop into an ever more vibrant, artistic, sophisticated, and cosmopolitan corpus of dramatic works that reflects changes in the Chicano people and their place in American society. In the last generation, from the 1960s to the 1990s, Chicano theater has rapidly evolved from its initial incarnation as a body of work expressing social protest and politically oriented short works dominated by one important creative figure. In recent times, Chicano theater has embraced a wider spectrum of theatrical activity. The sources of inspiration for this theater are also much more varied. Chicano theater shows much promise at the beginning of the twenty-first century.

Since the 1960s, with a tone ranging from consciousness-raising to rage, Chicano theater has been generating a new and different look. Further development and consolidation occurred in the 1970s as feminism entered the picture. In the 1980s—the Reagan years, a period that was declared the Decade of the Hispanic—changes, adjustment, nuances, and shadings in the twists and turns of a volatile art form offered a profile of a changing Chicano people. Innovative stage creations interacted with and reflected a naturally evolving social environment that continued to change in the 1990s. As in the previous era, Luis Valdez remained the major creator, leader, and innovator, but new trends, stars, and works also arose. The contributions of feminism and a host of women playwrights and their prolific theater productions became notable. So did changes in Chicano theater themes and subject matter, which evolved from the overwhelmingly dominant sociopolitical orientation of the 1960s to the deeper interiorization, psychological probing, and philosophical inquiries of more recent works. In addition, Chicano theater took a stab at the mainstream, if only as an "alternative" view; greater support from academic institutions and a greater sense of professionalism also took place.

While some social protest themes became less strident, exposure of Chicano perspectives became more widespread. Works such as *Corridos* and *I Don't Have to Show You No Stinking Badges,* both by Luis Valdez, were among the recent major hits, but for different reasons, as will be discussed below. A number of feminist works were innovative and controversial, ranging from Estela Portillo Trambley's *Sor Juana* (1983) to Josefina López's *Real Women Have Curves* and Cherríe Moraga's *Heroes and Saints* (1992). Important playwrights such as Carlos Morton and Denise Chávez made notable contributions, as did specific plays such as Judith and Severo Pérez's *Soldierboy,* among others. In short, the last three decades have been productive for theater by Chicanos and Latinos, marking an era of intense work and exciting results in the midst of a changing Chicano population and a steadily evolving American society heading toward diversity and multiculturalism.

Historical Antecedents

Because Chicano theater has so recently achieved wider public recognition and because Chicano theater works so often emphatically present current social and political concerns, it is easy to regard Chicano theater as a purely contemporary phenomenon. However firmly rooted in the present it might seem, contemporary Chicano theater did not develop in a vacuum. Indeed, it represents the culmination and synthesis of a long, rich tradition, although it is a tradition that has been generally ignored and neglected by the mainstream theatrical apparatus of literary historians, drama critics, the theater-going public, the popular press, and even scholarly publications. As part of the recent rediscovery and reevaluation of the Chicano past, critics and literary historians such as Luis Leal, Nicolás Kanellos, Tomás Ybarra-Frausto, Jorge Huerta, and others have written about the history of and the context behind Chicano theater.[1] In addition to the dramatic works of Americans and Western Europeans, there is the indigenous dramatic base as exemplified by *Rabinal Achí,* a Mayan work that, in modern multimedia fashion, combines chants, poetry, dancing, and religious motifs with drama. Although it is the only extant pre-Columbian play, there are references to other plays and fragments that suggest the rich dramatic tradition that was destroyed by the Spanish in their eagerness to eradicate all traces of "pagan" indigenous culture. The Spanish cultural heritage itself also includes a long and rich dramatic tradition that culminated in the masterpieces of the Spanish Golden Age soon after the conquest of Mexico. During the colonial period, the Spanish imposed on the Indians a steady theatrical diet of religious dramas, *pastorelas* (religious shepherds' plays dealing with the nativity),[2] and *autos sacramentales* (dramas for the purpose of evangelization). These didactic and evangelistic works sought to propagandize and educate the Indians in the glories of the Church, just as Luis Valdez's Teatro Campesino, many years later, would propagandize on behalf of La Causa. But even as the Spanish imposed their culture, the indigenous peoples continued to create theater, sometimes incorporating only partially understood Spanish themes, such as the eternal Spanish battle against Moors, a foe they had never seen. In addition, theatrical representations (later formalized into traveling theatrical troupes) took place throughout New Spain, developing a rich vein of popular comedy and entertainment that included political and social humor skits and domestic and melodramatic drama.[3] Not surprisingly, significant scholarly literature attests to the development of a Chicano theatrical tradition as an outgrowth of diverse antecedents. The view held by some that Chicano theater seemed to emerge full-blown in the 1960s is contradicted by more recent scholarly work.

The Backdrop: Chicano Theater in the 1960s

The advent of the Teatro Campesino (Farmworkers' Theater) in 1965, created as guerrilla theater to accompany César Chávez's Great Grape Strike of Delano, California, and the creation of the United Farm Workers Union, marked the beginning of contemporary Chicano theater. It was a period of remarkable social, political, cultural, and artistic ferment as Chicanos fought to establish their identity, reaffirm their dignity, and claim basic human and civil rights. Part of the all-encompassing struggles of La Causa, the Chicano renaissance of this period, was an explosion of creativity in the arts that expressed greater social, political, and economic consciousness and underlined the urgent need for change. In fact, theater, as well as the other arts (literature, art, music), often served as a backbone for militant resistance and revolutionary radicalism.

Luis Valdez, the creator of the Teatro Campesino, virtually single-handedly defined the nature of Chicano theater in the 1960s.[4] Influenced by Brecht, Cantinflas, the Comedia del Arte, and the San Francisco Mime

Troupe, Valdez led the Teatro Campesino in the creation of *actos*, short one-act plays, sketches, or vignettes that featured strong social protest leavened by humor and that were the result of collective improvisation. The work of a theater group with few resources for elaborate costumes or stage settings, the actos were performed in the flatbed of a truck by the side of a road, in the street, or wherever the Chicano audiences might be. Above all, the actos dealt with the Chicano experience, using Chicano characters, a Chicano point of view, and Chicano language, containing elements of both Spanish and English. They portrayed a collective social reality rather than individual neurosis or psychology. This was theater with a semi-Marxist orientation, a theater of social protest that sought to raise the consciousness of its audience and educate Chicanos to the injustice of their situation. But Valdez also wanted to support farmworkers and strikers, to raise their morale, and to inspire them to fight on. An important weapon for achieving these aims was humor, broad and bawdy at times, but aimed unerringly at Chicano enemies, wounding them with ridicule and satire. At the same time, Chicano audiences were hugely entertained. Outward frivolity merely reaffirmed a tremendously serious underlying social protest and political purpose.

Influenced both by Valdez and by the same white-hot fervor under which the Teatro Campesino had emerged, scores of theater groups were created. Many were based in universities, but some arose in the barrio, reflecting the reality that the majority of Chicanos were/are not farmworkers. For example, there was the Teatro de la Esperanza in Santa Barbara, California; the Teatro del Desengaño in Gary, Indiana; and the Teatro Urbano in Los Angeles. The politics of these theaters was radical and countercultural, militant and socialistic, Marxist and revolutionary.

In fact, 1960s Chicano theater was characterized by Brechtian theater techniques and theories mixed with a Cantinflas-like *rascuachi* flavor, fusing discontent, humor, and very clear evidence of the influence of Luis Valdez. What emerged from the Chicano theater of the 1960s was a portrait of La Raza from within, with Chicanos themselves portraying their own reality, in their own language, from their own perspective. If some of the urgency of this period has dissipated in subsequent years, there still remains a strong desire for an honest and authentic rendering of a Chicano reality from a Chicano point of view.

Brechtian theory was applied by Chicano playwrights to serve the need for social change.[5] An "unrealistic" production could produce the necessary distancing to bring about reflection in the audience, unlike the catharsis of

Aristotelian theater. The thinking audience, whose consciousness had been raised regarding the nature of social, political, and economic problems facing Chicanos, could now seek to effect reform, or at least change. Several of the actos, most notably *Los vendidos, Las dos caras del patroncito, No saco nada de la escuela,* and *Soldado raso,* seem to have achieved enduring popularity and are still performed by a new generation. Some of the techniques developed by the Teatro Campesino and other groups of the period can be seen, modified and extended, in the satirical sketches of groups such as Culture Clash and the Chicano Secret Service. Valdez himself has continued to develop as a playwright, director, creator, and producer at the forefront of innovations and developments in Chicano theater since 1965.

Setting the Stage: Chicano Theater in the 1970s

The early seventies were marked by increasing theatrical ferment but also by the tendency for theater groups to be affiliated with other sponsoring theatrical institutions, such as universities or community groups, and to receive grants and other forms of public subsidy. The idea of a theater that springs from the people and is sustained only by them, rarely more than a utopian ideal in the past, gave way to the practicalities of operating from an established base with the guarantee of at least modest resources.

This "institutionalization" of Chicano theater coincided with and perhaps made possible the development of professionalism and the entrance of Chicano theater into the mainstream of American drama, although by way of an "alternative theater" route that has not fully accepted Chicano or Latino theater. Dramatic productions by women also began to appear during this period as did deeper psychological insights and the plumbing of themes other than social protest. The net result was a growing corpus of Chicano dramatic works and the emergence of a Chicano theater canon. Not surprisingly, this period also saw the beginnings of serious scholarly study of Chicano theater.[6]

Certain gains and losses in the 1970s (and into the present) are clear when compared with theater of the 1960s. The continuing move to the mainstream was a step very often away from the barrio and the Mexican American community and toward the general dominant-culture theaters. Chicano theater productions were presented in regional theaters such as those found in Seattle, San Diego, Houston, Chicago, Los Angeles, and San Francisco and also in major world theater centers in New York, Paris,

Mexico City, and other major European and Latin American cities. As it evolved and developed, the quality, depth, and scope of Chicano theater demanded a much larger and more sophisticated stage than a makeshift street, truck-bed, or bare platform in an urban *colonia*. It even outgrew rural Chicano school-, church-, or community-based venues. As Chicano theater moved away from Valdez's acto format, with its specifically Chicano content, characters, conflicts, themes, and language, it also became a part of a "world theater" and the cosmopolitan attitude it promoted.

Theater among Chicanos could not maintain an insulated parochialism because it spoke to, of, and for the human condition as well as the universal conflicts and challenges created by human behavior and social conditions found worldwide. In the United States, even in Aztlán, the specific region of the American Southwest viewed as the homeland of the Chicano people, world conditions were also having a powerful effect. After the Cuban Revolution and the Vietnam War, global concerns continued to have an effect into the 1970s and beyond in the form of antiwar protests, pro-Cuba revolutionary militancy and inspiration, the ebb and flow of immigration, and anti-imperialistic currents. In the late 1970s Chicanos were deeply affected by Central American political and social turmoil, which added hundreds of thousands of Spanish-speaking refugees and exiles from Central America to the constant stream of undocumented workers that continued from Mexico, adding millions to the Latino population of the United States. Chicano theater, in its "purist" ethnic, culturally specific sense, had to expand its horizons to accommodate these different "Hispanic" or "Latino" elements, particularly because dramatic production is collaborative by nature. Indeed, even the labeling of Chicano theater as "Chicano" rather than "Latino" is an issue that is far too complex and peripheral to the basic aims of this chapter to be considered here in any detail, although it is an issue of great significance, as noted by Luis Leal, Rolando Hinojosa, Tomás Rivera, and many others.[7]

The 1970s also marked a transitional period between the nascent Chicano theater of the 1960s and the emergence of a more mature style of Chicano theater. The transition was led by Luis Valdez through his own dramatic productions as well as his creative leadership. With great generosity, Valdez allowed other grassroots Chicano theaters in the Southwest and beyond to use his actos. However, Valdez wrote the last of his actos in the early 1970s, after which he focused on the theme of the Vietnam War and turned to writing full-length Chicano plays. One such full-length play, *Zoot*

Suit, premiered in Los Angeles in 1977 to great acclaim and commercial, as well as critical, success.

Valdez's *Zoot Suit* has been much commented upon since it was presented commercially on Broadway and later released as a film. In *Zoot Suit,* Valdez explores the *pachuco,* the Mexican American rebellious figure attempting to find an identity in early 1940s Los Angeles. Notable in this dramatization of an historical event, the Sleepy Lagoon Trial, is Valdez's stylization: the blending of music, fantasy, Chicano language usage, myth mixed with convincing realism and strong social protest, and memorable characters such as the two central figures, El Pachuco and Henry Reyna. In the midst of all this, Valdez also manages to include psychological probing, references to indigenism as an important source for Chicano ideology, theatrical techniques involving self-reflection, and even philosophical considerations about the nature of reality. The play, focusing on a murder trial and the appeal process, is both ambitious and compelling. Critics on the East Coast were much less laudatory than those on the West Coast. Some were even hostile. The Chicano cultural specificity of the play and the bilingualism and biculturalism were apparently not something many East Coast critics could applaud. Chicano theater seemed to be a regional matter, evoking prejudice in the uninitiated and ignorant. *Zoot Suit,* however, still remains of central importance. Its publication in 1992 marked another important step in its continuing significance and emphasized the enduring importance of Luis Valdez and his work.

In addition to Luis Valdez, many other voices with different stories to tell emerged during the 1970s. For example, although Valdez is considered by many to be a *machista* writer, another strongly feminist writer also came forth.

Estela Portillo Trambley, of El Paso, published a poetic tragedy with a lesbian theme, *The Day of the Swallows* (1973).[8] Portillo Trambley also published a lighthearted musical, *Sun Images* (1976), with an El Paso–Juárez border setting that Nicolás Kanellos and Jorge Huerta judged to be a kind of "commodity" theater, with no serious social themes of consequence.[9] Other works began to identify more strongly with mainstream theater, including techniques such as psychological rather than social probing, a greater feel for individual characters, and stronger, deeper characterizations rather than characters acting in a mechanistic, deterministic fashion in response to the effects of purely external social forces. An internal perspective also came to be more characteristic in the humor directed both at Chicanos and their adversaries. At a technical level, more formalized sophistication, particularly the use of many more theatrical resources, became more common. Although the leadership and creative development of Luis Valdez often set the direction and innovations of Chicano theater, other significant influences were also at work during this period.

Toward Center Stage:
Chicano Theater Emerges as Distinct

From the 1980s on, Chicano theater moved further into the mainstream, with higher quality and more professional work. The move involved partial abandonment of "el pueblo Chicano" audience in favor of "explaining" the Chicano themes to a more general audience. Legitimacy, to some extent, was achieved through compromise. The harshly forceful political content of the "agit-prop" theater (theater with a propagandistic purpose that seeks to agitate its audience) of the 1960s moved from the streets and the labor fields to theaters that were part of mainstream Anglo American culture and society, the artistic home of a more or less liberal elite. The use of Spanish and Chicano slang terms, part of a unique Chicano discourse made necessary by a people between two cultures, had to be restricted in deference to the English-only audience. Occasionally, a colorful series of stereotypes emerged, confirming the worldview of a sometimes ignorant, uncaring Anglo American audience. At times, however, an important consciousness-raising function took place. Triumphs could be small—perhaps merely the affirmation of the existence of Chicanos and the creation of a viable theatrical representation. Chicanos were moving away from invisibility and toward a strong expression of theatrical talent. At least in theater circles, there was increasing awareness and recognition, again with Luis Valdez's works leading the way. A theatrical beachhead had been established, a part of the American and world stage had been claimed by Chicano theater. Naturally enough, Chicano diehards decried the compromises made by Chicano theater in the 1980s. Luis Valdez was charged with selling out, of compromising his integrity, of becoming more and more consciously commercial, and of focusing on a general mainstream audience of the dominant culture instead of the Chicano audience of old.[10] Times change, people change, one must adjust to new circumstances. Valdez kept defending himself, pointing out that as a middle-aged man he was definitely not the same radical revolutionary that he was when he was in his mid-twenties.[11] Positive reviews from critics in major cities in the Southwest echoed the popular and commercial success attained by Valdez and others entering the mainstream. Chicano theater could be considered primarily an entertaining art that probes the human condition, but with elements that are poorly understood by mainstream audiences, elements that may appear alien, exotic, social, ethnic, seemingly part of a secret cult.

In many ways, Valdez has continued to be prominent in the 1980s and 1990s. Yet, in contemporary Chicano theater, as we enter the twenty-first century, Valdez represents one significant voice among a number of voices, tendencies, playwrights, ideologies, perspectives, theater styles, and currents. Chicano theater of the 1980s and 1990s has become far more complex, diverse, and diffused than the work of one man. Feminism, whether radically militant or less militantly feminist, has become increasingly significant in presenting truth from a woman's perspective. Grassroots theater in the form of humorous sketches has become increasingly polished and professional, as in the works of Culture Clash. Political and social messages still maintain forcefulness, but the study of Chicano subjectivity is becoming more apparent. Psychological probing now coexists with an exploration of social forces. Historical inquiries by both playwrights and Chicano drama history scholars continue apace. Philosophical discourse is found both in contemporary Chicano drama and in the works of specialists in literary theory as they study the different levels and nature of reality in Chicano theater. Multiculturalism is also a factor. A production may be Latino or a reflection of a multicultural society, with, for example, a Chicano playwright portraying Chicana/o characters as merely part of a larger American society.

The most exciting and important trendsetter to emerge recently, Chicano playwright Octavio Solís, demonstrates this multicultural type of drama. Solís's work *Prospect* (1993), produced by the Teatro Campesino, demonstrates his great theatrical talent as well as this new multicultural tendency in Chicano theater. Solís, originally from Texas, portrays a Mexican American population in dramatic terms that are no less vital and vibrant than those portrayed in the Chicano theater of the past. In Solís's theater productions, however, Chicano characters interact with a number of highly important Anglo American characters. The work is no longer focused solely on the Chicano characters and their problems. Multiculturalism is a reality that Solís portrays naturally on the stage, thus pointing Chicano theater toward the mainstream, while maintaining a Chicano perspective. Contemporary Chicano theater, indeed, has evolved into something new as developments and changes move us into the new century.

It is quite fortunate that humor has remained a constant throughout the history of Chicano theater. The notion that ethnic and minority groups have no sense of humor, an irrelevant but persistent charge also leveled against feminists, is constantly disproved in Chicano theater. Valdez always leavened his plays with humor, and that tradition continues. As we enter the new millennium, Chicano theater also provides an alternative philosophy or ideology, part of "New Age" consciousness. Chicano theater of the 1960s and early 1970s was more localized, narrower in focus, and more culturally specific. A greater cosmopolitan perspective has emerged in more recent times, targeting a wider audience that includes other Latinos and the mainstream Anglo American audience. Though sometimes muted, political content continues to be an important part of Chicano theater, simply because it is such an urgent message for the theater to convey. Chicano theater is generated by those in a desperate social, political, and economic struggle, amidst the problems of discrimination, oppression, exploitation, injustice, and alienation.

Chicano theater of the 1980s and 1990s is certainly richer in some ways and poorer in other ways than it used to be. As mentioned, the sheer number of Chicano theater groups has decreased notably, from more than 100 in the 1960s to scarcely a score or so today, although exact figures are very hard to come by, given the regional and ephemeral nature of many small nonprofessional groups. College and university groups, as part of a spontaneous coming together of interested and committed students and faculty, have also declined, but there have been some gains in institutionalized theater. Officially sanctioned theater programs have been established at the University of California, San Diego, and the University of Southern California. Official support, established curricula, professional faculty, and more direct avenues for exercising a Chicano theater career have made the validation of Chicano theater possible. Theater classes and workshops are increasingly available in many southwestern colleges and universities and at the high-school level. Chicano and Latino theater have become an increasingly national phenomenon. In a few cases, theater specialists can devote themselves full-time, or virtually full-time, to Chicano theater at major universities in the Southwest.

Such situations are, unfortunately, relatively rare; among the exceptions are Carlos Morton and Jorge Huerta (at the University of California,

San Diego) and a few others in university settings. More often, opportunities are provided for Chicano theater at cultural centers that focus on Chicano arts. Notable examples include the Plaza de la Raza in Los Angeles, the Guadalupe Arts Center in San Antonio, the Centro Cultural de la Raza in San Diego, the Mission Cultural Center in San Francisco, the Casa de la Raza in Santa Barbara, and La Peña in Berkeley. These and a number of other such locations sometimes offer a ready-made stop for a touring Chicano play, for a local production, for Chicano theater classes and workshops, and for the awarding of Playwright in Residence fellowships. In addition to support from educational and cultural centers, professional groups such as the Teatro Campesino can also be crucial in the genesis of new works that require a playwright, director, cast, and technical and support personnel working in unison. For example, Judith and Severo Pérez's *Soldierboy,* a psychological antiwar drama and one of the best Chicano plays of the 1980s, was developed at the Teatro Campesino in San Juan Bautista under the tutelage of Luis Valdez, who directed the play's first production and nurtured it along as part of an innovative collaborative venture.[12] Similarly, the Teatro de la Esperanza, now based in San Francisco and thus much more multicultural than in its Santa Barbara days, provides opportunities for Chicano/Latino theatrical development. The movement away from a strictly barrio perspective to a multicultural, multiethnic, alternative theater is certainly a strong current in San Francisco among several groups, such as those in the Mission District and in the Fort Mason multiethnic complex of the arts. At times, Chicano theater literally has become part of general mainstream theater, as exemplified by Teatro Meta, the bilingual theater arm of the highly respected Old Globe Theater in San Diego. Cooperative ventures arise, which are often highly dependent on government, foundation, or corporation grants. A theater can also opt for some emphasis (depending on personnel, location, resources, audience interest, and the like) on Chicano or Latino theater, as in the case of the Group in Seattle, the Los Angeles Theater Center, the Mark Taper forum in Los Angeles, or the San Diego Repertory Theater, as well as many other groups in the Southwest and elsewhere.

Clearly, Chicano theater continues on a dynamic path away from the barrio and into the mainstream. Perhaps in some ways it is already a part of it, if only marginally. One basic ideal of Chicano theater is to remain true to its Chicano roots and essence while reaching for an enlightened general audience that can identify with its universality. Some grassroots agitation has been lost in the effort to make the theater not just more comprehensible, but more enjoyable and palatable to the general non-Chicano audience. Culturally specific materials must be altered. Linguistic usage, allusions, themes, and politics must be changed. This comes about at a time when students have the opportunity to study Chicano theater for credit, whereas in the past, the fervently committed would get together to create theater, without getting any credit, as a purely volunteer gesture to deliver urgent sociopolitical messages and to reaffirm Chicano culture.

Another problem that has arisen in the development of Chicano theater is the inevitable split between elite and folk productions. This split has become an ever-widening gap that is becoming more and more difficult to bridge. In many colleges and universities in the Southwest, Chicano productions have occasionally started out as experimental or student-directed works and evolved into mainstream productions.[13] Serious study in the field is now encouraged. Less relevant are the old barriers that blocked academic consideration of Chicano theater with such fundamental questions as: Does it exist? Is it worth studying? Exposure to the history and criticism of Chicano theater is more widespread now than ever at the university level. Many more scholarly works have been published, such as those by Nicolás Kanellos. The interest in ethnicity and a multicultural American experience means a simultaneous watering down of "authentic" Chicano theater just as dissemination is increasing. Of course, "authenticity" is more easily recognized than defined.

Theater Festivals

Theater festivals in the 1960s and 1970s were an especially important means to establish communication between different regional groups, allowing them to share materials and techniques while boosting morale. These often large and festive affairs offered an opportunity to become acquainted directly with a performing art that was often difficult to keep up with by its very nature. Notable among these prestigious and valuable affairs was the TENAZ Festivals (Teatro Nacional de Aztlán), spearheaded by Jorge Huerta. After a significant period of activity in the 1960s and 1970s, however, Chicano theater festivals began to change, at times almost disappearing.

Toward the end of the twentieth century, much of the fervent passion to create Chicano theater was inevitably dissipated, reflecting the more diffused nature of Chicano theater and the lack of communal solidarity. Such are the usual cycles, peaks, and valleys in the process of development. Losses can be counted, but so can some important gains. Such trade-offs as those experienced by Chicano theater through the 1980s and into the 1990s are a normal part of change, adjustment, and revitalization. Recently, for example, a number of new festivals and competitions have come to the fore. In Costa Mesa, in southern California, the annual Hispanic Playwrights' Festival features a number of plays and awards presentations. In New York, the late Joseph Papp instituted an annual Latino Festival that prominently features theater. Awards and recognition at international festivals such as these are clearly of great importance; but many other regional and general drama festivals also can bring prominence. Chicano theater festivals now have wider Hispanic and Latino dimensions and may involve not only Latino, ethnic, minority, or Spanish-language works but also general mainstream groups, regional works, and those specifically targeted for young playwrights. European and worldwide interest in Chicano theater continues to be significant. Interestingly enough, theatrical triumphs in Europe become more significant when word drifts back to the United States, helping Chicano theater achieve legitimacy.

Touring Theater Companies

Institutionalized professional theater companies now form a backbone for Chicano theater. The Teatro Campesino (in San Juan Bautista, California), led by Luis Valdez, is still the most important and prestigious of these companies. The Teatro Campesino, Carmen Zapata's Bilingual Foundation based in Los Angeles, and the Teatro de la Esperanza (in San Francisco) still make highly important, wide-ranging tours that present theatrical pieces to many thousands of viewers in hundreds of locations. Other groups, such as Jorge Huerta's student troupe at the University of California at San Diego, have also made significant tours throughout Europe.[14] Sketch comedy, involving short, sharp satirical segments, is currently represented by at least three professional groups—Latins Anonymous, Culture Clash, and the Chicano Secret Service. These groups, in a sense, are a throwback to the old acto tradition with their raw social commentary, political humor and satire, and topicality, but they are also more broadly representative of the sketch humor style developed by the television series *Saturday Night Live*.[15] Two recent presentations by Culture Clash, *A Bowl of Beings* (1991) and *S.O.S.* (1992), are illustrative of contemporary Chicano self-satire that simultaneously delivers stinging social and political criticism. The technique of social protest tempered by humor is as old, at least, as Aristophanes, but in Chicano theater circles it is most closely identified with the early works of Luis Valdez and the Teatro Campesino. These techniques are now being rediscovered, as Culture Clash and other theatrical groups make an impact on a new generation of audiences and critics and as Chicano/Latino theater continues to make greater inroads into the theatrical center stage.

Chicano theater of the 1980s and 1990s has also demonstrated other means by which to deliver Chicano theater to the public. One such variation is the individual touring play, exemplified by the work *I Am Celso,* adapted from the poetry of Leo Romero by Jorge Huerta and Rubén Sierra and performed as a one-man show by Sierra. *I Am Celso* has been presented in runs lasting a few weeks to both Chicano and non-Chicano audiences in large urban centers, particularly in southwestern cities with a vibrant Hispanic influence, such as San Antonio, Los Angeles, and San Diego. Much current Chicano drama balances the culturally specific and the more universal dimensions of the human condition to reach both Latino and mainstream audiences. Such a balance validates the Mexican American way of life for Chicanos while presenting an alternative philosophy of life (one of much greater hedonism, in the case of *I Am Celso*) to a naive but open-minded general audience. The fact that certain stereotypes—drinking wine, pleasure as foremost, a strong present-time orientation, a lighthearted carefree attitude—are confirmed for this general audience makes the message almost familiar and easier to take. Naturally, there has been strong criticism over the reinforcing of stereotypes in this play.

Media Coverage of Chicano Theater Productions

Since the 1960s (and even before) a number of scholarly publications have carried articles on Chicano theater. These productions had a powerful effect on mainstream media critics, who wrote important first articles, profiles and reviews in the *Los Angeles Times, Newsweek, The New Yorker,* and many other mainstream publications. The visibility increased as major theater publications, reviews, profiles, previews, interviews, and feature articles were published. Publications, information, and communications relating to Chicano theater changed as the productions became more universalized or, as some put it, more colonialized and directed, absorbed, and devoured by mainstream circles as a commercial entity, part of "commodity theater." In current parlance, Chicano theater is now part of postcolonial literature in the

United States. (Postcolonial literature, needless to say, is also a worldwide phenomenon.) As such, Chicano theater is a part of American theater, is frequently performed in English, and demonstrates its ties to the dominant culture and European American tradition.

Since Chicano theater has become part of the general interest media coverage, it has lost some of its distinctly underground edge. The publication TENAZ Talks Teatro, for example, has changed since the early 1970s, when it was an important annual publication of an alliance of Chicano theaters. In the seventies, TENAZ, under the strong leadership of Jorge Huerta, served an important purpose by communicating much information relating to the activities of Chicano theater groups. Huerta's valuable work continues, although the format and context have inevitably changed.

The Publication of Contemporary Chicano Drama

As Chicano theater became more popular, publication of these plays increased significantly, particularly in the form of anthologies. Two notable anthologies are Jorge Huerta's *Necessary Theater*, which contains six contemporary Chicano plays, and *On New Ground*, which brings together five Latino plays. These two anthologies contain such works as Cherríe Moraga's recently published *Giving Up the Ghost*, a feminist-lesbian drama. *Nuevos pasos*, an anthology edited by Nicolás Kanellos and Jorge Huerta, was originally published in 1978 and was republished by Arte Público Press. This work contains both Chicano and Puerto Rican plays but is predominantly Chicano drama. A number of other Chicano playwrights have published their plays in book form, including Estela Portillo Trambley (*Sor Juana*), E. A. Mares (*I Returned and Saw the Sun: Padre Martínez of Taos*, published in both Spanish and English),[16] and A. Hernández, who writes from a homosexual point of view and presents a scene in one of this plays where all the characters are nude.[17] The most significant development, without a doubt, is the project undertaken by Nicolás Kanellos with Luis Valdez to publish Valdez's complete works. Luis Valdez had published his original short plays, *Actos*, in 1971 through his own Cucaracha Press from his base with the Teatro Campesino in San Juan Bautista. Long out of print, the *Actos* have now been reprinted, along with other early works.[18]

Publication in and of itself is ordinarily such a straightforward process that one must wonder about the dearth of publication of Chicano theater in general and Luis Valdez's works in particular. According to Valdez, he has published so little because he always considered his plays to be "working versions," never quite finished, always to be adapted for a specific occasion. There are many other reasons why plays are infrequently published. Theater, as a performing art, is quite different by its very nature from other forms of literature. Theater often has a performance-based spontaneity and improvisation that may defy the printed page. Theater is generally presumed to be an illegitimate stepchild of literature, meant to be performed, witnessed, and experienced; only in exceptional cases does drama reach the printed page, and then it is often considered to be merely a "guide" for performance. The reading of plays in written form is regarded to be as inadequate as the reading of screenplays for movies. The play may be considered to be particularly ephemeral, no longer "relevant" or "valid," after even a short period. Given this general dearth of published theater works, it is not surprising that relatively few Chicano dramatic works have been published. The publication of Chicano drama has increased modestly since the period before the 1960s, when almost no Chicano plays were published, and even since the Chicano renaissance of the 1960s and the early 1970s. The emergence of published Chicano plays is an increasingly important current in contemporary Chicano theater.

Feminism on Center Stage in Contemporary Theater

Plays by women playwrights (such as Estela Portillo Trambley's *The Day of the Swallows, Morality Play,* and *Sun Images*) constitute a current of increasing importance in contemporary Chicano theater. Portillo Trambley's publication of *Sor Juana and Other Plays* (1981) was a milestone event—a woman, a Chicana, had published a book of mostly Chicano drama (only one of the four plays in the book has no relevance to the Chicano experience). More accurately, she had published a collection of Chicana plays; Portillo Trambley makes very clear her feminist ideology. The title play, *Sor Juana,* portrays the famous seventeenth-century Mexican nun (who was a precursor of women's liberation and all the more extraordinary for the context from which she emerged) as a full-blown, 1980s feminist. Portillo Trambley too obviously puts words in the mouth of Sor Juana, thus falsifying the character but also generating anachronistic laughs. Still, Portillo Trambley is articulate and highly intelligent. She has a gift for characterization, a notable skill in the creation of theater, an instinct for what works on stage. She continues to produce works that are among the best in Chicana/o drama. *Blacklight,* a remarkable play by Portillo Trambley, also harks back to both indigenous themes and the immigration of the undocumented.[19]

Other important new Chicana writers have surged forward more recently to continue this feminist trend in contemporary Mexican American theater. Cherríe Moraga, mentioned before, is the creator of *Giving Up the Ghost*, which has a strongly feminist theme that focuses on a lesbian love affair.[20] Moraga's *Shadow of a Man* is a harshly antimacho feminist work that destroys stereotypical ideas about female passivity, deplores the dysfunctional Chicano family, and clarifies the struggle between men and women in a troubled family.[21] In 1992, Moraga's *Heroes and Saints*, another work that is clearly feminist with veiled lesbianism, debuted in San Francisco. In this play, Moraga continues with the social drama of domestic and family dilemmas but also adds a significant fantasy construct to the play. In response to César Chávez's outcry over the effects of pollution, toxic pesticides, and poisonous field conditions for farmworkers in the Central Valley of California, Moraga's play deals with birth defects that ultimately reach the grotesque, thus using magical realism to blend the socially conscious with the fantastic. Moraga continues to solidify her career and establish the importance of the topics she chooses to illuminate.

Josefina López is the most exciting playwright to appear in recent years in Chicano theater. A young prodigy, she has won several play-writing contests since the age of 17 in 1987. Her two most important works to date are *Simply María* and *Real Women Have Curves*. Although both works are feminist, Josefina López seems much less strident than Moraga. López merely presents a truthful testimony from a woman's perspective; inevitably, her views and her works are feminist because she necessarily speaks of the need for freedom and liberation, of the need for self-determination, and of the search for an identity. Her sense of humor and exceptional talent for characterization infuse great vitality into her theatrical works. *Simply María* offers a portrait of a young Chicana in search of identity and her place in the universe, in American society, and in Chicana/o culture. Her subsequent *Real Women Have Curves* shows a remarkable advance. López presents an all-woman play with a cast of six, set in a garment sweatshop in Los Angeles, and unrolls important issues involving feminism, undocumented workers, machismo, social class differences, exploitation, discrimination, hopes and dreams, oppression, and obesity. The primary reason Josefina López has triumphed at such an incredibly young age is her uncommon skill at creating characters, believable characters that we can know and care about deeply.

The thematic concerns and social themes issue forth as natural and authentic expressions of this particular set of characters in this specific context. Both apparently autobiographical works focus on a young woman who wants to write, who wants to pursue art, who needs to find expression. The two works are truly feminist because they express the artistic and poetic truth of life from a woman's perspective, without manipulation, with total honesty, and with a will to create drama that moves us with its radical sincerity. López emphasizes the strength of character of the women. They may not be aware of the fine points of women's liberation, but they breathe the same air and act with strength and vigor.

Denise Chávez, author of *The Last of the Menu Girls* (1986), a novel/short story collection in the form of a Chicana bildungsroman set in New Mexico, has written a score of plays. As a playwright of great range and versatility in theme, form, characters, and approaches, she is similar to Estela Portillo Trambley and Luis Valdez. Chávez also has a strong vein of humor as well as a natural theatrical instinct. From musical to religious themes, her plays all show a lively quality of strong, sometimes quirky, characterizations and a poetic use of language that lends the works elegance and grace. One of her works, *Hecho en México,* which originated in 1983 as one segment of *Una Tardeada Nuevo Mexicana,* has as its central character Julia Mejía, described as "a Chicana who has grown up near the Mexican border, part of both cultures; a vibrant, joyous woman who, despite her heartaches and corns, manages to maintain a sense of humor and warmth."[22] This play deals with domestic workers and can thus be considered a Chicana proletariat play. Chávez has many other plays to her credit, including *Plaza* (presented at the Edinburgh Scotland Festival in 1984) and *Plague-Time* (1985), a musical about the Middle Ages. The latter was funded by the Rockefeller Foundation.

Luis Valdez and Corridos *(1983)*

Although women playwrights have come to the fore in Chicana/o theater recently, the extraordinary and pervasive presence of Luis Valdez—as playwright, director, and founder of the Teatro Campesino—has continued to be a leading force in Chicano theater. Valdez and his troupe have established the legitimacy of Chicano theater in New York with successful tours that received several OBIE (Off-Broadway) awards. His success in Europe has also validated Chicano theater, giving it visibility and prestige. As the steady erosion in the quantity of Chicano theater groups continues, the solid quality of Valdez's group is more and more evident. However, as a basically machista writer, creator, and director and a foil for the feminist theater that developed in the 1980s, Valdez's extraordinary presence in Chicano theater has become increasingly controversial.[23]

Indeed, Luis Valdez's career is exemplary for his strong leadership, creative drive, and unique innovations. In the field of Chicano theater since 1965, Valdez must always be reckoned with. He is the eye of the theatrical hurricane; he creates an impact and weathers the reactions. In recent times, the establishment's acknowledgments of his genius have brought charges that he is a *vendido*, a sell-out. The original creator of the classic acto "Los vendidos" is now himself so regarded, particularly by young, radical student elements. And the feminists have been accusing him of blatant machismo. On the other hand, Valdez's visibility and innovativeness as a creator and leader remain at a very high level. Popular success, especially with mainstream media and audiences, is a two edged sword. Material triumph in American cultural currents, in theater as well as in film, television, and publications, and the ensuing popularity and celebrity seem at odds with an authentic ethnic expression that Chicanos can intimately relate to. A conflict arises when trying to serve different masters simultaneously—"universal" or "Chicano-specific," "national" or "regional," "majority" or "English," "mainstream" or "marginal." The problematic is ever-present and always perilous. No doubt Chicano, and in general, U.S. Hispanic or Latino, theater has been in the process of development and growth. And at the center has been Luis Valdez, with all his talent, vision, creativity, energy, and ambition, setting himself up as a target for the ambivalence, confusion, contradictions, and ambiguity of the entire Chicano people.

In 1976 Valdez and the Teatro Campesino presented a televised play, *El corrido*, on PBS. Always interested in folklore, popular culture, and the sound of the voice of the people, Valdez returned with a new angle on the theme in 1983 in the work *Corridos*, which dramatized a number of Mexican or Mexican American *corridos*, or ballads, narrative folksongs of long-standing tradition that demonstrate the customs, values, and attitudes of the people. The old corridos were anonymous, often relayed news in the absence of media of mass communications, told stories, entertained, expressed feelings, and captured the essence of the people.[24] Valdez's idea was to dramatize these corridos and perform a number of them as part of a play, tied together by a structural device in the form of a master of ceremonies. He used thematic, dramatic, and character contrasts and comparisons to give the corridos a fuller, more authentic view of Mexican Americans and their heritage. *Corridos,* then, is a collection of these short adaptations, including such well-known ballads as "Rosita Alvírez" and "Delgadina." In 1983 the play opened in San Juan Bautista, the headquarters for twenty years of the Teatro Campesino. Initial success mandated the moving of the play seventy-five miles north to San Francisco, where it won fourteen awards in the annual San Francisco Drama Critics competition for outstanding theatrical work. In the fall of 1984, *Corridos* played at the Old Globe Theater in San Diego, an indicator of further mainstream acceptance. The critical and popular success of the play continued in Los Angeles. Nevertheless, disturbing charges were leveled at *Corridos* by Chicano critics—accusations of selling out, of woman-bashing, of the musical play being too "cute" and "picturesque," of superficiality, of grotesque and continual stereotyping of the Mexicans and Mexican Americans for the entertainment and reinforcement of negative or, at best "colorful," views held by the mainstream audience. According to Rodrigo Reyes in TENAZ Talks Teatro, most of the men are beasts and brutes and the women are frivolous flirts.[25]

Corridos is an entertaining work, in a sense, but deeply flawed. As a specifically Chicano work, *Corridos* is extremely limited; it is not even directed at Chicanos, though it is about Chicanos and their Mexican heritage. Many Chicano academics, though not most drama critics, seemed to view the play as a pretty picture postcard. José Antonio Burciaga described the musical as "caricaturesque." The segment on "Rosita Alvírez," he observes, seems to deny the image of the mother and the obedience owed to parents, cultural traditions long upheld as part of the family structure.[26] (To be fair to Valdez, however, it seems that this generation gap and rebellious defiance is built into the corrido itself, which Valdez merely adapted and interpreted in his own way while remaining more or less faithful to the original text.)

In fact, both the original ballad of "Rosita Alvírez" and its dramatized version portray a young, independent woman, flirtatious and even cruel, who is killed by a spurned lover. True, the victim seems to be responsible for her fate. Therefore, charges of machismo hurled at Valdez by, for example, Margarita Robles Segura may be taken seriously. The victim is the culprit. Violence is a typical trait of the macho. Men, she continues, seem to believe that women are mere possessions. The relationship between men and women depicted in this play could hardly be more negative.[27] Yet, is Valdez being indicted? Or should the attack more accurately be leveled against the play *Corridos,* Chicano theater, Chicano culture, or human nature? Is Valdez obliged to present only positive cultural icons? Are women only to be strong and forceful? (Actually, in many ways Rosita is a very strong-minded character who shows independence of thought.)

Another segment of the play, inspired by "Delgadina," also centers on a strong-willed woman who winds up as the victim of attempted incest on the part of her father. Patriarchy, machismo, male dominance, sexual abuse, lustful eroticism, the imposition of power, immorality, and hypocrisy triumph over Delgadina, who in turn represents purity, virginal innocence, religiosity, virtue, morality, and a strong-minded resistance that reaches extremely stubborn and self-destructive levels. This drama between good and evil, between honesty and hypocrisy, between lust and religion is powerful and certainly a highlight of *Corridos* as a whole. Yet, once again, the same basic charges of machismo have been leveled at Valdez.[28]

It is ironic that iron-willed protagonists such as Rosita Alvírez and Delgadina (among others) are singled out as such victims, such targets of antimachismo sentiment. But then both characters are not only losers and victims who ultimately capitulate in death, they are also perceived as partly responsible for their own downfall, as culprits and architects of their own defeats. Such is the complexity of life and of its artistic transmutation that contradictory, polemical arguments can be made against machismo or antimachismo sentiments embodied in a theatrical work.

Valdez found feminist critics descending upon him with accusations of promoting, not merely depicting, a patriarchal system. It was charged that Valdez, as a machista, deliberately presented the victimization of women, their weakness, frivolity, lack of resources, and failure to stand up to many aspects of the cultural system. The debate is, of course, endless and probably irresolvable, but it does show something of the cultural battlefield that Valdez has had to use as a stage for his dramas.

The mainstream media, daily newspaper reviews, awards committees, and the general public saw *Corridos* as a success: a hugely entertaining work made up of seven segments with vividly and swiftly etched characters, blazing conflicts, a colorful background of lovely music and attractive sets, smoothly professional in the cast and all other aspects of the play. It need hardly be mentioned that many Chicanos were also quite content with the dramatic expression Luis Valdez had given to Chicanos and their Mexican heritage. In 1987, a somewhat altered and shortened version of *Corridos* was presented on Public Television, with the winning of several Emmy and other awards following shortly.

Luis Valdez and
I Don't Have to Show You No Stinking Badges

In 1986, the prolific Valdez premiered a new play, *I Don't Have to Show You No Stinking Badges*, that moved in a more contemporary direction. The play deals with the Chicano family, media stereotypes, and attempts at assimilation. *Badges* reflects rising socioeconomic expectations among the Mexican American middle class as its greater education and suburban affluence create a different kind of dilemma from that faced by the farmworker. *Badges* is also a television situation comedy, with humorous wisecracks mixed with metaphysical and psychological overtones. There is, Valdez seems to say, a new and rather different Chicano problem that must be dealt with. Chicanos are largely urban, not rural. Many now have an education and focus on concerns other than the next meal. By using interiorization and subjectivity laced with philosophical social protest, Valdez tested new ways to explore the Chicano psyche in the multicultural context of the present-day American cultural landscape.

Badges focuses on the unexpected return of Sonny, who has dropped out of Harvard and returned to his parents' home. His parents have become successful as Hollywood bit players, playing stereotypical roles while managing a medical education for their daughter and Sonny's Harvard Law School education. Near a nervous breakdown, perhaps suicidal, Sonny now wants to become an actor. To complicate matters, he brings home his Japanese American girlfriend. An identity dilemma is set up, using techniques such as interior duplication (a mirror-image, "play-within-a-play" device).

Badges demonstrates a number of differences when compared with other works by Valdez.[29] Unlike his other works, *Badges* has a much deeper subjectivity and interiorization and probes for metaphysical meaning. It also portrays psychological conflict within the individual, to the point of neurosis and nervous breakdown. The social context and the individual's psychology meet on a common ground. Unusual also is the fact that the play is strictly contemporary, featuring Chicanos who live a suburban existence, attend Harvard Law School, and live in an upper-middle and professional social class that is not directly struggling against uncomfortable economic realities. Instead of worries about paying the rent, the characters suffer from neurotically anguished thoughts about the meaning of life, an identity crisis, and a struggle to stay afloat between stress and motivation. Also, the situation comedy format of the play is more closely related to popular culture and the media than Valdez's old fascination with folklore, the legacy of the common people. But, yes, times do change.

Judith and Severo Pérez and Soldierboy

Soldierboy (1984), originally developed under the tutelage of Luis Valdez at the Teatro Campesino in San Juan Bautista in 1982, has been extensively revised several times since then, as frequently occurs with a "working version" of a play. Recently, again with further revision, the work was published in a more definitive form by Jorge Huerta in his anthology of Chicano theater, *Necessary Theater*.[30] This antiwar drama continues the social protest that Chicano theater works directed against the Vietnam War in the sixties and seventies. However, like Rubén Sierra's *Manolo*, this play deals with the readjustment of a Chicano veteran, this time from World War II, a different historical era that illuminates the present by focusing on the past. The play is also a domestic drama that sheds light on the Chicano family and its dynamics.

In essence, *Soldierboy* focuses the return of the soldier Frank from service during World War II to his Chicano family in San Antonio. The family is an extended family, including his wife and son, his brother, and parents. Psychological scars, family problems, and societal lack of concern, even discrimination, make the adjustment process of the returning "war hero" problematic and difficult. The play is built on a structure that deftly interweaves various plot strands with highly effective characterizations that are ultimately extremely absorbing.

The play extends the meaning of a social drama by presenting the message from the psyche of an individual, going, one might say, from Brecht to Arthur Miller. Discrimination against the returning Chicano soldier-hero is still present, still ironic, still particularly bitter. But so are the nightmares, anguish, flashbacks of an intense psychological nature. The play continues the tendency toward interiorization, toward the exploration of the psyche, toward the dramatic representation of trauma as it affects the individual. The greater penetration into both individual and family psychology in the context of a particular historical period, the complex socioeconomic, political, and cultural forces of San Antonio in the forties, represents a further advance for Chicano theater. Nor is social criticism muffled; it is heightened by convincing characterization. Alienation as part of the continuing Chicano dilemma is underlined. A generation gap arises between the returning

"Soldierboy" and his parents, who look at the situation with an outmoded submissiveness. The humor in the play is significant in conveying an authentic reality, just as the nightmarish scenes, the memories of war-time trauma, also engross the audience. With these sophisticated, complex symbolic representations of the psyche, Chicano theater goes beyond the literal, the simple, the superficial. As layers of straightforward representation are shed, Chicano theater moves forward into newly discovered realms of subtlety, complexity, and interiorization. Chicano subjectivity and multifaceted characterization reach new heights in the representation on the stage of the Chicano as individual, family, and group within general American society.

Conclusions and Recommendations

Since its origins, Chicano theater has been a remarkably distinct phenomenon with a long, rich tradition. In more recent times, Chicano theatrical productions have become ever more visible, with their presence increasingly felt in ever larger theatrical circles. Although traditional roots have sometimes been cast aside, gains have been recorded. Playwrights in the eighties—the Decade of the Hispanic—did water down Chicano specificity as they broadened the potential solidarity of a larger, more united Latino form that would include the Chicano component. Most recently, two anthologies have appeared: *José, Can You See? Latinos On and Off Broadway* and *Puro Teatro, A Latina Anthology*.[31] Present trends point in the same direction as we move into the new century. Still, Chicanos remain the largest and most significant component under this Latino banner. The mainstream has validated Chicano theater by providing grants and academic support, just as commercialization has softened its more strident social protest element, which, in any case, seemed directed toward the already initiated true believer. The professionalization and institutionalization of Chicano theater as a fundamental part of contemporary drama became more and more significant in the eighties and nineties. New dramatic talent rose to join the few great pioneers of the sixties Chicano theater period. The consciousness-raising function of Chicano theater has become more and more of a reality, though one wonders about the actual accomplishment of substantive social change. Co-optation by the mainstream, whether the university, the arts establishment, or the media, has become the rule as we head into the new century.

Yet gains have been notable. First, acknowledgment of existence of Chicano theater took place. Further curiosity has revealed the unique character and high quality of and the inherent interest in Chicano drama. Plays, troupes, and artists continue to flourish, as do their creators and those who provide a venue for them. Yet, is it too little, too late? Has Chicano theater sold out? Is the dominant culture so powerful that it envelops and devours everything, relegating Latino works in general, and Chicano theater in particular, to the merely quaint and picturesque segment of the theatrical season? Will the future hold homogenization or a theatrical Chicano ghetto, colorful but innocuous? Is part of the social protest muzzled because of sponsorship, or are playwrights perfectly free to preach a social message, which is heard only by the already converted?

If developments proceed apace, one can foresee more Chicano artists, playwrights, and theatrical personnel coming to the fore, propelled by the recent developments in Chicano theater. And inevitably, these figures will head for the mainstream. The question of separatism, whether from the mainstream or from other Latino groups, versus assimilation will continue to be a burning issue, one of those irresolvable questions ultimately settled by prestige, impact, influence, and the box office. Meanwhile, Chicanas/os and Chicano theater will straddle the extremes. To proceed as in the recent past is to let certain natural forces of the society come together with individual ideologies and group agendas to ultimately determine the contours of Chicano theater. Those who are committed to the mainstream continue to make inroads but perhaps need a more systematic approach. Clearly, Chicano theater remains distinct and diverse, yet a part of the whole. Generally, activism and forceful assertion of efforts have resulted in university programs, professional affiliations with established theaters, and the broad visibility and viability of contemporary Chicano theater. This kind of action must continue on more fronts to ensure the continuing development of a vibrant Chicano theater tradition.

Notes

1. See, for example, several books by Nicolás Kanellos: *A History of Hispanic Theater in the United States: Origins to 1940* (Austin: The University of Texas Press, 1990); *Two Centuries of Hispanic Theater in the Southwest* (1982); *Hispanic Theater in the United States* (1984); and *Mexican American Theater, Then and Now*, ed. Nicolás Kanellos (1983). All were published by Arte Público Press in Houston. Kanellos also published *Mexican American Theater; Legacy and Reality* (Pittsburgh, Penn.: Latin American

Literary Review Press, 1987). See also Jorge Huerta, *Chicano Theater: Themes and Forms* (Tempe, Ariz.: Bilingual Review/Press, 1983). Luis Leal's literary history studies include references to theater in works such as "Mexican American Literature: A Historical Perspective," in *Modern Chicano Writers*, eds. Joseph Sommers and Tomás Ybarra-Frausto (Englewood Cliffs, N.J.: Prentice-Hall, 1979), 18–30. Also see Tomás Ybarra-Frausto, "Chicano Theater: Punto de Partida," *Latin American Theater Review,* IV (1971).

2. For Christmas 1991, Luis Valdez and the Teatro Campesino combined several of these elements in an English-language version of *La pastorela,* the traditional Spanish Christmas play transformed into contemporary Chicano theater, mixing farce and piety in a Chicano context. A videotape version is available through Teatro Campesino.

3. This is particularly important in the previously cited studies by Nicolás Kanellos. Especially, see *Hispanic Theater in the United States: Origins to 1940* (Austin: The University of Texas Press, 1990). Also notable are references by Luis Valdez that the Teatro Campesino (Farmworkers' Theater) and contemporary Chicano theater did not emerge from a vacuum. See two significant early articles by Luis Valdez in *Aztlán: An Anthology of Mexican American Literature,* eds. Luis Valdez and Stan Steiner (New York: Vintage, 1972), specifically, "Notes on Chicano Theater," 354–58, "El Teatro Campesino," 359–61, and a note on 353. Also Jorge A. Huerta traces the historical development in "From the Temple to the Arena: Teatro Chicano Today," in *The Identification and Analysis of Chicano Literature,* ed. Francisco Jiménez (New York: Bilingual Press/Editorial Bilingüe, 1979).

4. For information and criticism on Luis Valdez, see Tina Eger, *A Bibliography of Criticism of Contemporary Chicano Literature* (Berkeley: Chicano Studies Library Publications, 1982), 62–79. Also a biographical-bibliographical article appears in *Chicano Literature,* eds. Francisco Lomelí and Julio Martínez (Westport, Conn.: Greenwood, 1984). See also Nicolás Kanellos, ed., *Biographical Dictionary of Hispanic Literature in the United States* (Westport, Conn.: Greenwood, 1989). Also see Francisco Lomelí and Carl Shirley, eds., *Dictionary of Literary Biography,* vol. 82, *Chicano Writers: First Series* (Detroit: Gale, 1989).

5. The influence of Bertolt Brecht on the Teatro Campesino has been extensively studied in a number of articles. One such is by Barclay Goldsmith, "Brecht and Chicano Theater," in *Modern Chicano Writers,* eds. Sommers and Ybarra-Frausto, 167–75.

6. See the studies listed in note #1. Also, consider some other studies: Francisco Jiménez, "Dramatic Principles of the Teatro Campesino," in *The Identification and Analysis of Chicano Literature,* 117–32; and Carlota Cárdenas de Dwyer, "The Development of Chicano Drama and Luis Valdez' Actos," in *Modern Chicano Writers,* eds. Sommers and Ybarra-Frausto, 160–66.

7. See Luis Leal, "The Problem of Identifying Chicano Literature," 2–6, and Rolando Hinojosa, "Mexican American Literature: Toward an Identification," in *The Identi-*

fication and Analysis of Chicano Literature, ed. Jiménez, 7–18. Both Leal and Hinojosa return to the same theme in *Criticism in the Borderlands: Studies in Chicano Literature, Culture, and Ideology,* eds. Héctor Calderón and José David Saldívar (Durham, N.C.: Duke University Press, 1991). See Rolando Hinojosa's foreword, "Redefining American Literature," xi–xv; and Luis Leal, "The Rewriting of American Literary History," 21–27. The entire framework and context have changed and such reformulations are indispensable.

8. Originally published in *El espejo/The Mirror* (Berkeley: Quinto Sol, 1972), 151–93.

9. "Sun Images," in *Nuevos Pasos: Chicano and Puerto Rican Drama,* eds. Nicolás Kanellos and Jorge Huerta (Houston: Arte Público Press, 1979), 19–42.

10. Margarita Robles Segura, José Antonio Burciaga, Rodríguez Reyes, and Tomás Ybarra-Frausto are Chicano critics with a negative view toward *Corridos,* cited by Carlos Morton, "Critical Response to *Zoot Suit* and *Corridos,*" *Chicano Studies Occasional Paper,* series #2 (El Paso: The University of Texas at El Paso, August 1984), 9–13.

11. Note this statement by Luis Valdez: "We're still cultural, still political, but first and foremost, theater is what we do for a living. We're not afraid to sell tickets; this may seem at variance with our radical theater origins, but it's reality. We've got to pay the rent, pay taxes, provide a decent living for our actors and staff." Quoted in Morton, "Critical Response," 13.

12. See my article "*Soldierboy,* Una muestra de la eficacia del teatro chicano de hoy," in *La Comunidad,* Sunday cultural supplement to *La Opinión* (Los Angeles), 24 de mayo de 1987, 12–13.

13. For example, in the recent past I noted *Soldierboy* by Judith and Severo Pérez as a mainstay production at California State University, Sacramento. *Latina* by Milcha Sánchez-Scott has likewise been presented at California State University, Stanislaus. Other examples could be mentioned.

14. Among university and academic theater circles, Jorge Huerta of the University of California, San Diego, has perhaps most ambitiously and persistently pursued student theater programs, productions, and tours, both nationally and internationally. Most recently, his touring productions have included *Johnny Tenorio* and *The Trials of Don Eduardo.*

15. See the review, for example, of Culture Clash, *A Bowl of Beings,* by Sylvie Darke, *Los Angeles Times,* 21 June 1991, F-1, F-18. A video collection of these six sketches has been presented on PBS and is available as a videotape from Cinewest (Hollywood, 1992).

16. See Estela Portillo Trambley, *Sor Juana and Other Plays* (Ypsilanti, Mich.: Bilingual Review Press, 1983). Also see E. A. Mares, *I Returned and Saw Under the Sun: Padre Martínez of Taos* (Albuquerque: University of New Mexico Press, 1989, in separate Spanish and English versions).

17. Alfonso Hernández, *The False Advent of Mary's Child and Other Plays* (Berkeley: Justa, 1979).

18. Luis Valdez, *Early Works: Actos, Bernabé and Pensamiento Serpentino* (Houston: Arte Público Press, 1990). Luis Valdez, *Zoot Suit and Other Plays* (Houston: Arte Público Press, 1992).

19. *Blacklight* is one of the plays in Estela Portillo Trambley's collection *Sor Juana and Other Plays*.

20. Cherríe Moraga, *Giving Up the Ghost: Teatro in Two Acts* (Los Angeles: West End, 1986).

21. Published in *Shattering the Myth: Plays by Hispanic Women,* selected by Denise Chávez, ed. Linda Macías Feyder (Houston: Arte Público Press, 1992).

22. Quoted from theater program.

23. See some feminist criticisms in Morton, "Critical Response," 10–13.

24. The literature on the Chicano *corrido* (ballad) is especially extensive. A good initial source is Américo Paredes, *"With His Pistol in His Hand": A Border Ballad and Its Hero* (Austin: University of Texas Press, 1958); and Paredes, *A Texas-Mexican Cancionero* (Urbana: University of Illinois Press, 1976).

25. See Morton, "Critical Response."

26. José Antonio Burciaga, quoted in Morton, "Critical Response," 11.

27. Margarita Robles Segura, quoted in Morton, "Critical Response," 11–12.

28. Debate continues on this matter, also extending to many other sources. See, for example, Cordelia Candelaria, "Social Equity in Film Criticism," 64–70, and Sylvia Morales, "Chicano-Produced Celluloid Mujeres," 89–93, in *Chicano Cinema,* ed. Gary Keller (Ypsilanti, Mich.: Bilingual Review Press, 1985).

29. The play appears in Luis Valdez, *Zoot Suit and Other Plays* (Houston: Arte Público Press, 1992). For *I Don't Have to Show You No Stinking Badges,* see 155–214.

30. See Jorge Huerta, *Necessary Theater* (Houston: Arte Público Press, 1990). For Judith and Severo Pérez's *Soldierboy,* see 20–75.

31. Alberto Sandoval-Sánchez, ed., *José, Can You See? Latinos On and Off Broadway* (Madison: University of Wisconsin Press, 1999); and Alberto Sandoval-Sánchez and Nancy Saporta Sternbach, eds., *Puro Teatro, A Latina Anthology* (Tucson: University of Arizona Press, 1999).

Breaking the Silence: Developments in the Publication and Politics of Chicana Creative Writing, 1973–1998

EDWINA BARVOSA-CARTER

. . . when she transforms silence into language a woman
transgresses.
Gloria Anzaldúa, *Making Face, Making Soul*

Creative writing by Mexican American women has not enjoyed a long
history of frequent publication. Rather, Chicana writers have often
faced limited opportunities for publication and myriad obstacles to dis-
seminating their prose, poetry, and drama. Moreover, Chicana writers have
written in contexts in which gender, racial, and ethnic discrimination, as
well as economic and political subordination, have resulted in disempowerment, lack of opportunity, and silence. Yet, silence has not reigned. Since the
mid-1970s, Chicana writers have published an increasing number of literary
works. Increased publication and dissemination of Chicana creative writing
has, in turn, brought heretofore marginalized voices to greater public attention. Now, in the new millennium, literature by Chicana writers is closer
than ever to taking a central place in the U.S. literary landscape.[1]

This story of breaking the silence, however, remains largely untold.
Critics and others who recount Chicana/o literary history often tell a tale of
Chicano literature and male literary success.[2] Several recent anthologies, for
example, almost entirely neglect the unique development and specificity of
Chicana writing and publication. One collection went so far as to conflate

Chicana with Chicano writing by describing the anthology as a volume with "an amazing autobiographical homogeneity, as if one supreme creator . . . were responsible for every one of its pages."[3] Another anthology devoted to Chicana literature does describe the social and historical context of recent Chicana writing and the unique transformation of its themes. Yet it refers only briefly to the long struggle Chicana writers have undertaken to introduce their words into the public domain.[4]

The aim of this essay is to recount the often-neglected but significant recent developments in the publication of Chicana creative writing and to point out some dimensions of its social and political significance. I focus on the publication of books of poetry, prose fiction, and drama written by Chicana writers between 1973 and 1998. In relation to this, I outline three interrelated components: 1) the social and historical context in which contemporary Chicana writing is embedded; 2) the changing opportunities and trends in publication between 1973 and 1998; and 3) the potential social and political significance of many of the themes raised by Chicanas in their creative writing. These three interconnected components reveal that Chicana writers have not only broken the silence since the 1970s but also claimed critical, exploratory, and dissenting voices. As Francisco Lomelí puts it, the "[l]iterature written by Chicanas not only has become a significant voice of the Chicano experience but also [has become] a mainstay in more contemporary trends with the purpose of breaking new ground and exploring new areas of human experience."[5]

Drawing from these three components, I consider the publication of literature by Chicanas on two levels. First, I regard the struggle of Chicana creative writers to publish their work as an *act* of claiming voice, as a political phenomenon in which heretofore marginalized voices consciously circumvent a variety of obstacles to raise issues of personal, social, and political significance. Second, I view this literature in terms of its *content,* as an important literary development that has introduced new ideas and interpretations of social and political significance. Among the significant themes probed by Chicana writing is the transformation of subjectivity arising from cultural difference and complexity. Many Chicana writers have fought long and hard to bring their writing and perspectives to public view, and many of their voices are well situated to speak to issues of social and political urgency. It remains for critics, theorists, and other thinkers to engage fully with the personal, social, and political insights delivered by their words. This essay contributes to that task.

Critical Contexts

It is helpful to view contemporary Chicana literature in terms of the historical and intellectual contexts that have influenced many Chicana writers. The postwar civil rights movements are among the most influential of these contexts. Numerous writers describe the influence these political movements have had on their writing and personal perspectives.[6] The Chicano movement, the women's movement, the anti-Vietnam War movement, and the black civil rights movement of the sixties and seventies captured the attention and influenced the writing of two generations of Chicana writers. The first of these writers include Lucha Corpi, María Herrera-Sobek, Angela de Hoyos, Beverly Silva, and Alma Villanueva. They have been joined by a second wave of Chicana writers including Ana Castillo, Lorna Dee Cervantes, Sandra Cisneros, and Helena María Viramontes. These writers and others now stand at the forefront of Chicana creative writing.

It is misleading, however, to focus solely on the postwar social and political context of Chicana writing. The diversity of Chicana experience has also been influenced by the long and complex history of the geographical region now divided into the United States and Mexico. Chicana/o literature itself can be divided into three periods: the Spanish colonial and Mexican National period, the postannexation period of 1848 to 1950, and the Chicano Renaissance from 1950 to the present. The historical context relevant to Chicana/o writing thus extends back to the ancient pre-Columbian cultures of the Americas and reaches forward through the colonial period to the subsequent centuries when Mexicanos established settlements in the vast southwestern regions of North America. Over time, Mexican peoples came to dominate southwestern North America, and only relatively recently have these lands become part of the United States. It was not until 1845, for example, that the United States formally annexed Texas. It was only 150 years ago, in 1848, that the United States annexed the lands that are now California, New Mexico, Arizona, and parts of Nevada, Colorado, and Utah in the postwar Treaty of Guadalupe Hidalgo.

The forced secession of these lands in 1848 and the influx of Anglo settlers connected with the California gold rush of 1849 dramatically changed the lives of Spanish-speaking peoples in these regions. In this postannexation period Mexicanos were dispossessed of land they had held in many cases for hundreds of years. Property and political rights guaranteed by treaty to Mexicans remaining in the United States were systematically violated.

Increasingly landless and impoverished, Mexican Americans were denied equal economic and political opportunities. Over the next several decades, inequitable social dealings became institutionalized, and systematic racial discrimination against Chicanas/os, including segregation and the denial of civil rights and liberties, became entrenched in the American sociopolitical structure.[7] The systematic subordination of Mexican Americans by the dominant Anglo society during this period continues to be one of the most important contexts of Chicana/o writing.

Poverty and economic marginalization are also crucial contexts of contemporary Chicana/o creative writing and are intertwined with the dynamics of racial and ethnic discrimination. In 1910, the Mexican Revolution created a wave of immigration from Mexico to the United States. This group of Mexican immigrants (some the grandparents and parents of contemporary Chicana writers) experienced both discriminatory Anglo culture and the effects of exploitative labor practices that forced them into conditions of extreme poverty. Deep poverty among Mexican Americans occurred across the U.S. Southwest and as far north as the steel, meatpacking, and railroad barrios of Chicago. Well before the depression era and the purge of welfare repatriation, many Mexican Americans were struggling to survive. Subsequent waves of new Mexican immigration and postwar economic advancement have never eradicated the widespread poverty among Mexicans and Mexican Americans in the United States. Impoverishment and economic marginalization remain critical dimensions influencing much Chicana/o writing.

Large-scale cultural contradictions are another important context that has influenced Chicana writing. During the 1950s and 1960s, racial and ethnic discrimination against Mexican Americans persisted, and contradictory cultural messages continued to abound. On one hand, Chicanas/os were directed to speak and act as assimilated members of the white American mainstream. On the other hand, they were consistently identified as culturally distinct from and inferior to the Anglo population. Chicanas/os responded differently to these conflicting cultural messages. Cultural assimilation and separatism were two diametrically opposed responses. Some Mexican American families attempted to assimilate into Anglo culture by suppressing their Spanish language and traditional customs. Others, often already segregated in the barrios of southwestern or midwestern cities, retreated into family life and into the enclave of Chicana/o society. Between these two extremes, other Chicana/o families acculturated to both cultures by balancing multiple languages and sets of social practices within daily life. This middle ground (described by Gloria Anzaldúa as life in the "borderlands") has increasingly become a site of cultural transformation where Mexican, Chicana/o, indigenous (Native American), and Anglo cultures reciprocally influence and transform one another.[8] Many contemporary Chicana writers are themselves members of families in which the convergence of multiple cultural dynamics was part of everyday life. For these women, the dynamics of cultural mixture (itself definitive of all Chicanas/os as mestizos/as) thus became a matter of profound influence on their lives and writing. As mature writers, many of these women have written prose and poetry that portrays and grapples with life as it is lived in and through a multiplicity of crosscutting cultural values, meanings, and practices. Their work attends to the intersecting and fluctuating borders of gender, sexuality, economic status, physical ability, educational advantage, subculture, religion, ethnicity, race, and so on. As I will stress below, this context of Chicana writing is the source of some of the most important social and political insights offered by contemporary Chicana writing.

Finally, the large-scale political movements of the 1960s and early 1970s marginalized some Chicanas in ways that profoundly influenced many Chicana writers. For many Chicanas within the Chicano movement, for example, political alliances with Chicanos were often fraught with the tension of gender oppression and long-standing machoistic norms.[9] Likewise, connections with the feminist movement became difficult for Chicanas and other women of color, whose voices were disregarded by wealthy white perspectives that dominated the movement.[10] Ana Castillo describes being caught between these conflicting movements as one of the most difficult times in her life. She writes, "I was crucially aware that departing as a woman from the Latino Movement's goal of seeking retribution on the basis of race, ethnicity, and social status—but *not* on gender—would be a lonely path. Addressing such issues, especially those related to sexuality, was seen as the territory of privileged white women and even interpreted as a betrayal by many Latino activists, both men and women."[11] Like Ana Castillo, many Chicanas found themselves both associated with and disassociated from the Chicano and feminist movements. The attitude of many Chicanas toward these movements became increasingly ambiguous. The result was a set of crosscutting identifications and exclusions akin to those created by large-scale cultural contradictions. Both of these contexts—life amid conflicting cultures and life amid conflicting movements—placed Chicana writers in an "in-between place." Writing from this in-between place has proved to be a central element of much Chicana poetry and prose.

Limits, Trends, and Opportunities

From their in-between places, Chicana writers have generated a stream of literary publications that began in 1973. Initially, Chicana writers had difficulty publishing their creative writing, especially in book form. The initial rate of book publication was slow and restricted to small-scale publication with limited distribution. Several factors probably contributed to this difficult beginning. First, at a general level "[t]he exclusion of Chicanas from literary authority is intimately linked to the exclusion of Chicanas from other kinds of power monopolized by privileged white males."[12] Hence, the difficulty Chicanas had asserting their voices in an existing system of literary privilege was part of their overall disempowerment in a variety of domains (e.g., political, social, economic) as (often poor) women of color. Subjected to ethnic, class, and gender discrimination, "Chicana writers share[d] with all women writers the problem of breaking into a male-dominated industry."[13] Established inroads to publishing certainly did not exist for Chicanas writing in the 1970s and early 1980s. Few publishers handled Chicana prose, poetry, or drama.

Second, institutional, financial, and emotional obstacles have also undermined the publication of Chicana works. Some of the most successful Chicana poets and writers describe having had a general lack of institutional support for their writing. This lack of support ranged from active discouragement by writing teachers to the dearth of mentors who could advise them through the publication process.[14] Lorna Dee Cervantes, for example, describes the publication of her poetry collection *Emplumada* as very accidental, arising from a long struggle with many questions about an approach to publication.[15] Limitations on time and financial support also hindered literary production and publication. Beverly Silva, for example, stresses that for her, "[t]he high cost of living keeps me away from my writing. All my work has been done without support and in spare moments of my life."[16] Moreover, the internalized concept of women's intellectual labor as valueless and illegitimate held by many Chicanas (and/or those around them) has also been a significant emotional obstacle to some Chicana writers.

To these cultural, institutional, material, and emotional obstacles to publication another difficulty was added. This difficulty was the interplay between the Chicano movement and the canonization of Chicano writing during the 1970s. The Chicano Movimiento fostered a burst of Chicano art and literature known as the Chicano Renaissance. This convergence of politics and heightened cultural production in turn generated a literary canonization process that took the Chicano movement's concerns as its primary frame of reference. Juan Bruce-Novoa argues that, consequently, particular Chicano novels were privileged and canonized during the sixties and seventies, "as much a result—if not more so—of implicitly or explicitly expressed needs and ideologies as of formal excellence."[17] Overt political expression and the portrayal of a standard Chicano identity became the hallmarks of the preferred texts in the growing Chicano canon.[18] The result was a heightened attention to a handful of male writers and the marginalization of other writers—both female and male—whose writing did not seem sufficiently political (e.g., Josephina Niggli and John Rechy). Poet Lorna Dee Cervantes refers to this state of affairs as the reason behind her founding of Mango Publications in the mid-1970s. She states, "I felt there was a lot of serious writing being done, and a lot of it was not blatantly political. And a lot of poets who[m] I was meeting and traveling around [with,] who were very good, were real hesitant about publishing, and especially publishing their work as a Chicano or under that label, being afraid of those definitions. When I met Gary [Soto], for instance, that was how he looked at things, 'You know, if that is Chicano poetry, I am not a Chicano poet.' And the magazines, the *revistas*, at that time were emphasizing that they were distinctly looking for material that was political."[19]

The prevailing emphasis on overtly political literature and a single Chicana/o identity described by Juan Bruce-Novoa gave critics, publishers, and others in the literary domain a particular bias in their approach to Chicana/o literary works. This bias led critics and others to focus on blatantly political texts in a way that drew attention away from Chicana writing that was either less overtly political or that defined politics broadly to encompass more than just political protest and electoral activity. The resulting inattention to Chicana literature in the 1970s and early 1980s was clear. One commentator noted in 1985 that most critics had not yet engaged with Chicana literature enough "to determine and decipher the [Chicana] author's intentions with respect to the literary standards they challenge. The underlying implication is that the issues women writers raise are not of great magnitude or importance. This conclusion can be easily verified by citing the astonishingly scarce bibliographical entries that deal directly with

Chicana novelists."[20] This inattention to Chicana writing is also consistent with trends to favor portrayals of a single Chicana/o identity—an identity that much Chicana writing turns upside down.

Considering this range of obstacles to Chicana publishing, some scholars have stressed that "male control of Chicano publication enterprises is a most important element in the analysis of Chicana literary production."[21] Certainly there is evidence that dominant preconceptions about the appropriate terrain of Chicana/o prose and poetry produced circumstances in which "[C]hicana authors have suffered undue hardships in the area of publication due to their status as a marginal group within a marginal group."[22] Although some male writers would have suffered from these preconceptions as well, the inequitable treatment of Mexican American women writers made their work virtually invisible during the 1960s and 1970s.[23]

Facing these combined obstacles, some Chicana writers attempted to combat the invisibility of their work during the 1970s by turning to small presses for publication. One example is Alma Villanueva's alliance with Place of Herons Press, founded in 1974 by James Cody. Described as an "ethnic publisher," Cody published Villanueva's *Bloodroot* in June 1977 and her *Life Span* in 1984.[24] Cody took an interest in Villanueva's poetry, originally thinking that it was written by a man. To him, her poems had a "universal quality, embracing all subjects and passions, that seemed . . . almost only to come from the writings of men."[25] In better praise of Villanueva, Cody remarked, "one of the outstanding qualities of Alma's work . . . is her sensitivity, a kind of sensitivity that very few male poets ever permit themselves to show. . . . It would be well if male poets would begin to look at Villanueva in a search for it."[26] Villanueva's persistence in seeking publication resonates in her remark that "[w]riting takes all your courage—to stand by your work and see it through to publication. . . ."[27] *Bloodroot* was reprinted in 1982. Yet, like many early chapbooks of Chicana poetry published by small presses, it remains difficult to find. The scarcity of these texts certainly contributes to the limited critical and popular attention given to many excellent works by Chicanas.

Despite Villanueva's experience with Place of Herons, opportunities with small presses were few in the late 1970s. In Ana Castillo's words, "[f]or the poet, especially, small presses offer[ed] a long-desired trap-door to the larger world. However, again for Latina/o poets these avenues were—and are to date—still limited."[28] Consequently, some Chicana writers, including Castillo, ultimately found it necessary to publish their work themselves. Castillo self-published her first two chapbooks of poetry, *Otro Canto* in 1977 and *The Invitation* in 1979.

To further broaden publication opportunities, a few writers across the country also established their own small publishing firms in order to publish their writing. One important example is M & A Editions, of which Angela de Hoyos is copublisher and general editor. Through the press, de Hoyos published *Arise Chicano! and Other Poems* in 1975 and *Chicano Poems for the Barrio* in 1976. In 1978, M & A Editions also published Evangelina Vigil's book of poetry *Nade y nade*. Similarly, Bernice Zamora self-published *Restless Serpents* with Diseños Literarios in Menlo Park, California, in 1976. Margarita Cota-Cárdenas, co-owner of Scorpion Press, published her *Noches despertando inConciencias* in 1977. Lorna Dee Cervantes also founded her magazine, *Mango*, and Mango Publications in 1976 to provide a multicultural forum for poets and writers who were hesitant about publishing.[29] These and other writer-owned presses played a critical role in making Chicana writing available in print in the 1970s.

Against many obstacles, the persistent efforts of Chicana writers established a small but steady output of Chicana prose, poetry, and drama in the 1970s. The publication of contemporary Chicana literature is typically considered to have begun in September of 1973 with a special issue of the Quinto Sol journal *El Grito* entitled *Chicanas en la literatura y el arte*.[30] The issue was edited by Estela Portillo Trambley, and it was the first anthology of Chicana creative writing. The year 1975 marked the beginning of contemporary book publication by Chicanas. In that year Portillo Trambley published a book of short stories entitled *Rain of Scorpions and Other Writings* with Quinto Sol. Also in 1975, Angela de Hoyos published a volume of poetry, and Berta Ornelas published her novel *Come Down from the Mound*. In 1976, Bernice Zamora and Angela de Hoyos published their works through their own presses, and as the United States celebrated its bicentennial, Isabella Ríos's novel *Victuum* went to press.

By 1977, a stream of publications—an average of four titles per year—had been established. Villanueva's *Bloodroot* was published in 1977, as was Castillo's *Otro canto*. This rate of publication remained steady through the first half of the 1980s. In 1980, for example, El Fuego de Aztlán published Lucha Corpi's *Noon Words*. Lorna Dee Cervantes's Mango Publications published Sandra Cisneros's chapbook of poetry *Bad Boys,* and Rossetta Press released Denise Chávez's *Life Is a Two-Way Street*. The following year, *Emplumada,* Lorna Dee Cervantes's widely acclaimed collection of poetry, was published by the University of Pittsburgh Press, and Maize Press, founded in 1977 by Xelina and Alurista, published Gina Valdés's *There Are No Madmen Here*. In 1982, Evangelina Vigil's *Thirty an' Seen a Lot* was released by Arte Público Press.

In 1983, Bilingual Press entered the Chicana book publishing scene with Beverly Silva's *Second St. Poems*. Gary Keller founded Bilingual Press (and its companion journal *Bilingual Review*, established in 1974) because, in Keller's words, "[t]here was a tremendous need for an outlet for Chicano, Puerto Rican, Cuban-American . . . and other Hispanic citizens of the United States . . . [who] had no place to publish or very few places to publish. . . ."[31] Together with Arte Público Press, established by Nicolás Kanellos in 1979, Bilingual Press has played a key, and at times dominant, role in the publication of Chicano and Chicana creative and critical writing.[32] Also in 1983 and 1984, Estela Portillo Trambley, Carmen Tafolla, and playwright Cherríe Moraga all published creative works with other small presses, including M & A Editions and Boston's South End Press.

By 1984, however, two changes had occurred. First, the annual rate of publication of Chicana literature perceptibly increased. The number of publications jumped from four to more than six per year. At this time Chicana prose and poetry were increasingly anthologized, and the amount of critical attention received by Chicana writing likewise escalated. Credit for this transformation may be attributed to the earlier successes of Chicana writers who had pressed hard to publish their work during the preceding decade. As María Herrera-Sobek put it, "The initial success of vanguard writers such as Alma Villanueva, Bernice Zamora, Lucha Corpi, and Lorna Dee Cervantes in the late 1970s and early 1980s encouraged Chicano-oriented publishing houses to 'risk' investing in Mexican American women writers. The success of these initial ventures [has] been greatly instrumental in helping minority women get their works in print and in the market place where they can be made accessible to the reading public as well as to academic critics."[33] These early publishing successes and increasing critical acclaim influenced publishers. By the mid-1980s more Chicana literature was being published than ever before.

The second major change to occur in the mid-1980s was the increasing concentration of Chicana publishing. By 1985, Arte Público Press and Bilingual Press were publishing an increasingly higher percentage of all of the Chicana literary works published. In a survey I have taken (see fig. 8.1), forty-five presses published Chicana creative writing between 1975 and 1998.

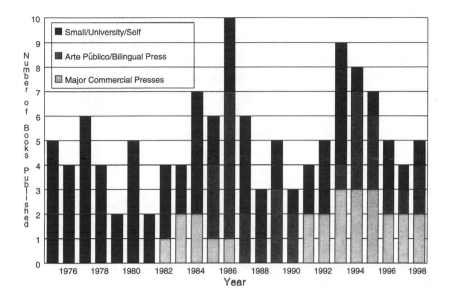

FIGURE 8.1 Profile of presses publishing Chicana books from 1975 to 1998.

Among these publishers, 42 percent of their combined total output—almost half—was produced by only four publishers. Of the number of published books surveyed here, the two largest Latino-oriented publishing houses, Arte Público Press and Bilingual Press, together published more than 34 percent (20 percent and 14 percent, respectively). Between 1985 and 1989 alone, Arte Público Press and Bilingual Press published 62 percent of Chicana works brought to press. Among these were Pat Mora's *Chants*, Helena María Viramontes's *The Moths and Other Stories*, Denise Chávez's *Last of the Menu Girls*, Angela de Hoyos's *Woman, Woman*, Lucha Corpi's *Delia's Song*, Alma Villanueva's *La chingada* and *UltraViolet Sky*, Ana Castillo's epistolary novel *The Mixquiahuala Letters*, Beverly Silva's *The Cat and Other Stories*, and Patricia Preciado Martin's *Days of Plenty, Days of Want*.

Although Arte Público Press and Bilingual Press came to dominate Chicana and Chicano publishing in the mid-1980s, other small presses remained active. Among these were Maize Press, which published Gina Valdés's *Eating Fire* in 1986; Relámpago Press, which published Margarita Cota-Cárdenas's novel *Puppet* in 1985; and West End Press, which published Cherríe Moraga's play *Giving Up the Ghost* in 1985. In addition, two other presses specializing in works by or of interest to women of color began to take a larger place in the publication of Chicana writing. These were Aunt

Lute Books and Third Woman Press. Joan Pinkvoss founded Aunt Lute Books in San Francisco in 1978 with the express purpose of publishing "multicultural, feminist material."[34] Particularly well known in Aunt Lute's catalog is Gloria Anzaldúa's mixed-genre book of creative and critical prose and poetry *Borderlands/La frontera: The New Mestiza*, published by the press in 1987.

In the early 1990s, publication patterns for novels and book-length collections of poetry and prose by Chicanas changed yet again. This new trend was characterized by greater commercial successes and increased publication by major mainstream presses. The publication history of *My Wicked Wicked Ways* by Sandra Cisneros exemplifies this shift. After its first publication by Third Woman Press in 1987, this poetry collection enjoyed considerable popular success. By 1990, sales had led to a second printing, and in 1992 the poems were printed yet a third time. In that same year, Random House opted to publish *My Wicked Wicked Ways* in hardcover. Around this time, Random House also published much of Cisneros's other work. In 1991, for example, Random House republished *The House on Mango Street* with the Vintage Contemporaries imprint. The first edition of this award-winning book was published by Arte Público Press in 1984, and a revised version was published by Arte Público in 1989. The book received a great deal of critical praise as being both beautifully crafted and socially and politically astute. Both a commercial and critical success, *The House on Mango Street* is probably Cisneros's best-known work. Another highly acclaimed collection of Cisneros's short prose, entitled *Woman Hollering Creek and Other Stories*, was originally published in hardcover by Random House in 1991 and later published in paperback in 1992 as a Vintage Contemporaries edition. *Loose Woman* was published in early 1994 by Alfred A. Knopf, which provided a highly visible promotion for the book. The publication of Sandra Cisneros's works by large mainstream publishing houses represented an important shift in the publication of literature by Chicanas. This shift is illustrated in the figure, which shows a clear contrast between the early limits to and subsequent broadening of publication opportunities open to Chicana writers.

In general, the 1990s ushered in a period of increasing market success for Chicana poetry and prose published by small presses. In turn, this growing market success has incited a new willingness among large mainstream commercial presses to publish the works of Chicanas. Within this new trend, Sandra Cisneros has garnered perhaps the most attention from large mainstream publishers. Yet, she is by no means the only Chicana writer to be published by major commercial presses during the 1990s. Ana Castillo's epistolary novel *The Mixquiahuala Letters* (1992) and *Sapogonia* (1994) were both published by Doubleday and Company. In addition, Castillo's collection of poetry *My Father Was a Toltec* (1995) and her novel *So Far from God* (1993) were both published by W.W. Norton. *So Far from God* was issued in paperback and promoted by Penguin/Plume in 1994. Alma Villanueva's *Naked Ladies* was published by Anchor Books/Doubleday in 1994, the same year that Farrar, Straus, and Giroux published Denise Chávez's *Face of an Angel.* Harcourt Brace also published Kathleen Alcalá's *Spirits of the Ordinary* in 1998, following its original publication by Chronicle Books in 1997.

In most of these cases, small presses had first published books that were later published by the major presses. More recently, however, major mainstream presses have initially published an increasing number of books by Chicanas. Books in this category include Sandra Cisneros's *Loose Woman,* published by Knopf in 1994; Helena María Viramontes's novel *Under the Feet of Jesus,* published by Dutton in 1995; Ana Castillo's book of short stories *Loverboys,* published by Norton in 1996; and Sylvia López-Medina's second novel *Siguiriya,* published by Harper Collins in 1997. The serial publication of works by established Chicana writers, the publication of previously unpublished material by Chicanas, and the increasing number of Chicana writers published by major presses suggest two things. First, deepening relationships are developing between particular writers and their publishers, resulting in ongoing publication support for these particular writers. Second, there seems to be an increasing commitment among some major presses to offer publishing support to (at least a few) Chicana writers with whom they have not yet worked. It would seem that the inroads to publishing that were lacking for Chicanas in the 1970s are becoming rapidly established.

Considering these developments, the 1990s became the most successful decade to date for the publication of Chicana creative writing. In addition to works published by large mainstream presses, small publishing houses have continued to publish Chicana works in increasing numbers. The most active small presses include Aunt Lute Press, Third Woman Press, Bilingual Press, Arte Público Press, and several university presses. The University of New Mexico Press, for example, has been active in publishing Chicana creative writing, including Mary Helen Ponce's autobiographical novel *Hoyt Street* and Pat Mora's *Nepantla: Essays from the Land in the Middle,* both published in 1993. Other writers who published in the

1990s include Alicia Gaspar de Alba, Lorna Dee Cervantes, Lucha Corpi, Tina Juárez, Ofelia Dumas Lachtman, Pat Mora, Cherríe Moraga, Terri de la Peña, Emma Pérez, Patricia Preciado Martin, Gina Valdés, and Bernice Zamora.

Unfortunately, some Chicano writers and critics have not taken the increasing success of Chicana writers altogether gracefully. A few Chicano critics, editors, and publishers continue to ignore the quality and hard-won success of Chicana writing. In recent years the success of many works by Chicanas has outstripped that of contemporary Chicano writers, some of whom are also active critics. Numerous Chicano critics acknowledge and engage with Chicana writing.[35] Others, however, ignore Chicana writers or restrict their attention to a few select writers while ignoring the work of a large number of others.[36] Still other Chicano critics openly display their displeasure at recent developments in the publication of Chicana writing. Ray González had this to say about Ana Castillo's novel *So Far from God:* "A novel like *So Far from God* may represent the unfortunate side of the triumph of multiculturalism: One of the dangers today is that glamorous, high-powered agents and publishers place pressure to produce on minority writers who may not be quite ready. New York wants *the* Chicana novel so bad it hurts."[37] In a response to González, Gerald Howard, Ana Castillo's editor at W.W. Norton, charged González with "blaming the writer for her publisher."[38] He further responded, "I wish [González] would acknowledge that a forty-year-old writer with four collections of poetry and two previous novels to her credit is more than 'ready' for as large an audience as can be found for her."[39]

The response of Castillo's editor and the efforts of large publishing houses to promote works by Chicanas reinforce the suggestion that there is an increasing commitment on the part of major publishers to take Chicana writers seriously. Critics who fail to extend serious attention to Chicana writing often continue the long-standing refusal (traceable to the 1960s and 1970s) to engage critically with Chicana literature in terms of the creative intentions of individual Chicana writers.[40]

Comments such as those of González offer explicit and implicit opposition to efforts that encourage Mexican American women's writing. Because of this, encouragement and commensurate opportunities for Chicana writers are still needed. Although I have outlined the dramatic increase in the publication of Chicana creative writing over the last twenty-five years, it would be false to conclude that the publication of works by Chicanas (or other minority women writers) is firmly established and widespread.[41] Several Chicana authors have become very successful. Books by Sandra Cisneros and Ana Castillo can be purchased in bookstores nationwide. Yet, only about 120 book titles by Chicana creative writers have been published in the last quarter-century. Moreover, the list of Chicana creative writers who publish regularly but who have had no opportunity to publish a book-length piece far exceeds the list of Chicana writers with book credits to their name. If these and other still-unknown writers are to disseminate their work, and if new Chicana writers are to develop, then forms of discouragement and discrimination must give way to a more supportive environment. Movements to offer constructive criticism of existing Chicana literature and encourage the production of more literary works are of critical importance. Such movements may take a variety of forms that appeal to anyone interested in creative writing involving skilled word-craft, original expression, and significant meaning. Whether some critics, publishers, educators, and others in the literary field will continue to undermine existing movements to engage and support Chicana writing remains to be seen. What is clear, however, is that Chicana writers will continue to produce and publish creative works that merit both critical and popular attention. Their work merits attention not only for the beauty, imagination, and excellence of composition but also, as we shall see in the following pages, for the socially and politically significant insights to be found among its topics and themes.

Social and Political Significance

Thus far I have described Chicana writers in the act of transforming silence into language. In essence I have focused on the *act* of writing and publication as a form of social and political dissent in which Chicana voices are raised. Claiming voice where it has previously been denied constitutes an act of dissent in that it defies existing forms of marginalization based on gender, sexuality, physical ability, class, ethnicity, race, and other dimensions. Voices, once claimed, will further challenge injustice and marginalization and help produce social and political transformation. Thus, it is important to engage with Chicana literature not only as an *act* but also in terms of its *content*, that is, in terms of the ideas, images, and expressions to be interpreted from the poetry or prose itself.

While political and social ideas have long been a part of Chicana creative writing, the style of their expression has varied. In the earliest writings, some

Chicanas addressed social and political actuality in fairly direct terms.[42] Voices in this poetry or prose frequently questioned and dissented, but often in generalized ways. Such an engaged-yet-generalized voice speaks in these emphatic lines by Lorna Dee Cervantes:

> I believe in revolution
> because everywhere the crosses are burning,
> sharp-shooting goose-steppers round every corner,
> there are snipers in the schools . . .
> (I know you don't believe this.
> You think this is nothing
> but faddish exaggeration. But they
> are not shooting at you.)[43]

These expressions drew energy from the Chicano and other civil rights movements. Later, political expressions in Chicana writing began to focus instead on the contradictions created by limits to the social justice achieved by the civil rights movements. The civil rights movements increased the educational, political, and economic opportunities open to many Chicanas/os. Bilingual education, ethnic studies programs, educational and economic affirmative-action policies, and the strengthening of civil rights protections benefited many, including a small but growing Mexican American middle class. Many contemporary Chicana writers took advantage of the educational opportunities (though often at great sacrifice) and are now more or less upwardly mobile. Advancements for some, however, did not eliminate the poverty, lack of opportunity, economic and political exploitation, and discrimination experienced by most Mexican Americans and Mexican immigrants in the United States. Despite real improvements, millions of Mexican Americans continue to be sequestered in low-paying jobs. Thus, many have been left behind by the economic, educational, and political advances of the postmovement era, even while these advances are now under renewed attack.

Not surprisingly, these circumstances have been explicit themes in much Chicana writing since the 1980s.[44] At that time, many voices in Chicana writing took on a more personal tone, and the language of personal experience became increasingly prevalent. This personalization recharacterized the social and political content of the literature and echoed the then-common statement, "the personal is the political."[45] Such a personalized political voice is found, for example, in Pat Mora's poem "Echoes," in which themes of social inequality, economic exploitation, and cultural identification are mingled with the imagery of a party:

> In her white uniform, Magdalena
> set the table remembering such laughter
> at fiestas in Zacatecas, enjoying
> the afternoon's songs and games,
> trying to snare English words floating
> in the air like the children's
> carefree balloons.
>
> Her smile wavered when I spoke
> to her in Spanish. Perhaps she wondered
> why I'd leave the other señoras,
> join her when she served, why I'd
> drift to the edge.
> Again and again I hear:
>   just drop the cups and plates
>   on the grass. My maid
>   will pick them up.
> Again and again I feel
> my silence, the party whirring round me.[46]

Stylistic and thematic changes in some Chicana writing may also reflect a reciprocal influence between creative writing (as well as Chicana critical writing) and concurrent intellectual developments. Among these possible influences are the rifts in feminism that opened in the 1970s and widened in the 1980s. These rifts diversified feminist thought into different feminisms, some of which, like much Chicana writing itself, actively emphasized and drew attention to the experiences of Third World, lesbian, and poor working-class women. In addition, scholarly thought on race, ethnicity, and (post)colonialism related to much of Chicana literature in its emphasis on the differences in social categories such as race and gender. Based on these and other intellectual developments, emphasis on difference, race, ethnicity, gender, and sexuality began to play a larger part in the U.S. cultural mainstream during the 1980s. Debates and backlashes involving "identity politics"; multiculturalism; gay civil rights; feminism; and postmodernist, poststructuralist, and postcolonial thought spilled over into popular media and influenced educational and political structures. This context both supported and challenged Chicana creative (and critical) writers who continued in the 1990s to grapple with and explore a range of themes including sexuality, rape, familial and other interpersonal relationships, language, cultural practice, social and political conflict, subjectivity, and personal transformation, in short, the experiences of human frailty, degradation, pain, empowerment, and joy.

These and other themes in Chicana writing provide powerful social and political insights in addition to their aesthetic offerings. Of particular sociopolitical importance, in my view, is the theme of multiple identity in the work of many Chicana writers including Ana Castillo, Sandra Cisneros, Pat Mora, Gloria Anzaldúa, Lorna Dee Cervantes, Marina Rivera, and Alicia Gaspar de Alba, to name only a few. As has already been stressed, the historical context of much Chicana writing has typically involved the negotiation of intersecting social borders. These borders separate languages, nation states, genders, sexual preferences, cultures, subcultures, ethnic groups, races, degrees of physical ability, and classes. Negotiating and challenging these borders has caused many Chicanas (like other border dwellers) to internalize and maintain a range of different identities, identities that they assume as they proceed through everyday life.[47] Chicanas and other border dwellers thus live in and through a variety of different (mutually conditioning and contradictory) roles and frames of reference to survive. More and more, therefore, Mexican American women view their Chicana selfhood as a personal, complex, and always transforming weave of Mexican, indigenous, Anglo, and other cultural components.

By using the theme of shifting and permeable borders between different components of life, much Chicana writing highlights multiple identity. In doing so this literature explores a mode of being in which contradictory and mutually conditioning identities exist within our overall identity structures. Multiple identity is characteristic, for example, of Esperanza, the young protagonist of Sandra Cisneros's short stories in *The House on Mango Street*.[48] The theme of multiple identity is also used in various works by Ana Castillo and Gloria Anzaldúa, who cast Chicana *mestizaje* as a site not only of oppression and discomfort but also of empowerment. In *Borderlands/La frontera*, Anzaldúa describes "mestiza consciousness" as a mode of being that balances, *but does not deny,* the ambiguities and flux caused by living in multiple (and contradictory) frames of meaning and practice. Most important, Anzaldúa suggests that multiple identity that commingles multiple sets of meaning and reference can prevent the intolerance and violence unleashed by the insecurity of encountering differences in others.[49] This suggestion merits our particular attention. It is important because the project of how to live peacefully and democratically in the context of countless human differences is among the most pressing political tasks of our time. Much Western political thought ill prepares us for this task, often insisting that cultural homogeneity is necessary to peaceful democratic regimes.[50] In contrast, much Chicana writing speaks to the workings of diverse polities by forming complex modes of thought and behavior amid conflicting cultural forces.

The treatment that some Chicanas have given multiple identity in their creative writing is important not only for Chicanas/os but for anyone who grapples to understand contemporary social and political life. Political, economic, and technological transformations increasingly break down existing political, linguistic, and cultural borders. At the same time, countervailing social and political dynamics re-emphasize the diversity of human experience and increase the number of recognized divisions within and among existing human societies. As a consequence of these diametric forces, everyone is to some extent a border dweller. Our borders lie at many levels and are continually transforming. These transformations force us to either catch up and balance complexity or retrench and bulwark our lives against the endlessly changing borders within and around us. Recourse to the latter can result in isolation, fear, violence, and political failure. By questioning and elaborating the complex human experience of living and moving among very different forms of social and political life, Chicana literature presents us with ideas and interpretations that we may draw upon to address and understand our current political dilemmas. Engagement with this literature may generate new political thought on identity, political discourse, commonality and difference, citizenship, and democratic practice.[51]

Emma Pérez has described the history of Chicanas as one in which "[w]e [as Chicanas] have not had our own language and voice in history. We have been spoken about, written about, spoken at, but never spoken with or listened to."[52] From this voiceless point of departure, Chicana writers have acted over the past twenty-five years to break silence by struggling to publish their creative works and bring them to public attention. This struggle continues. Some Chicana writers have already transformed their long-imposed silence into a language of beauty, originality, and insight. Contemporary thinkers and readers would do well to listen carefully to the voices of these writers and to seriously consider the messages their voices bring.

Notes

Author's Notes: I would like to give special thanks to María Herrera-Sobek for her guidance and encouragement of this project. My thanks also go to Seyla Benhabib for her support, to Cheryl-Ann Michael for her comments on an early draft, and to William Barvosa-Carter for his comments and technical assistance. I am also grateful to Yolanda Broyles-González, Mario T. García, and Francisco Lomelí for their help-ful questions and critical comments at the final stage. All errors and omissions remain my own.

Epigraph quote from Gloria Anzaldúa, ed., *Making Face, Making Soul: Creative and Critical Perspectives by Women of Color* (San Francisco: Aunt Lute Books, 1990), xxii.

1. In this essay I focus on contemporary trends in book publication (novels and collections of prose, poetry, and drama) by Chicanas. In my survey I have made every effort to be as inclusive as possible. Any omissions or errors are unintentional. In addition, I have not focused on publications by Chicanas prior to 1960. A growing wealth of new scholarship, however, is focusing on earlier publications, and some earlier texts are coming back into print. Arte Público Press, for example, has recently republished María Amparo Ruiz de Burton's 1885 work *The Squatter and the Don* (Rosaura Sánchez and Beatrice Pita, eds., 1993). See also María Herrera-Sobek, *Reconstructing a Chicano/a Literary Heritage: Hispanic Colonial Literature of the Southwest* (Tucson, Ariz.: University of Arizona Press, 1993).

2. For example, see Ilan Stavans, "Labyrinth of Plenitude," *The Nation*, 18 January 1993, 65–67. Stavans does mention Sandra Cisneros (and two other Latinas) as having published with large mainstream presses. His historical account of Latino literature on a "voyage from the periphery to the center of culture, from marginality to acknowledgment," however, never mentions women writers, either Chicana or Latina; see especially p. 66.

3. Harold Augenbraum and Ilan Stavans, eds., *Growing Up Latino: Memoirs and Stories* (New York: Houghton Mifflin Co., 1993), xii–xiii.

4. Tey Diana Rebolledo and Eliana S. Rivero, eds., *Infinite Divisions: An Anthology of Chicana Literature* (Tucson, Ariz.: University of Arizona Press, 1993), 23.

5. Francisco Lomelí, "Chicana Novelists in the Process of Creating Fictive Voices," in *Beyond Stereotypes: A Critical Analysis of Chicana Literature*, ed. María Herrera-Sobek (Binghampton, N.Y.: Bilingual Press, 1985), 30.

6. Wolfgang Binder, ed., *Partial Autobiographies: Interviews with Twenty Chicano Poets* (Erlangen, P.F.G.: Verlag Palm & Enke Erlangen, 1985).

7. Juan Gómez-Quiñones, *Roots of Chicano Politics, 1600–1940* (Albuquerque, N. Mex.: University of New Mexico Press), 191–293.

8. Gloria Anzaldúa, *Borderlands/La frontera: The New Mestiza* (San Francisco: Aunt Lute Books, 1987), preface.

9. Much has been written on gender bias within the Chicano movement. For a more detailed description, see Marta Ester Sánchez, *Contemporary Chicana Poetry: A Critical Approach to an Emerging Literature* (Berkeley, Calif.: University of California Press, 1985), 4–6; and Cynthia Orozco, "Sexism in Chicano Studies and the Community," in *Chicana Voices: Intersections of Class, Race and Gender,* eds. Teresa Cordova et al. (Albuquerque, N. Mex.: University of New Mexico Press, 1990), 11–18; and for a variety of pieces dating to the period, see Alma M. García, ed., *Chicana Feminist Thought: The Basic Historical Writings* (New York: Routledge, 1997).

10. For an account of this development, see Cherríe Moraga and Gloria Anzaldúa, eds., *This Bridge Called My Back: Writings by Radical Women of Color* (Watertown, Mass.: Persephone Press, 1981).

11. Ana Castillo, *My Father Was a Toltec and Selected Poems 1973–1988* (New York: W.W. Norton, 1995), xix.

12. Yvonne Yarbo-Bejarano, "Chicana Literature from a Chicana Feminist Perspective," in *Chicana Creativity and Criticism: Charting New Frontiers in American Literature,* eds. María Herrera-Sobek and Helena María Viramontes (Houston, Tex.: Arte Público Press, 1988), 139.

13. Yvonne Yarbo-Bejarano makes this point in her introduction to Helena María Viramontes's collection of short stories *The Moths and Other Stories* (Houston, Tex.: Arte Público Press, 1985), 7. Poet Beverly Silva agrees that in her experience "as a minority woman, getting published has been difficult." Bryan Ryan, ed., *Hispanic Writers: A Selection of Sketches from Contemporary Authors* (Detroit, Mich.: Gale Research Inc., 1991), 443.

14. Lorna Dee Cervantes and Sandra Cisneros, for example, both describe the active discouragement they received from writing teachers and others in educational settings. See Binder, *Partial Autobiographies,* 39–74.

15. The publication in periodicals of Cervantes's poetry also began with some degree of happenstance. She was first published by Nicolás Kanellos who, after hearing Cervantes give a poetry reading at the 1974 Teatro Festival (in Mexico City), approached her about publishing poems in *Revista Chicano-Riqueña.* Binder, *Partial Autobiographies,* 42–43.

16. Ryan, *Hispanic Writers,* 443.

17. Juan Bruce-Novoa, "Canonical and Noncanonical Texts: A Chicano Case Study,"

in *Redefining American Literary History,* eds. A. LaVonne Brown Ruoff and Jerry W. Ward, Jr. (New York: Modern Language Association of America, 1990), 200.

18. For Juan Bruce-Novoa these privileged texts were also typically characterized by particular themes including the preservation of family and ethnic tradition, working-class solidarity, anti-assimilationist goals, and the specter of ignoring these objectives. "Canonical and Noncanonical Texts," 200. Nationalist overtones also favored inattention to the diversity among Chicanas/os and to the diversity within individual Chicana/o identities.

19. Binder, *Partial Autobiographies,* 52–53.

20. Francisco Lomelí, "Chicana Novelists," 32.

21. Herrera-Sobek, *Beyond Stereotypes,* 11. This is an important point. The presence of gender bias in the Chicano movement and the close connection between the movement's ideological themes and the canonization of Chicano texts makes the influence of gender bias in the literary domain of the 1970s more than plausible. The degree of this influence, however, is difficult to isolate and would require further examination well beyond the scope of this essay.

22. Herrera-Sobek, *Beyond Stereotypes,* 10.

23. Rosaura Sánchez, "Chicana Prose Writers: The Case of Gina Valdés and Sylvia Lizárraga," in *Beyond Stereotypes,* 61.

24. Len Fulton, ed., *International Directory of Little Magazines and Small Presses,* 27th ed. (Paradise, Calif.: Dustbooks, 1991).

25. James Cody's preface to *Bloodroot* by Alma Villanueva (Austin, Tex.: Place of Herons Press, 1982), i.

26. Ibid., iv–v.

27. Ryan, *Hispanic Writers,* 495.

28. Castillo, *My Father Was a Toltec,* xviii. Castillo continues: "Thus a few Latino/as across the country began their own publishing imprints. And if even that narrow opportunity to publish was not available, a poet might decide to print her work herself. This is why I 'published' my two chapbooks, *Otro Canto* and later *The Invitation,* mostly with the support of friends."

29. Binder, *Partial Autobiographies,* 52.

30. According to Francisco Lomelí this early publication constituted both an end to silence but also "a critical stage of inner reflection . . . the year 1973 can perhaps be regarded as the key point of departure for contemporary writings by Chicana authors whose inclinations were to accentuate an experimental perspective that focused on a woman's world view, her immediate sphere of social interactions, and concerns of a feminist nature." "Chicana Novelists," in *Beyond Stereotypes,* 30.

31. Gary D. Keller, general editor and founder of Bilingual Press, taped interview by author, Simmons College, Boston, Massachusetts, 16 November 1993.

32. Arte Público Press's companion journal, *The Americas Review,* was established in

1974. Note that for both Bilingual Press/ *Bilingual Review* and Arte Público Press/ *The Americas Review,* the press (and therefore book publication) began several years *after* the journals had been established and had become important places for the periodical publication of Chicana/o prose and poetry.

33. María Herrera-Sobek and Helena María Viramontes, eds., *Chicana Creativity and Criticism: Charting New Frontiers in American Literature* (Houston, Tex.: Arte Público Press, 1988), 9.

34. Len Fulton, ed., *International Directory of Little Magazines and Small Presses,* 27th ed., (Paradise, Calif.: Dustbooks, 1991), 48.

35. Francisco Lomelí is a notable example.

36. Sandra Cisneros is often singled out in this way. See, for example, Meier and Ribera, *Mexican Americans,* 237. See also Ilan Stavans, "Labyrinth of Plenitude," *The Nation,* 18 January 1993, 65–67. In this review of new Latino fiction, Stavans refers to the work Cisneros has published with a major press as "quite impressive," but he does not mention any other Chicanas; see also note #3 above. His brief mention of Cisneros instead segues into a dig at her and other Latinas that imputes to them opportunism in their choice of publishers. He writes, "To be sure, for years many of these writers had been loyal to small university-based presses like Arte Público in Texas and Bilingual in Arizona. But a handsome advance and the possibilities of enviable exposure became magnets for those interested in making it big," 65.

37. Ray González, "A Chicano Verano," *The Nation,* 7 June 1993, 772–73.

38. Gerald Howard, Letter to the Editor, *The Nation,* 19 July 1993, 86.

39. Ibid.

40. Ray González, for example, overlooks complex themes in Castillo's *So Far from God* such as the transformation of subjectivity within a hybridized culture. Failing to engage the novel on these more sophisticated levels, González imports a vague standard of realistic fictionalization, charging Castillo with "romanticizing" ethnicity through characters "too 'ethnic' for their lives to be believable, even in the supernatural world . . ." *The Nation,* 7 June 1993, 772–73.

41. The suggestion that there is widespread publication of works by minority women is often made even in publishing industry literature. See, for example, the special issue on multicultural literature and the publishing industry's commitment to diversity in *Publishers Weekly,* 9 August 1993, 31–36. bell hooks discusses the falsity of the conception that literature by women of color is now sufficiently published and engaged with in "black women writing: creating more space," in *Talking Back, Thinking Feminist, Thinking Black* (Boston, Mass.: South End Press, 1989), 142–47.

42. Although I describe this language as direct, it was perhaps not direct enough to be considered overtly political in the canonization process of the 1970s.

43. Excerpt from "Poem for the Young White Man Who Asked Me How I, an

Intelligent Well-Read Person, Could Believe in the War between Races," from *Emplumada,* by Lorna Dee Cervantes, © 1981. Reprinted by permission of the University of Pittsburgh Press.

44. For an example of this contrast as drawn in a creative work see Lorna Dee Cervantes's poem, "For Virginia Chávez," in *Emplumada,* 16–18.

45. Tey Diana Rebolledo also makes this observation in relation to critical writing by Chicanas. She argues that "[w]hat is different about these [more recent] essays from those written in the 1960s is the personal tone, the direct voice of the author, questioning herself and her society." *Infinite Divisions,* 27.

46. Pat Mora, "Echoes," in *Borders* (Houston, Tex.: Arte Público Press, 1986).

47. More than speculation, this concept of multiple identity is an increasingly dominant one in empirical psychology where "personality is not [seen as] a self-unifying system, but rather . . . a collection of selves that operate independently in different contexts." Richard M. Ryan, "Psychological Needs and the Facilitation of the Integrative Process," *Journal of Personality* 63, no. 3 (1995): 396.

48. For a reading of *House on Mango Street* in terms of multiple identity, see Renato Rosaldo, "Changing Chicano Narratives," in *Culture and Truth: The Remaking of Social Analysis* (Boston, Mass.: Beacon Press, 1989), 160–67.

49. Gloria Anzaldúa, *Borderlands/La frontera: The New Mestiza* (San Francisco, Calif.: Aunt Lute Books, 1987), see especially pp. 77–88.

50. John Stuart Mill, for example, emphasized that representative government was virtually impossible in regimes with different linguistic and cultural groups. See his *Considerations on Representative Government,* ed. Geraint Williams (London: J.M Dent; Rutland, Vt.: C.E. Tuttle, 1993). This view has remained conventional among many contemporary political scientists despite increasing attention to the dynamics of multicultural democracies. See, for example, Arendt Lijphart's classic, *Democracy in Plural Societies: A Comparative Exploration* (New Haven: Yale University Press, 1977), 1.

51. I draw upon Chicana poetry and prose, for example, to explore the connection between multiple identity and contemporary democratic citizenship in a book currently in progress entitled *A Wealth of Selves: Multiple Identity and Contemporary Citizenship.*

52. Emma Pérez, "Sexuality and Discourse: Notes from a Chicana Survivor," in *Infinite Divisions,* 26.

Trends and Themes in Chicana/o Writings in Postmodern Times

FRANCISCO A. LOMELÍ, TERESA MÁRQUEZ, AND MARÍA HERRERA-SOBEK

*C*hicano literature definitely came of age in the 1980s and 1990s. Literary production in these two decades reached a new phase within the theoretical parameters of what Rosaura Sánchez describes in her essay "Postmodernism and Chicano Literature." Our study explores the literary texts published in the aforementioned decades and focuses on such emergent themes and trends as the explosion of Chicana publications, the new detective novel, and the continued popularity of Mexican immigrant themes.

The Chicano movement's new crop of writers is composed of men and women with a wide range of interests, some of which are different from the initial movement's ideologically driven goals of the previous decades. The exigencies of cultural nationalism are currently less overt, and writers can now begin to focus on the individual, or on *la petite histoire*, as well as on the group. Some of our contemporary writers stress understanding the various dimensions of identity in addition to establishing and validating them. These "little stories" or microcosms of life are important because they can be viewed as emblematic of everyday existence and can help us decipher how everyday experiences are internalized by the psyche. When the messianic zeal of the Chicano movement, undeniably evident in the sixties and seventies, subsided or at least became less visible in the eighties, new discursive strategies emerged. Chicano writers in the last two decades have opted to create new themes and blur boundaries instead of targeting the unbridled political passions of the previous decades. The objective seems to be a greater introspection—more vertical than horizontal—into a wide array of manifestations that document Chicano social spheres. The muralistic realism of the sixties and seventies, comprised of broad characterizations, has given way to an examination of slices of life that deal with conflicts generated by complex societal factors. For instance, the early literary strategies of Tomás Rivera, Rolando Hinojosa, and Miguel Méndez consisted of structuring epic stories characterized by sweeping cultural significance. These strategies were a type of realistic social perspective bent on reclaiming a sense of historicity. This inclination, to a certain extent, has given way in some authors' works to a more individualized examination of their personal lives. For example, note the popularity of the autobiographical mode in many of the contemporary Chicano texts. Postmodernism has derailed the search for absolute truth. Contemporary writers, although greatly conditioned by their Chicano background, are now seeking answers in the personal experience. Whereas for some writers from the 1960s ethnicity figured as an end unto itself in literary production, contemporary writers examine this same ethnicity with regard to its evolving qualities. No longer conceptualized as static and essentialist in nature, ethnicity is appreciated for its inherent diversity and in particular for its hybridity. Ethnicities that are fluid, constantly changing, and eclectic allow for a more dynamic configuration. Ethnicity has consequently shed its exotic cloak—as perceived from the outside—and has become a human trait conditioned by historical and geographic factors. Chicanos no longer perceive of themselves as purely victims of a one-way socialization process but rather as human beings who are socially constructed via a confluence of interfacing societal processes. In the process, Chicanos have come to properly value their cultural heritage while continuing to insist on their rights as citizens in American society.

The decade of the 1980s, denominated the "Decade of the Hispanic" by the federal government, began with much fanfare and promise. The sudden proliferation of the term "Hispanic" exploded into the national conscience, and a resurgence of political and economic power was eagerly anticipated. The term gained currency and undermined the usage of more ethnically accurate labels, such as "Chicano" and, in some cases, even "Mexican American." The term "Hispanic" attempted to provide a more generalized sense of an interethnic identity and was meant to satisfy political circles in Washington D.C. Consequently, the ethnic designation of "Hispanic" was adopted by government institutions throughout the nation. Many Chicanos optimistically hoped that the enthusiasm generated by the publicity associated with the Decade of the Hispanic in the media would translate into bona fide social and economic progress. Some even counted on finally achieving the American Dream and assumed that cultural and racial conflicts would be resolved. Needless to say, this dream has not been fully realized. By the end of the 1980s, Chicanos and other Hispanics felt that they had been seduced by a publicity stunt that had only co-optation and assimilation as its objective. The subtext underlying the Decade of the Hispanic was the imperative to blend in and not to manifest too overtly any ethnic qualities. The publicity campaign was designed to instill hope of a better future and to avoid any destabilization of the status quo or questioning of hegemonic society.

The 1980s had started on an upbeat note but soon became marred by an event that Anglo mainstream society considered threatening: massive immigration to the United States due to civil war in Central America. The targeting of immigrants appeared as a new form of institutionalized racism. Furthermore, the illusory economic programs of the Reagan administration mortgaged the future with long-term loans while ignoring the deficit. The Reagan "trickle down" economic policies favored the upper classes, and the "glass ceiling" at the workplace became entrenched and functioned as an insurmountable barrier against the advancement of upwardly mobile Latinos. What at first seemed a potential breakthrough for Chicanos and other Hispanics soon turned into politics as usual. These events resulted in economic hardship for the working class and impeded social and economic progress for people of color.

The beginning of the 1980s marked a low point in Chicano literary production, a shift in focus and spirit from the many accomplishments achieved in the 1970s when literary experimentation had reached a high point. As evinced in Necochea et al. (1982), Chicano authors in the early eighties seemed uncertain about which direction to turn with their creativity. This low point was characterized by a sense of self-doubt in the Chicano community and by fears that a revolutionary window of opportunity was fast disappearing. The collective engagé spirit of the 1970s, oftentimes inspired by Mexican myths and legends, suddenly found itself facing a practical "me-first" generation of the 1980s. The gut-wrenching searches for a collective identity by such figures as Oscar Zeta Acosta, Alurista, and Ricardo Sánchez seemed far removed from the new era of self-absorption. There was a general feeling that since the literary stature of Tomás Rivera, Miguel Méndez, Rudolfo Anaya, Luis Valdez, Rolando Hinojosa, Estela Portillo

Trambley, Bernice Zamora, José Montoya, Gary Soto, and others had been secured, what else could the literary movement possibly offer? A search for identity and the construction of myths took on new parameters of inquiry, judging from the works of Richard Rodríguez and Ana Castillo.

The year 1980 marked a turning point in which the literature lost some of its protest edge in favor of a more personalized view. The examination of the intrahistorical took root at this time and had many followers. A perspective from inside out prevailed, and a number of works were produced, especially by Gary Soto, that concentrated on small events from which to extract greater meaning and significance. Suddenly, innuendo, language variants, and even self-history became important in narrating stories, organizing fiction, and constructing poetry. As Francisco A. Lomelí observed, "Whereas technique had been the central point of consideration [in the 1970s], the shift became more one of utilizing technique to unveil a cross-sectional disclosure of multifaceted experiences covering gender, class, [and] psychological and social determinants" (Lomelí 1993, 102).

By the mid-1980s, an exciting new group of writers emerged on the Chicano literary scene, changing it forever. This group viewed culture as more a fluid experience than a prescribed form of defining worldview. Prominent in this new group were a sizable number of Chicana writers. The year 1985 marks the date of the rise of what we term the "Contemporary Chicana Generation." This group has exerted a great deal of influence since then and promises to continue to do so into the twenty-first century. A new poetics also emerged in 1985 as the result of a desire to experiment with genres that focused on gender egalitarianism and the meaning of culture from a variety of perspectives. The possibility of joining a redefined mainstream appealed to many authors in their quest to discover and gain new readers. Part of this shift in literary taste can be traced to the previous decade, when Chicano writing displayed excesses that became somewhat formulaic and contrived. Writing Chicano works only for Chicanos became a burden to some because the motivation to break boundaries and expand the Chicano presence seemed a loftier goal. This shift in the genre resulted in a new-found interest in Chicano literature, and in particular in Chicana/Latina writings, by established commercial outlets, who now played a central role in dissemination. The feelings of relative isolation and disenfranchisement of the 1970s were not completely erased but were incorporated under the postmodernist rubric of decentralization.

| By the mid 1980s, Chicano literature found a wider audience, in large

part due to its connection to a European readership (surprisingly enough, less so to a Mexican one). International attention was first captured by Marcienne Rocard's book, *Les fils du soleil: la minorité mexicaine à travers la littérature des États-Unis* (Sons of the Sun: The Mexican Minority through the Literature of the United States), and Tino Villanueva's *Chicanos: antología histórica y literaria* (Chicanos: A Historical and Literary Anthology), which both appeared in the 1980s. Furthermore, the first and second International Conference on Chicano Culture and Literature in Germersheim, Germany (in 1984), and Paris, France (in 1986), played a key role in promoting the general appeal of Chicano literature. Subsequently, other international conferences have taken place in numerous cities, such as Barcelona, Madrid, and Granada (Spain), Taxco (Mexico), Groningen (Holland), and Bordeaux and Marseilles (France). Mainstream U.S. society was no longer the target audience, but ironically, it too began to take notice of these fast-moving literary developments. In addition to the conference proceedings from the first two meetings of the International Conference on Chicano Culture and Literature, the books *Missions in Conflict: Essays on U.S.-Mexican Relations and Chicano Culture* (1986), by Renate von Bardeleben et al., and *European Perspectives on Hispanic Literature of the United States* (1988), by Genevieve Fabré, were particularly instrumental in challenging Chicano provincialism, American canonicity, and U.S. indifference toward change. The result was an expanded readership that raised new theoretical questions and methodologies and a European perspective that was different from what Chicanos had faced within their geographical boundaries. Chicano literature began to take on a more international profile and to communicate with new and unfamiliar ethnic traditions. This dialogue became a means through which Chicanos could profitably explore differences between ethnic groups while projecting a facet of Americanism that was unknown abroad.

The global arena contributed much toward a better understanding between European and Chicano critics, who learned critical theories and approaches from both sides of the Atlantic. Writers themselves also began to look beyond their respective regions and beyond their Chicano and other American circles. Internationalization, on the one hand, produced greater mainstreaming, but on the other hand it made writers reflect on the basic principles that had previously guided their literary endeavors.

If the 1970s demanded that Chicanas/os re-create themselves for local consumption, the 1980s demanded that they reconfigure themselves and export images to foreign cultures who were less familiar with and knowledgeable about Chicanas/os. Some of the initial international works that shed new light on Chicano literature were Wolfgang Binder's *Partial Autobiographies: Interviews with Twenty Chicano Poets* (1985), Lia Tessarolo Bondolfi's *Dal mito al mito: la cultura di espressione chicana: dal mito originario al mito rigeneratore* (From Myth to Myth: The Culture of Chicano Expression: From Primordial to Regenerative Myth, 1987), Yves-Charles Grandjeat's *Aztlán, terre volée, terre promise: les pérégrinations du peuple chicano* (Aztlán: Stolen Land, Promised Land; The Pilgrimages of the Chicano People, 1989), María Eugenia Gaona's *Antología de la literatura chicana* (Anthology of Chicano Literature, 1986), Elyette Benjamin-Labarthe's *Vous avez dit chicano: anthologie thematique de poesie chicano* (Have You Said Chicano: Thematic Anthology of Chicano Poetry, 1993), Heiner Bus and Ana Castillo's *Recent Chicano Poetry/Neueste Chicano-Lyrik* (1994), and Rosamel Benavides's *Antología de cuentistas chicanas: Estados Unidos de los '60 a los '90* (Anthology of Chicana Short Story Writers: United States from the '60s to the '90s, 1993).

Despite the slow beginning in Chicana/o creative production in the 1980s, this decade later became synonymous with the literature's great successes both commercially and aesthetically speaking. The frontline of such cutting-edge literary production in the 1980s was led by a vanguard of well-trained and inspired Chicana writers who came together more by circumstance than design. Their success became so well documented that eventually the 1980s became known as the "Decade of the Chicana." A feminist ethos emerged and inscribed itself in a literary movement that aspired to represent Chicanas' lives in more accurate, complex, and authentic ways. Chicana writers helped produce a movement within a movement and became a definite tour de force because of their originality, verve, sensibility, and determination. The important constellation of Chicana literati who published landmark works in or near 1985 includes Helena María Viramontes (*The Moths and Other Stories*, 1985), Cecile Pineda (*Face*, 1985; *Frieze*, 1987), Sandra Cisneros (*The House on Mango Street*, 1984), Cherríe Moraga (*Giving Up the Ghost*, 1986), Denise Chávez (*The Last of the Menu Girls*, 1986), Pat Mora (*Borders*, 1986), Mary Helen Ponce (*Taking Control*, 1987), Laura del Fuego (*Maravilla*, 1989), Gloria Anzaldúa (*Borderlands/La frontera: The New Mestiza*, 1987), and Margarita Cota-Cárdenas (*Puppet*, 1985). Other writers such as Ana Castillo, who had published chapbooks such as *The Invitation* (1979), became a significant voice in Chicana/o writer circles;

she eventually gained prominence with her novel *The Mixquiahuala Letters*. Castillo and Sandra Cisneros are two of the most prominent and influential spokespersons within the Chicana/o literary movement today.

Each of the Chicana writers listed above published her first substantial publication in 1985 or shortly thereafter, and each made an indelible impression in the literary world. As a group, their focus on feminist and gender issues spawned a renaissance of literary production. This production focused on the reconceptualization, re-presentation, and recovery of women's voices. Their new aesthetics underscored a woman's worldview. Without a doubt, the convergence of such a high-powered group sparked a new synthesis with respect to how Chicano culture came to define itself. These writers added experiential depth, creative vigor, and international visibility to the literature.

The Decade of the Chicana did not happen by chance but was the result of challenges set originally in 1975, a year denominated as the "International Year of the Woman." Once the literature written by men leveled out in terms of its nationalistic zeal and its grandiose cultural agenda—including the ego-driven one-man "cult shows" of personas and personalities—Chicanas were determined to fill in the gaps with relevant stories and impressions on how they saw and experienced the world, oftentimes framed within a feminocentric folklore. In a real sense, they proposed to re-create or establish significant portions of a Chicana epic, that is, a story that had remained silent, untold, forgotten, ignored, minimized, and even repressed. Their interests included l) the examination of women as "theoretical subjects"; 2) the cultivation of a wide assortment of literary forms; 3) the incursion into the psyche or what we might term "experiential inwardness"; 4) the portrayal of social elements from a "herstorical" approach; 5) the presentation of texts from a genderized political and cultural perspective; 6) the objective to either challenge, defy, or break traditional boundaries or borders of any kind (including textual and sexual); and 7) the desire to reach others in order to exercise some kind of inspirational influence among subsequent generations.

The writers of the above-mentioned generation, who continued to dominate the literary scene in the 1990s, have become the most important postmodern trendsetters and innovators. Their many contributions to style and to the artful, even daring, blurring of different genres are well recognized. They mix art forms freely to break down barriers or simply blend divergent forms by contradicting, undermining, or interrogating otherwise "straightjacket" limitations. Their main concerns focus on issues such as maturation, the effects of cultural institutions and social conditioning, the role of family and upbringing, an awareness of sexuality, a sense of otherness, a challenging of conventional literary forms, the passing of generations, and the discovery of an interlingual and intercultural social grouping (Lomelí, p. 104). With respect to identity, Eliana Ortega and Nancy Saporta Sternback point out that "The question of identity arises as a result of the negation, marginalization, and silencing of Latinas' history by official discourse, that is, the dominant culture's version of history." This talented group indeed set the stage for a new vanguard poetics that will set the tone for decades to come.

Although no single writer served as guru, epicenter, or trailblazer for the Contemporary Chicana Generation, what distinguished this generation from the previous ones was that each genre was well represented, without any one necessarily dominating. The authors usually produced transgeneric works with unique and unconventional compositions. Examples include Ana Castillo *(The Mixquiahuala Letters)*, Sandra Cisneros *(The House on Mango Street)*, and Norma Cantú *(Canícula: Snapshots of a Girlhood en la Frontera)* in the novel; Helena María Viramontes *(The Moths and Other Stories)* in the short story; Cherríe Moraga *(Giving Up the Ghost)* and Denise Chávez ("Novenas narrativas: ofrendas nuevomexicanas") in theater; Pat Mora *(Borders)* and Naomi Quiñónez *(Sueño de colibrí/Hummingbird Dream)* in poetry; and Gloria Anzaldúa *(Borderlands/La frontera: The New Mestiza)* in the creative essay. If gender was their main concern as a social issue, then the discussion of sexuality as intrinsically relevant to identity also was center stage, along with the theoretical question of what metamorphosed genre should be used to accommodate such expression. In fact, in some cases the focus on gender and sexuality highlighted an area that had been previously rebuffed, censured, or repressed. From this vantage point Chicana authors managed to propagate a discourse and a subjectivity that opened up new avenues of expressing and representing women within society in general and with respect to other women, especially other Latinas, in particular. The potential for recovering untold histories of women's lives became infinite. At the same time, this generation redirected their attention toward overcoming restrictive notions of Chicana/o culture through a feminocentric perspective, especially one shaped by a Chicana viewpoint.

In conjunction with this charismatic group of women writers who changed the direction of Chicana/o literature forever, two important events occurred. First, with its headquarters at the University of Houston, the Recovering the U.S. Hispanic Literary Heritage Project launched an aggressive campaign to reconstruct the literary history of Hispanics while recovering forgotten texts written prior to 1965. Second, a series of authors who made their mark in the 1970s recaptured some of their luster at the end of the 1980s. In the first category, significant recoveries included *The Squatter and the Don* (1992), originally written by Amparo Ruiz de Burton, but reintroduced by Rosaura Sánchez and Beatriz Pita. In the second category, Gary Soto, Jimmy Santiago Baca, Nash Candelaria, Alejandro Morales, Rolando Hinojosa, Miguel Méndez, Tino Villanueva, Rudolfo Anaya, Alurista, John Rechy, Lorna Dee Cervanates, and Juan Felipe Herrera made a comeback with important contributions. Even José Antonio Villarreal, Sabine R. Ulibarrí, and Américo Paredes, whose antecedent works date back to the 1950s and, in Paredes's case, to the 1930s, reappeared with significant new works.

Rolando Hinojosa and Gary Soto remain the most prolific authors and are further solidifying their position as masterful storytellers. Hinojosa, on the one hand, continues to explore a mythic region, Belken County, through a metatext he calls the "Klail City Death Trip Series." His narratives provide an in-depth portrayal—a horizontal and vertical view of history, geography, and culture—of what can easily be surmised to be the southern Texas and northern Mexico regions. *Partners in Crime: A Rafe Buenrostro Mystery* (1985) and *Korean Love Songs from Klail City Death Trip* (1980), for example, continue to explore border issues. His most recent novel, *Ask A Policeman: A Rafe Buenrostro Mystery* (1998) continues the Buenrostro story with greater character profiles in a mythic region that continues to expand. Soto, on the other hand, offers a series of poignant stories about youths in the process of maturation in a series of novels particularly aimed at a young audience (*Summer on Wheels*, 1995; *Buried Onions*, 1997). His prose and poetry takes place in the San Joaquín Valley in California. In this central California setting, the anecdote is magnified to show the human drama of constantly adapting and adjusting to small-town circumstances. Among his best works during this period are *Living up the Street: Narrative Recollections* (1985), *Black Hair* (1985), and *A Summer Life* (1990).

Another talented poet is Jimmy Santiago Baca, whose novel *Martín & Meditations on the South Valley* (1987) narrates a person's physical and spiritual journey through a specific region. The final representative of this group that resurfaced in the late 1980s is Juan Felipe Herrera, who published *Akrílica* in 1989. This work is a collection of highly experimental poetic accounts that mix theater with memoirs, and journalism with plastic arts, thus creating a bilingual potpourri of rhythms and neologisms.

Several important new voices appeared during the 1980s. Arturo Islas, with his *The Rain God: A Desert Tale* (1984) and *Migrant Souls* (1990), introduced new themes and family genealogies. It was the Chicanas, however, who began to achieve greater national recognition. Ana Castillo, with her novels *The Mixquiahuala Letters* (1986) and *Sapogonia: An Anti-Romance in 3/8 Meter* (1990), came the closest to becoming a literary leader in this decade. Sandra Cisneros became the guidepost by which we could measure the commercial reception of Chicana literature in mainstream circles. Together, Castillo and Cisneros have generated the most interest and provided the most visibility for Chicana literature during the 1980s and 1990s.

Cisneros's *The House on Mango Street* garnered a great deal of fanfare for its highly poetic prose about a young protagonist who feels at odds with her immediate environment, including her family. Her character, Esperanza, goes through a series of adventures and close calls as she crisscrosses the streets of her Chicano neighborhood in a large city. Esperanza relates her stories from the vantage point of an innocent child, and in the process, a distinct community emerges with many of the typical social problems plaguing it: poverty, racism, and the community's negotiations with assimilation. In addition, other issues surface such as the quest for identity, the role of the writer vis-à-vis her responsibility to her Chicano community, and women's oppression in both the barrio and society in general. Cisneros's second major work is *Woman Hollering Creek and Other Stories* (1991), an excellent collection of short stories that poignantly capture the lives of women and their predicaments and social trappings in Texan and Mexican surroundings. The poetic prose offers much depth and insight into the experiences of prepubescent girls and young women. The gripping stories burst out with humor and pathos; this strategy allows the reader to explore the character's psyche with great interest and profound respect.

Ana Castillo, in her novel *The Mixquiahuala Letters* (winner of an American Book Awards prize in 1987), displays a flair for experimentation with form and narrative strategies while creating convincing female characters who depend on each other for psychological and moral support. This highly original work, in the form of a multigenre diary, introduces perhaps the most profound character representations of two women who are different yet complement each other. Her later work, *Sapogonia: An Anti-Romance in 3/8 Meter*, creates a metaphorical construction of a country through which gender relations can be explored. In a later novel, *So Far From God* (1994), she injects elements of magical realism through a family of women who learn to deal with outsiders who are diametrically opposite to them. She continues expanding her brilliant storytelling abilities in her most recent works: *Loverboys: Stories* (1996) and *Peel My Love Like an Onion* (1999). Castillo also expands Chicana themes in other works, such as her poetry collection *My Father Was a Toltec and Selected Poems* (1995). In this slim volume of poems she explores different family situations where patriarchy continues to rule as an institution. Some of the poems included in *My Father Was a Toltec* underscore the Chicana/o heterogeneous racial makeup (such as in "We Would Like You to Know"), whereas others suggest alternative social orders ("In My Country"). Castillo also offers some groundbreaking, provocative, and insightful essays in *Massacre of the Dreamers: Essays on Xicanisma* (1995), in which she effectively deconstructs various forms of colonialism ranging from spirituality to sexuality. She has also edited the anthology *Goddess of the Americas: Writings on the Virgin of Guadalupe* (1996), a collection of provocative essays exploring the meaning of the Virgin of Guadalupe for contemporary Chicanas/os and Latinas/os. The deciding factor that makes Cisneros and Castillo such outstanding authors is their talent for poetically creating strong, difficult-to-forget female characters. Together, they and other Chicana/Latina writers have forged what is considered to be a second Latina/o literary boom. This renaissance is now part of a multicultural forum in which Puerto Ricans, Cuban Americans, Chicanos, and other Latinos are creating a significant corpus of literary writings.

Literature Produced in the 1990s

The 1990s have ushered in a new wave of Latina/o writers whose writings are characterized by a greater interethnic cross-fertilization, a Latin Americanization or "tropicalization" in themes, a definite diversity in terms of experiential perspectives, a new poetic prose alongside proselike poetry, and especially an experimentation with forms (such as memoirs, [auto]biography, journals, *testimonios*, and ethnographies), thereby producing a vital unpredictability and a hybrid freshness never before witnessed. In some cases, such as Norma Cantú's *Canícula: Snapshots of a Girlhood en la Frontera* (1995), Sheila Ortiz Taylor's *Coachella* (1998) and *Imaginary Parents: A Family Autobiography* (1996), Alicia Gaspar de Alba's *Sor Juana's Second Dream*

(1999), and Pat Mora's *Agua santa/Holy Water* (1995), *House of Houses* (1997), and *Aunt Carmen's Book of Practical Saints* (1997), conventional literary forms are challenged, molded, fused, or defied for the sake of creating a literature that makes the insignificant significant. The everyday thus becomes central and manifests itself with a sophisticated apparatus, telling a story that seems deceptively simple. The literature in its most contemporary expression displays a distinct maturity and confidence and delves into new realms of experience. It is a literature reinventing itself beyond the margins.

Chicana/o literature has matured beyond being a one-dimensional social discourse or an essentialist formula of identity-building. Heteroglossia and heterogeneity are common elements that operate as subtexts, regardless of what the constraints of genre might imply. Spurred on partly by postmodern aesthetics (sometimes anti-aesthetics), many Chicano works demonstrate polyphonic qualities whereby the protagonist tends to be uncertain, sometimes splintered, or at least shared by various voices. This decentralization causes the reader to reconsider narrative strategies not as monolithic constructions but rather as attempts to unveil the complexities of a reality in its fullest frame. Chicana/o writers in the 1990s, perhaps more than ever before, create texts that defy easy classification as literary products. If in the 1970s this blurring of genres or mixture of forms and styles appeared as processes that challenged hegemonic literary production, then the most recent works are more than a sign; rather, they embrace various styles and constructions and suggest that the message exists somewhere between *how* something is told and *what* is told. That explains the authors' flair in constructing the intergeneric overlapping so commonly seen during the decade. Furthermore, the experiential narration or poetic utterance requires free movement from one genre to another, thus avoiding becoming a slave to any one form. The result is significant because authors now blend form and subject more than ever before by avoiding restrictive notions of literature. Chicanas/os, consequently, appear more and more as writers who crisscross, even conflate, the gamut of human environments as they explore otherness, often paradoxical, shifting identities and varying notions of diversity. A good example is Graciela Limón's *The Memories of Ana Calderón* (1994), which combines testimonio with the more typical immigration novel by presenting the trajectory of a woman's hardships and obstacles vis-à-vis patriarchy and cultural values that perpetuate it.

Numerous examples confirm that, literarily speaking, Chicanas/os are prepared for the twenty-first century. Some of the transitional writings

by Ana Castillo, Sandra Cisneros, Gloria Anzaldúa, and Helena María Viramontes serve as points of continuity as they continue to produce important works. New writers, nevertheless, have emerged. A significant number
of authors abound in this new postmodern era; among them are Luis J.
Rodríguez, *Always Running: La Vida Loca; Gang Days in L.A.* (1994); Rubén
Martínez, *The Other Side: Notes From the New L.A., Mexico City, and Beyond*
(1992); Norma Cantú, *Canícula: Snapshots of a Girlhood en la Frontera*
(1995); Benjamín Alire Sáenz, *Dark and Perfect Angels* (1995), *Carry Me Like
Water* (1995), and *The House of Forgetting* (1997); Dagoberto Gilb, *The Magic
of Blood* (1993) and *The Last Known Residence of Mickey Acuña* (1994);
Graciela Limón, *In Search of Bernabé* (1993), *The Memories of Ana Calderón*
(1994), and *Song of the Hummingbird* (1996); Maricela Norte in her numerous poetry readings (unpublished); Sylvia López-Medina, *Cantora* (1993)
and *Siguiriya* (1997); Louie García-Robinson, *The Devil, Delfina Varela, and
the Used Chevy* (1993); Luis Urrea, *Across the Wire: Life and Hard Times on
the Mexican Border* (1993); Yxta Maya Murray, *Locas* (1997); Demetria Martínez, *Mother Tongue* (1994); Alfredo Véa, Jr., *La maravilla* (1993) and *The
Silver Cloud Café* (1996); Manuel Ramos, *The Ballad of Rocky Ruiz* (1993) and
The Ballad of Gato Guerrero (1994); Montserrat Fontes, *First Confession*
(1991) and *Dreams of the Centaur* (1996); Erlinda Gonzales-Berry, *Paletitas de
guayaba* (1991); Michele Serros, *Chicana Falsa and Other Stories of Death,
Identity, and Oxnard* (1993); and Juan Estevan Arellano, *Inocencia ni pica ni
escarda pero siempre se come el mejor elote* (1992). Some authors, such as
Miguel Encinias, in *Two Lives for Oñate* (1997), continue the line of historical
chronicles originally developed by Nash Candelaria in the 1980s. Francisco
Jiménez, on the other hand, revisits the migrant experience in *The Circuit:
Stories from the Life of a Migrant Child* (1997), a topic originally popularized
by Tomás Rivera.

The most recent group of writers exemplifies tremendous versatility
and talent in that they do not subscribe to one literary agenda or trend.
Their themes explore new areas of socialization and human predicaments.
Multivalence and the exploration of new realms seem to be at the core of
their inventiveness, their playfulness. "Hard-core" topics, for example, have
now been expanded and are dominated by women characters, as for example in *Locas* (1997) by Yxta Maya Murray. This novel poignantly shows
another side of an experience in the urban barrios. Chicanas/os are more
and more perceived as complex beings with multiple identities. Among the
many literary manifestations in the 1990s, two major trends in Chicana/o

literary production have emerged, the detective novel and the Mexican immigrant novel.

The Detective Novel

Until recently, the detective/mystery novel had been virtually nonexistent
in Chicana/o literature. However, within the past several years a modest
yet vigorous boom has set off what may well be the beginning of the Raza/
Aztlán detective tradition or the formation of the Chicana/o detective persona. In the process, Raza writers have shaped and reshaped the detec-
tive/mystery genre for specific cultural, political, and social purposes to
comment on issues of class, gender, race, and sexual orientation or preference. These writers are producing new literary models that may be viewed
as forms of social criticism and cultural representation. Moreover, these
writers are modifying the genre by transforming the detective protagonist
from white and middle- or upper-class, as in the classical tradition introduced by Edgar Allen Poe and honed by Sir Arthur Conan Doyle, to Raza
working-class personas.

Detective/mystery writers Rudolfo Anaya, Lucha Corpi, Rolando Hinojosa, Michael Nava, and Manuel Ramos are notably changing the detective fiction formula as they create first-person narratives to investigate the
issues mentioned above in relation to cultural and criminal environments.
This significant change has been noted, for example, by Juan Bruce-Novoa,
who proposes in "Who's Killing Whom in Belken County: Rolando Hinojosa's Narrative Production" (1987) that Hinojosa's work can be read as an
extended detective novel, characterized by murders and crimes in the lives of
southern Texans. He further offers that Hinojosa's "Klail City Death Trip"
series, including *Partners in Crime,* manifests characteristics of the detective
novel: the disappearance of people, lost ancestry, facts and incidents, and a
search for justice.

Some Chicano writers such as Rudy Apodaca and Max Martínez, however, do not create Chicano detectives but rather have white male personas
as protagonists. Apodaca's *The Waxen Image* (1977) is described in its jacket
blurb as the first mystery-suspense novel by a Chicano writer. The protagonist is an advertising executive named Ross Blair, who lives in San Francisco
and travels to New Mexico after he receives a mysterious telephone call from
his former wife to tell him that their daughter is missing. Antonio Márquez

refers to *The Waxen Image* as a potboiler filled with "cardboard characterizations that match the tourists' view of New Mexico" (Marquez 1989, 255–65).

In Max Martínez's *White Leg* (1996), a novel compared to the hard-core novels by Jim Thompson and James M. Cain, the central character, Gil Blue, a small-time criminal, is pursued relentlessly and tenaciously by the FBI, the Texas Rangers, and the local police, who want him dead. Even his boss, who practically owns the small town of White Leg, Texas, wants him dead. In both novels, the authors develop a number of secondary Chicano characters: *curanderas* (folk healers), farmworkers, and service workers, for example.

The increasing body of detective/mystery novels, including those of Apodaca and Martínez, forms a microcosm of the Chicano world into which the readers are drawn and shown an aspect of life and thought. These novels not only reflect the oral tradition and the custom of storytelling found in Chicano/Mexicano folklore but also share an emphasis on signs, symbols, behaviors, and manners. These characteristics distinguish the Raza detective/mystery novel from other novels in the genre. Moreover, these qualities are usually communicated by the narrators, often the protagonists, who express their attitudes, sensibilities, sense of community, and personal values. Frequently, the protagonists behave in ways that demonstrate a strong sense of identity with and close connections to their communities; these attachments help bring about successful conclusions to their investigations and also help create order out of chaos in their surroundings. For instance, Manuel Ramos's protagonist, Luis Móntez, and Lucha Corpi's Gloria Damasco persist in restoring their sense of justice and honor in their communities when these ideals are violated, regardless of time spent or dangers encountered. The two characters, Móntez and Damasco, painstakingly solve murders that occurred twenty years before, during the Chicano Movement, to bring order to their communities.

Another distinguishing attribute of the Raza detective/mystery novel is that the protagonist can be as brash as the hard-boiled detective, but unlike the hard-boiled gumshoe, the Chicano protagonist takes time to nurture personal and family relationships or to be involved in romantic relations. For example, in Michael Nava's mystery series, his protagonist, Henry Ríos, is involved in a long-term relationship with his lover, who is dying of AIDS. Anaya's Sonny Baca, in *Rio Grande Fall* (1996), has a year-long relationship that might eventually lead to marriage. In addition, Baca has a strong friendship with Don Eliseo and his *compañeros,* Doña Chona and Don Toto, the elderly keepers of the Rio Grande Valley traditions that go back to the seventeenth century. Sonny, at ease with the old people, respects Don Eliseo and his knowledge. In Ramos's series, Luis Móntez is also respectful toward his elderly father and his old ways, even though at times his father is cantankerous and difficult. And he respects his lover's grandfather, an old man who tells long, rambling stories about his family and Pancho Villa. Anaya's and Ramos's tough detectives show respect and care for the elders in their communities. Even more unlike the classic hard-boiled personas, Raza detectives are "complex, multitalented, and possessed of a social consciousness," and they are interested in the social and political milieu because of connections to their communities. Nava's character, Henry Ríos, gives the reader an insight into his private life and his compassion for those who suffer because of their sexual orientations. In *Golden Boy* (1988) Ríos, shocked by the physical appearance of his friend dying of AIDS, agrees to defend a young gay man who is charged with murder. Ríos does so out of friendship and compassion for his dying friend. Because Ríos is openly homosexual and has written a document on gay rights, he is often called on for help. Similarly, Corpi's Gloria Damasco and Ramos's Luis Móntez become involved in the Chicano Movement because they seek to bring about changes in the social and political conditions of La Raza.

Although the texts tend to focus more on plot than on character development, Raza detectives are more than "cardboard" characters. Anaya's and Ramos's detectives have personal lives, family histories, strong connections to their communities, interesting careers, and a well-developed social and political consciousness. Readers are privy to the private thoughts and actions that make the protagonists appear as fully developed persons, whereas the rest of the characters are much less developed.

Cityscapes are another characteristic of Chicano novels. Except for *White Leg, The Waxen Image,* and *Partners in Crime,* the novels take place in cities such as Albuquerque, Denver, San Francisco, and Los Angeles. The protagonists are quite familiar with and comfortable in their urban surroundings; cityscapes are well integrated into the plots and form atmospheres that help shape the protagonists. Often the descriptions of cities and portraits of the characters from the barrios and the streets draw as much attention as the criminal activities. For example, in *The Death of Friends* (1996), Michael Nava describes his neighborhood and other parts of Los Angeles during and after an especially devastating earthquake.

A characteristic that Raza detective novels share with other novels in the genre is the presentation of city police and detectives as incompetent officials who have difficulty in solving crimes and the "superior" knowledge of the nonprofessional detective. The Raza detectives, in the Sherlock Holmes tradition, pay close attention to details. Details of ordinary everyday life are what give significance or importance to motives, landscapes, and characters and help develop social and political meanings. For example, in *The Ballad of Gato Guerrero* (1994), Ramos describes his protagonist's encounter with a homeless and mentally unstable young man who shouts racial slurs at him. Ramos, in detailing this incident, comments on the social conditions of the homeless and on race relations. In *Cactus Blood* (1995), Corpi describes and discusses the serious medical condition of the murder suspect, caused by pesticide contamination as a teenager. Corpi's exact details of the cause and effect of the contamination dramatize the victimization of the farmworkers and offer a social critique of these conditions.

Another characteristic of the Raza mystery is the difference in world view. Unlike the hard-boiled or classic detectives, who represent solitary existential perspectives, Raza detectives represent a community view. As stated before, the Raza persona is community-oriented, with a personal history that includes religious values. In *Rio Grande Fall*, Anaya's detective is given spirituality and religious values; in addition, Anaya provides Sonny Baca with a spirit animal, a coyote, who guides and protects him. In *Cactus Blood*, not only can Corpi's curandera read Gloria Damasco's spirit, but she can also assist the body and spirit to be in balance. Ramos's protagonist possesses a worldview suggesting some hope of improvement for the poor people who live in the barrios, although he is critical of corrupted white power structures. And as stated, Corpi's protagonist Gloria Damasco's worldview is critical of an agricultural industry that uses dangerous pesticides and herbicides with blatant disregard for the farmworkers and their health.

Another attribute of Chicano detective fiction is that writers do not stress physical violence as a major characteristic and keep its action and description to a minimum. In texts where writers follow the hard-boiled tradition, the protagonists are inductive, they follow their instincts and react instinctively. Yet another distinctive characteristic of the Chicano detective novel is that the detective is always conscious of racism and social injustice, and many texts examine the issues of class, race, gender, and sexual preference. An illuminating book written by Stephen F. Soitos, *The Blues Detective* (1996), cites W. E. B. Du Bois as suggesting that racism forces African Americans to view themselves as second-class citizens first and then as Americans, thereby creating a double consciousness. The Raza detective also manifests this double consciousness and uses this awareness to better grasp the criminal mentality.

This double consciousness is expressed through repeated references to music, dance, food, and religion, which make Raza detective fiction culture-specific. Furthermore, the use of these referents helps define the uniqueness of Chicano culture. For example, *curandería* (folk medicine), still very much a part of the culture, expresses a worldview anchored in spiritual awareness and a connection to the natural environment. One of Anaya's characters in *Rio Grande Fall* is a young curandera who uses her powers of divination to help Sonny Baca fight the evil forces of the Raven, Baca's nemesis. Anaya's use of curandería is an attempt to recognize its significance in Raza cultural identity and survival. As references to these iconographies reoccur from novel to novel, the concept of a Raza detective fiction is reinforced.

The new Raza detective fiction is transforming the traditional detective formula for social, political, and cultural objectives. Chicano writers use their work to comment on issues of race, class, gender, and sexual orientation. This new detective fiction is further defined by cultural manifestations, often expressed by working-class detectives. Cultural identity, one of the major themes that marks the texts, frequently is associated with double consciousness, a distinctive worldview, and community values; these characteristics strongly emphasize positive aspects of Chicana/o identity. As Chicana/o detective fiction writers continue to explore and transform the traditional detective formula, the Raza detective promises to become a vigorous agent for social and cultural change.

The Mexican Immigrant Novel

Historical memory reminds us that Mexican immigration to the United States is not new and that it has served as subject matter for artistic expression for a century and a half. The Mexican immigrant has been traveling to the United States since 1848, when Mexico's northern provinces were lost in the Mexican-American War of 1846–1848. Mexican immigration as thematic material surfaced in *corridos* (Mexican ballads), film, theater, and other artistic cultural expressions. In the 1990s a significant number of novels have appeared in which the principal theme is Mexican immigration. In this section, we examine the prolific production of Chicana/o novels evidencing this theme in the nineties.

As stated earlier, the immigrant as protagonist in Mexican American literary works dates back to the middle of the nineteenth century. Ballads or corridos such as "El corrido de Kiansas," "Los enganchados," "Corrido de Pensilvania," and many others have been sung throughout the history of Chicanos in the United States. Many folk songs present the immigrant odyssey from the perspective of the immigrants themselves. The corrido has the longest tradition of immigrant representation but, as David Maciel and María Rosa García-Acevedo have pointed out in their studies on the representation of the Mexican immigrant in films, the movie industry also has had a long history of immigrant representation (Maciel and García-Acevedo, 1998: 149–202). Recently such films as *Contrabando humano* (Human Contraband), *Memorias de un mojado* (The Memoirs of a Wetback), *Mojado Power* (Wetback Power), *Jaula de oro* (Golden Cage), *Ni de aquí ni de allá* (Neither from Here Nor from There), *Frontera* (Borderlands), *Maldita miseria* (Damned Poverty), *El vagón de la muerte* (The Boxcar of Death), and *El jardín del Edén* (The Garden of Eden) are all recent examples of the popularity of the immigrant theme in Mexican films.

In a similar vein, the Chicana/o narrative has included the immigrant theme within its plot. A paradigmatic novel about Mexican immigration first appeared in 1926 bearing the title *Las aventuras de Don Chipote o cuando los pericos mamen* (The Adventures of Don Chipote or When Parrots Suckle their Young). The novel was written in Spanish by a Mexican national. In 1959 the first contemporary Chicano novel appeared: *Pocho,* by José Antonio Villarreal. The novel's plot begins with what has become the starting point for many Chicano novels: the history of the immigrant experience of the first generation, the settlement history of the second generation, and sometimes the assimilation process of the third generation. Other novels that follow this structure are *Barrio Boy, Chicano, Macho!, Trini, Peregrinos de Aztlán, Rain of Gold,* and many others.

In the nineties the Chicana/o narrative continues to reproduce the paradigmatic immigrant history. The basic structure of current immigration-oriented novels consists of recounting the journey from Mexico undertaken by the immigrant, his/her integration into North American society, and the assimilation of generations descended from the original immigrant. Within this group of novels we can include *The Dark Side of the Dream,* by Alejandro Grattan-Domínguez, a Chicano-Irish writer. As the title indicates, this novel has a negative view of the immigrant experience in which the American dream is more of a nightmare for Mexican nationals. Ofelia Dumas

Lachtman's novel *The Girl from Playa Blanca* (1995) is directed toward a young audience. The narrative traces the experiences of a young girl who travels from Mexico to the United States in search of her father. Demetria Martínez offers us an interesting variation in her novel *Mother Tongue,* in which the immigrant coming to the United States is from El Salvador rather than Mexico. Martínez's novel depicts the love relationship between a war-scarred Salvadoreño and a Chicana. Graciela Limón's work deviates from the typical immigrant novel in that her main protagonist in her Mexican immigrant saga, *The Memories of Ana Calderón* (1994), is a woman. Likewise, Pat Mora, in her novel *House of Houses* (1997), features a woman protagonist who traces the family tree back to Mexico and Spain and tells of subsequent immigration to the U.S. Southwest.

In a second group of novels with Mexican immigrant themes, the immigrant is a secondary character who nevertheless plays an important role within the narrative plot. Of particular interest are those novels produced by Chicana writers such as Helena María Viramontes, who wrote the novel *Under the Feet of Jesus* (1995). The novel features Perfecto Flores as a Mexican immigrant who joins Estrella's family, who are migrant workers in the fields of California. Estrella is a young adolescent girl and is the main protagonist in the novel.

Norma Cantú introduced the immigrant theme through various characters, not just a single immigrant. The Texas-Mexico border towns of Laredo and Nuevo Laredo and the crossing of the characters to and from Mexico are integral to the plots of her vignettes.

A most innovative novel by Tina Juárez, *Call No Man Master,* is structured as an historical novel, with the action taking place in the nineteenth century during Mexico's War of Independence (1810–1812) and up to the 1830s. The novel is set in Guanajuato, Mexico, and features a brave woman-soldier protagonist, Carmen Rangel, who has joined the rebel soldiers of the priest Miguel Hidalgo y Costilla. When she is captured by the Spanish army, she escapes to San Antonio, Texas, where she takes up residence. The novel ends before the Texas-Mexico war in 1836 and before the battle at the Alamo takes place.

In the last four decades we have witnessed in the United States a particular sense of crisis in relation to Mexican immigration. We agree with historian David Maciel and political scientist María Rosa García-Acevedo, who wrote in a recent article, "The Celluloid Immigrant: The Narrative Films of Mexican Immigration" (1998, p. 149), that

Mexican undocumented emigration to the United States is the single most complex and difficult issue currently facing these two countries. The controversy concerning Mexican undocumented workers in the United States includes economic, political, legal, social, cultural, and even moral considerations. Mexican migration has, in fact, become one of the salient political issues of the 1990s. The question has intensified in the political discourse of both countries and has received considerable attention from the academic community, policy makers, and the printed and mass media.

Paradoxically, even though one cannot deny the hostility against Mexican immigrants on the part of the Anglo population, there does exist a love/hate relationship or one of repulsion and attraction. It goes without saying that despite the official line promulgated by the United States against immigration, this country needs immigrants, and particularly the Mexican immigrant. Agribusiness as well as the service industry needs these workers. Therein lies the perennial call to renew the discredited Bracero Program of the 1942–64 era. As numerous studies have demonstrated, both the U.S. economy and the Mexican economy need Mexican immigrants to continue trekking along the historical migratory routes to El Norte. As long as Mexican workers continue to migrate legally or illegally to the United States, some Chicano literary production will continue to focus on this important phenomenon, and we will continue to read about the adventures, the sorrows, the heroism, the deaths, and triumphs of Mexican immigrants.

Bibliography

Alurista. *Zeros* (Tempe, Ariz.: Bilingual Review Press/Editorial Bilingüe, 1995).

——. *Et tú . . . raza?* (Tempe, Ariz.: Bilingual Review Press/Editorial Bilingüe, 1994).

——. *Spik in Glyph* (Houston: Arte Público Press, 1980).

——. *Nationchild Plumaroja* (San Diego, Calif.: Toltecas en Aztlán Productions, 1972).

——. *Floricanto en Aztlán* (Los Angeles: University of California, Chicano Studies Cultural Center, 1971).

Anaya, Rudolfo Alfonso. *Río Grande Fall* (New York: Time Warner, 1996).

——. *Zia Summer* (New York: Warner, 1995).

——. *Albuquerque* (Albuquerque: University of New Mexico Press, 1992).

——. *Tortuga* (Berkeley: Editorial Justa, 1979).

——. *Heart of Aztlán* (Berkeley: Editorial Justa, 1976).

——. *Bless Me, Ultima* (Berkeley: Quinto Sol Publications, 1972).

Anderson, Benedict. *Imagined Communities* (New York: Verso, 1991).

Anzaldúa, Gloria. *Borderlands/La frontera: The New Mestiza* (San Francisco: Spinsters/Aunt Lute, 1987).

Apodaca, Rudy. *The Waxen Image* (Mesilla, N. Mex.: Titan Publishing Co., 1977).

Arellano, Juan Estevan. *Inocencia ni pica ni escarda pero siempre se come el mejor elote* (México: Editorial Grijalbo, 1992).

Arias, Ron. *The Road to Tamazunchale* (Reno, Nev.: West Coast Poetry Review, 1975).

Baca, Jimmy Santiago. *Martín and Meditations on the South Valley* (New York: New Directions, 1987).

Bardeleben, Renate von, Dietrich Briesemeister, and Juan Bruce-Novoa. *Missions in Conflict: Essays on U.S.–Mexican Relations and Chicano Culture* (Tubingen, Germany: G. Narr, 1986).

Benavides, Fray Alonso. *Benavides' Memorial of 1630*, trans. Peter P. Forrestal, C.C.S.C. (Washington, D.C.: Academy of American Franciscan History, 1954).

Benavides, Rosamel. *Antología de cuentistas chicanas: Estados Unidos de los '60 a los '90* (Santiago, Chile: Editorial Cuarto Propio, 1993).

Benjamin-Labarthe, Elyette. *Vous avez dit chicano: anthologie thematique de poesie chicano* (Bordeaux, France: Editions de la Maison des Sciences de l'Homme d'Aquitaine, 1993).

Binder, Wolfgang. *Partial Autobiographies: Interviews with Twenty Chicano Poets* (Erlangen, Germany: Palm & Enke, 1985).

Bruce-Novoa, Juan. "Who's Killing Whom in Belken County: Rolando Hinojosa's Narrative Production," *Monographic Review/Revista Monografica* (Odessa, Texas), 3.1–2 (1987): 288–97.

Burton, Amparo Ruiz de. *Who Would Have Thought It?* (1872; reprinted by Houston: Arte Público Press, 1995).

——. *The Squatter and the Don* (1885; reprinted by Houston: Arte Público Press, 1992).

Bus, Heiner, and Ana Castillo. *Recent Chicano Poetry/Neueste Chicano-Lyrik* (Bamberg: Universitätsbibliothek Bamberg, 1994).

Cabeza de Vaca, Fabiola. *We Fed Them Cactus* (Albuquerque: University of New Mexico Press, 1954).

Campa, Arthur L., ed. "Coloquio de los pastores," in *Spanish Religious Folktheater in the Southwest*, special edition of *The University of New Mexico Bulletin* 5, no. 2. (Albuquerque: University of New Mexico Press, 1934): 55–94.

Cantú, Norma. *Canícula: Snapshots of a Girlhood en la Frontera* (Albuquerque: University of New Mexico Press, 1995).

Castillo, Ana. *Peel My Love Like an Onion* (New York: W.W. Norton, 1999).

——, ed. *Goddess of the Americas = La diosa de las Américas: Writings on the Virgin of Guadalupe* (New York: Riverhead Books, 1996).

——. *Loverboys: Stories* (New York: W. W. Norton, 1996).

——. *Massacre of the Dreamers: Essays on Xicanisma* (New York: Penguin, 1995).

——. *My Father Was a Toltec and Selected Poems* (Novato, Calif.: West End Press, 1988; New York: W. W. Norton, 1995).

——. *So Far from God: A Novel* (New York: Plume, 1994).

——. *Sapogonia: An Anti-Romance in 3/8 Meter* (Tempe, Ariz.: Bilingual Press/Editorial Bilingüe, 1990).

——. *The Mixquiahuala Letters* (Binghamton, N. Y.: Bilingual Review Press/Editorial Bilingüe, 1986).

——. *Women Are Not Roses* (Houston: Arte Público Press, 1984).

——. *The Invitation* (n.p., 1979).

Chávez, Denise. *Face of An Angel* (New York: Farrar, 1994).

——. "Novenas narrativas: Ofrendas nuevomexicanas," in *Chicana Creativity and Criticism: Charting New Frontiers in American Literature,* eds. María Herrera Sobek and Helena María Viramontes (Houston: Arte Público Press, 1987).

——. *The Last of the Menu Girls* (Houston: Arte Público Press, 1986).

Cisneros, Sandra. *Loose Woman* (New York: Random House, 1994).

——. *My Wicked, Wicked Ways* (New York: Vintage Books/Random House, 1992).

——. *Woman Hollering Creek and Other Stories* (New York: Random House, 1991).

——. *The House on Mango Street* (Houston: Arte Público Press, 1984).

Corpi, Lucha. *Black Widow Wardrobe* (Houston: Arte Público Press, 1999).

——. *Cactus Blood* (Houston: Arte Público Press, 1995).

——. *Eulogy for a Brown Angel* (Houston: Arte Público Press, 1992).

Cota-Cárdenas, Margarita. *Puppet* (Austin: Relámpago Book Press, 1985).

Encinias, Miguel. *Two Lives for Oñate* (Albuquerque: University of New Mexico Press, 1997).

Escobedo, Fray Alonso Gregorio de. "La Florida," in *Pirates, Indians and Spaniards: Father Escobedo's "La Florida,"* ed. James W. Covington, trans. A. F. Falcones (St. Petersburg, Fla.: Great Outdoors Publishing Co., 1963).

Espinosa, Aurelio Macedonio. "Romancero de Nuevo Méjico," *Revista de Filología Española,* Añejo LVIII (Madrid: Consejo Superior de Investigaciones Científicas, Patronato "Menéndez Pelayo." Instituto "Miguel Cervantes," 1953).

——, ed. *Los Comanches: A Spanish Heroic Play of the Years Seventeen Hundred and Eighty,* special edition of *The University of New Mexico Bulletin* 1, no. 1 (Albuquerque: University of New Mexico Press): 27–46.

Espinosa, Fray Isidro Félix. *Crónica apostólica y seráfica de todos los colegios de propaganda fide de esta Nueva España.* Primera Parte (México: Viuda de Don Joseph Bernardo de Hogal, 1746); trans. Carlos E. Castañeda, *History of Texas 1673–1776* (Washington, D.C.: Academy of American Franciscan History, 1964).

Fabré, Genevieve. *European Perspectives on Hispanic Literature of the United States* (Houston: Arte Público Press, 1988).

Fontes, Monserrat. *Dreams of the Centaur* (New York: W. W. Norton & Co., 1996).

——. *First Confession* (New York: W. W. Norton & Co. 1991).

Fuego, Laura del. *Maravilla* (Encino: Floricanto, 1989).

Galarza, Ernesto. *Barrio Boy* (Notre Dame: Notre Dame University Press, 1971).

Gaona, María Eugenia. *Antología de la literatura chicana* (México: Centro de Enseñanza para Extranjeros, UNAM, 1986).

García-Robinson, Louie. *The Devil, Delfina Varela, and the Used Chevy* (New York: Anchor Books, 1993).

Gaspar de Alba, Alicia. *Sor Juana's Second Dream* (Albuquerque: University of New Mexico Press, 1999).

Gilb, Dagoberto. *The Last Known Residence of Mickey Acuña* (New York: Grove, 1994).

——. *The Magic of Blood* (Albuquerque: University of New Mexico Press, 1993).

Gonzales, Jovita. *Caballero: A Historical Novel* (College Station: Texas A&M University Press, 1996).

Gonzales-Berry, Erlinda. *Paletitas de guayaba* (Albuquerque: El Norte Publications, 1991).

Grandjeat, Yves-Charles. *Aztlán, terre volée, terre promise: les pérégrinations du peuple chicano* (Paris: Presses de l'Ecole Normale Supérieure, 1989).

Grattan-Domínguez, Alejandro. *The Dark Side of the Dream* (Houston: Arte Público Press, 1995).

Herrera, Juan Felipe. *Maya Drifter: Chicano Poet in the Lowlands of America* (Philadelphia: Temple University Press, 1997).

——. *Akrílica* (Santa Cruz: Alcatraz Editions, 1989).

Herrera-Sobek, María. *Northward Bound: The Mexican Immigrant Experience in Ballad and Song* (Bloomington: Indiana University Press, 1993).

Hinojosa, Rolando. *Ask a Policeman: A Rafe Buenrostro Mystery* (Houston: Arte Público Press, 1998).

——. *The Useless Servants* (Houston: Arte Público Press, 1993).

——. *Partners in Crime* (Houston: Arte Público Press, 1985).

——. *Mi querido Rafa* (Houston: Arte Público Press, 1981).

——. *Korean Love Songs from Klail City Death Trip* (Berkeley: Justa Publications, 1980)

——. *Generaciones y semblanzas* (Berkeley: Justa Publications, 1977).

——. *Klail City y sus alrededores* (La Habana: Casa de las Américas, 1976).

Horno-Delgado, Asunción, Eliana Ortega, Nina M. Scott, and Nancy Saporta Sternbach, eds. *Breaking Boundaries: Latina Writings and Critical Readings* (Amherst: University of Massachusetts Press, 1989).

Islas, Arturo. *Migrant Souls* (New York: Morrow, 1990).

——. *The Rain God: A Desert Tale* (Palo Alto, Calif.: Alexandrian Press, 1984).

Jaramillo, Cleofas. *Romance of a Little Village Girl* (San Antonio: The Naylor Company, 1955).

——. *Shadows of the Past* (Santa Fe: Seton Village Press, 1941).

Jiménez, Francisco. *The Circuit: Stories from the Life of a Migrant Child* (Albuquerque: University of New Mexico Press, 1997).

Juárez, Tina. *Call No Man Master* (Houston: Arte Público Press, 1995).

Lachtman, Ofelia Dumas. *The Girl from Playa Blanca* (Houston: Piñata, 1995).

Lea, Aurora Lucero-White, ed. "Las cuatro apariciones de la Virgen de Guadalupe," in *Literary Folklore of the Hispanic Southwest* (San Antonio: The Naylor Company, 1953), 86–106.

——. "Los moros y cristianos," in *Literary Folklore of the Hispanic Southwest* (San Antonio: The Naylor Company, 1953), 107–12.

Limón, Graciela. *Song of the Hummingbird* (Houston: Arte Público Press, 1996).

——. *The Memories of Ana Calderón* (Houston: Arte Público Press, 1994).

——. *In Search of Bernabé* (Houston: Arte Público Press, 1993).

Lomelí, Francisco A. "Contemporary Chicano Literature, 1959–1990: From Oblivion to Affirmation to the Forefront," in *Handbook of Hispanic Cultures in the United States: Literature and Art* (Houston: Arte Público Press, 1993), 86–108.

López-Medina, Sylvia. *Siguiriya: A Novel* (New York: Harper Collins Publishers, 1997).

——. *Cantora: A Novel* (New York: One World–Ballantine, 1993).

López-Stafford, Gloria. *A Place in El Paso: A Mexican American Childhood* (Albuquerque: University of New Mexico Press, 1996).

Maciel, David, and María Rosa García-Acevedo. "The Celluloid Immigrant: The Narrative Films of Mexican Immigration," in *Culture across Borders: Mexican Immigration and Popular Culture,* ed. David Maciel and María Herrera-Sobek (Tucson: University of Arizona Press, 1998), 149–202.

Márquez, Antonio. "Algo viejo y algo nuevo: Contemporary New Mexico Hispanic Fiction," in *Paso por aquí: Critical Essays on the New Mexican Literary Traditions 1542–1988,* ed. Erlinda Gonzales-Berry (Albuquerque: University of New Mexico, 1989), 255–65.

Márquez, Teresa María. "Asesinato en Aztlán: El investigador hispano." Paper presented at La Construcción de la Identidad Española e Hispánoamericana: Cine y Literatura (hosted in Valladolid, Spain by the Instituto de Estudios de Iberoamerica y Portugal, Universidad de Valladolid; and Duquesne University), June 1997.

Martínez, Demetria. *Mother Tongue* (Tempe: Bilingual Review Press, 1994).

Martínez, Max. *Layover* (Houston: Arte Público Press, 1997).

——. *White Leg* (Houston: Arte Público Press, 1996).

Martínez, Rubén. *The Other Side: Notes from the New L.A., Mexico City, and Beyond* (New York: Random House, 1992; Vintage edition, 1993).

——. *The Other Side; Fault Lines: Guerrilla Saints and the True Heart of Rock n' Roll* (New York: Verso, 1992).

McKenna, Teresa. *Migrant Song: Politics and Processes in Contemporary Chicano Literature* (Philadelphia: Temple University Press, 1997).

Méndez, Miguel. *Peregrinos de Aztlán* (Tucson: Editorial Peregrinos, 1974).

Mora, Pat. *Aunt Carmen's Book of Practical Saints* (Boston: Beacon Press, 1997).

——. *House of Houses* (Boston: Beacon Press, 1997).

——. *Agua santa/Holy Water* (Boston: Beacon Press, 1995).

——. *Borders* (Houston: Arte Público Press, 1986).

——. *Chants* (Houston: Arte Público Press, 1984).

Moraga, Cherríe. *Heroes and Saints and Other Plays* (Albuquerque: West End, 1994).

——. *Giving Up the Ghost* (Los Angeles: West End Press, 1986).

——. *Loving in the War Years: Lo que nunca pasó por sus labios* (Boston: South End Press, 1983).

Moraga, Cherríe and Gloria Anzaldúa. *This Bridge Called My Back: Writings by Radical Women of Color* (New York: Kitchen Table: Women of Color Press, 1983).

Morales, Alejandro. *The Rag-Doll Plagues* (Houston: Arte Público Press, 1992).

——. *The Brick People* (Houston: Arte Público Press, 1988).

——. *Reto en el paraíso* (Ypsilanti, Mich.: Bilingual Review Press/Editorial Bilingüe, 1983).

——. *Caras viejas y vino nuevo* (México: Editorial Joaquín Mortiz, 1975).

——. *La verdad sin voz* (México: Editorial Joaquín Mortiz, 1975).

Murray, Yxta Maya. *Locas* (New York: Grove Press, 1997).

Nava, Michael. *The Death of Friends* (New York: G. P. Putnam, 1996).

——. *Golden Boy* (Boston: Alyson, 1988).

Necochea, Fernando de, Luis Leal, Francisco A. Lomelí, and Roberto G. Trujillo (eds.) *A Decade of Chicano Literature (1970–1979): Critical Essays and Bibliography* (Santa Barbara: Editorial La Causa, 1982).

Niza, Fray Marcos de. *The Journey of Fray Marcos de Niza,* trans. Cleve-Hallenbeck (Dallas: University Press in Dallas, 1949), 30–34.

Núñez Cabeza de Vaca, Alvar. *La relacion que dio Aluar nuñez cabeca de vaca de lo acaescido en las Indias en la armada donde yua por gouernador Panphilo de narbaez desde el año de veynte y siete hasta el año de treynta y seis que boluio a Seuilla con tres de su compañia* (Zamora, 1542).

Otero-Warren, Nina. *Old Spain in Our Southwest* (New York: Harcourt Brace Jovanovich, 1936).

Paredes, Américo. *A Texas-Mexican "Cancionero": Folksongs of the Lower Border* (Urbana: University of Illinois Press, 1976).

——. *"With His Pistol in His Hand": A Border Ballad and Its Hero* (Austin: University of Texas Press, 1958).

Pineda, Cecile. *Frieze* (New York: Viking, 1986; New York: Penguin Books, 1987).

————. *Face* (New York: Viking, 1985).

Ponce, Mary Helen. *Taking Control* (Houston: Arte Público Press, 1987).

Portillo Trambley, Estela. *Trini* (Binghamton, N.Y.: Bilingual Review Press/Editorial Bilingüe, 1986).

————. *Sor Juana and Other Plays* (Ypsilanti, Mich.: Bilingual Review Press/Editorial Bilingüe, 1983).

————. *Rain of Scorpions and Other Writings* (Berkeley: Tonatiuh International, 1975).

————. "The Day of the Swallows," *El Grito* (spring 1971): 4–47.

Quiñónez, Naomi. *Sueño de colibrí/Hummingbird Dream* (Los Angeles: West End Press, 1985).

Ramos, Manuel. *Blues for the Buffalo* (New York: St. Martin's Press, 1997).

————. *The Last Client of Luis Móntez* (New York: St. Martin's Press, 1996).

————. *The Ballad of Gato Guerrero* (New York: St. Martin's Press, 1994).

————. *The Ballad of Rocky Ruiz* (New York: St. Martin's Press, 1993).

Rebolledo, Tey Diana, and Eliana S. Rivero. *Infinite Divisions: An Anthology of Chicana Literature* (Tucson: University of Arizona Press, 1993).

Rechy, John Francisco. *Rushes* (New York: Grove Press, 1979).

————. *The Sexual Outlaw: A Documentary* (New York: Grove Press, 1977).

————. *Numbers* (New York: Grove Press, 1967).

————. *City of Night* (New York: Grove Press, 1963).

Ríos, Isabella. *Victum* (Ventura, Calif.: Diana-Etna Incorporated, 1976).

Rivera, Tomás. . . . *Y no se lo tragó la tierra/ . . . And the Earth Did Not Part* (Berkeley: Quinto Sol Publications, 1971).

Rocard, Marcienne. *Les fils du soleil: la minorité mexicaine à travers la littérature des États-Unis* (Paris, France: G. P. Maisonneuve et Larose, 1980).

Rodríguez, Luis J. *Always Running: La Vida Loca, Gang Days in L.A.* (New York: Simon and Schuster, 1994).

Rodríguez, Richard. *Hunger of Memory* (Boston: D. R. Godine, 1981).

Ruiz de Burton, Amparo. *The Squatter and the Don* (Houston: Arte Público Press, 1992).

Sáenz, Benjamín Alire. *The House of Forgetting: A Novel* (New York: Harper Collins Publishers, 1997).

————. *Carry Me Like Water* (New York: Hyperion, 1995).

————. *Dark and Perfect Angels* (El Paso, Tex.: Cinco Puntos Press, 1995)

————. *Calendar of Dust* (Seattle: Broken Moon Press, 1992).

Salmerón, Fray Gerónimo de Zarate. *Relaciones,* trans. Alicia Ronstadt Milich (Albuquerque: Horn and Wallace Publisher, 1966).

Sánchez, Rosaura. "Postmodernism and Chicano Literature," *Aztlán* 18 (fall 1987): 1–14.

Serra, Junípero. *Writings of Junípero Serra* (vols. I–IV), ed. Antonine Tibesar, o.f.m. (Washington, D.C.: Academy of American Franciscan History, 1955).

Serros, Michele. *Chicana Falsa and Other Stories of Death, Identity, and Oxnard* (Culver City, Calif.: Lalo Press, 1993).

Soitos, Stephen F. *The Blues Detective* (Amherst: University of Massachusetts Press, 1996).

Soto, Gary. *Buried Onions* (San Diego, Calif.: Harcourt Brace, 1997).

——. *Summer on Wheels* (New York: Scholastic, 1995).

——. *A Summer Life* (Hanover, N. H.: University Press of New England, 1990).

——. *Black Hair* (Pittsburgh: University of Pittsburgh Press, 1985).

——. *Living up the Street: Narrative Recollections* (San Francisco: Strawberry Hill, 1985).

——. *The Tale of Sunlight* (Pittsburgh: University of Pittsburgh Press, 1978).

——. *The Elements of San Joaquín* (Pittsburgh: University of Pittsburgh Press, 1977).

Taylor, Sheila Ortiz. *Coachella* (Albuquerque: University of New Mexico Press, 1998).

Taylor, Sheila Ortiz, and Sandra Ortiz Taylor. *Imaginary Parents: A Family Autobiography* (Albuquerque: University of New Mexico press, 1996).

Tessarolo, Lia Bondolfi. *Dal mito al mito: la cultura di espressione chicana: dal mito originario al mito rigeneratore* (Milan, Italy: Jaca Books 1987).

Urrea, Luis. *Across the Wire: Life and Hard Times on the Mexican Border* (New York: Anchor Books, 1993).

Valdez, Luis. *Zoot Suit and Other Plays* (Houston: Arte Público Press, 1992).

——. *Actos* (San Juan Bautista, Calif.: Cucaracha Publications, 1971).

Vásquez, Richard. *Chicano* (New York: Doubleday, 1970).

Véa, Alfredo, Jr. *The Silver Cloud Café* (New York: Dutton, 1996).

——. *La maravilla* (New York: Dutton, 1993).

Venegas, Daniel. *Las aventuras de Don Chipote o cuando los pericos mamen* (Houston: Arte Público Press, 1998).

Villagrá, Gaspar Pérez. *La historia de la Nuevo México, 1610,* trans. and ed. Miguel Encinias, Alfredo Rodríguez, and Joseph P. Sánchez (Albuquerque: University of New Mexico Press, 1992).

Villanueva, Alma. *The Ultraviolet Sky* (Tempe: Bilingual Review/Editorial Bilingüe, 1988).

——. *Bloodroot* (Austin: Place of Herons Press, 1977).

Villanueva, Tino. *Chicanos: Antología histórica y literaria* (México: Fondo de Cultura Económica, 1980).

Villarreal, José Antonio. *Pocho* (New York: Doubleday, 1959).

Villaseñor, Edmundo. *Rain of Gold* (Houston: Arte Público Press, 1991).

——. *Macho* (New York: Bantam Books, 1973).

Viramontes, Helena María. *Under the Feet of Jesus* (New York: Dutton, 1995).

——. *The Moths and Other Stories* (Houston: Arte Público Press, 1985).

Zamora, Bernice. *Restless Serpents* (Menlo Park, Calif.: Diseños Literarios, 1976).

Contributors

EDWINA BARVOSA-CARTER is assistant professor of Chicano Studies and political science at the University of California, Santa Barbara. She earned her Ph.D. in political science from Harvard University in 1998 and completed her master's degree at Cambridge University in social and political science in 1993. Her research interests are in contemporary social and political identity. She is currently completing a book on the political implications of multiple identity.

ROBERTO R. CALDERÓN is assistant professor in the Division of Bilingual/ Bicultural Studies at the University of Texas, San Antonio. He received his B.A. in political science from Brown University and his M.A. and Ph.D. in history from the University of California, Los Angeles. His areas of teaching and research include the fields of cultural, labor, and political history. He is the recipient of a Ford postdoctoral fellowship through the National Research Council. He has published several essays in various publications and has contributed articles and interviews to university and community newspapers since the 1970s. His major publications include *South Texas Coal Mining: A Community History* (1984), *Directory of Organizations for Immigrant Rights* (1996), *Mexican Politics in Texas: Laredo, 1845–1910* (2000), and *Mexican Coal Mining Labor in Texas and Coahuila, 1880–1930* (2000).

VIRGINIA ESCALANTE, a former journalism professor at the University of Arizona and Pulitzer Prize-winning journalist at the *Los Angeles Times,* is earning her doctorate in communication at the University of California, San Diego.

JUAN GÓMEZ-QUIÑONES is a professor of history at the University of California, Los Angeles. His areas of teaching and research include the fields of political, labor, intellectual, and cultural history. In 1990 Professor Gómez-Quiñones received the Scholar of the Year Award from the National Association of Chicano Studies. He has more than thirty publications including *Mexican American Labor, 1790–1990; The Roots of Chicano Politics, 1600–1940; Sembradores, Ricardo Flores Magón y el Partido Liberal Mexicano: A Eulogy and Critique; Chicano Politics: Reality and Promise, 1940-1990; 5th and Grande Vista: Poems, 1960-1973;* and *Mexican Nationalist Formation: Political Discourse, Policy and Dissidence.* He has served as a member of the Board of Trustees, California State Universities and Colleges; commissioner of the WASC Accrediting Commission for Senior Colleges and Universities; and member of the board of directors of the following civic organizations: MALDEF (Mexican American Legal Defense and Education Fund), The Latino Museum, The Mexican Cultural Institute, OSIEC (One-Stop Immigration and Education Center), and El Pueblo de Los Angeles Commission.

FRANCISCO LOMELÍ currently serves as chair of the Department of Chicano Studies and professor in the department of Spanish and Portuguese at the University of California, Santa Barbara. His areas of specialization are Chicano and Latin American literary analysis. He has been the recipient of Fulbright, Ford, and Rockefeller fellowships. He has served as guest editor of the literary journals *De Colores, Confluencia,* and *Discurso literario.* He has served as editor or coeditor of *Handbook of Hispanic Cultures in the United States, Aztlán. Essays on the Chicano Homeland, Chicano Studies: A Multicultural Approach,* and *A Decade of Chicano Literature, 1970–1979.*

TERESA MÁRQUEZ is director of the Government Information Department, a regional federal depository library at the Zimmerman Library, University of New Mexico. She is also the bibliographer for Chicana/o Studies. She is coeditor of the journals *Las mujeres hablan* and *Cosecha.* She has compiled bibliographies for *The Magic of Words, Pasó por aquí,* and *Rudolfo A. Anaya: Focus on Criticism.* She has written two articles on the Chicana/o mystery genre. She is also the coordinator for two literary awards for criticism, the Premio Aztlán and Critica Nueva.

SUSAN RACHO is a Los Angeles–based, Emmy Award–winning producer/writer. A twenty-four-year veteran of film and television, she most recently produced and directed "Taking Back the Schools," a documentary episode of the PBS series *Chicano: History of the Mexican American Civil Rights Movement.* In her early career, she produced for the *Realidades* series (KABC).

Racho's diversified production credits include Carlos Fuentes's *The Buried Mirror*, Carl Sagan's *Cosmos*, *La Raza: A Working People*, *Jazz in America*, and *Trumbo Remembered*. Her work has been featured at the San Sebastian Film Festival. Recently, she coproduced a feature film entitled *Never Trust a Serial Killer*. She is currently writing and producing a feature-length documentary for HBO entitled *The Bronze Screen: The Latin Image in American Cinema*.

ARTURO RAMÍREZ, professor of Chicano and Latino Studies at Sonoma State University in California, is originally from south Texas. He received his three degrees, including his Ph.D. in 1973, from The University of Texas at Austin. He has published numerous scholarly works, articles, and reviews, which have appeared in such journals as *The Latin American Theatre Review*, *The Journal of Popular Culture*, *Hispania*, *The American Review*, *The Journal of Latin American Studies*, *MELUS*, *The Southwest Review*, and a number of other journals and quarterlies. He has also published short stories, essays, and other works. He has directed several Chicano university drama productions to accompany his writings on the theater. Professor Ramírez has presented scores of papers at local, regional, national, and international conferences. As coeditor, he has published the Chicano art anthology series *Chicano Culture and Folklore* (1997). Ramírez has received a number of awards, including three from the National Endowment for the Humanities. He has taught at several colleges and universities, including Whittier College, Idaho State University, Colby College, the University of California at San Diego, and San Diego State University.

DIANA I. RÍOS is an assistant professor in the Department of Communication Sciences and associate director of the Institute for Puerto Rican and Latino Studies at the University of Connecticut, Storrs. She conducts survey and field research on Chicana/o and Latina/o audience use of English- and Spanish-language television, newspapers, U.S. and Mexican cinema, and other forms of mediated communication. Her most recent projects include Caribbean-heritage audiences and their relationship with media, and older-generation Latina and European American women's memories of Golden Age cinema stars. She teaches and publishes in the interdisciplinary areas of mass communication and Latina/o Studies. She has served as an officer of the Minorities and Communication division of the Association for Education in Journalism and Mass Communication for five years.

GEORGE VARGAS attended the University of Michigan, where he received a B.F.A., followed by an M.A. and a Ph.D. in American studies with an emphasis on Latino art history and racial/ethnic studies. He has taught both Western art history and Latin American art and has worked as an arts administrator and a museum educator for major cultural organizations in the Midwest and Southwest. In 1990–91, he received a Ford Fellowship, serving in art museums in Chicago. His interests also include mural art, border art, and film studies. He lives in Austin, Texas, where he was a visiting scholar at the Center for Mexican American Studies at The University of Texas. He is currently writing a book on Chicano art.

Index

About the Editors

DAVID R. MACIEL is professor of history and chairperson of the Department of Chicano/a Studies at California State University, Domínguez Hills. His teaching interests and research fields include Chicana/o history, Mexico, modern Latin America, and the U.S. Southwest. He has held academic appointments at the University of New Mexico, the University of Arizona, Arizona State University, and the University of Houston. In addition, he has been a visiting professor at the National Autonomous University of Mexico; the University of California, San Diego; the University of Arizona; the University of California, Irvine; the University of California, Los Angeles; Centro de Investigación y Docencia Económica; and the University of Guadalajara. He has been the recipient of two Fulbright teaching and research postdoctoral fellowships to Mexico and research fellowships from the Ford Foundation, the National Endowment for the Humanities, the Fidecomiso para la Cultura México-Estados Unidos, and the Fondo Nacional para la Cultura y las Artes. He has served as a media consultant on the film *Break of Dawn* and on numerous documentaries in the United States and Mexico. His published research has focused upon the Chicano community, Mexican cultural history, and film. He has written or edited several books including *Ignacio Ramírez: Ideólogo del liberalismo social en México; Aztlán: historia del pueblo chicano; Al norte del Río Bravo: Pasado inmediato 1930–1982; El México olvidado; El Norte: The U.S.–Mexican Border in Contemporary Cinema; El bandolero, el pocho y la raza: imágenes cinematográficas del chicano; Mexico's Cinema: A Century of Films and Filmmakers*, coedited with Joanne Hershfield; *Chicanas/Chicanos at the Crossroads: Social, Economic, and Political Change*, coedited with Isidro D. Ortiz, and *Culture across Borders: Mexican Immigration and Popular Culture*, coedited with María Herrera-Sobek. He has also published numerous articles, book chapters, and reviews in scholarly journals from the United States and Mexico. Currently, he is completing a monograph on the cinema of Mexico.

ISIDRO D. ORTIZ is professor of Chicana/Chicano Studies at San Diego State University. His teaching interests and fields include Chicano/Latino politics, California and American politics, and political movements. He completed undergraduate studies in secondary education with a specialization in history and political science at Texas A&I University and pursued graduate studies in political science at Stanford University. He has received several institutional research grants as well as a grant from the American Political Science Association. He has published articles and book chapters on various aspects of Chicano/Latino politics in the United States and Mexico. He has also served as coeditor of *Chicano Studies: A Multidisciplinary Approach* and *Chicanas/Chicanos at the Crossroads: Social, Economic, and Political Change* and editor of *Chicanos and the Social Sciences 1970–1980: A Decade of Development*. His current research focuses on Chicano/Latino political strategies and the relationship between politics and popular culture.

MARÍA HERRERA-SOBEK holds the Luis Leal Endowed Chair and is professor of Chicano Studies at the University of California, Santa Barbara. She has taught at the University of California, Irvine, and was a visiting professor at Stanford and Harvard universities. She has published several books including *The Bracero Experience: Elitelore versus Folklore* (1979); *The Mexican Corrido: A Feminist Analysis* (1990); and *Northward Bound: The Mexican Immigrant Experience in Ballad and Song* (1993). She has edited or coedited numerous anthologies including *Beyond Stereotypes: The Critical Analysis of Chicana Literature* (1985); *Chicana Creativity and Criticism: Charting New Frontiers in Chicana Literature* (1988 and 1996); *Gender and Print Culture: New Perspectives on International Ballad Studies* (1991); *Reconstructing a Chicano/a Literary Heritage: Hispanic Colonial Literature of the Southwest* (1993); *Chicana (W)rites: On Word and Film* (1995); *Saga de México* (1991); *Culture across Borders: Mexican Immigration and Popular Culture* (1998); *Santa Barraza: The Life and Work of a Mexica/Tejana Artist* (2000); *Recovering the U.S. Hispanic Literary Heritage: Volume III* (2000), and *Power in Academe: Race and Gender–Strangers in the Tower?* (2000).

In addition, Professor Herrera-Sobek has published more than 100 scholarly articles, book chapters, book reviews, and numerous poems in journals. She is one of three poets featured in the book *Three Times a Woman* (1989). She is currently editing several anthologies and writing a book on Chicana writers and ecological theory.